Praise for

Designing Web-Based Training...

Horton has done it again! He's addressed the cutting edge problem of Web-based training design with his pragmatic, research-based approach. His work is task-oriented and down-to-earth. He doesn't waste our time with excessive educational philosophy. In short—comprehensive overview, practical advice, engaging presentation.

Robert E. Horn
Author, *Visual Language: Global Communication for the 21st Century*

As each new media wave is adopted for instructional purposes, there is a lag in effective exploitation of the unique features the medium brings for supporting learning. *Designing Web-Based Training* bridges the gap by providing a rich and detailed reference. All the chapters present guidelines and examples that illustrate effective ways to instructionally exploit the unique features the Internet provides while adapting to the technical constraints. Additionally there is ample guidance on effective supporting resources such as course announcement pages, course descriptive pages, mechanisms to support learner motivation that are needed to make any WBT product a success. In particular I found the chapter on using the web to promote collaboration including tips and examples on use of chats, message boards, and discussions especially useful.

Ruth Clark, Ed.D.
President, Clark Training & Consulting

Until Bill Horton wrote this book on *Designing Web-Based Training* there was more hype than substance. Designers have been seeking guidance on how to exploit the Web's distribution potential while combining it with powerful instructional programs. Horton provides structure, stimulation and substance in this important book. A lot has happened in the field of interactive learning. Web-based training is definitely what is happening now. *Designing Web-Based Training* will be a de facto classic in the field.

Gloria Gery
Principal, Gery Associates
Author, *Making CBT Happen*

Designing Web-Based Training

How to teach anyone anything anywhere anytime

By

Esther Alukpe.
Nov. 2001.

William Horton

New York • Chichester • Weinheim • Brisbane • Singapore • Toronto

Publisher: Robert Ipsen

Editor: Theresa Hudson

Managing Editor: Frank Grazioli

Book Design and Composition: William Horton Consulting, Inc.

Trademarks

Many words in this publication in which the Author and Publisher believe trademark or other proprietary rights may exist have been designated as such by use of Initial Capital Letters. However, in so designating or failing to designate such words, neither the Author nor the Publisher intends to express any judgment on the validity or legal status of any proprietary right that may be claimed in the words.

This text is printed on acid-free paper.

This publication is designed to provide accurate and authoritative information in regard to the subject matter covered. It is sold with the understanding that the publisher is not engaged in rendering legal, accounting, or other professional service. If legal advice or other expert assistance is required, the services of a competent professional person should be sought. FROM A DECLARATION OF PRINCIPLES JOINTLY ADOPTED BY A COMMITTEE OF THE AMERICAN BAR ASSOCIATION AND A COMMITTEE OF PUBLISHERS.

Library of Congress Cataloging-in-Publication Data:

Horton, William K. (William Kendall)

    Designing Web-based training / William Horton
       p. cm.
    Includes bibliographical references and index.
    ISBN 0-471-35614-X (paper/website : alk. paper)
    1. Employees--Training of--Computer-assisted instruction. 2. World Wide Web. I. Title.

    HF5549.5.T7 H635 2000
    658.3'42404--dc21
                                           99-088038

Printed in the United States of America

10 9 8 7 6 5 4 3

FAQ about this book

SHOULD I BUY THIS BOOK?

Yes, of course! My publisher will make a profit and I'll get a couple of dollars in royalties. You'll have an impressive tome to decorate your bookshelf and to which you can point as the reason for anything you do remotely connected with Web-based training.

SHOULD I READ THIS BOOK?

Better question. If you need to train somebody and you think Web technologies might help, this book is for you.

DO I HAVE TO BE A PROGRAMMER TO READ THIS BOOK?

No, everyone is welcome. You do not need a lot of technical expertise to understand the basic design issues for Web-based training. True, some technical knowledge docs help. You need experience navigating the Web. It would help if you have at least lurked in a chat room or asked a question in a newsgroup, but it is not essential. You do not have to be a certified Java programmer, but you should know that Java programming is more than specifying "drip" on the coffee grinder at the grocery store. If you have created your own Web page, you have most of the knowledge you need to get started with this book.

IS THIS BOOK FOR SCHOLARLY STUDY?

My sisters and brothers in the academic community are welcome to read this book, but no one should expect a scholarly work crammed with footnotes and hesitant generalizations. This book is for practitioners who cannot wait for all the research to be done and need advice now.

HOW SHOULD I READ THIS BOOK?

You shouldn't, not in the conventional sense of starting at Page 1 and plodding through to the end. Definitely not. This book is designed as a handbook you use to get advice in little pieces as your design matures. Look it over, read the introductory parts, and skim the rest. When you have a design problem or need some inspiration, thumb through the appropriate section or dive into the index.

IS THIS ANOTHER ONE OF THOSE TOOLS-FOR-FOOLS BOOKS?

No way. I figure you are smart enough to read the manual—and take the tutorial that comes with the tool. Anyway, this book is for designers, not tool operators. And, in this book, we are not going to spend much time on design issues related to a particular product.

My strongest advice is to design first and then buy the tool that best realizes that design. If you start with a tool, you are limited to what it can do. The history of design is full of unsuccessful examples of designing to fit that box.

If you need a book on choosing tools, pick up Brandon Hall's *WBT Cookbook* [1].

SO WHAT IS THIS BOOK?

This book is quite simply my advice to you. "Say, Bill, you've been doing this WBT stuff for a while and I'm just getting started. What do I need to know?"

It assumes you are intelligent enough to evaluate the advice and see whether it applies to your situation and how. This book is not for those who want to know what buttons to press in which order in a particular authoring system. It is not for those who believe there is some rote procedure that will guarantee effective training without any tough decisions and painful compromises. This book is for fellow thinkers and real designers.

WHO ARE YOU TO GIVE ADVICE?

If you want to see my immodest press-release biography, you can pick it up at www.horton.com. Here's the more modest version.

I have been at this awhile. I created my first network-based course in 1971 as an undergraduate at MIT. I was hired to teach a course in computer simulation of social systems at MIT's Center for Advanced Engineering Study to mid-career engineers and business officials. With the arrogance and naïveté of youth, I had not bothered to ask whether the course existed before I took the job. I needed the money. I soon realized that I would be developing the course only a few days ahead of the students. There was not time to copy exercises and notes and other materials. So I hit upon the idea of storing them on the computer used to run simulation programs. Students could print out the materials and assignments on a clackety-clack Teletype machine. Students loved the fact that they could print out the instructions for an assignment right where and when they performed it.

Since then I have spent close to three decades helping people put training materials and documents onto computers. For the past 12 years, I have earned a significant fraction of my income teaching courses on these subjects in industry training centers and hotel meeting rooms. I have had considerable first-hand field experience observing successful training. I created my first full-scale Web-based course in 1996 and survived.

I am a designer. I love to design things. I have won international awards for user interfaces, manuals, technical papers, and books I have created. A kitchen and bath I co-designed with my wife were featured in *Better Homes and Gardens*. Along the way, I have written books on designing online documents [2], icons [3], graphics [4], and Web pages [5].

In preparing to write this book, I took a good bite of over 200 Web-based courses. I learned more than I ever thought possible about the Java programming language, Windows NT servers, and obscure HTML tag attributes. I also learned firsthand that some design techniques work better than others.

I also talked to many course designers, instructors, administrators, and learners about their experiences creating and taking WBT. I confirmed my belief that personal preferences—even my own—were not a good guide for design.

As a consultant, I've learned a lot from the successes and failures of my own and of my clients. Although I have not made all the mistakes that can be made, I have made enough to have good instincts about what leads to disaster. And I've learned the importance of careful design.

ISN'T WBT TOO NEW FOR CLEAR ADVICE?

Although WBT is too new to have an extensive track record or research history, we can use past experience with related technologies and techniques that apply to WBT.

▸ **Related forms of education.** Experiences and research in adult education and distance learning help us understand how remote adult learners behave and how they respond to technological advances in training. We can trace the history of distance learning from correspondence courses through educational radio and television, programmed instruction and teaching machines, audiocassette courses, and satellite-broadcast courses.

▸ **Electronic documents and courses.** WBT uses many of the same media, hypertext-linking, and display mechanisms as other forms of electronic communications. We can learn a lot from the experiences of designers of disk-based CBT, online help and online documentation, and non-training Web sites.

▸ **User-interface design.** WBT is a computer application with a user interface. Many of the same principles that apply to designing the user interface for a word processor or database application apply to WBT as well.

Designers of WBT should not ignore, dismiss, or remain totally ignorant of the lessons learned from these related fields.

WON'T THIS ADVICE LIMIT ME?

Advice should provide a floor but not a ceiling. It should make it easier to create instructionally competent courses—and with some additional effort—instructionally excellent ones. It should not limit those with the technical knowledge, pedagogical knowledge, and passion to do better. Remember two important pieces of advice about taking this advice:

Follow these guidelines completely—unless you have a good reason not to.

Never follow these guidelines more than 85% of the time.

HOW IS THE BOOK ORGANIZED?

Early in the design of this book, I considered doing away with chapters and just having separate topics of advice. But this is a book after all and uses chapters to draw together related design issues. Here's what you will find in each chapter.

1 Meet Web-based training — What is WBT? Where did it come from? Why is it important? What do I need to do before starting on a project?

2 Evaluate WBT — Is WBT really the best solution? And how much does it cost? Take an objective look at the advantages and disadvantages of WBT.

13   **Venture beyond courses**   We learn by more than taking courses. Shop a catalog of Web-based alternatives, including libraries and museums, guided tours and field trips, job aids, conferences, and simulations.

14   **Contemplate the future**   Join us for a few pages of speculations about what may happen next.

ARE THE EXAMPLES REAL?

No, they are all fake. All the examples really work and they are all based on real-world examples, but getting legal releases or smuggling them out through the firewall was too much work. So we re-created them, putting them in a common format and simplifying them to focus attention on the point they exemplify. And, no, there is no company called ZipZapCom.

All the examples, unless otherwise noted, run in a 4.0-level browser—without additional plug-ins or add-ons. Some use Microsoft Active Server Pages scripts on the server to communicate with a database, and a few others require a discussion group or chat server— all pretty standard stuff these days. Beyond that, we have tried to note any other special software behind the examples.

You can see many of the examples on the companion Web site for this book at www.wiley.com/compbooks/horton/, and on the William Horton Consulting site at www.horton.com/DesigningWBT/.

WHO IS RESPONSIBLE FOR THIS BOOK?

I (William Horton) wrote it. I am responsible for the logical lapses, the begging questions, and the irreverent attitude. Most of the conceptual designs are my fault, too.

Most of the examples and artwork were done by Katherine Horton, my business partner, high-school sweetheart, and co-conspirator in life.

Kurt Matthies of Mesa Interactive tried to explain some of the technical errors to me and Marilyn Brown pointed out lots of grammatical errors and misspellings, which I replaced with new grammatical errors and misspellings. Jeff Kandyba did the chapter graphics. Terri Hudson of John Wiley and Sons convinced me to recant my vow to never ever *ever* write another book.

Beyond that there are thousands of people responsible for the hundreds (well at least 200) of WBT courses I took while researching this book. If there are any good ideas in this book, they probably came from designs by children, for they were the best I found. Children— undaunted by technical hurdles, unaffected by training fads, and unfettered by dogma— design naturally and directly. I hope I was as good a student as they were teachers.

Contents

2 EVALUATE WBT 17

3 PICK AN APPROACH 53

4 BUILD THE FRAMEWORK 77

5 ORGANIZE LEARNING SEQUENCES 135

6 ACTIVATE LEARNING 191

7 TEST AND EXERCISE LEARNING 273

8 PROMOTE COLLABORATION 333

9 TEACH IN THE VIRTUAL CLASSROOM 397

10 MOTIVATE LEARNERS 417

11 GO GLOBAL 439

12 OVERCOME TECHNICAL HURDLES 481

13 VENTURE BEYOND COURSES 519

1

Meet Web-based training

What is WBT and why do you want to use it?

For tens of thousands of years, human beings have come together to learn and share knowledge. Until now, we have had to come together at the same time and place. But today, the technologies of the Internet have eliminated that requirement. Soon anybody will be able to learn anything anywhere at any time, thanks to a new development called Web-based training.

WHAT IS WEB-BASED TRAINING?

Web-based training (hereafter called WBT) marshals Web technologies to the task of training. Several definitions of WBT are common. Some people hold that WBT is limited to what takes place entirely within a Web browser without the need for other software or learning resources. Such a pure definition, though, leaves out many of the truly effective uses of Web technologies for learning.

As author of this book, I am empowered to coin whatever definition I want, though it only applies within the covers of this book. Being more practical than theoretical, I want a definition that reflects what clever designers are doing today. I define WBT as:

> Any purposeful, considered application of Web technologies to the task of educating a fellow human being.

Notice a couple of things about this definition. The two adjectives *purposeful* and *considered* emphasize the fact that WBT is not just a Web site thrown together without thought for learning. The second point is that the word *educating* was chosen rather than *training*—not because *educating* is more esteemed than *training*, but because there no longer seems to be any clear difference.

WBT is the term that is used most often to describe the use of Web technologies for learning within industry, while the terms *Web-based education* and *Web-based instruction* are more common within universities. We will stick with *WBT* because the primary emphasis of this book is the kind of training provided by business organizations, though most of the advice here could be applied to designing courses for use within academia.

Heritage and history of WBT

Web-based training is the confluence of three social and technical developments: distance learning, computer-conveyed education, and Internet technologies.

It draws on the technologies, traditions, and techniques of all three areas. And it can learn from the triumphs and mistakes of all three.

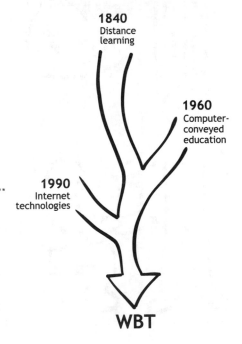

Distance learning

Distance learning has its roots in the correspondence education that developed in the United States, France, Germany, and the United Kingdom during the mid 1800s [6]. By 1840, Sir Isaac Pitman was teaching his shorthand system by mail. About that time Scottish educator James Stewart of Cambridge University began offering off-campus lectures. In the US, Illinois Wesleyan University began a home-study program in the 1870s, and a "Correspondence University" was founded in Ithaca, New York, in 1883. In the 1890s, the International Correspondence Schools (ICS) grew out of home-study courses in mine safety developed the decade before by Thomas J. Foster. ICS eventually supplied home-study courses to workers at 150 different railroad companies.

Correspondence education was a remarkable social innovation. It made education and training available to those who lived in remote areas or worked jobs during school hours. It also opened the doors of education to women, who could not enroll in male-only institutions, and to those whose physical handicaps prevented them from attending conventional schools.

Today, distance education is a large, multi-faceted endeavor. The Public Broadcasting Service (PBS) transmits courses to 2000 institutions. The US Army's Logistics Management College in Fort Lee, Virginia, conducts video and audio training at over 70 remote locations. The US Air Force's Air Technology Network provides similar training at all Air Force bases in the mainland United States. The Open University in the UK teaches most of its 200,000 learners by distance learning methods.

Distance education has readily adopted new technologies to reach wider audiences and teach more effectively. In 1925, radio courses were first offered by the State University of Iowa, and in the 1940s, educational television added capabilities to broadcast live presentations to distant learners. In the 1980s, teleconferencing allowed teachers and learners to talk together, even though distances and political boundaries separated them. In the 1980s and 1990s, satellite television networks let learners see and interact with instructors a world away. WBT is just the latest technology to advance distance learning.

Computer-conveyed education

Several forms of computer-conveyed education preceded WBT. These forms all use computer systems to store and deliver educational lessons. These forms take various names, the most common being *computer-aided instruction (CAI)*, *computer-based education*, *computer-based instruction*, and *computer-based training (CBT)*. The term *CAI* is typically used to describe systems by educational institutions and *CBT* to describe systems in industry.

The roots of computer-conveyed education go back before anyone thought of using computers to teach. During World War II the US military forces had to train large numbers of farm boys to operate sophisticated weapons and other equipment. Military trainers experimented with many techniques, from comic books to Hollywood-style films. These trainers discovered that audiovisual materials were effective, not just as aids to paper and classroom training, but also as the core method of training. This style of training, which uses film and audio-recordings along with richly illustrated training manuals, became known as *audiovisual education*.

With the value of technology in conveying knowledge proven and widely accepted, it is not surprising that early computer systems would see use as educational tools. The first widespread use of the computer in training occurred in the late 1950s when Stanford University teamed with IBM to offer computer-aided instruction in elementary schools. Most of the early CAI consisted of drill-and-practice sessions and required expensive mainframe computers.

The first real breakthrough occurred in the 1960s when the University of Illinois planned and Control Data Corporation developed the PLATO system. PLATO stands for Programmed Logic for Automatic Teaching Operations, and it allowed the sophisticated branching necessary for teaching complex subjects. By 1985, over 100 PLATO systems were in service in the US, and learners had logged 40 million hours of instruction.

The requirement for a mainframe computer system and distributed terminals limited the use of CAI. With the arrival of the personal computer and the almost immediate development of training and education programs to run on it, computer-conveyed education took its next giant leap. As multimedia capabilities were added to personal computers, the principles of audiovisual education were revived on an individual scale. Incompatibilities of hardware and operating systems, however, limited the use of personal computers.

Apple's Macintosh and later the Microsoft Windows operating system provided a standard platform on which programmers could develop training programs. Applications were becoming available for these platforms that let even non-programmers develop training. Since then, we have seen a steady development and refinement of technologies for delivering training on personal computers, including simpler programming tools such as HyperCard for the Macintosh and Visual Basic for Windows, multimedia development tools, courseware authoring tools, and CD-ROMs. Each advance made training easier and less expensive to develop and deliver. Yet this training was limited to single computer systems or proprietary networks. The next development was to erase that limitation and open the way to true WBT.

Web technologies

Many of the technologies essential to WBT actually predate the Web. Some go back to the invention of the Internet or before. It is ironic to think the Internet evolved from technologies designed to fight World War III. The basic network protocols that let my computer send an e-mail message to your computer originated in research intended to create a communications network that could survive a nuclear attack. The goal was to enable one military base to send a Teletype message to another surviving base even though most of the other bases on the network were now dust in the upper stratosphere.

Once such a network was developed, a true swords-into-ploughshares metamorphosis began to take place. The few universities that—by dint of their critical defense research—were allowed on the network began finding more and more uses for it. The results were e-mail, file-transfer programs, newsgroups, and repositories of text documents. And eventually—as the system was opened to the general public—the Internet.

But the Internet was not easy for most people to use. It required memorizing cryptic commands, loading several different programs, and typing long and hard-to-remember names of things. The World Wide Web was not intended to solve that problem but rather a more modest one. Developed at CERN, the particle accelerator research facility in Switzerland, what became the Web was simply intended as a way that researchers could share their academic papers over the Internet. Instead of footnotes, researchers would insert hypertext links to cited papers. Readers could point at a link, click it, and voilà the cited paper appeared.

To format and organize their pages, the creators of the Web defined a simple set of tags called HyperText Markup Language or HTML. The secret ingredient of HTML was simplicity. Unlike its techno-nerdy cousin SGML, HTML was simple. It was so easy that just about anybody could use it. Soon universities and private companies were creating programs called browsers to display HTML documents on UNIX, Macintosh, and Windows systems.

The Web quickly became a graphical user interface for the valuable but complex resources of the Internet. Now millions could enjoy and profit from the Internet's bounty—and millions could contribute to it. Training was an obvious application.

WBT is born

In a sense, WBT began the first time someone read a Web page and learned something. The first "purposeful, considered" use of the Web for training was probably the dozens of informal tutorials on how to use HTML to create Web pages. These tutorials were little more than paper pages on the computer screen. They conformed to no educational theory and followed little of the advice you will find in this book. And yet, some of us learned enough HTML from them to write books about designing Web pages [5].

Vendors of CBT tools, such as Allen Communication, Asymetrix, and Macromedia, quickly began offering plug-ins to enable Web browsers to display modules developed with their CBT tools. These vendors soon realized that the large, integrated file formats optimized for storage on CD-ROMs posed problems for the slower network connections and packet-oriented communications protocols of the Internet. Within months, they began updating their file formats. Macromedia, for example, introduced the Shockwave format for Authorware to offer greater compression, embedded fonts, and a streaming feature so learners could begin interacting with a module before the whole file downloaded. These vendors developed separate products, such as Allen Communication's Net Synergy and Macromedia's Flash, specifically for authoring materials for the Web.

In 1998 and 1999, the intense competition of the "browser wars" between Netscape and Microsoft yielded several advancements that made their browsers better equipped to deliver WBT on their own. Capabilities like Dynamic HTML, richer scripting languages, and the ability to display XML documents encouraged more WBT developments. To take advantage of some of these advancements, new authoring tools, like Macromedia's Dreamweaver Attain Objects made it simpler to create interactive WBT that did not require plug-ins.

In this same time frame, private companies and universities began offering complete server-based WBT authoring and delivery systems. Integrated packages include WBT Systems's TopClass and Docent's Docent Enterprise.

By late 1999, WBT was clearly walking on its own. Some would say sprinting.

Not just electronic classrooms or CBT over a wire

Most early attempts at Web-based training just dumped classroom materials online or let learners download and play existing CBT modules. Some attempts succeeded, some did not, but few lived up to their potential.

Almost all early attempts at WBT suffered from what I call *horseless carriage syndrome*. Early in this century, the devices we now call automobiles were called horseless carriages. That's what they were. For a decade or so, most of them came with buggy-whip holders as standard equipment. The first few hundred motion pictures were made by filming stage plays from the fourth row center. No one thought to move the camera or to splice together pieces filmed separately.

Have you seen films of early television news broadcasts? What did you see? A man sitting, smoking a cigarette, reading from sheets of paper, never making eye contact with the viewer. He was a radio newsreader just doing his job as he had for decades.

Whenever any new technology comes along, we seem to spend a decade or so using it exactly the way we did the previous technology. In hindsight, such mimicry seems stupid or silly. At best, it wastes valuable years that could have seen innovation and growth.

With so many possibilities, we must ask, which is the best way for our learners to master the subject? Not what is the best way in the classroom or the best way on the computer screen, but what is best way *period*. How, using Web technologies, as well as other technologies and conventional means, can we effect the same learning processes?

What does WBT change?

WBT is part of the biggest change in the way our species conducts training since the invention of the chalkboard or perhaps the alphabet. The development of computers and electronic communications media has removed barriers of space and time. We can obtain and deliver knowledge anytime anywhere.

According to Nobel Laureate Herbert Simon, the verb *to know* used to mean, "having information stored in one's memory. It now means the process of having access to information and knowing how to use it" [7].

WBT does not change how humans learn, but it does change how we can teach them. People learn with WBT pretty much as they have for 50,000 years. But what WBT does change is the economics and capabilities of *delivering* training. WBT makes it easier and less expensive to produce certain kinds of learning experiences for people at a distance.

The fundamental responsibility of the instructor does not change. Instructors still create an experience that causes someone else to learn. That experience may be a presentation, or it may be a simulation, a game, a field trip, an assigned reading, or a team project.

In WBT, the responsibility to provoke effective learning experiences may be divided. Producing effective WBT is a large job requiring several different skills: instructional design, writing, visual design, programming, and group leadership. The day when one person can comfortably perform all these necessary activities is still a ways off. Till then, the joint role of designer-producer-presenter enjoyed by many classroom instructors may be distributed among a team.

WBT IS JUST IN TIME FOR JUST-IN-TIME TRAINING

Many of the reasons for implementing WBT come not from the characteristics of WBT but from the exploding demand for training—especially training in technical knowledge, which WBT is well suited to teach.

Shortage of trained technology workers

A lack of trained technology workers restrains corporate growth and profits. The International Technology Training Association estimates that in 1998 there were 350,000 unfilled positions for programmers, computer scientists, and systems analysts [8]. And the need will not be filled any time soon. The U.S. Department of Commerce estimates that between 1996 and 2006 the number of people needed in these fields will increase 108%, or by more than a million jobs.

International Data Corporation reported in its "1997 Global IT Survey" that 20% of Information Technology executives in the U.S. felt that the lack of skilled workers was the greatest limit to their business growth [9]. The lack of training raises support costs for products. As many as half of the calls to help desks require on-the-spot training to resolve the problem [10].

However, traditional educational institutions are not meeting that need. According to the American Electronics Association, between 1990 and 1996 the number of graduates in high technology fields dropped by 5%, and the decline seems to be continuing.

Workers want more training

Management is not alone in recognizing the urgent need for training. Workers clearly seek more training, often on their own time at their own expense. A survey conducted by the Gallup Organization of 1012 U.S. workers in May and June of 1998 found that 99% of workers felt they needed additional training [11].

Many are returning to universities. By 2001, more than 15 million adults in the U.S. will be enrolled full- or part-time in college and university programs [12].

However, most workers prefer to learn on the job. That same Gallup Organization survey of 1012 U.S. workers found that workers strongly preferred informal on-the-job training and self-paced training to formal classroom training [11].

Corporations are responding. In 1998, U.S. organizations budgeted $60.7 billion USD for training [13]. That's about the same amount as spent on education by all U.S. universities.

WBT IS WELL UNDER WAY

WBT and the technologies on which it is based are advancing rapidly and growing exponentially.

Technology advances daily

The core technologies of WBT are literally growing exponentially. Computer processor speed doubles every 20 months. Memory doubles every 20 months. Disk space doubles every year. Communications speed doubles every 24 months.

As a result, the computers we have today have eight times the processor speed and memory, communicate three times faster, and have disks thirty-two times larger than the ones we had five years ago—and cost 40% less.

The Web is growing even faster

According to a Netcraft survey, the number of Web sites increased fivefold in just two years, reaching 5 million in April 1999. In 1993, there were 130 Internet domain names registered. In 1998, there were 3,000,000.

WBT is growing just as rapidly

The growth in WBT matches that of its technologies. According to International Data Corporation (IDC), WBT is growing at a rate of over 100% per year. Expenditures for WBT should reach about $2.4 billion USD in 2000, $5 billion in 2001 and $10 billion in 2002. According to IDC, sales of intranet- and Internet-delivered educational content and equipment will reach $1.1 billion USD in 1999—double the figure for 1998 [14].

Training professionals seem to agree. Seventy-eight percent of respondents in a survey reported in *The 1999 CBT Report*, said that WBT was growing, while almost none felt it was shrinking [15]. The numbers bear out these predictions. Attendance at the Online Learning conference soared from 750 in 1997 to 3000 in 1998—a 400% increase in just one year. Use of WBT by learners preparing for IT certification exams rose threefold between 1997 and 1998 [16]. UOL Publishing increased the number of online students from 8,000 in 1997 to 80,000 in 1998.

Corporations are already training over the Web

The list of corporations with major WBT efforts is long and growing. From 1994 to 1999, corporations spent $600 million USD on online training [17]. In 1999, 41% of large organizations had some form of online training, and 92% planned to implement some form of training over their intranet by the end of the year.

To aid in its process re-engineering efforts, Boeing developed 18 courses, each made up of four or five half-hour lessons. Over 40,000 Boeing employees have completed one or more of these courses [18] for a total of over 190,000 course completions.

According to Brandon Hall, in his "Hall Monitor" column, which appears in *Inside Technology Training*, Novell will soon offer all customer courses over the Web. Field representatives for MCI WorldCom undergo 40 hours of WBT before they hit the road. DaimlerChrysler is using WBT to train 13,000 workers in Germany.

Dow Chemical is moving the training of its 40,000 employees to WBT. By the year 2000, Dow Chemical expects to conduct 80% of its 700,000 hours of training over the Web [19].

Cisco has made 125 hours of video sales presentations available over the Internet to its sales representatives and distributors [14].

Over half of universities and colleges use WBT technology

CGA Consulting reports that almost half of U.S. universities and colleges provide some form of education online [20]. According to the Campus Computing Project, 44 percent of college courses already use e-mail. About 33 percent of college courses use the Internet and 23 percent use the Web as part of the course itself. By 2007 almost half of all university and college students will take some courses through distance education technologies [21].

WHY DO YOU WANT TO USE WBT?

Before you begin designing a course, understand why you are doing so. What are you trying to do for your organization and for your learners?

What will you do for your organization?

Identify your business goals first. Only then can you decide whether training is the best solution and whether WBT figures into that training.

What are you trying to accomplish for your organization? Before you start listing the things you will accomplish for learners, think about what you will do for your organization, your sponsor, or your financial backers. What does your business or university hope to accomplish? Your list might look something like this:

▶ Reduce costs of training by 50% over the next year

▶ Quickly prepare a global marketing plan to sell a new line of products.

▶ Reduce misdiagnoses of battery failures by 90%

▶ Earn $200,000 by selling courses

▶ Recertify 150 nuclear power plant operators

Keep the business objective in the back of your mind as you make other decisions. Write it on a note card and tack it to your wall so you never stray too far from this objective.

What will you do for learners?

What will you teach and to whom? Start off by setting specific teaching objectives. Good objectives specify which learners will accomplish what results under what conditions and to what degree of success.

Note: I distinguish **teaching** objectives from **learning** objectives. Teaching objectives are what *you* want to teach someone, and learning objectives are what *learners* want to learn. If you have chosen well, your teaching objectives match learners' learning objectives perfectly, and only a grammatical shift from "the learner" to "you" is necessary.

Write clear objectives

There are no magic formulas for writing objectives, but four elements seem essential to all well formulated objectives:

▶ Who are the learners?

▶ What will training accomplish for them?

▶ How will they apply what they learn?

▶ What degree of success will they accomplish?

Let's take a closer look at each of these questions. They can help us set objectives that are both practical and worthy.

Who are the learners?

Whose knowledge, skills, and attitudes are you trying to alter? What groups of learners are you designing for?

Describe learner characteristics pertinent to your goal so that instructional designers can gauge:

▶ What are the learners' current levels of knowledge, biases, skills, and attitudes?

▶ What are their expectations and attitudes toward training?

▶ What motivates them to learn?

▶ How well prepared are they to use WBT technologies?

Such intimate knowledge may require conducting surveys, interviews, and testing.

What will training accomplish for them?

What exactly will learners accomplish by taking your course? As a result of your course what will they:

▶ **Do?** In completing the course, what will learners accomplish or create?

▶ **Be able to do?** What skills will they acquire?

▶ **Believe?** How will the learners' preconceptions and biases be altered?

▶ **Feel?** What attitudes and emotions will learners experience?

▶ **Understand?** What conceptual knowledge will learners gain?

How will they apply what they learn?

We teach so that learners can *apply* what they learn, not merely *accumulate knowledge*. People apply knowledge, skills, and attitudes in real world circumstances. As part of the objective, we need to specify what those circumstances are. That way, designers can tailor the training to accomplishing results in these circumstances. *Circumstances* is a pretty broad term. It can include any of these factors if relevant to the learner's ability to apply learning:

▶ What events will trigger application of the training?

▶ What resources can the learner draw on? Books? Calculators? Access to the Web? Memory only?

▶ What assistance will the learner have? A supervisor to guide the learner? Peers with whom to discuss problems?

What degree of success will learners accomplish?

We like to think that all learners will be perfectly successful in accomplishing the intended results. Ironically, though, designing for a goal of perfect performance often leads to worse, not better, results. Thus, for each objective, we should state realistically how successful learners should be in applying what they learn.

Quantifying the degree of success is not easy, but we can at least set metrics such as these:

▶ Percent of learners who will accomplish the objective perfectly

▶ Average error rate

▶ Time required to perform the task

▶ Amount produced in a specified period of time

▶ Reduction in frequency of problems or increase in rate of favorable incidents

Examples of teaching objectives

Here are some examples of teaching objectives from different courses:

Learners	Results	How applied	Degree of success
Full-time foresters with less than five years' experience	Openly and objectively consider controlled burns as a means of forest management.	Foresters will give recommendations when asked. They will have access to Web-based resources.	Novice foresters will recommend controlled burning with the same frequency as more experienced foresters.
Visual Basic programmers working on database projects	Be able to retrieve and write data from remote databases using ADO and RDS.	Programmers will have access to all online documentation and other Web-based resources.	At least 85% will be able to write routines to retrieve, alter, and rewrite data within 10 minutes.
Customer support technicians	Correctly identify the cause of battery failures.	When answering customer complaints over the phone.	Reduce the current rate of misdiagnosis by 90%.
Individual investors	Develop a balanced financial plan to accomplish their individual objectives.	Using Web-based resources during the course.	Over 90% will complete their plans.

Make your organization's goal your goal

In preparing your teaching objectives, keep your business objectives in mind. Research and experience warns that unless teaching objectives support business objectives the project will fail [22]. State clearly how your goal relates to those of your overall organization. Why do you want to do what your plan proposes? For example:

Most misdiagnoses of battery problems are caused by lack of knowledge among customer support technicians about the modes of battery failure and the symptoms they can produce. By training customer support technicians, we can reduce the rate of misdiagnosis by at least 90%.

Create a bridge connecting the business objectives and the teaching objectives so that both business managers and instructional designers can see how the objectives work together.

Defining curriculum

When setting the scope for a course or series of courses, consider whether definitions of the body of knowledge already exist. For the scope of your course or curriculum, do any of the following exist?

▶ Defined criteria of knowledge by government bodies or industry associations.

▶ Certification or licensing requirements.

▶ Standard reference works that cover an area.

▶ Professional associations that represent an area.

Such a definition can save you months of debate and hair-splitting in defining the limits and boundaries of your course.

DESIGN FIRST, LAST, AND IN BETWEEN

This book is about design. Many people think design is what occurs only at the beginning of a project. That view cannot withstand the realities of the design process. The process of design is simple in theory but complex in practice.

Design is a process

First you analyze your requirements and design the course. Then your build it and test it. Oops! Better analyze the results and redesign a bit. Then you need to build in a few changes and test again. And so it goes.

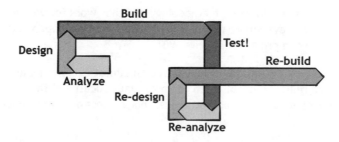

The design process proceeds in a cycle of analyze, design, build, and test. Thus, design is a series—sometimes a seemingly endless series—of decisions. The design process is essentially cyclical, corkscrewing in from high level to detailed issues while continually revisiting the same requirements over and over again.

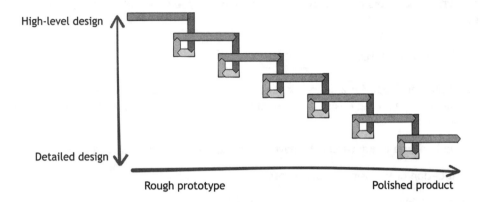

The design process involves top-down design gated by testing at every level and tempered by a willingness to back up and start over where called for. At the beginning, you deal with high-level issues and work with a crude prototype, perhaps nothing more than a stack of sketches on index cards. At the end of the process, you are fine-tuning individual pixels of the final course.

Religious issues and why we avoid them

This book does not prescribe an educational theory or a development methodology. It was written so that you can fit its advice into your current theory or methodology. What is important is that you design the course to accomplish its objectives, not to fit a narrowly defined theory or to accommodate an inflexible authoring tool.

Many designers treat educational theories and development methodologies like strict religion. And only their religion is the true religion. An exogenous constructivist considers Designer's Edge a tool of the seven-horned devil. Devotees of Information Mapping guffaw at the foo-foo-puffery of the Microworldians.

If you have a theory and development methodology and they work for you, good. WBT is flexible—and learners are even more flexible. If you keep your eyes open and apply your theory sensitively, you can produce effective WBT.

I have seen effective WBT courses developed based on almost every popular theory, even "I just did what seemed right." I do not mean to imply that educational theory and development methodology are not important, just that success does not depend on any particular one.

50,000 years of instructional design in a nutshell

1. Show them.
2. Tell them.
3. Let them try.
4. Repeat.

If this does not work—or if you want to be part of the latest educational fad—change the order of the steps until you find a combination that works.

LET PEOPLE LEARN AS THEY ALWAYS HAVE

Rather than use WBT to mimic existing methods of education, perhaps we should broaden the perspective to include all the ways people learn. Think of all the ways you have learned throughout your life. Here is a brief list of ways people learn with some notes on how WBT and its components can be used to enable anybody anywhere to learn that way.

We learn by ...	How we can learn this way in WBT
Listening to lectures, interviews, debates, sermons, speeches, stories, testimonials, and discussions among experts	Webcasts (p 195) using audio and video. Case-study activities (p 226). Online conferences (p 548). Virtual response pads (p 361). Audioconferencing (p 363) and videoconferencing (p 364). Presentation sequences (p 199). Event-playback pages (p 163).
Seeking advice from parents, mentors, co-workers, bosses, psychologists, religious leaders, consultants, and friends	Mentoring (p 542). E-mail roster (p 110) along with biographies of the instructor (p 94) and learners (p 109). Discussion groups (p 348) and other collaboration mechanisms (p 346). Guest speakers in Webcasts (p 195). Scavenger hunt activities (p 204).
Reading books, manuals, papers, articles, poems, stories, reports	Presentation sequences (p 199). Related Resource pages (p 154) and Course resources pages (p 113). Virtual libraries (p 520). Search-the-Net pages (p 115).
Watching presentations, demonstrations, performances	Webcasts (p 195). Presentation sequences (p 199). Event-Playback pages (p 163). Whiteboard (p 358) and screen-sharing sessions (p 359).
Examining exemplars. Visiting and touring museums, factories, historical sites, other countries and cultures. Critiquing the work of others.	Virtual museums (p 525). Online conferences (p 548). Virtual field trips (p 559) and guided tours (p 554). Featured Example (p 158) and Code Sample (p 161) pages. Group-critique activities (p 237).
Critiques by experts, bosses, parents, peers, and self.	Discussion groups (p 348) and other collaboration mechanisms (p 346). Group-critique activities (p 237). Mentoring (p 542).

We learn by ...	How we can learn this way in WBT
Modeling the behavior of parents, teachers, experts, and heroes. Examining the behavior of others.	Mentoring (p 542). Webcasts (p 195) with guest experts. Case-study activities (p 226). Role-playing activities (p 232). Simulators used as courses (p 567), learning games (p 251), and tests (p 296).
Exploring. Trying things out. Taking things apart and putting them back together again. Finding our own way. Playing games.	Guided tours (p 554). Simulators used as courses (p 567), learning games (p 251), and tests (p 296). Virtual laboratories (p 242). Hands-on activities (p 246). Exploratory tutorials (p 143). Choice pages (p 165). Brainstorming activities (p 223).
Discussing ideas with experts and peers.	Discussion groups (p 348), chat sessions (p 354), and other collaboration mechanisms (p 346). Mentoring (p 542). Online conferences (p 548). E-mail roster (p 110).
Practicing skills and abilities over and over again. Drill and practice sessions.	Simulators used as courses (p 567), learning games (p 251), and tests (p 296). Drill-and-practice activities (p 202). Role-playing scenarios (p 232). Virtual laboratories (p 242). Hands-on activities (p 246). Procedure pages (p 166).
Memorizing by mnemonics. Repeating affirmations.	Drill-and-practice activities (p 202). Presentation sequences (p 199).
Conducting research. Finding and analyzing information on our own.	Scavenger hunt activities (p 204). Guided research (p 207) and guided analysis (p 211) activities. Case studies (p 226). Exploratory tutorials (p 143).

IN CLOSING ...

The rest of this book will guide you in realizing the potential of WBT. Use it to assess the various techniques provided by WBT and to shape them to your objectives and the needs of your learners.

> The illiterates of the 21st century will not be those who cannot read and write but those who cannot learn, unlearn, and relearn.
>
> — Alvin Toffler

2

Evaluate WBT

Advantages, disadvantages, and costs of WBT

One of the first major design decisions you confront is whether to use WBT at all. Before you commit to WBT technologies, you should weigh the potential and requirements of WBT to decide whether WBT offers the best solutions for your needs. You should also estimate the costs and make sure you are willing to pay them.

You cannot make the decision based on a mathematical weighing of promised advantages and feared disadvantages. Promised advantages do not pop ready-to-run out of the box. You have to coax and lure them out with good design and hard work. Likewise, the disadvantages that others have experienced are not inevitable. Workarounds and countermeasures can neutralize many of them. As you consider the advantages and disadvantages of WBT, think about how to achieve the advantages while scheming how to avoid the disadvantages.

As you consider this long list of advantages and disadvantages, remember that the only ones that matter are the ones that pertain to your course. If, for example, you do not plan to use collaboration mechanisms, then you get none of their advantages or drawbacks. Always keep your course in mind.

> Before beginning to compose something, gauge the nature and extent of the enterprise and work for a suitable design. Design improves even the simplest structure whether of brick and steel or of prose. You raise a pup tent from one sort of vision, a cathedral from another.
>
> — E. B. White

THE IDEAL USE OF WBT

Let's start with the best situation for using WBT. If your situation matches this ideal, you can probably skip the rest of this chapter and start right in designing your course.

The ideal learner

New technologies and techniques are not for everyone. Certain groups can better take advantage of such advances [23, 24].

Who are the ideal learners for WBT? They are people who:

▶ Learn independently and view learning positively

▶ Are self-disciplined, manage time well, and enjoy working alone

▶ Express themselves clearly in writing

▶ Have good basic computer skills and value the role of technology in business and learning

▶ Need to acquire new knowledge now but cannot easily attend traditional training, for example those who travel or live in a remote location

▶ Laugh at small technical glitches and revel in solving problems

▶ Have a definite goal, such as certification, a degree, or the ability to perform a specific task

▶ Are moderately experienced in a field and already understand the basic concepts of that field

Know any ideal learners? Neither do I, but the more your learners match this profile, the easier your task of designing WBT to meet their needs.

The ideal course

What is the ideal WBT project? WBT excels at efficiently teaching precisely defined objective knowledge, such as:

▶ Step-by-step procedures

▶ Scientific and business concepts

▶ Syntax and vocabulary of human and computer languages

▶ Mechanical skills that must be performed speedily

For your first Web-based course, pick an existing instructor-led course that covers such well-defined knowledge. Select a course that is well designed but that is not working because it costs too much, occurs too infrequently, or cannot keep up with demand. Make that course your first Web-based course and the odds are in your favor.

ADVANTAGES OF WBT

Although WBT is a relatively new phenomenon, it has already demonstrated some distinct advantages over traditional classroom training and over disk-based computer-based training (CBT). WBT has all the advantages of disk-based CBT, such as constant availability, non-judgmental testing, and instant feedback. WBT does not offer the ability to use multimedia freely but does have some advantages of its own:

▶ Access to Web-based resources

▶ Centralized storage and maintenance

▶ Collaboration mechanisms

WBT combines the collaboration of face-to-face training and the anywhere-anytime availability of CBT. And WBT is just in its infancy. Everyone agrees it is going to get better and better.

WBT can save vaults of money

The fuel propelling adoption of WBT is money. Potential cost savings have energized corporations and universities to begin using WBT now. Technology-conveyed training, including WBT, is typically 40-60% less expensive than training delivered by traditional means [25].

What kinds of costs are saved?

How does WBT save money? Mainly by reducing some of the largest costs for training. Here are some cost savings you should consider for your project.

Travel expenses

Up to 40% of the cost of corporate training is for travel [26]. Aetna estimated that for training 1200 employees, travel expenses alone would cost $5 million USD—that's $4166 per person [27]. Travel expenses can include airfare, mileage, parking, taxi fares, lodging, meals, and phone calls back to the office.

Facilities and supplies

WBT reduces capital costs for training facilities. Because learners take the class from their own offices or homes, the need for classrooms, chairs, desks, tables, whiteboards, easel pads, and other classroom supplies is reduced or eliminated. Virtual laboratories (p 242) and simulations (p 251) can replace expensive laboratories and test equipment. Because many of the instructional resources are on the Web, the need for libraries, bookstores, copying machines, and storerooms is cut.

These savings allow companies and schools to deliver more learning without adding more facilities. Kent State University, working with IBM and ILINC, built a distributed learning network that enabled Kent State to increase enrollment by 30% without adding additional buildings [28].

Reduced administrative costs

Some WBT systems can perform—or at least simplify—many time-consuming administrative chores:

- ▶ Distributing course catalogs

- ▶ Registering students

- ▶ Distributing course materials and handouts

- ▶ Recording grades and "attendance"

- ▶ Compiling critiques

Salaries

Employees are usually paid for the time they are in training. Although the time spent learning may not be less with WBT, the time spent traveling to training definitely will be less. For a three-day classroom course, learners may spend a day traveling to the training and a day returning, thus three days of training can cost five days of salary. With WBT three days of training cost just three days of salary. And, if employees choose to take training on their own time, it can cost less still.

Lost opportunity costs

Almost no cost comparisons consider lost-opportunity costs, the costs incurred or revenues not generated because someone is in training and not on the job. Sales representatives book no orders while they are in training. Consultants record no billable hours. The basic work of the organization does not get done while people are in training.

Organizations report big savings

Many separate organizations report substantial savings from their initial forays into WBT.

▶ **Buckman Laboratories** reduced the costs of training employees to use e-mail and other technologies. Costs fell from $2.4 million USD to $400,000 when Buckman switched to online training [29].

▶ **Hewlett-Packard** cut the cost of training 700 engineers on a new chip from $7 million USD to $1.5 million. The training was performed in 30 days instead of the year projected for on-site classroom training [30].

▶ **ASK International** replaced a weeklong classroom course providing product knowledge to sales representatives with a six-hour course made up of self-paced materials and an on-site workshop. The costs dropped from $2500 USD per learner to $500 [31].

▶ **Eli Lilly & Company's** Web-based training program saved the company $800,000 USD in travel and salary costs over classroom training during the new program's first year [32].

▶ **MCI WorldCom** used online training to save $5.6 million USD in 1998 [27]. MCI WorldCom's Career Enhancement University, a virtual classroom, saved the company $2.8 million in travel, facilities, and salaries ($1500 per learner). As of June of 1998 CEU had trained 3,825 students in 369 classes. These savings resulted from an investment of $300,000 in communications infrastructure and 3200 person hours of development. As of October 1998, CEU had produced a 237 percent return on investment [33]. MCI WorldCom used its virtual classrooms to train 7000 network technicians at 800 locations.

▶ **Aetna** saved $3 million USD by using online training to educate 3000 employees. Online learners achieved 4% higher levels of expertise than those in traditional training [27].

▶ **MetLife**, according to Asymetrix, was able to train 9000 field sales representatives to use a new computer application for $30 USD each.

▶ **Cisco** reduced the $1200 - $1800 USD cost per learner of instructor-led training to $120 with WBT [34].

▶ **Novell** certification can be an expensive process. The price of a four-day classroom course for Novell certification was $1800 USD, not including travel, lodging, meals and time away from the job. The same training now costs $700 to $900 delivered by WBT [34].

What are realistic costs?

Costs for WBT and other forms of training are not easy to estimate. (See the section on cost estimating, p 43, for some tips.) If you need a quick estimate and you do not care whether it is accurate or not, try one of these two methods of guided guessing:

▶ **Consider what you are spending now.** Total up the amount your organization has invested in classrooms, administrative offices, whiteboards, chairs, classroom computers, and so forth. Expect to spend one-quarter to one-half that much on the infrastructure (servers, networks, and computers) for WBT. Now count the number of instructors, managers, administrators, instructional designers, janitors, and subject-matter experts you employ now. Dedicate one-half that number to WBT.

▶ **Count the number of people you must train**. As a rule, WBT will be cheaper if you have over 300 to 500 learners. If development costs or per-student delivery costs are especially high, WBT may be less expensive with fewer learners.

WBT improves learning

Although WBT is new, there is already evidence that instructional designers need not sacrifice quality of learning to move to WBT.

WBT enables better teaching techniques

WBT that implements effective instructional design may actually provide a better learning experience than classrooms or disk-based CBT.

WBT activates learners

Well-designed WBT challenges learners. To progress in a WBT course, learners must actively navigate the course. They may be required to select which lessons to take and in what sequence. Activities and practice sessions alternate with presentations. Learners cannot just sit back and listen to a lecture or passively watch video. They must think and respond. They must actively learn. Although it is possible to design WBT in which learners are passive, it is just as easy to include meaningful interaction and interactivity.

With WBT, learners feel more in control of their learning. Because learners feel in control, they take more responsibility and learn more effectively [35].

WBT exposes learners to real-world data

WBT can expose learners to a whole world of data and experiences. Access to the real world can make learning concrete and pertinent. The real world provides a sounding board for ideas. For example, an 8th grade science class in the U.S. investigated microorganisms found in pond water. They contacted similar classes in the United Kingdom, South Africa, and Japan. The U.S. students believed that the organisms found in these different lands would be different from those in local ponds. After all, how could such tiny, fragile organisms travel great distances? When they examined photographs posted by the Japanese class, however, they found the same organisms. The real world forced them to revise their theories and think more deeply about the issues they were studying [35].

The Web can expose learners to realistic data for study and analysis. Because learners can copy the data into their spreadsheets, they can analyze large collections of data almost as easily as typing in the paltry sets of data used for classroom examples. And the real-world data has all the irregularities, exceptions, and messiness that learners must deal with on the job anyway. Having access to such large messy datasets was found useful by 85.7% of learners in one experiment [36].

Thanks to government agencies and universities, the Internet is loaded with statistical analyses, data collections, and scientific reports on economics, medicine, astronomy, crime, biology, geology, and dozens more subjects. For some fields, such as weather and finance, real-time feeds provide up-to-the-moment data.

WBT provides a more in-depth learning experience

WBT can make learning more complete and comprehensive by exposing learners to more aspects of a subject. All elementary and high school teachers interviewed in one project felt that "well-designed, effective technology-supported projects provided students with a more in-depth learning experience than do traditional approaches …" [35].

WBT can develop better thinking skills

Learners who use Web technologies to discuss issues, research questions, and solve problems improve their critical reasoning, problem solving, and creativity [37]. In writing classes, learners asked more substantive questions and commented more constructively on the writing of peers [38]. Learners expressed their reasoning more clearly and made more specific suggestions for improvement.

WBT lets learners reflect before responding

When events are conducted by e-mail or discussion groups, learners can take their time answering questions. Learners take longer to respond and think through their answers more deeply [39]. Most say they learn better when they have time to think before speaking or writing.

WBT promotes collaborative learning

Web technology promotes collaborative learning [35]. Learners can discuss, debate, and brainstorm with colleagues from throughout the company, across the country, or around the globe.

WBT uses effective learning technologies

WBT is based on several new technologies and the use of technology in learning is a bit, well, controversial. Designers can take heart, though. Recent studies indicate that learning technology can improve learning. Over half of universities and colleges surveyed by CCA Consulting rated the effectiveness of learning technology "high" or "very high" in improving student attitudes toward learning, enhancing student achievements, in increasing interaction among students and instructors, and boosting the self-esteem of students [40]. And technology can enable students to explore advanced subjects. Seventh-grade mathematics students at Norwood Middle School in New Jersey used Geometer's Sketchpad to explore concepts traditionally taught only two grades later [35].

WBT emphasizes learning not butts in seats

With WBT, training departments cannot be evaluated merely by the number of numb posteriors occupying classrooms. WBT and other new methods of delivering training are emphasizing the amount of learning accomplished rather than merely the number of person-hours spent in the classroom [41, 42, 43].

WBT helps learners identify knowledge resources

Part of learning is identifying resources that can answer questions now and in the future. Libraries are such resources. Library research helps learners identify valuable sources of knowledge, but the library is across town and not open all day. Resources identified on the Internet can be bookmarked or added to a personal jump page, where they are never more than a couple of mouse clicks away. As our definition of learning shifts from memorizing knowledge to gaining the ability to solve problems, such resources become an essential part of learning.

WBT is just as effective as classroom training

Many attempts at comparing the effectiveness of WBT and classroom training found that early attempts at WBT performed on a par with established classroom courses.

The no-significant-difference effect and its significance

Tom Russell of North Carolina State University has published a bibliography of 355 research papers, reports, and summaries over the years that have found no statistically significant difference in effectiveness in learning in the classroom, by correspondence, through videotapes, by interactive video, through CBT, or by WBT [44]. This finding is called the "no-significant-difference phenomenon."

Cited examples of no significant difference for WBT include these:

▶ A Web-based course achieved the same level of performance as a lecture-format course [45]. Students with access to both, did, however, perform better.

▶ Online and face-to-face learning were equally effective [46].

▶ Community college students felt that an online course design was as effective as a traditional classroom and were highly satisfied with their learning experience [47].

▶ Studies of computer-mediated learning at universities typically find no difference in effectiveness from traditional education [48].

▶ "Grades and performance of the online learners proved neither better nor worse on the average than traditional section students" [49].

From the studies showing no significant difference, Moore and Kearsly [50] conclude:

(1) there is not sufficient evidence to support the idea that classroom training is the optimum delivery method; (2) instruction at a distance can be as effective in bringing about learning as classroom instruction; (3) the absence of face-to-face contact is not in itself detrimental to the learning process; and (4) what makes any course good or poor is a consequence of how well it is designed, delivered, and conducted, not whether the students are face-to-face or at a distance [50].

Pay special attention to point (4). That is what this book is all about.

Note that not everybody agrees that the no-significant-difference effect really exists or matters. Bill Orr of Auburn University has published a rebuttal list of studies that found online training superior [51]. Later in this chapter (p 26), we list some studies in which WBT performed better.

More just-as-good cases

I unearthed a few more studies in which WBT did as well as classroom training:

▶ Students taking a Web-based course in exercise physiology scored as well on their final exam as those taking a lecture-based version. And they liked WBT: 88% said they would "take another Internet-based course given the opportunity" [52].

▶ Students in a new Web-conducted geography course offered by Western Michigan University achieved the same results as those in traditional classroom courses. Ninety percent expressed satisfaction with the course [53].

▶ A comparison of an initial offering of six WBT business courses at Nova Southeastern University found that the WBT courses were just as effective as their traditional classroom counterparts [54].

Even tie-scores are a victory for WBT

Comparisons that show no significant difference between WBT and conventional training are themselves a strong recommendation for WBT because in most of these studies the WBT was a first effort. In many cases it was:

▶ The first WBT course created by the authors

▶ The first WBT course taken by the students

▶ The first WBT course taught by the instructor

▶ The first time learners had used several new technologies

▶ The first experience of the technical and support staff supporting a WBT course

▶ The first use of new or newly converted material

▶ Built by converting existing materials optimized for the traditional environment rather than developing new material for the WBT environment

WBT is sometimes significantly better

In many cases, WBT is not just as good as classroom training but better. Here are a handful of examples:

California State-Northridge statistics course is statistically better

A virtual classroom version of a course in social statistics scored 20% higher on midterm and final exams than the same course taught in a traditional classroom. Students in the virtual class spent more time on class work and understood the material better. At the end of the class they felt more positively toward math. The virtual class provided more perceived contact with peers and appeared more flexible to learners [55].

Office Depot trained more people better

Office Depot used a virtual classroom to simultaneously train students in Florida, California, and Texas, thus increasing enrollment by a factor of three while increasing student satisfaction by 20% [56]. Retention increased by 25%, student satisfaction by 30%, and demand by 30%. Costs decreased by 80% [28].

Merrill Lynch improved test scores

Merrill Lynch converted instructor-led courses to create 12 intranet-based courses providing over 30 hours of instruction. Test results improved over the classroom courses [57].

Mortgage bankers learn in more depth

In courses by the Mortgage Bankers Association of America, learners covered the same material as in the classroom but at greater depth and with greater access to experts [58].

Toys "R" Us delighted learners with more flexible training

Toys "R" Us used WBT collaboration mechanisms to train employees in 19 regional distribution centers how to operate new computer programs [59]. The training was enthusiastically received by employees who liked the frequency of classes and the flexibility this provided, the access to remote experts, and the cost savings.

WBT learners are satisfied

Though learning satisfaction is not a reliable measure of learning, it certainly beats learning dissatisfaction. And, as a whole, initial WBT learners appear satisfied.

▶ After completing one WBT course, 81% of learners said they preferred WBT [60].

▶ Courses on managed healthcare and on interviewing were rated highly by learners at Rhone-Poulenc Rorer [57].

▶ Students in a Web-based Computer Foundations course at Macon State College in Georgia all agreed that the course met their expectations, that they received help from the instructor when they needed it, and that they were encouraged to ask questions [61].

▶ At Northern Indiana University 90% of distance learners in human resources development courses were satisfied with the effectiveness of their learning experience [62].

▶ Although they felt the online class required more work, 80% of students in a University of Dallas course said they would take another Internet-based course [63].

Other advantages for learners

Learners benefit from other aspects of WBT besides a more effective learning environment. Here are some of the additional advantages that learners say are important to them.

Learners can get the best instruction available

"I want to know I am getting the best training possible. I can shop around for the best course on the Web."

With courses available on the Web, learners can select the best courses, the best schools, the best instructors, and the best fellow learners. As more courses go on the Web, competition will develop and choices increase. Corporations will realize the advantages of providing employees with more choices than provided by local vendors or in-house training departments.

True, a lot of the courses on the Web today would have to improve just to achieve mediocrity. But more and more vendors offer sample courses or even money-back guarantees so learners can try out a course before parting with their training budget. At least with the Web, learners are not limited to the choices provided by their in-house training department or local training providers.

Furthermore, the quality of self-directed courses is consistent for all learners. The learners are not at the mercy of the instructor assigned to teach the course this particular session.

Discussions get needed time

"Discussions can continue outside of class—for days or weeks. If you think of a witty retort a week later, no problem, just add it to the discussion."

When using e-mail and discussion groups, learners can take time to compose replies. They can attach supporting materials, cite sources, and prepare graphics and other media.

Training occurs just in time

"I need training now. Not next quarter, not next month, not next week. I need training right now."

With WBT, learners can get training right when they need it. With self-directed WBT, learners do not have to wait for a class to form and they can proceed at their own pace. When a need arises, they can learn what they require. They can learn about a new product the night before pitching it to a potential customer. They can brush up on interviewing skills a few hours before an interview.

Learners set the pace and schedule

"My schedule is too full and changes too much for me to attend regularly scheduled classes. And I travel a lot."

Many busy workers cannot fit training into their schedules. In an effort to accommodate them, many training organizations are now offering classes on Saturday mornings and Sundays. WBT goes further, making courses available 24 hours a day, 7 days a week.

No one is completely happy with the pace of an instructor-led course. It is too fast for some and too slow for others—and the instructor is always checking the clock on the wall.

With WBT, learners have more flexibility in learning at their own speed. Many WBT courses do not require consecutive time. Learners can take the course at their own pace. Some can study full-time while others devote a few hours a week to the course. Learners can repeat lessons they find especially interesting or difficult and skip others they have already mastered or do not need.

Learners get better access to the instructor

"I could 'talk' to the instructor. I could ask my questions and get help on my problems."

Often learners report that they actually had more frequent and more effective communication with their instructors than in classroom courses. After completing a University of Dallas online course, one student said, "Believe it or not, I actually felt that my asynchronous instructor was easier to approach with questions than my classroom teachers" [63].

Learners showcase their work

"Everybody could see what I was learning—even my five-year-old daughter."

Writing a paper or doing a project that will be seen only by an instructor lacks the motivation of preparing materials that will be posted on the Web for the whole world to see [35]. That *Whole Watching World* includes bosses, potential employers, family and friends, professional colleagues, and even potential mates.

Training adapts to the learner's style

"For the first time I learned the way I like to learn."

WBT accommodates many different learning styles. People learn in the way most efficient for them:

- ▶ Visual or verbal
- ▶ Analytical or experiential

WBT also works for varied personalities:

- ▶ Morning-people or evening-people
- ▶ Sprinters or plodders
- ▶ Extroverts or introverts

Many learners say they like the freedom to be themselves and concentrate on learning rather than on social appearances. With WBT they can take the course in a tee shirt and sandals or in pajamas and fuzzy slippers. They can sneeze, yawn, and burp without embarrassment.

Learners get immediate feedback

"Getting feedback immediately made exams seem like puzzles or games. They were fun."

One advantage cited again and again by WBT veterans is immediate feedback. Learners liked not having to wait days and days to see how they did on a test. Students love the immediate feedback of automatically scored tests—especially if they are just practice tests and the scores are not recorded.

Learners are treated more equally

"Grading is more evenhanded. Flattery and flirting do not play a role. You have to get by on your ideas."

WBT provides a cloak of anonymity that lets learners control their on-screen personas and diminishes personal characteristics like race, nationality, and gender. More attention is focused on ideas and less on irrelevant characteristics.

Although in its early years the Internet seemed the domain of male techno-nerds, it has since moved into the mainstream with corresponding demographics. In general—and there are exceptions—women are as likely to use the Internet for research, publication, and commerce as males. Girls send e-mail, chat, and surf the Web with about the same frequency as boys of the same age.

WBT saves money for learners

"When I added up all the things I didn't have to buy, I was amazed at how much money I saved."

With WBT, the hidden costs of training are minimal. Because travel is unnecessary, WBT cuts wear and tear on automobiles, gasoline, bus fare, insurance, and parking fees. Since most materials are on the Web, they are free. Learners do not need to purchase, store, or recycle books, course packs, and hundreds of pages of handouts.

For learners who take courses on their own computers, WBT requires less computer power than multimedia-heavy CD-ROM-based CBT.

WBT saves time for learners

"I saved gobs of time. With WBT, almost all of my training time was spent learning."

With traditional classroom training, much of the learner's time is spent on non-training activities: traveling to the city where training is conducted, driving or riding to and from the classroom building; finding a place to park; walking to the classroom, going to the library, running by the bookstore only to discover the course packs are not available yet, going on field trips, and waiting to ask the instructor a question after class. WBT cuts out this wasted time.

WBT produces positive side effects

"I learned a lot more than the subject of the course. My computer skills are better, and I am learning to write again."

Taking a WBT course is not always easy. But the effort of doing so may have side benefits beyond mastering the subject of the course. Learners:

► Gain general technical knowledge about computer and Internet technologies they can apply on their jobs

▶ Acquire specific online learning and reading skills they can use in future courses

▶ Develop self-discipline needed to stay on schedule with a multi-month project

▶ Come to view learning as their responsibility rather than that of the instructor

▶ Improve their writing skills [35]

These intangible benefits are seldom included in calculations of benefits and costs.

Other advantages for instructors

Instructors moving from classroom to WBT may not immediately see the advantages WBT offers and how it can help them conduct classes more effectively and conveniently. Some of these advantages mirror those for learners; others are new.

Instructors can teach from anywhere

WBT benefits mobile instructors as much as mobile learners. The instructor can teach the course from any location with an Internet connection. This opens up the ranks of instructors to experienced, active experts who cannot meet the demands of regular classroom meetings.

For example, Ilya Zaslavsky, an assistant professor at Western Michigan University in Kalamazoo, Michigan, was able to conduct his geography classes while on leave in San Diego [53].

Instructors travel less

Because instructors do not have to travel to remote sites to conduct training, they spend more time on productive and enjoyable activities. Instructors can spend more time planning, producing, and polishing their courses. They can also conduct classes more often. Instructors may spend more time with their families and, if they travel less, they are less prone to exhaustion and burnout.

Course content can be dynamic

Instructors can "add to the course pack" as the course progresses. They can do this from home at two in the morning when an inspiration hits, from the beach on vacation when they remember something that was left out, or in the office in response to an e-mail message from an amateur proofreader.

Instructors can more quickly respond to changes in subject matter. A procedure is updated, a price-list revised, or the terms of a contract amended. The course can be kept up to date with minimal cost—no reprints, errata sheets, or updates to the updates.

The content can grow and change to respond to learners' needs, to correct mistakes and omissions, and to incorporate better content. Revising the course becomes a routine, continual activity, not a frantic effort between class offerings.

Instructors save time

WBT reduces the "administrivia" of running a course. Many of the routine, but time-consuming tasks of administering a course can be automated. With WBT, the instructor is freed from:

▶ Having handouts and course packs printed

▶ Handing out assignments, notes, and other papers

▶ Collecting assignments

▶ Returning graded assignments

▶ Making announcements

Instructors can check learners' facts and references

Access to the Web lets instructors quickly verify facts, confirm quotations, and check citations. Citations to a Web source take just a mouse click to verify. Availability of special Web-based calculators can make checking mathematical computations a snap.

Other advantages for organizations

WBT saves organizations money. But the benefits do not end there. Let's look at some of the bounty from an organizational perspective.

WBT delivers consistently high-quality training

WBT can ensure that all the appropriate people in the organization get the same quality of training at the same time. They hear the same message presented in much the same way. With instructor-led WBT more people can attend the classes.

In one day, using Web training technologies, master trainers at ProSoft can train 50 trainers throughout the U.S. on complex software packages [10]. And, with self-directed WBT learners can easily fit the training into their busy schedules.

All learners can reach a specific level of mastery. WBT can easily certify that a workforce has mastered a subject area.

WBT provides training around the globe without travel

WBT provides training to the whole world as it reduces the need for travel. More people spend more time at their desks and in the field—doing their jobs. Rensselaer Polytechnic Institute in Troy, New York, conducted live training of learners 11 time zones away in Hong Kong [64]. Lucent's Wireless University makes WBT courses available in 90 countries [65].

WBT gives organizations flexibility

Web-based technologies are flexible. They provide many choices for how to deliver learning, provide interaction and interactivity, and price units of learning. You can use Web technologies to implement any learning methodology you choose from recidivist behaviorism to exogenous constructivism [66]. Courses can be revised midstream. Material can be added, revised, or deleted, as the course is going on. Courses can be adapted to the needs of a specific class or individual learner. Producers can bill by course, by enrollment, by student, by site, by topics accessed, or by time and length of access. Such flexibility makes it easier for managers to fit training into their budgets.

WBT integrates training with work

Learning takes place in the learner's work environment where the knowledge will be applied. This communicates the message that learning is a natural part of work, not an unwanted interruption or an entertaining but unrelated vacation.

WBT creates valuable learning resources

WBT courses generate valuable learning resources. Chats and forum discussions can be archived and abstracted. Feedback forms provide valuable tips on how to improve the course. Student projects provide a starting point and exemplars for future classes. Some student projects can generate works of value outside the course.

WBT leaves records that can be analyzed and studied. Lucent's Network Wireless Group tracks education level, product experience, and job skills to see how these factors relate to success for learners taking WBT through Lucent's Wireless University [65].

WBT keeps experts on the job

With WBT, specialists with rare knowledge can spend more time applying it and less time communicating their knowledge to others. Boeing found that its WBT efforts let its 300 process designers focus on their jobs rather than on developing classroom training [18].

WBT helps recruit workers

Increasingly, workers seek out employers who provide the training that their employees need to develop and maintain their skills. Home Depot capitalizes on this trend by touting its "Office Depot Interactive" training on the Careers part of its Web site.

DISADVANTAGES OF WBT

WBT is not all advantages and benefits. It has costs, requires compromises, and poses serious risks. Most of these negatives can be overcome with good design—but only if you acknowledge and understand them.

The purpose of this section is not to scare you out of using WBT but to balance the scales a bit. WBT is not an educational panacea. This section gives you information you need to honestly evaluate WBT and decide whether it meets the needs of your particular project. If this section provides ammunition to kill off an ill-conceived WBT project, then you will have paid for the cost of this book many times over—without having to read all of it. Killing off a bad WBT project does as much to advance WBT as commissioning a good project.

WBT requires more work

Lacking the slick tools of CBT development and the finely honed management procedures of classroom training, WBT courses require more time and effort to design, to teach, and to take.

More instructor effort required

Many instructors report that electronic delivery requires 40 to 50% more effort on their part [67]. Many teachers using technology in elementary and high schools complain about the increased amount of time and effort such courses require of them [35].

Students, lacking face-to-face contact, demand more attention and feedback from instructors. Some instructors felt they had become, in effect, private tutors [68].

Complaints from instructors about a higher workload diminish as they gain experience. By the third course, the workload may be no more than a conventional course [69].

Solutions

- ▶ Invest in better tools and templates.

- ▶ Delegate duties to learners. Make them more responsible for their own learning.

- ▶ Limit contacts to official office hours when the instructor will be available electronically.

- ▶ Use professional course authors for creating courses.

Conversion efforts take longer than expected

Converting existing classroom courses to WBT has proven harder than many designers expected. Faculty of Florida's Nova Southeastern University found that converting six undergraduate business courses to WBT took much more time than expected [70].

Designers quickly discover that the **Save As HTML** command in their word processor or presentation graphics program does not do the whole job. And they realize that a course requires more than electronic versions of the class overheads and handouts.

Solutions

▶ Perfect conversion techniques on a small pilot project of a single course or part of a large course.

▶ Automate the conversion process as much as possible.

▶ Consider redesigning the course rather than converting it.

More effort required by learners

Often learners report that WBT courses take 20 to 40% more time and effort than traditional classroom courses [63]. Online discussions, brainstorming sessions, and problem-solving activities purportedly take longer than their face-to-face counterparts [71]. Lacking the feedback of facial expressions, body language, and tone of voice, participants in online communications must spend more time apologizing for unintended insults, correcting misinterpretations, and clarifying ambiguities. As a result, learners spend less time on the matter of the discussion.

To benefit from technology, learners must use it. However, if learners feel that the benefits of the technology are not worth the extra effort required to master it, they may resist using the technology [72, 73].

Solutions

▶ Point out benefits of learning technologies that learners may have missed.

▶ Teach learners how to collaborate and how to learn efficiently in WBT.

▶ Moderate discussions and give guidance, tips, and hints where needed.

Superb instructional design and production required

WBT requires superb instructional design and materials. In classroom training, a good instructor can adapt, supplement, and compensate for a weak curriculum.

Because the instructor is not present to correct minor mistakes and clear up misunderstandings, course materials for WBT must be more complete, accurate, and precise.

> For IT subjects every detail needs to be correct because computers are so pedantic that if even one command is not precisely written, an entire exercise can fail. It is very time consuming to produce materials that attain this level of perfection. – Philip Rutherford [74].

Many projects fail to budget the time and detailed attention necessary to achieve this level of quality.

Solutions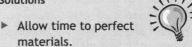

▶ Allow time to perfect materials.

▶ Perform quality control testing. Conduct a beta-test class.

▶ Institute a problem-reporting mechanism to help identify quality defects.

▶ Immediately correct problems and announce availability of improved materials.

Learners fear losing human contact

Many instructors and learners fear that with WBT they lose the human touch of classroom instruction. Though their fears seem greater than warranted by experience, the fears can become reality if learners refuse to take WBT courses or do not commit themselves in them.

Many claim that distance learning is impersonal

There is a widespread belief that the lack of face-to-face contact means that distance learning is impersonal [60]. If the Web is used merely to broadcast learning materials, "human contact is lost, students are isolated, and the educational experience is passive, limited, and alienating" [75]. Many instructional designers fear that learners, lacking face-to-face contact with the instructor and fellow learners, may fail to develop required social skills.

Such dire fears are not borne out by the decades of self-paced distance learning delivered by mail and satellite video. And we must ask how much interpersonal interaction there is in the average lecture class?

The real problems (and solutions)

Let's consider the real fears often expressed by learners new to WBT and what we can do to relieve them.

Problem	Description	Solution
Meanings are misinterpreted.	It is hard to tell what people mean when you cannot see their body language, gestures, and facial expressions or hear their tone of voice. Jokes become insults and subtle praise seems sarcastic.	▶ Encourage students to make their emotions clear and to follow up with others: "Are you making a joke or trying to insult me?" ▶ Teach the use of smileys. ▶ Tell students to develop thick skins.
Who will get me unstuck?	Many learners fear that they will not be able to get help when they are perplexed or frustrated by something in the course. This feeling is exacerbated by the technical glitches, bugs, and downright complexity of some WBT software.	▶ Provide phone or chat support. ▶ Enable learners to help each other. ▶ Encourage collaboration for all kinds of questions and issues. ▶ For more tips, see Chapter 12.
How will I ask questions?	Learners customize mass education by the simple process of asking questions in class. They rely on this ability to clarify misunderstandings and to fill gaps.	▶ Conduct regular chat sessions with the instructor. ▶ Set up ongoing discussion groups among learners. ▶ Hold office hours.
I won't learn from my classmates.	Many learners feel they learn more from conversations with their fellow learners than from the instructor or textbook. Some really do learn more.	▶ Set up online discussion groups. ▶ Include collaborative activities. ▶ Let groups of students conduct their own chat sessions.
Solo learning is lonely.	Learning by yourself can seem cold and sterile to some. (Yet others prefer learning alone.) Some need the interaction, competition, and social pressure of a class to motivate them.	▶ Provide access to a facilitator at any time. ▶ Implement discussion groups and chat sessions. ▶ Publish a schedule with deadlines. ▶ Conduct team activities.

2

Evaluate WBT

Technical requirements are difficult to meet

Some of the most formidable barriers to WBT are technical. Many learners never get started because they cannot get the course to display in their browser. Even when they do get started, technical glitches make for a frustrating, stressful experience. Little is learned except that WBT is no fun.

Many Web-based courses are "dead on arrival." That is, learners never get started because they cannot meet the technical requirements for the course. They cannot figure out how to download and install the required browser, plug-ins, and other software (p 482). They cannot get their laptop to dial out of the hotel, signal a phone card number, or log in through the maze of the corporate intranet firewall. Many potential learners just say, "This is too much trouble. I give up."

Even minor technical glitches can interrupt progress and thwart learning. Long download times, temporarily unavailable pages, and browser crashes can plague even the best system.

Promises of 24 x 7 availability are seldom met in practice. A backhoe cuts a fiber optic cable in the front lawn of the service provider. The disk housing the course develops a slight imbalance a millisecond before converting itself to shrapnel, slicing through casing and shorting out the processor board. The server sometimes has to be shut down for maintenance or to transfer the course to another server. It is hard to have backups for every component.

A complex course may rely on multiple servers for Web pages, for e-mail, for forums, for chat, for uploading and downloading files. Not all of them may be working all the time. If Yahoo!, E*TRADE, and AOL can have outages, so can your course.

Having to deal with unfamiliar and not entirely reliable technology may subject learners to additional stress and distractions. As a result, they spend less time on the subject matter of the course, so their time is used less effectively [75, 76].

Technical difficulties pose such a serious problem that we have dedicated a whole chapter to them. In Chapter 12, you can find some good ideas for overcoming technical barriers.

WBT disrupts established ways that work

Classroom training has low technology but very refined technique. The procedures of classroom training are thoroughly understood and effectively entrenched. Lectures go back 2500 years to the ancient Greeks, and textbooks have been around for over 500 years. Despite limitations, classroom training works.

WBT is new, different, and crude. To use WBT effectively, you must replace processes and techniques that have served civilization for hundreds of years. Nostalgia, paranoia, and genuine skepticism greet the advocate of WBT.

Lectures are not so bad

One reason that the lecture form of instruction persists is that it works—as practiced, not as decried by educational theorists. In a real-world classroom, especially one in industry where instruction is the instructor's full-time job and where learners are not a captive audience, the lecture is not a predetermined one-way broadcast. Lecturers pause after major points to scan the facial expressions and body language of listeners to see how well the last point was understood. They answer questions, and if none are forthcoming, they ask questions of the listeners. Each offering of the class may be different in pacing or even path from the previous one. Good lectures are as interactive as good WBT.

Many learners prefer a traditional format

Often first-time WBT learners express frustration with the lack of a traditional format [63]. An independent evaluation of an experimental statistics course found that 92.9% would have preferred a standard lecture-and-tests course [36].

Because many learners prefer traditional formats, some WBT designers feel, as Ilya Zaslavsky at Western Michigan University states, that "it is very important to preserve some of the traditional elements of classroom teaching so this change isn't traumatic for the students" [53].

Some professionals may feel threatened by WBT

Because WBT uses new technologies, employs new strategies, and foregoes many established communications channels, it may face resistance from those who must now adopt new roles and responsibilities to support it. When Aetna developed an intranet-based training program to train 3000 employees, 2 of 33 trainers chose to transfer to other jobs [17].

Expect some attrition among instructors, say 5 to 10%, especially if the role of the instructor changes substantially.

Solutions

▶ Explain that the ability to design and conduct WBT courses is a valuable skill.

▶ Provide training so instructors can gain confidence in their ability to conduct WBT courses.

▶ Help those who cannot make the adjustment find new jobs elsewhere.

Some fear fast obsolescence

Teachers who learn to write on a blackboard while facing the students have acquired a skill they can use the rest of their career. A teacher who has learned to use a new software package has acquired a skill that will soon be obsolete

Many course designers, likewise, are reluctant to commit their work to a system that may be obsolete in a few years. They foresee an expensive conversion effort to the next great technology or tool.

Solutions

▶ Pick tools and technologies that will be in use for several years. Let others experiment with techno-fads.

▶ Adopt technologies that are easy to learn.

▶ Remind instructional designers that tools change rapidly but principles of effective design change little.

WBT can distort learning

Not all aspects of WBT further learning. WBT poses its own distractions and annoyances. Let's take a look at some of these obstacles and what we designers can do to overcome them.

Obstacles		What we must do to compensate
Too many disruptions	Many learners find it is hard to learn at the office or at home because of the constant interruptions.	▶ Make lessons and topics shorter. ▶ Show learners how to bookmark lessons. ▶ Suggest setting aside learning times and hanging a "Do not disturb" sign on the door.
Web is distracting	The Web is seductively distracting. Undisciplined learners can get sidetracked into exciting forays that, though pleasant, contribute little to the goals of the course.	▶ Make your Web pages cover most of the screen. ▶ Include few external links and put them at the ends of lessons. ▶ Publish and enforce deadlines.
Computer as authority figure	Some students may give more credence than warranted to information presented by the computer [75, 76]. Many Internet sources undergo no critical review process and are little more than unfounded opinions. Some learners may not be aware of this limitation.	▶ Warn learners of the variable quality of Web sources. ▶ Have learners compare contradictory sources. ▶ Conduct a scavenger hunt (p 204) for contradictions and nonsense.

Obstacles		What we must do to compensate
Hypermedia chaos	Free-form hypertext linking has "the potential to make matters worse, creating a sprawling network of items lacking even topical organization" [77].	▶ Organize the course well. ▶ Limit the number of external links. ▶ Include a map showing the organization of the course.

Traditional training is viewed as a reward

Many learners view training as a personal reward. They get to travel at company expense, stay in a nice hotel, eat nice meals, make new friends, and forget about their problems back at the office. Even nearby classroom training provides respite from the monotony of daily work and a change of work environment. Training is often viewed as a vacation given to employees as a reward for hard work.

WBT is no vacation. It may teach. It may qualify the learner for a new job. It may even entertain a bit. But it is no vacation. Learners expecting a vacation may feel short-changed.

Solutions

▶ Publicize WBT as the Next Big Thing and make those taking courses feel special.

▶ Give early participants gifts of coffee mugs, mouse pads, and so forth.

▶ Point out how much classroom training costs and remind participants that the financial health of the organization is in their interest.

Dropout rates may be high

It is widely claimed that distance-learning formats suffer from a low rate of completion relative to classroom training [28]. For WBT, the claims are more severe. As many as 70 to 85% of those with little learning technology experience may drop out [16, 78].

However, there is little compelling evidence that the high dropout rate is common. Some learners have just had bad experiences with poorly designed CBT or early WBT. Many of the cases cited are courses with voluntary enrollment and no fee. Many of the dropouts may have just been taking a taste of online learning.

In any case, even a low dropout rate may be too high.

Solutions

▶ Make your WBT interesting.

▶ Encourage learners to try it out first.

▶ Actively motivate learners. See Chapter 10.

▶ Require learners to commit to finishing the course.

WBT cannot teach certain subjects, right?

Although WBT seems well suited for teaching objective knowledge, especially technical and business knowledge, its fit with other areas is not as clear. In fact, many experts claim that WBT is not suited at all for teaching soft skills and psychomotor skills [79]. While the number of successful examples of WBT used for these purposes is few, that alone does not mean that WBT cannot teach these subjects. It just means that we need to carefully consider whether WBT can teach the soft skill or psychomotor skill we need to teach.

WBT is soft on soft skills

Soft skills, such as team leadership, dealing with difficult people, and giving effective feedback, are difficult to teach by any means. Soft skills involve making subtle judgments and being sensitive to nuances of emotion. Physically present instructors can make such judgments and possess such sensitivity, it is claimed. Since computers cannot do these things, WBT cannot teach these skills.

Before giving up on WBT, let's take a closer look at the things that people do better than computers. The list may look something like this:

▶ Get others unstuck. Help people ask the right question.

▶ Inspire others.

▶ Recognize complex patterns of symptoms that have never occurred before.

▶ Communicate genuine emotion. Sympathize and empathize.

▶ Deal with incomplete and contradictory information

▶ Recognize emotional subtleties

▶ Brainstorm to generate possible solutions

▶ Synthesize new solutions.

Now, put a check mark by each activity that is essential for your course. For each of these essential human abilities, decide which ones human instructors can accomplish through the media and mechanisms of WBT. Consider brainstorming activities (p 223), team design projects (p 219), learning games (p 251), and all the various collaboration mechanisms of WBT (p 333).

Keep in mind that WBT is not taught by a computer. The computer merely delivers the learning experiences engineered by the designer and instructor. The important question, for soft skills training, is whether WBT delivers the kinds of interaction necessary.

Everybody knows WBT cannot teach psychomotor skills

Psychomotor skills require learning to perform complex motions fluently—without conscious control of each separate movement. Psychomotor skills include typing, dance, and playing sports. Psychomotor skills require commanding muscles to make precise, timed, three-dimensional motions, while responding to tactile feedback and muscular tension—all without conscious thought. No wonder I didn't get that sports scholarship.

Probably the ideal way to teach psychomotor skills is with a coach to model the required skill, monitor the learner's performance, and supply encouraging but critical feedback.

I know of no examples of psychomotor skills taught entirely by WBT. And I cannot imagine how to do it. Perhaps that means that other designers are as dull-witted as I—or that they are not bothering to try. A walk through my local bookstore gives me hope though. There I find books purporting to teach ballroom dancing, improve your golf swing, and teach keyboarding (the activity formerly known as typing). If books can teach these skills, then WBT can, too.

If you want to try using WBT for at least part of the task of teaching psychomotor skills, here are a few ideas to get started:

▶ Use WBT to teach any background knowledge about the skill, such as when it is performed and how to recognize a successful performance.

▶ Instruct learners on how to perform the motions. Use clearly written text illustrated with pictures of the critical positions in the motions. Include notes on tactile feedback ("If you feel a burning sensation at the back of your thigh, relax your leg immediately.")

▶ Use small video clips to teach each part of a complex movement.

▶ Have learners work with partners who can monitor their performance. Provide objective criteria for evaluating performance.

▶ Use WBT to prescribe and track a practice regimen. Have the learners enter practice results in a Web form and submit them to a database. The database can then send friendly reminders if they fall behind schedule or warn them if they are overdoing certain activities.

▶ Motivate. Use WBT to supply stories about famous dancers or athletes, emphasizing the difficulties they overcame and how much they had to practice, practice, practice.

Teaching psychomotor skills by WBT will not be easy or inexpensive. Perhaps the best approach is to use WBT only for those parts of the training that WBT clearly does well.

ESTIMATING COSTS

WBT is so new and so diverse that cost estimating is more a matter of wishful thinking than scientific method. Few organizations report costs, especially for projects that run over budget. Even the available figures are hard to interpret. What exactly is an hour of instruction? What costs are included? Are costs of instructional design and subject-matter research included? How complex was the project? And, oh yes, how effective was it?

Let's look at a very simple analysis of the costs of a WBT project. The first compares total costs of WBT to those of classroom training. The second analysis calculates the return on investment garnered by switching from classroom training to WBT.

Back-of-the-envelope analysis

The following spreadsheet shows a comparison of costs between classroom and WBT versions of a course. It illustrates the kind of comparison you might do before beginning a WBT course.

	Classroom	WBT	
Per-course costs			
Course length	8	8	hours
Development time rate	50	200	hours development/course hour
Development cost rate	$ 50	$ 100	USD/hour development
Total	$ 20,000	$ 160,000	USD
Per-class costs			
Instructor salary	$ 800	$ 800	USD
Instructor travel	$ 1,500	$ -	USD
Facilities	$ 500	$ 50	USD
Subtotal (per class)	$ 2,800	$ 850	USD
Class size	20	20	learners
Number of learners	200	200	learners
Number of classes	10	10	classes
Total class costs	$ 28,000	$ 8,500	USD
Per-learner costs			
Learner's travel	$ 1,500	$ -	USD
Learner's salary	$ 800	$ 800	USD
Instructor's salary	$ 25	$ 50	USD
Subtotal (per learner)	$ 2,325	$ 850	USD
Number of learners	200	200	learners
Total learner costs	$ 465,000	$ 170,000	USD
Total costs	$ 513,000	$ 338,500	USD

In the following sections we will explain this comparison of costs line by line.

Keep in mind that this analysis is very simple. I have completed other estimates that took into account hundreds of factors but have not found them more accurate than those that considered only the most important factors. It seems that we can make precise estimates, just not accurate ones.

Per-course costs

Per-course costs represent the costs that the course producer pays once for each course created. These costs consist mostly of development costs.

Course length

In a perfect world, or just a bit smarter one, cost estimates for learning would be based on the amount learned rather than a unit of time spent taking a course. In cost-estimating WBT, an hour is a silly, fictional unit of learning. Making estimates based on hours of instruction originates with the pretense that learning occurs at a uniform rate during the time period the learner is sitting in a classroom or reading a book. Using hours as a unit of measurement makes even less sense when applied to WBT. Each learner may take a different path through the course and, therefore, can hence spend a different amount of time in it.

WBT designers are well aware of this fiction. Most just shrug and interpret it to mean the amount a competent instructor could teach on average in one classroom hour.

So how many hours does a course contain? If the course has many paths and loops and optional branches, the answer is not easy to calculate. Some simulations can go on forever. In some courses, an individual learner may experience only 10% of the content of the course.

Here's a simple procedure I use to estimate the number of learning hours. If a course has definite, albeit branching, paths, I base the course-hours on the aberrant learner who visits every page and completes every activity. If the learner frequently repeats pages, as in a simulation, I base it on the average length of time a learner spends in the course. (Only testing—or keen instincts honed through years of experience—can accurately estimate the average length of time a learner will spend in the course.) I then adjust the development time required upward to reflect the complexity of designing pages that do not grow stale with repeated visits.

The example course for the cost comparison consists of eight mythical instruction-hours. In a classroom course it might consist of six hours of classroom work and two hours of readings. For WBT, it might consist of a total of eight hours of screen-time spread over several days or weeks.

Development time rate

The development time rate refers to the number of person-hours of development required for each finished hour of instruction. The development time rate depends on the complexity of the project and the experience of the design team. No exact formula is possible, though some general rules can help.

▶ For a moderately complex project done by a moderately experienced team, figures of 200 person-hours per instruction-hour are common, though estimates often run from 100 to 600 hours [26, 28, 80]. I would caution against using a figure on the low end of this range as such figures seldom include the additional instructional design necessary to truly exploit the strengths of WBT.

▶ A simple text-and-graphics page-turner created from an existing classroom course and textbook by an experienced team using templates may require 50 hours of development per hour of instruction. On the other hand, an immersive virtual reality simulation done from scratch by neophytes may require 500 or even 1000 hours of development for each hour of instruction learning [81].

▶ One primary factor is the complexity of the course. Is the course a simple linear sequence of static pages? Does it involve drill and practice? Does it incorporate graphics, animation, and video? Will it require lots of custom programming—for simulations, for instance?

▶ Do not forget to budget for the time needed to research the subject and organize your findings. According to Mike Huffman, manager of educational products development at Novell, it takes only half as long to create each hour of instruction if the material already exists in written form [82].

▶ Another factor is the experience of the team designing and building WBT. Experience takes into account whether this project is a first effort, how familiar designers are with the subject matter of the course, how experienced they are with WBT technologies, and whether they have developed templates, code snippets, and other reusable components.

The example uses figures of 50 hours for classroom training and 200 hours for WBT.

Development cost rate

The development cost rate refers to the cost of each person-hour of development work. Such rates range from $50 to $200 USD for work done in the United States. Rates for internal development (done by employees of the company producing the course) are about half those of external vendors. However, as a self-serving external consultant, I am quick to remind my clients that many internal rates do not reflect the full costs of paying, provisioning, and pampering employees who remain on the payroll after the project ends.

Development cost rates also depend on the complexity of the work. If a project requires extensive programming and multimedia development, its rate will be higher than for a project that requires simply arranging text and graphics in an HTML editor. Notice that complexity has a multiplicative effect: It increases the number of development hours required and the cost of each of those hours.

The example course has development rates of $50 USD for the classroom version and $100 per hour for the WBT version.

Total per-course costs

To calculate the total per-course costs, multiply the length of the course in hours by the development time rate and by the development cost rate.

	Classroom		WBT	
Per-course costs				
Course length	8		8	hours
Development time rate	50		200	hours development/course hour
Development cost rate	$ 50	$	100	USD/hour development
Total	$ 20,000	$	160,000	USD

As you can see, the WBT version costs considerably more to develop. This increased cost is almost always the case. The additional development costs represent an investment aimed at reduced per-class and per-learner costs.

Per-class costs

Most instructor-led WBT courses are offered as classes. That is, a group of learners proceed through the course together. Each time a class is offered there are certain expenses beyond the costs of developing the course. These consist mainly of the time of the instructor and other staff members.

If a course is not taught in classes, no per-course expenses are incurred. Most self-paced courses lack a class structure and hence have no per-class costs.

The example WBT course is taught in classes and has some appreciable class costs, though less than those for the classroom version. Let's look at how these costs are calculated.

Instructor's salary (and benefits)

Each time a class is taught, the instructor must prepare and perform certain activities independently of the number of learners in the class, so salary is primarily a per-class cost. Costs that depend on the number of learners are per-learner costs and are tabulated separately.

For instructor's salary, calculate the amount of the instructor's time needed each time the course is offered and convert this time to the amount of salary paid over that period. Also include any other costs required to keep instructors on staff. These include routine benefits such as medical insurance, vacation time, office space, and pencils pilfered from the supply closet. These extra costs typically add 50 to 100% to the base pay rate of the instructor.

For both the classroom and WBT version, the example assumes the instructor's salary is $800 USD.

Instructor's travel

If the instructor must travel to a different site to teach the class, the costs of travel will be charged against the course. These costs will typically include airfare, rental car, hotel, and meals.

For our example, we assume that the instructor must travel to a regional training center at a cost of $1500 USD. For WBT, we assume the instructor can conduct the class from his or her base location.

Training facilities

For classroom training, facilities consist of rooms, chairs, whiteboards, easel pads, and the like. Each class may be charged a classroom rent or apportioned a fraction of the costs of maintaining a training center. For WBT, facilities are usually inexpensive, consisting of a fraction of the cost of maintaining a Web server. However, if we are using specialized video-conferencing systems or must pay to upgrade the corporate intranet, facility costs can be quite high.

The example assumes a facilities cost of $500 USD for the classroom course and $50 for the WBT version. These figures are based on costs for renting classrooms and storage space on Web servers.

Class size

Before we can calculate the number of classes we must offer to train the required number of learners, we must decide on the class size. Although extremely large WBT classes are possible, most instructors recommend keeping class size small, at least for the first few WBT courses a learner experiences. I agree.

For both the classroom and WBT versions, the example assumes 20 learners per class.

Number of learners

Now we come to one of the most critical factors in the success of WBT: the number of people you must train. We consider it here because it affects the number of classes required.

The example assumes that we have to train 200 learners either by WBT or classroom training.

Number of classes

To calculate the number of classes, we just divide the number of students by the class size. If the result is not a whole number, we round upward to the next whole number.

This procedure assumes that we fill classes to the extent possible. Often that is not the case. If you cannot fill classes to their limits, use the average enrollment as the class size rather than the maximum class size.

For our example we will assume that we can train 200 people in 10 classes of 20 people each. Since the WBT and classroom versions have the same number of learners and same class size, they both require the same number of classes.

Total per-class costs

To calculate the total per-class costs we just multiply the per-class cost by the number of classes.

Per-class costs	Classroom		WBT	
Instructor salary	$	800	$ 800	USD
Instructor travel	$	1,500	$ -	USD
Facilities	$	500	$ 50	USD
Subtotal (per class)	$	2,800	$ 850	USD
Class size		20	20	learners
Number of learners		200	200	learners
Number of classes		10	10	classes
Total class costs	$	28,000	$ 8,500	USD

Notice that the class costs are less for WBT than for classroom training.

Per-learner costs

The per-learner costs are those incurred for each additional learner we train. These costs consist of the salary and travel costs of the learner while in training and of the instructor's salary while working with this individual learner.

Learners' travel costs

Learners may need to travel to receive training. When they travel, they incur costs for airfare, rental cars, taxis, hotels, meals, and incidental expenses. The example assumes that learners incur travel costs of $1500 USD on average for classroom training but that WBT requires no travel by learners.

If your company has a travel department, they can help you estimate the basic costs of transportation and lodging. You can probably fill in the costs of meals by consulting the restaurant receipts crammed away in the corners of your billfold. And do not forget to throw in a little for incidental expenses such as tips, laundry for long stays, permitted phone calls, and so forth.

Learners' salaries

While learners are completing a course they are still drawing their salaries. Another way to think of this cost is that of lost production. Learners are being paid for work that is not getting done.

To calculate such a figure, just add the annual costs of benefits to the learner's annual salary and divide by the number of workdays per year. Then multiply this daily salary figure by the number of days the learner is off the job.

For both the WBT and classroom versions, the example assumes that the learner draws a salary of $800 USD while in training. The example probably underestimates the costs of classroom training because it does not take into account the extra time the classroom learner must spend traveling to the training site.

Instructor's salary

Didn't we already pay the instructor? Yes, but not enough. Each learner may require some individual attention and effort from the instructor. The instructor must answer questions by e-mail, in chat, or in discussion groups. The instructor must grade assignments and may counsel the learner. That time may not be much for each individual student but may mount up when tallied for hundreds of learners.

For our example, we assume about $50 USD of the instructor's salary goes for efforts to help each individual learner in WBT, but only $25 is expended in the classroom version. WBT learners will have more technical problems than classroom learners.

Total per-learner costs

To calculate the per-learner costs, add up the learner's travel costs and salary and the instructor's salary costs. To get a total of the per-learner costs for all learners, multiply by the number of learners.

	Classroom		WBT		
Per-learner costs					
Learner's travel costs	$	1,500	$	-	USD
Learner's salary	$	800	$	800	USD
Instructor's salary	$	25	$	50	USD
Subtotal (per learner)	$	2,325	$	850	USD
Number of learners		200		200	learners
Total learner costs	$	**465,000**	$	**170,000**	USD

In the example, WBT is really saving money for each learner trained.

Total costs

To calculate the total project costs, we just add up the per-course, per-class, and per-learner costs.

	Classroom	WBT	
Per-course costs	20,000	160,000	USD
Per-class costs	28,000	8,500	USD
Per-learner costs	465,000	170,000	USD
Total costs	$ 513,000	$ 338,500	USD

In our example, WBT saves $175,500 over classroom training.

Return on investment

Many organizations evaluate proposed projects based on their return on investment.

Return on investment is a simple concept. You invest money in a savings account at your local bank. They pay you interest on the money you have on deposit. That interest is the return on your investment. If the bank pays 5% on savings accounts, your deposit has a 5% return on investment, or ROI for short.

A corporation may have money to invest. Should it invest in a savings account, in buying another company, in reroofing the corporate headquarters, or in developing WBT courses? How can it decide which is the best investment? One way to evaluate a potential investment is to compare the return on each investment. In this case, return on investment represents the annual savings or income generated by an investment.

Since we assume our sample project is complete within a year, we can calculate an approximate ROI by dividing the savings produced by WBT by the additional initial investment it requires. For this latter figure, we compute the additional development costs for WBT, beyond those that would be required for classroom training.

$$ ROI = \frac{(\text{Total costs for classroom training}) - (\text{Total costs for WBT})}{(\text{Development costs for WBT}) - (\text{Total costs for classroom training})} $$

$$ = \frac{\$513{,}000 - \$338{,}500}{\$160{,}000 - \$20{,}000} $$

$$ = \frac{\$174{,}500}{\$140{,}000} $$

$$ = 125\% $$

You do not have to be Chairman of the Federal Reserve Board to know that this is a very good return on investment. You also do not need to be a financial genius to treat any such back-of-the-envelope analysis with the healthy skepticism it deserves. All this analysis proves is that WBT is certainly worth a second look.

IN CONCLUSION ...

Summary

- ► WBT lets people learn where and when they need training.

- ► WBT works best for teaching well-organized objective knowledge to mature, motivated learners who cannot participate in conventional training.

- ► WBT can reduce training costs such as travel, facilities, administration, and lost time by 30 to 80%. WBT typically costs much more to develop than conventional training but much less to deliver.

- ► WBT can improve learning by exposing learners to real-world examples and cases, by enabling collaboration and cooperation with distant partners, by encouraging reflection instead of mere reaction, and by emphasizing results rather than attendance.

- ► WBT is more work than classroom training—for designers, instructors, and learners. It requires more detailed design, more careful production, and greater participation.

- ► With WBT learners may miss direct face-to-face contact with the instructor and other learners, though Web collaboration may fill this void for some.

- ► Numerous comparisons find WBT courses as effective as classroom training—or better.

For more ...

Trade magazines serving the training community frequently carry articles on the merits of various forms of training and on calculating their costs and benefits. Check back issues of:

- ► *Training and Development* (www.astd.org/virtual_community/td_magazine/)

- ► *Inside Technology Training* (www.ittrain.com)

- ► *Technical Training* (www.astd.org/virtual_community/tt_magazine/)

Search the Web for: **WBT advantages** or **WBT costs**.

> Education costs money, but then so does ignorance.
>
> — Sir Claus Moser

3

Pick an approach

Design decisions that affect the course as a whole

With WBT you can create many kinds of courses. This chapter guides you through the big-picture decisions that determine the basic nature of your course. It guides you in deciding the basic kind of course you want to create; suggests some alternatives to pure WBT; and helps you set technology standards, pick a metaphor, and name the course wisely.

CHOOSE THE KIND OF COURSE

With Web technologies, we can create several different kinds of courses, each providing learners with a distinctive type of learning experience and each suited to different situations. Some courses are led by an instructor who charts the path and sets the pace for a group of learners. In other courses, learners find their own way, set their own pace, and interact only with the computer. Let's consider the design decisions that will determine the nature of your course.

Instructor-led or learner-led?

One of the first and most important decisions facing designers is the role (or lack of a role) for an instructor. WBT does not eliminate the value of an instructor.

> The teacher's role in coaching, observing learners, offering hints and reminders, providing feedback, scaffolding and fading, modeling, and so on, are powerful enhancements to any learning situation [83].

However, WBT gives us choices as to who leads: the instructor or individual learners. This choice is not limited to pure instructor-led or pure learner-led forms but includes a spectrum of possibilities in between these two extremes, as shown here:

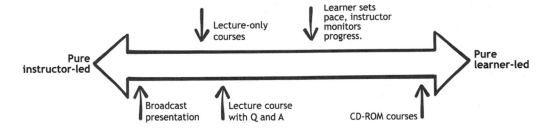

The choice is not between pure instructor-led and pure learner-led training, but rather a range of possibilities between these two extremes. Pure instructor-led training is limited to short events such as broadcast presentations. Most so-called instructor-led training allows learners some freedom to pursue optional topics and to schedule their own time between instructor-scheduled events. As we move toward the learner-led end of the spectrum, the role of the instructor fades to that of a facilitator—on tap but not on top. The instructor's role can become that of just another learning resource that learners can summon at a mouse click. Pure learner-led WBT courses do exist and resemble stand-alone disk-based CBT.

Both instructor-led and learner-led training offer advantages:

Advantages of instructor-led training	Advantages of learner-led training
▶ The instructor can answer questions and solve problems as they arise.	▶ Learners develop self-reliance they will need after the class.
▶ Instructors provide authority that some learners may need for motivation.	▶ Learners are not required to conform to the instructor's schedule.
▶ An instructor can adjust the course to suit the needs of a particular class.	▶ Instructors add substantially to the cost of delivering courses.
▶ Instructors can grade activities and tests too subtle for automated scoring.	▶ All learners get the same quality of learning experience.
▶ Instructors can sympathize, empathize, urge, cajole, and inspire learners.	▶ Learners appreciate the anonymity and privacy. No "teacher's dirty looks."

Many WBT courses deliberately shift from instructor-led to learner-led during the progress of the course. The course starts with the instructor firmly in charge, setting the pace, making assignments, presenting information, and grading results. As the course progresses, the instructor's role fades, with the instructor's responsibilities being taken up by teams and eventually individuals. By the end of the class learners are prepared to apply their learning alone.

Synchronous or asynchronous?

One of the most important design decisions is whether to make WBT synchronous or asynchronous. Unfortunately, no two terms cause more confusion than *synchronous* and *asynchronous*. One expert will call a course synchronous while another will call the same course asynchronous. This confusion masks an important design issue: Can learners control when they learn?

What do you mean by synchronous or asynchronous?

The terms *synchronous* and *asynchronous* apply better to individual events and activities than to whole courses.

Synchronous	Asynchronous
In a strict sense, the term *synchronous* means that everyone involved in an activity must perform their part at the same time. Such events are sometimes called *real-time* or *live* events. Such events include chat sessions, screen-sharing and whiteboard sessions, and videoconferences.	*Asynchronous* activities are ones that participants can experience whenever they want. Permanently posted Web pages and automatically scored tests are clearly asynchronous—learners can read them at any time.

The problem with these definitions is the meaning of "at the same time." Some take it to mean within minutes or seconds, while others take it to mean a span of hours or days. Is an e-mail message answered in two days asynchronous or synchronous? How about a discussion group where learners can add to messages at any time but require checking every day or so to keep up with discussions?

Courses are not purely synchronous or asynchronous

Courses are not purely synchronous or asynchronous. Courses are made up of a mix of activities and events that can be synchronous or asynchronous. Still other events and activities take place over a different period of time for each learner. Rather than considering *synchronous* and *asynchronous* as mutually exclusive terms, perhaps we should use a scale indicating how much latitude learners have in completing activities.

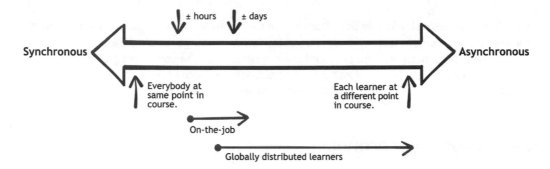

Courses considered synchronous probably include some activities and events that learners can partake of at their own pace. And an "asynchronous" course can still have deadlines, timed tests, and "respond immediately" tests. Courses that must be taken by busy professionals while on the job must be scheduled around meetings and other scheduled events. These courses can only be synchronous within a few hours. If learners are distributed around the globe, in many different time zones, in countries with different business and religious holidays, it will be difficult for learners to stay closer than a day or two in sync with one another.

Industry goes asynchronous, academia synchronous

Most industrial WBT uses an asynchronous model while most WBT within universities is primarily synchronous. According to the ASTD '99 Panel "Leveraging Instructional Technology Through the Use of Online Learning," 75 to 85% of all WBT is neither synchronous nor class-bound. A perusal of university catalogs, however, will show that most of their Web-based offerings use a synchronous virtual-classroom model. Why the difference? I speculate that universities are attempting to use the Web to extend their existing courses with minimum trauma to instructors, administrators, and students, while industrial training departments are facing adult learners with schedules too filled to meet the strict meeting times required for synchronous events. It will be interesting to see if these two models soften as WBT and our experience with it evolve.

Pick the right approach

Your course can be asynchronous or have a mixture of synchronous and asynchronous activities. In designing your course, consider the advantages of each approach:

Choose synchronous activities when ...	Choose asynchronous activities when ...
▶ Learners need to discuss issues with other learners at length	▶ Learners are from a wide span of time zones and countries
▶ Learners need the motivation of scheduled events reinforced by peer pressure	▶ Learners have inflexible or unpredictable work schedules
▶ Most learners share the same needs and have the same questions	▶ Learners cannot wait for a class to form
	▶ Learners have unique individual needs

What size class?

In WBT a class is a group of individuals learning the same material on the same schedule. Unlike classroom training, the size of a WBT class is not constrained by physical architecture but by decisions of the course designer. Classes of ten thousand are technically feasible, though seldom wise.

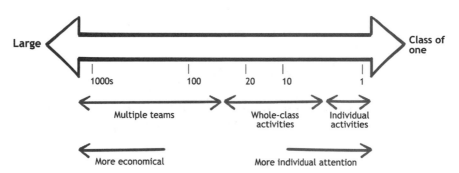

While larger classes are more economical, they provide learners with less individual attention. The class size also affects the possibilities for collaboration. With very small classes, most work must be done by individuals. With moderate class sizes, say up to 30, the class as a whole can participate in activities. In larger classes, learners must be divided into teams. Clearly the size affects the design of activities and other course materials.

Advantages of different class size

The size of the class is an important issue as it affects both the economics and instructional effectiveness of the course. The size determines the number of times the course must be offered, how often a class starts, the learner-teacher ratio, and the potential for team activities. Let's look at the advantages of each class size:

Large class size	Small class size	Class of one
▶ More economical ▶ More people taught in less time ▶ More classmates to interact with	▶ More individual attention from the instructor ▶ Whole-class activities are practical ▶ Classes start more frequently	▶ Learner gets a private tutor or mentor ▶ No waiting for a class to form ▶ Learning is private

What to consider

To decide on a class size, you need to consider both your business and teaching objectives:

▶ Budget. How many class sessions can you afford to offer?

▶ Frequency of need. How long can learners wait for a class to form?

▶ Expectations. What class size are learners accustomed to?

▶ Critical mass. How many learners are needed for essential collaborative activities?

▶ Individual attention. How much of the instructor's time does each learner require?

▶ Instructor load. How many learners can each instructor successfully serve?

Where will learners take the course?

Imagine your learners taking your course. Where are they? Are they in their offices, at home, on the road, or in a corporate training center? Where should they be?

Both a decision and a prediction

The success of a course can depend on where people take it. For designers, this is both a decision and a prediction. I know designers who decided that learners would take courses on specially equipped high-performance workstations in a quiet, calm, corporate training center. After they deployed their course they found the expensive training center vacant as most learners took the course from outdated laptop computers in hotel rooms and from their children's home computers, both using slow-speed dial-up connections. As a designer you **may** recommend where learners should take courses but you **must** predict and design for where learners will actually take the courses.

Why is *where* important?

Where people take lessons controls what computer they use and what kind of network connection they have. It also affects how much noise and how many distractions they must contend with. The choice of computer in turn affects the ability of the course to display information and to play multimedia. The network connection limits the use of media, participation in live events, and use of confidential or secret information in the course. The environment of the learner affects how much attention learners can give the course, how long they can participate in an activity, and how often they must put a hand over the screen to hide confidential information. Almost every aspect of the course is affected by where the learner takes the course.

What are my choices?

People take WBT courses in four main environments. Let's look at each in turn, weighing its advantages and disadvantages while noting the design requirements it imposes for the course.

In the learner's office or cubicle

Many of the cited advantages of WBT assume learners take courses at their desks. And this locale certainly has some advantages. Consider the ideal situation: There are absolutely no travel costs, and learners can sandwich learning among other tasks, as time is available. Their computers are attached to a relatively fast network and in-house technical support is available to help set up the computers and repair them when necessary. The greatest advantage is the fact that learning takes place where it will be used, thus making it easier for learners to apply what they learned.

Taking WBT at the learner's office does have disadvantages in practice. The office is often a place of continual interruptions. Cubicles can be noisy and visitors frequent. Furthermore, the learner's computer may not be ideal for taking WBT. A computer tuned for accounting or drafting or software development may not welcome the plug-ins and other software needed for WBT.

For courses that will be taken in this setting:

▶ Create the course with short, self-contained modules so the learner can fit modules between interruptions.

▶ Teach learners to bookmark their position so they can return to it after an interruption.

▶ Use large graphics and multimedia if the speed of the network allows them to load quickly.

▶ Caution learners about leaving their workstations with confidential or proprietary information displayed.

Learning center

Many companies are setting up special rooms where employees can take WBT and CBT courses. These rooms are called *learning centers* or *learning labs* or *individual learning facilities*. Learning centers are designed to provide a quiet place where people can learn without the noise or interruptions of their workplace and without the hassles of having to set up their own computer. Most learning centers contain desks or carrels with computers specially equipped to run courses. Such computers have all the necessary software installed and set up. They also have high-speed network connections. Some learning centers feature a facilitator or technician to greet learners, get them started, and provide help when requested.

Unisys set up learning centers where its employees could come to take courses. The company felt that such quiet, well equipped centers provided a better environment than the employees' offices, where they were exposed to the distractions and interruptions of work, or their homes, where they were often too tired to concentrate adequately [29].

Learning centers do have some drawbacks though. Learning takes place in an environment different from the one in which it will be applied. Learning centers require people to be away from their desks for significant periods of time. Some require learners to schedule time days in advance.

Learning centers are expensive to set up and administer. Unless all employees work on a single campus, multiple learning centers will be required. Learning centers are of little use to employees who travel or are stationed in small remote offices.

If your learners will be taking courses mainly in learning centers, take advantage of the facilities' strengths and compensate for their weaknesses:

- ▶ Loosen your technical requirements. Use multimedia, advanced browser capabilities, and large graphics freely.

- ▶ Budget for centers. If centers must host your learners, the centers may require compensation.

- ▶ Train center staff to support your courses. Document the technical requirements, and show facilitators how to get learners started.

Home

Many employees take WBT at home during evenings and on weekends. Most of these employees say they cannot find enough quiet time at the office to complete lessons. Others have better computers at home than at work, especially those whose work computers are old or configured for purposes other than learning. Multimedia home computers sold today are quite capable of running WBT courses. Some companies encourage their employees to take courses on their own time. A smaller number subsidize the purchase of the home computer.

Taking courses at home is not without its drawbacks. Many learners find they have traded office distractions for family distractions. A child needs help with homework, the dog wants to be walked, or the spouse does not like being ignored. Except for computer-proficient children, most homes lack a technical support staff. Learners at home must typically access courses by dialing into the corporate intranet, oozing through the firewall, and logging into the course. They may find their access to confidential or secret material blocked. Their communications speed is less than that of learners connected directly to the network.

If learners will take courses from home:

▶ Limit the size of pages so they download quickly even at modem speeds.

▶ Design the course to accommodate frequent interruptions.

▶ Increase efforts to motivate learners (Chapter 10)

▶ Minimize the technical requirements (p 67), especially the number of plug-ins the learner must download and set up.

▶ Plan for how you will handle potential security problems.

▶ Streamline the process of accessing the course from outside the firewall.

The road

More and more professionals are mobile, spending increasing portions of their time away from the office. They check into their hotel room, unplug the phone, plug in their laptop computer, and fire up your course.

At first, this might seem like the worst possible place to take WBT. The laptop computer may be old or damaged from years of travel. The process of dialing out of a hotel's phone system, into a corporate intranet, through the firewall, and onto the course server can be complex and unreliable. Modem connections may be slow and phone bills high. A laptop can be stolen, and its cached or downloaded materials read by malicious eyes. Furthermore, learners may be forced to take courses while suffering from jet lag, sleep deprivation, and indigestion. Not an ideal learning environment.

But learning while traveling does have some advantages. Learners are free of the distractions of office and home. Many find that WBT courses ease the loneliness of travel, especially if the course includes collaborative activities. One traveling technician put it this way: "It keeps me from hanging out at the hotel bar." For many traveling professionals, though, WBT provides the only practical way to get the training they need.

If many of your learners will take courses while traveling:

▶ Minimize the technical requirements. Base course designs on what works on a two-year-old laptop.

▶ Let learners download entire lessons, or package the entire course on CD-ROM.

▶ Limit use of confidential or secret information in the course.

▶ Make live events optional. Let learners download a summary or transcript of the event.

Summary

As you consider where learners will take WBT, keep these limitations in mind:

Characteristic	Where WBT is taken			
	Office	Learning center	Home	Road
Who can take courses in this location?	Employees with desktop computers	Those near training center	Those with adequate home computers	Those with adequate mobile computers
Interruptions and distractions	High	Low	High	Moderate
Technical capabilities	Moderate	High	Moderate	Low
Time away from work	Minimal	High	Minimal	Minimal
Availability of technical support	Good	Very good	Poor	None

CONSIDER ALTERNATIVES TO PURE WBT

Classroom courses and disk-based CBT both have strengths that can benefit WBT learners; they also have weaknesses that WBT can overcome. For many training needs, the best solution may not be pure WBT, pure disk-based CBT, or pure classroom training, but an intelligent hybrid mingling the best features of each. Organizations with large investments in classroom training and disk-based CBT may prefer to reuse their well-tested training materials during a transitional period while they redesign their courses for WBT.

Hybrid of WBT and classroom training

WBT and classroom training offer complementary strengths that inventive and brave designers are combining to create interesting hybrids.

Mix WBT and classroom training

WBT and classroom techniques can be combined in several ways to take advantage of the strengths of each.

Use WBT for the main presentation

Some designers precede and follow a WBT course with classroom sessions.

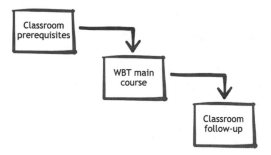

Typically the first classroom session is used to orient learners, introduce them to the instructor and fellow learners, and to motivate them to complete the WBT session. The follow-up classroom session lets learners ask questions, clear up misunderstandings, and resolve conflicts that arose during the WBT portion.

Use WBT for preparation and reinforcement

Other designers reverse the previous pattern by sandwiching a conventional classroom course between two WBT mini-courses.

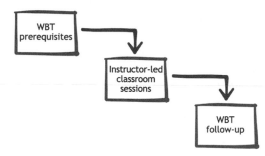

The first WBT course reviews prerequisite material to ensure that all learners are productive from the start of the classroom course. The WBT follow-up course provides optional topics, more chances to practice skills, and refresher sessions for those who need them.

Use a facilitator to guide WBT learners

In facilitated WBT, a human facilitator guides learners as they take WBT lessons. Learners take WBT at scheduled times in a classroom with a facilitator present. Every few weeks an instructor may conduct a traditional class.

As an alternative, the instructor may phone students or conduct conference calls with groups of students while they are taking the course.

Use WBT materials in the classroom

Rather than move the classroom to the Web, you can move a WBT course into the classroom. The instructor can project the WBT course and use it to teach and demonstrate points within the classroom. If you use WBT courses in a classroom, provide an alternative interface to make WBT materials more convenient to use in the classroom. Such an interface may consist of an outer frameset with a special table of contents and navigation buttons.

If materials will be used in a classroom:

▶ Limit dependencies between modules of the WBT materials.

▶ Provide special introductions to sequences of material.

▶ Write instructions for teachers.

▶ Make selected parts of the materials printable (for overheads, for example).

Start with an effective course ... and redesign it

If you want to create WBT from an existing classroom course, start with one that works well as a classroom course. Unless the underlying instructional design is strong, the conversion may fail [54]. Even strong design may require updating:

> Current courses taught in the traditional lecture-based format cannot be transported to a distance-learning environment without modification [84].

Consider what aspects of the classroom course are independent of the classroom environment and which will require simulating classroom techniques or finding Web-based substitutes.

Create a halfway house for classroom training

An instructionally sound classroom course can benefit from elements of WBT as it prepares to make the leap to full WBT. Such a halfway approach may be better than jumping directly to 100% Web delivery. It gives the instructional designer and learners time to learn to use the various technologies of WBT. The resulting Web-enhanced classroom course may be better than the old classroom course and better than a full WBT version.

Here are some ways to start down the road to true WBT:

▶ Distribute handouts via the Web. Let learners download and print out paper activities from the classroom course.

▶ Put readings and other easily converted materials on the network where learners can access them before class.

▶ Use the Web to communicate with learners. Let learners submit assignments by e-mail. Conduct quizzes by the Web. Conduct surveys and gather feedback by Web forms.

▶ Set up a Web-based discussion group for conversation beyond the classroom.

▶ Make routine announcements on a Course Home page (p 111). Post the class syllabus (p 400), reading list, assignments, and test dates to the course Web site. Add the course policies (p 97) and other reference information, too.

▶ Make recorded lectures, slides, and notes available to those who could not attend live events and to those who want to review the materials.

▶ Add exercises that require using the Web for examples or research.

Hybrid of WBT and disk-based CBT

CBT programs on CD-ROM (or downloaded to a local disk) are common and widely used, especially in industry. The CD-ROM provides generous storage and fast loading that make WBT designers salivate. Conversely, WBT allows centralized updating and collaborative activities that have never been available to CBT designers. By combining these two forms, designers can create forms of learning impossible a few years ago.

Mix WBT and disk-based CBT

How can we combine the best of WBT with the best of disk-based CBT? Let's look at some of the learning cocktails served up by clever designers.

Use CD-ROM for heavy media

In a Web-based course, you can send learners a CD-ROM containing video clips, animations, graphics, sounds, and other media you do not want to have the learner download. David Iadevaia includes a CD-ROM in the "course pack" for his Internet course on astronomy [68]. The CD-ROM contains multimedia and application programs students use in the course.

Add dynamic content to a CBT course

Supplement a CD-ROM course by adding dynamic information, such as specifications, prices, and data sheets. Post such information on a Web server. You can also use the server for updates to the CD-ROM course and for optional modules.

Add collaboration to a CBT course

From a CD-ROM class, link to Web-based collaboration tools. Provide e-mail links to communicate with a facilitator or instructor. Set up a discussion group so learners can share and debate ideas. Add more sophisticated human-graded activities that learners submit from Web forms.

Make the course run from CD-ROM

A couple of years ago, about two weeks before I was to install a WBT course onto my client's server, the client notified me that the server would not be ready but the training must proceed as scheduled. We scrambled and converted the WBT course so that it could run from a CD-ROM. All interaction had to be with the computer or via e-mail with the instructor. Having the course on CD-ROM, though, removed the requirement of a high-speed Internet connection.

TechnoTip: For a course to run from CD-ROM you must either install a small Web-server on each learner's computer or you must eliminate any requirement for "server-side processing." This second case means that all auto-scoring and interactivity must be provided by scripts executed by the browser and that no database access is practical.

Download the course to local disk

Some organizations prefer to store the bulk of course materials on the learner's local hard disk. Employees at Unisys, headquartered in Blue Bell, Pennsylvania, found that downloading and playing courses was more convenient than waiting for them to be shipped on CD-ROM or enduring sluggish access over the corporate intranet [29]. Storing courses on the user's disk eliminates delays when accessing individual modules. It also lets learners access modules while disconnected from the Internet. Learners can connect to the Internet temporarily when they need services or resources only available there.

Note: If you must download large files, do it during off-peak hours for the server. Remember that the server may be in another time zone than you are.

Avoid the dangers of a hybrid approach

Hybrid approaches entail compromises. Not all compromises succeed. Hybrid approaches may lead to some problems that you should prepare for:

▶ **Material on CD-ROM can become out of date.** Learners sometimes fail to throw away the old CD-ROMs. **TechnoTip:** Have your course read a file from the disk to check the date of the disk and display a warning if it is out of date.

▶ **CD-ROMs are complex to produce and ship**. You must master, manufacture, package, label, and ship the disks to learners in multiple countries. Painful solution: Subcontract this work with a firm that can do it more efficiently than you can.

▶ **What drive is the CD in?** The lesson must know in which drive the CD-ROM is loaded. The CD-ROM may be Drive D on one computer, Drive E on another, and Drive Q on yet another. When I undock my laptop the CD-ROM that was Drive G is now Drive E. Some computers sold today come with both a CD-Rewritable drive and a DVD drive. Both can read CD-ROMs. **TechnoTip:** When the course starts the first time, ask the learner to find a file on the CD-ROM. Store the first part of this file's path in a cookie that other pages can use to locate needed media.

▶ **Hybrids require unique technical solutions.** Hybrid implementations tend to require idiosyncratic solutions to problems. These solutions often require custom programming that cannot be reused on other projects.

Migrate disk-based CBT to WBT

If you have a well-designed CBT course you want to move from disk to Web, consider these steps to add the advantages of the Web while preserving the best features of your course:

▶ Divide a long course into smaller modules that can download and play independently. Replace the all-in-one file with a linked collection of much smaller files.

▶ Convert to Web-friendly versions of multimedia formats. For example, convert Macromedia Authorware and Director modules to Shockwave format.

▶ Reduce reliance on specific fonts and on file formats unique to a specific operating system.

▶ Add e-mail links so that learners can ask questions of a facilitator, instructor, or mentor.

▶ Set up discussion groups for learners to share, brainstorm, and debate ideas.

▶ Add human-graded activities. Use these for questions and issues too subtle for scoring by computer.

▶ Use the Web to post updates and additional material. Let learners download updated modules.

▶ Create a jump page to relevant resources on the Web.

SET TECHNOLOGY STANDARDS

WBT depends on technology. As such, WBT designers must take into account their goals and limitations as they lay down some basic rules about what technologies the course will rely on. These are important if the course is being created by separate teams or outside vendors.

Designate target browsers

First decide what browser learners can use to take your course. Limit this list to one or two specific browsers. In this case, each version of a particular brand is a different browser. For example:

Netscape Navigator 4.5

Internet Explorer 5.0

If HTML features are supported by all of your target browsers, use them freely. If features are supported by some of your targeted browsers and ignored cleanly (that is, without causing any error) by the others, use the features for non-essential information, for decorations, and experiments. If features are not cleanly ignored by some of the target browsers, either do not use the feature or prepare two versions of the page.

Consider requiring a late model browser rather than an earlier one that requires multiple plug-ins. For example, the Dynamic HTML supported in Version 4 browsers may be adequate for simple animations that would require a plug-in with Version 3 browsers.

Specify file formats for materials

The choice of allowable file formats has several critical implications for designers. Some file formats will require proprietary plug-ins that learners must download and install. Information in one format may download quicker and display more smoothly than in another. Not all formats can be displayed in all versions of all browsers. The choice of file formats may limit the choice of tools for creating course materials. Pick formats that everyone can display safely.

Favor widely used file formats

So that as many people as possible can take your course with the minimum amount of time spent downloading and installing plug-ins, pick file formats that play in the browsers most people already have.

Start with browser-native formats

Start with formats displayed directly by the browser itself without assistance from other software, such as plug-ins. These formats displayed by the browser are called *browser-native* formats. They depend on the brand and version of browser you have selected. For example, here are browser-native formats for Internet Explorer 5.0:

- ▶ HTML, including Dynamic HTML, and Cascading Style Sheets (CSS)

- ▶ Text (ASCII and Unicode)

- ▶ JavaScript 1.2

- ▶ GIF, JPEG, and PNG graphics

- ▶ XML, including XSL style sheets

- ▶ Java

Next consider platform-independent formats

Platform-independent formats are ones that can be reliably displayed, albeit with plug-ins, in multiple browser versions on multiple operating systems. Though plug-ins are required, they exist for most browsers and are either inexpensive or free. Platform-independent formats are usually industry standards rather than proprietary formats. Some industry-standard formats include:

- ▶ **Music:** MIDI

- ▶ **Video:** MPEG

- ▶ **Virtual Reality:** VRML

Then think about popular Web formats

Next consider some proprietary formats that are already widely used and for which technical support is readily available. Many learners will already have the required plug-in installed, and, if they need to install one, help is available. Here are some formats in this category:

- ▶ **Sound:** WAV, Real Audio, MP3

- ▶ **Multimedia:** Shockwave Director, Shockwave Flash, Shockwave Authorware, QuickTime, AVI

▶ **Documents:** Adobe Acrobat PDF, Rich Text Format (RTF)

At this point, consider licensing requirements. Some formats can be distributed freely over the Web from a server but require a license to distribute on CD-ROM.

Finally, consider popular proprietary desktop formats

Finally, consider formats common in specific work environments. These might include desktop applications and other tools used by target learners. For example, some businesses have standardized computer setups that include a suite of applications such as Microsoft Office. Such a company could include Microsoft Word and Excel documents in their courses. Remember to check for licensing restrictions.

Avoid obscure and unsupported formats

I do not recommend using formats that require a rare plug-in or one for which technical support is not readily available—unless you are prepared to provide that support.

Often university courses will include files that require a plug-in that was created as part of a computer science department project last semester without considering whether a better alternative already exists. Often the plug-in has not been thoroughly tested and support is only available three hours a week.

Prefer virus-proof formats

Prefer virus-proof formats. For example, a Java applet is more virus-proof than a Java application. A word-processing document without embedded macros is more virus-proof than one with macros.

Limit file sizes

Unless all learners have high-speed network connections **all the time**, consider suggesting limits for the total file size for each page, that is, the size of the HTML file **and all the files it automatically loads.** Here are some guidelines that should get most pages down the cable in less than ten seconds:

If learner's connection speed is:	Limit each page to a total size of:
14.4 Kbps	10K
28.8 Kbps	20K
56 Kbps	40K
128 Kbps	80K
1 Mbps	640K
Faster	1 Megabyte per Mbps

CONSIDER A METAPHOR

There remains one more course-level decision to make. Should you use a metaphor to help organize and style your course? If so, which metaphor?

A metaphor is a consistent design that models the structure and appearance of the course on something familiar to learners. A metaphor can be an extended analogy, theme, motif, ongoing scenario, or overall question. Such metaphors, analogies, and explicit comparisons can help people learn [85]. A good metaphor lets people apply what they know about a real-world environment to the task of navigating the WBT course. It also gives the course a unified and consistent appearance and organization.

Examples of metaphors in WBT courses

Metaphors are common in online training, though we often take them for granted. Let's consider a couple of examples of how a metaphor can contribute to organizing and imparting learning.

Solar theater

The Yohkoh Public Outreach Project (solar.physics.montana.edu/YPOP/) chose the metaphor of a movie theater for a collection of tutorials, activities, and scientific data on the physics of the sun.

> The project never really took off until we had a unified version as expressed through a theme. Solar physics just isn't a theme that immediately grabs people's attention; instead we use the theme of a movie theater. We selected the movie theater because the real highlight of the project is a long-term scientific-quality movie of the Sun. So, each aspect of the site is created to be consistent with this theme. There is a program that contains a site-map, a lobby that has attraction posters, a projection room that has background information on the satellite, and interview with the star of the movie (the Sun) and a solar classroom [86].

Note the use of something familiar and fun (a movie theater) to organize and present something potentially boring (scientific data).

ASK Internet Camp

ASK organizes its basic course on using the Internet as a summer camp (www.askintl.com). The Welcome sign hangs from wooden poles. The main menu is a mountainside camp covered with waterfalls, cabins, hiking trails, and lots of happy campers. The discussion group is called "Campfire stories" and the instructor is a counselor.

Consider proven metaphors

Before you churn your creativity to a froth to find an entirely new metaphor, consider whether an established metaphor may suit your needs.

For a virtual classroom, use a school metaphor

If your class is taught as a virtual classroom, design a metaphor that mimics the structures and procedures of a physical classroom—or do not use a metaphor at all. Any other metaphor would contend with learners' habitual expectations.

Map each Web mechanism to the analogous function or object in the physical classroom:

Represent this item:		As this:
Learner	→	Student
Instructor	→	Teacher
Training center or department	→	School
Discussion group	→	Study groups, student lounge
Real-time events	→	Class meetings
Tests	→	Exams or quizzes
Jump page for external resources	→	Library
Reference materials on course site	→	Handouts
Chat sessions with the instructor	→	Office hours
Assigned activities	→	Laboratories

Use a structural metaphor in asynchronous courses

For courses where learners determine the path through the course, pick a metaphor that clarifies the organization of the course and makes navigating within it predictable. Here are some examples of structural metaphors:

Metaphor	Home page	Web Page	Lesson	Course	Collection of courses
Book	Title page	Third-level heading	Chapter	Volume	Library
Building	Lobby, directory	Room	Floor	Building	Block, campus, office park
City	Overview, simple map	Building	Neighbor-hood	City	Province, metropolitan area, county

Metaphor	Home page	Web Page	Lesson	Course	Collection of courses
Factory	View of factory floor	Work-station	Machine tended by several workers	Whole factory	Industrial park
Office	View of whole office	Object or piece of paper	File drawer, box, desk	Whole office	Building
Magazine	Cover	Article	Section	Individual issue	Volume or whole archive of past issues
Television	Brief program listing	Program	Miniseries Channel	All programs available.	

Use a 3D metaphor as a starter only

Consider a spatial, three-dimensional metaphor, such as a building or a town, for new users, but let them switch to an index, menu, table of contents, or search facility when they want more efficiency. Navigating through three-dimensional space one mouse click at a time can become tedious.

Use a puzzle for complex activities

For a complex learning activity, use the metaphor of a puzzle. Each activity or lesson supplies one piece of the puzzle. The student must then put the pieces together to see the big picture, solve the puzzle, and win the game.

Pick a metaphor wisely

In considering a metaphor, determine how it will make your course more predictable, more unified, and more fun.

Maximize overlap with the real world

A good metaphor makes the learning environment more predictable. Learners can guess what to do next. The key requirement is a good overlap between the metaphorical world and the real world. Everything in the metaphorical world should have an analog in the real world and vice versa.

A good metaphor is already familiar to learners. It contains objects and actions corresponding to real-world objects and actions of interest to the learner.

Pick a rich metaphor

A good metaphor is rich enough to cover the entire subject and flexible enough to adapt to everything you want to represent. It can be extended as the system grows. It is sufficient to represent all navigational features without recourse to a second metaphor.

Pick a metaphor meaningful to learners

Consider what is familiar to your learners. In a comparison of a paper and a control-panel metaphor by mechanical engineering students 63% preferred the control-panel metaphor [87]. A desktop metaphor may not work well for factory workers. Likewise, a schoolhouse metaphor may not work for those who do not look back on their early schooling with fondness.

Deploy the metaphor naturally

Metaphors work best when they seem to grow naturally out of the organization or subject matter. A heavy-handed or artificial application of a metaphor can seem confusing or just plain silly.

Express the metaphor in words and pictures. Express the metaphor in the names and appearances of the objects and actions learners encounter in the course. Apply the metaphor in the design of page titles, banners, emblems, and buttons. Apply it in naming the divisions of the course and the actions learners can take.

Announce the metaphor clearly. If a course, lesson, or other learning unit uses a metaphor, state it explicitly in the introduction to the unit. Our metaphor may not be obvious to the harried, anxious learner.

Distinguish the metaphor from content. Display the metaphor in such a way that no one confuses the metaphor with what you are trying to teach. Make the metaphor consistent with the subject—but distinct from it. You can graphically distinguish metaphorical components with a distinctive color, drawing style (freehand or technical), or thematic shape (triangle, rounded rectangle).

Use the metaphor at top levels only. Use the metaphor for navigation of only the top and second level of the site. Few metaphors provide more than two levels of division. Use the metaphor to guide the learner to the right neighborhood—then admit it is really just a course.

Use a consistent metaphor for modularity. For modularity, all units must use the same metaphor or none at all. A distinctive metaphor or graphical theme will mean that a module cannot be combined with modules that do not use the same metaphor or theme.

NAME COURSES CAREFULLY

Often the title is all users see to entice them to click on a link for more information. Name a course so that learners can predict the goals, approach, and subject of the course just by reading the title.

> Project management—advanced level simulator

> Selling the Model 329/X – Self-paced tutorial

> Developing your financial plan: Web seminar for individual investors

Think about how a course will be retrieved and sorted in an online catalog. Put the most important part first. That way, it is where learners look in an index or alphabetical listing, and their rapidly scanning eyes notice these important words.

IN CONCLUSION ...

Summary

- ▶ Many types of WBT courses are possible, depending on a few fundamental choices. Consider where your course should fall along each of these scales:

Pure instructor-led	to	Pure learner-led
Pure synchronous	to	Pure asynchronous
Large class	to	Class of one

- ▶ Specify where learners should take the course. Then design it for where they will really take it.

- ▶ Pure WBT may not be the best approach to training. Consider alternating WBT and classroom sessions, having instructors lead learners through WBT, or using WBT materials in a classroom.

- ▶ Also consider mixing elements of disk-based CBT and WBT, perhaps using disks to store multimedia and using the Web for dynamic content and collaboration.

- ▶ Specify what technologies can be used in your course. Prefer technologies that are reliable, available to many, and fully supported by their vendors.

- ▶ Consider a metaphor to organize the course, unify its parts, and add interest and appeal for learners. Pick a metaphor familiar to learners and express it in labels and images.

For more ...

The International Society for Performance Improvement (www.ispi.org) publishes papers and holds conferences with lots of discussion on the proper modes for training and plenty of block diagrams showing correct sequences.

Margaret Driscoll, in her book *Web-Based Training,* classifies WBT into four distinct categories: Web/Computer-Based Training (W/CBT), Web/Electronic Performance Support Systems (W/EPSS), Web/Virtual Asynchronous Classroom (W/VAC), and Web/Virtual Synchronous Classroom (W/VSC) [79].

If you have opted to create an instructor-led course, be sure to review Chapter 9 on teaching in the virtual classroom and Chapter 8 on collaboration mechanisms. If you lean more toward an asynchronous course, stop in at Chapter 7 on testing, much of which can be automatically scored, and at Chapter 13 which has some ideas for going beyond conventional courses for just-in-time training.

4

Build the framework

Routine but necessary parts of the course

There is more to a successful course than instructional content. Successful courses require a framework to entice learners, to register and orient them, to keep them informed about the course and the people associated with it, to help them navigate the course reliably, and to congratulate them when they are done. Such a framework or "shell" provides a sturdy home for the lessons and other learning materials of the course.

WHAT IS A COURSE FRAMEWORK?

A course framework consists of all the routine parts of the course that do not teach subject matter but that are nevertheless an essential part of the course. They are the Web pages that describe and introduce the course, register learners, help administer the course, gather feedback, supply technical and administrative support, make individual topics easily accessible, and provide access to additional learning materials. The course framework is sometimes called the shell because it protects and contains the valuable core.

The course framework is not the heart of the course and creating it is not the most creative or glamorous aspect of designing WBT. However, the course framework often makes the difference between a course that meets its business and teaching objectives and one that does not.

Here is a diagram showing the components of a complete course framework:

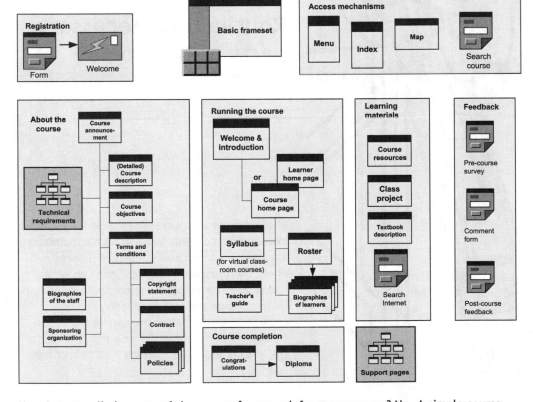

Must I create all elements of the course framework for every course? No. A simple course will not need all elements. A self-paced course can omit the elements for the class members and the instructor. Often, simple courses combine multiple elements into a single page.

Once you have created a course framework for one course, you can re-use it for the next course and the next and the next. Each framework can serve as the template for the next one.

This diagram might look daunting, but observe that pages are grouped into a few main functions. And we will step through them one at a time. You can decide whether you need each and learn how to design it.

TELL LEARNERS ABOUT THE COURSE

Before learners register for a course, they may want to know about it. Why should I take it? What will it teach me? What does it require of me? What must I do to get ready for the course? Even learners who have begun the course may want to glance back at this information. Let's consider some of the pages you may need in order to fully inform learners about the course. Throughout this section, we will use the course *Secrets of User-Seductive Documents* for examples of the course framework elements.

Course Announcement page

The Course Announcement page is a concise overview of the course with links to more detailed information. It can take several forms and go by several names: *About the Course*, *Course Catalog Entry*, *Course overview*, *Course Description*, and *Course Identification*. Here is an example of a simple course announcement:

The announcement is not designed to provide complete, detailed information about the course. Its goals are modest. The announcement helps learners decide whether to investigate the course. It simplifies obtaining more details by linking directly to them.

(Detailed) Course Description page

The Course Description page is one of the most important marketing and support tools for your course. It provides complete details about the course. It tells learners everything they need to know in order to sign up for the course and prepare for the first activity. As such, the Course Description page may be long. You may want to suggest printing it out.

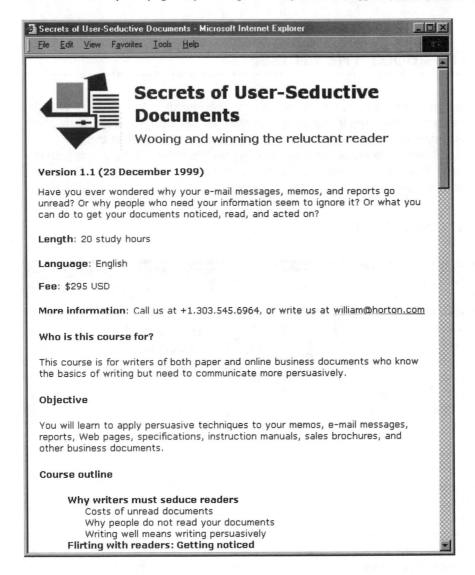

There is no set formula for what the description must contain. Let's review a list of the kinds of details commonly found in course descriptions.

Identification

Start the course description with a complete identification of the course: Number, title, subtitle, version, and revision date.

Secrets of User-Seductive Documents

Wooing and winning the reluctant reader

Version 1.1 (23 December 1999)

Enticement to take the course

Next include an inviting statement telling why the learners should take the course. This statement is not necessarily intended to sell the course but to motivate the potential learner to read further in the description.

Here are some motivational formulas that have hooked learners:

Have you ever wondered: _____? _____? _____?

Have you ever asked yourself: _____? _____? _____?

Have you ever wanted to _____?

Notice how the following example makes the reader aware of the problem the course solves:

```
Have you ever wondered why your e-mail messages, memos, and reports go
unread? Or why people who need your information seem to ignore it? Or what you
can do to get your documents noticed, read, and acted on?
```

Course specifications

Now that you have the reader's attention, you can quickly identify the nature of the course. In a concise format, list the most important characteristics of the course, such as length, languages in which it is offered, and fee. For example:

```
Length: 20 study hours

Language: English

Fee: $295 USD
```

For more information

Tell potential learners whom to turn to for more information. Give them an e-mail address and phone number for questions not answered in the description.

> **More information**: Call us at +1.303.545.6964, or write us at william@horton.com

Who should take the course

Tell learners the intended audience for the course. Is it for a particular professional group, such as mechanical engineers or human resources executives? Is it aimed at a particular skill level, say beginner or advanced? Does it solve a problem experienced by a large number of potential learners?

> **Who is this course for?**
>
> This course is for writers of both paper and online business documents who know the basics of writing but need to communicate more persuasively.

Credits awarded

Specify if the course earns credits toward a degree, certification, or prize.

> This course earns three Continuing Education Units.
>
> This course earns five credits toward the Associate Degree in Mechanical Drafting.
>
> This course fulfills 30 of the 60 hours required by the State of New South Wales for retraining.

Coverage

What subject matter does the course cover? What are the main points covered in the course? Start with a brief statement of objectives.

> **Objective**
>
> You will learn to apply persuasive techniques to your memos, e-mail messages, reports, Web pages, specifications, instruction manuals, sales brochures, and other business documents.

List only the main objective here. If you have more than a couple of objectives, list them in a bulleted list. If the objective statement is complex, include the full set of objectives in a separate page (p 90) and link to them.

You may also want to include a one- or two-level outline of the topics covered in the course.

Course outline

> **Why writers must seduce readers**
>> Costs of unread documents
>> Why people do not read your documents
>> Writing well means writing persuasively
> **Flirting with readers: Getting noticed**
> **Small talk: Getting and keeping the reader's attention**
>> Hooking the reader's interest
>> Smooth transitions
>> Making sure the reader comes back again
> **Sensual pages**
>> More show and less tell
>> More visual formats
>> Appealing to other senses
> **Toward a lasting relationship with the reader**

Focus the outline on what potential learners want to know. Emphasize the real-world benefits the learner will gain. Omit unimportant, unavailable, or discouraging entries. Although teachers may like a long list of content and its pedagogical excellence, it will only bore learners who just want to know what they will get out of the course.

For a complex course, a simple outline may not provide enough detail to fully preview the course. In that case you can link to a more detailed outline or to the complete course syllabus (p 400).

Special incentives

Tell learners why they should take this course now, as in this example:

Bonus

Register now and receive a copy of William Horton's book *Secrets of User-Seductive Documents*.

By registering for this course you qualify for a 15% discount on any additional courses. You also get access to our library of white papers and reports on documentation and training.

Are there any special incentives for taking your course? Be sure to list all these:

▶ Bonuses or prizes

▶ Ways this course is better than other courses on the same subject

▶ Reduced price

▶ Discount on additional courses

▶ Special resources such as a library

> ▶ Members-only areas or events

> ▶ Advance notice of courses and first choice of dates

Prerequisites

What prior knowledge and skills must the learner possess before enrolling in your course?

Prerequisites

To profit from this course you must be able to:

- Write basic business documents in simple, understandable English.
- Navigate a Web site using hypertext links.
- Fill in and submit Web forms.
- Send and reply to e-mail messages.

List what learners must know or be able to do. Must they possess specific knowledge? Must they have experience in a particular field or area of knowledge? Must they have taken prior courses? Must they have achieved a minimum grade level in those courses? What computer skills and online learning technology skills must they possess?

Enrolling

Give learners the information they need to enroll in the course.

Available: After 15 March 2000

Class size: This course does not have formal classes but enrollment is limited to 15 students at any time.

Register now.

Tell learners:

> ▶ **Availability** of the course ("Open enrollment")

> ▶ **When the class starts** ("Next available class starts 15 June")

> ▶ **Approvals required,** for example, the learner's supervisor or the instructor

> ▶ **Class size.** Is it an intimate 5 or a dizzying 10000?

> ▶ **Deadline for enrolling** ("Register by 8 June")

Include a link to the page on which learners can register for the course.

Is the course required?

If a course is in any way required, state so clearly in the description. Is the course required:

▶ By all employees?

▶ For certain jobs?

▶ For access to certain areas?

▶ To renew a license?

▶ Periodically as a refresher?

Style of instruction

Describe how learners will learn. Help learners imagine themselves taking the course.

How you will learn

This is no boring page turner. You won't feel you are reading *Moby Dick* from a computer screen. You will get lots of opportunities to practice what you learn. You'll get immediate, anonymous feedback from dozens of automatically scored activities and practices. You can discuss the course, ask questions, and get help with special problems through the course discussion group or through e-mail exchanges with your facilitator. As part of the course you will receive personal advice as you revise one of your own documents to make it more seductive.

Will the course consist mainly of reading Web pages, of watching lectures, or of running simulations? In what ways will learners interact with the instructor, with each other, or with course materials? Will learners interact as a whole class, in small teams, or only as individuals? What media are used to present information? Text and graphics? Multimedia? Virtual reality? What collaborative tools are used: e-mail, discussion groups, chat, video-conferencing, or others? What types of activities will help learners practice applying what they learn? Will learners produce documents or other work products as part of their class work?

Versions available

Is the course available in multiple versions? Learners may be shopping for a special version or may just want to sample the course. Tell learners if you have a:

▶ Sample or demonstration version

▶ Low-bandwidth version

▶ Printable version

Required behaviors

Tell learners what the course requires of them. Does it require certain traits and skills, such as tact, self-discipline, and time-management? Does it require the learner to commit to interact with fellow learners, to stay on schedule, and to finish the course?

What this course requires of you

If you are new to self-directed learning, you may find this style of learning fresh—and a bit frightening. You can set your own pace. No one will nag you or criticize you for not participating. You learn by participating actively. You alone are responsible for your own learning. That means you must have the drive and discipline to see the course through.

This course also requires interacting with other learners. It is your job to help them learn, just as it is theirs to help you. You are expected to practice the tact and politeness expected of business professionals.

Welcome and good luck.

Include a polite but clear statement alerting learners that they are expected to behave as responsible adults.

Tell how long the course will take

Tell learners how much time the course will take to complete and how much effort it will require. Be realistic. If you say a course takes 20 hours, learners should not find themselves one-tenth of the way through after 15 hours.

Time required

You can take this course at your own pace, but to complete it will require 15 to 25 hours of work. To complete the course in four weeks, for example, you must work about one hour per business day.

Give a range. For the high end, give the amount of time required for a learner with the minimum prerequisite knowledge to master all the material in the course. For the low end, give the amount someone with thorough prerequisite knowledge would require to learn the minimum necessary to meet the course objectives.

How do you get these figures? Test. And revise after the first few dozen learners. Try to state limits such that 85% of learners finish within the time limits.

Technical requirements

Make clear what hardware and software is required to take the course. For example:

Technical requirements

This course will run on Macintosh and Windows systems. It requires the equivalent of a 200 MHz Pentium PC with 24 megabytes of memory running Windows 95, 98, or NT or a Macintosh running OS 8 or later. It runs in either Netscape or Internet Explorer browsers of Version 4.0 and later. It requires no plug-ins but some optional examples do require the Adobe Acrobat 3.0 plug-in.

If your course requirements are any more complex than this, include a separate Technical Requirements page (p 493) linked to sources of help for meeting the requirements. See Chapter 12 for suggestions on how to help learners over hurdles posed by such technical requirements.

How to get the most out of this course

Give the learner tips for success in the course, for example:

To get the most out of this course

Do all the activities. They do not take long and they let you practice what you have learned.

Review the readings after you complete the activities. The activities will make clear how you can apply the readings.

Participate in the discussion groups. Ask questions, debate issues, and help others. Especially help others.

If the list is long, make it a separate page and link to it.

Fees and costs

Explain exactly what the basic fee includes and any extra charges that may apply. List the basic fee as well as the fee for materials, network accounts, and so forth. If taxes apply, mention them, too.

Fees

$295 USD.

Includes access to the course for one year from the date of registration.

Author or instructor of the course

Many technical authorities are well known in their field, and learners will sign up for a course just for the opportunity to learn from such an expert. If the teacher or author of your course is an authority, feature the fact. Provide a brief biography of the authority and a link to a more complete biography.

> **Author and facilitator**
>
> This course was developed and is facilitated by William Horton, president of William Horton Consulting, Inc. William Horton, author of five books on designing effective documents, has won several international awards for his designs.

Grading policy and procedure

Tell prospective learners if the course is graded and how a grade is assigned. Will students receive a letter or numeric grade? Or just a pass/fail grade? Are grades optional? What parts of the course contribute to the final grade? Here is an example of such a description:

> **Grading policy**
>
> This course is normally ungraded. If you require a grade, you may request one— **before you start the course**. The grade will be based equally on your class project, submitted activities, and participation in discussion groups.

If the policy is at all complex, link to the part of the Course Policy page that details the grading method (p 101) or to a separate Grading Policy page.

What to do before the first event

List things the learner should do before the first class meeting or lesson. Are there things they need to buy, read, or set up? Do they need to get an e-mail or other computer account? In this example, we just remind learners to make sure they meet the technical requirements.

> **Before you start**
>
> There are no pre-class readings or activities. However, please review the prerequisites in this description and the separate list of technical requirements to make sure that you meet all of them.

Links to alternative sources

Consider providing a rich set of links to alternative sources for those who decide the course is too basic, too advanced, or not the right aspect of the subject.

Encourage printing the description

If the course description is long, complex, requires careful reading, or has legal implications, encourage students to print it and read it from paper.

> **Print this page?**
>
> This page is rather long and contains important details we do not want you to miss. If you find reading from paper easier, we encourage you to print this page.

You probably want to put this invitation earlier on the page, either at the top under the banner or at the bottom of the first scrolling zone.

Link to continue

At the end of the description, include a link to the Registration page (p 105) so the motivated learner can act immediately. Phrase the link as a provocative, rhetorical question? "Sounds great! But how do I get started?"

> Don't let school interfere with your education.
>
> — Mark Twain

Objectives page

The Objectives page tells learners in detail what they will get out of taking the course. Use an Objectives page for a large, complex course where learners may have a lot of questions about what the course accomplishes, and where they need strong motivation to commit to completing it. Here is an example.

This example, which is from a different course than the other examples, tells learners what they will gain by taking the course.

Do not make a big deal about objectives. Just tell people what they will do, be able to do, understand, and believe by taking the course.

Use objectives to motivate

Objectives statements are often so boring that most learners just hit the Next button to get past them. That is a shame because well-written objectives provide a strong motivator for learners.

Try imagining a learner jumping out of bed exclaiming, "Hurrah! Today I'm going to learn to _____."

Write objectives so that learners will say, "Yeah, I want that!"

Translate teaching objectives to learning objectives

Unfortunately, the words we use to express teaching objectives (what **we** want to teach **them**) are especially effective at discouraging **them**. They have their own list of what they want to do. Use words that reflect what learners want to do, not what we want to do to them.

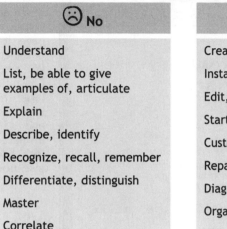
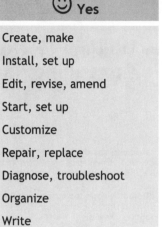

☹ No	☺ Yes
Understand	Create, make
List, be able to give examples of, articulate	Install, set up
Explain	Edit, revise, amend
Describe, identify	Start, set up
Recognize, recall, remember	Customize
Differentiate, distinguish	Repair, replace
Master	Diagnose, troubleshoot
Correlate	Organize
	Write

Stress application of training

Revise objectives statements so they clearly communicate how learners will apply the knowledge and skills they gain in training.

☹ No	☺ Yes
▶ After successfully completing the course, the learner will be able to:	▶ After successfully completing the course, you will be able to:
▶ Articulate what the product is.	▶ Identify groups of customers for whom this product is appropriate.
▶ Describe where the product fits within the product line.	▶ Show these customers how the features of the product benefit them.
▶ Explain the most important capabilities and features of the product.	▶ Quickly, confidently, and accurately answer the most common questions about the product (price, availability, requirements, main features, etc.).
▶ Enumerate the customer benefits inherent in the product.	▶ Show advantages over competing products.
▶ Identify relevant product specifications.	▶ Quickly find answers to specific, detailed questions about this product.
▶ Recall competitive advantages of the product.	

Sponsoring Organization page

A Sponsoring Organization page identifies the training vendor, training department, or university offering the course and any advantages it provides to learners who take its courses.

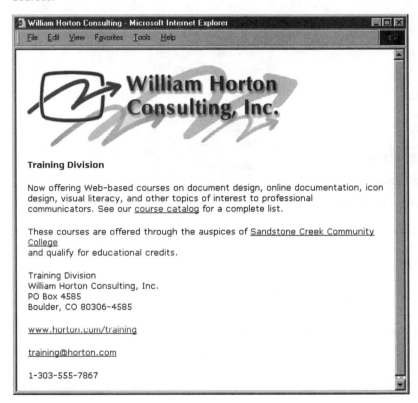

This example shows an Organization page. It is designed as if William Horton Consulting were large enough to have divisions and as if it were affiliated with a local educational institution.

The Organization page may be part of the Web site for the course or part of the Web site for the organization itself.

Give the full, official name of the organization

Give the complete, official name of the organization that offers the course. If the organization is a department of a larger organization, name both.

> Training Department
> ZipZapCom Incorporated

Spell out any acronyms:

> NTI – Nassau Technical Institute

Likewise, if the organization is known by another name, include that as well. If the organization is known by an abbreviation or department number, state that too.

> You may know us as ZZTD

Kiruna Mining Division Training (KM/T)

No one should have any doubt as to which organization produced, sponsored, offers, and supports the course.

Provide complete contact information

Tell learners how to contact the organization offering the course. Include full details for mail, telephone, and Internet contact.

▶ Mailing address

▶ Phone number (including a toll-free one)

▶ Fax number

▶ Web home address

▶ E-mail address

Mission

If the mission or scope of the organization is not clear from its name, include a brief description of the goals and offerings of the organization. Are there other courses this learner might be interested in?

> ZZTD offers both classroom and Web-based training on how to set up, operate, maintain, and program ZipZapCom's line of computer peripheral devices. These courses are available to both customers and internal staff. For a listing, see our Course Catalog.

Keep the statement short, just a sentence or two. Link to more detailed descriptions as necessary.

State the educational authority

What gives this organization its educational authority? Is it part of a larger system, consortium, or program?

> Province of Manitoba Certified College

> Authorized by the IACC Engineering Recertification Board

Is the organization accredited?

> ZZU holds full accreditation from the Central Florida Association of Trade Schools.

If certificates are awarded, make clear what value these have as credentials.

Biographies of staff members

People are naturally curious about people, especially people they are asked to trust and rely on for their own success. Because learners may not have face-to-face contact with instructors and other course staff, you should include a complete but brief biography of the course instructor, author, and others that learners may need to interact with.

Here is an example for our ongoing case study.

 ## Meet your instructor

A little bit about William Horton

Highlights

Name
William Horton

Position
President
William Horton Consulting, Inc.

Awards and honors
IF-Industrieform Seal of Quality
ACM Rigo Award
Fellow of the Society
for Technical Communication

Contact
E-mail: william@horton.com
(I prefer this method)

Voice: +1.303.545.6964

Post:
William Horton Consulting, Inc.
838 Spruce Street
Boulder, CO 80302 USA

Hello! I'm looking forward to meeting and working with all of you in the coming class.

We are engaging in a whole new way to learn—and it's very exciting. I look forward to your thoughts and feedback about this class, so I hope you won't hesitate to contact me.

About Bill

William Horton has been in the forefront of electronic information design since 1971. He specializes in applying ergonomics to the task of getting information from one human brain to another. He helps organizations and teams make the transition from traditional media to electronic media.

For over 15 years Bill has conducted seminars internationally on subjects ranging from multimedia design and visual literacy to user-interface design, online documentation, and Web-based training.

Bill is a sought-after lecturer and keynote speaker. Most recently he keynoted the 1995 and 1996 Interactive Conferences, Influent Technology Group's 1997 Conference series, the EDS Global Communications Conference, and the 1997 International Technology Training Association Conference in Barcelona.

Bill is a prolific author. His books include *Designing and Writing Online Documentation* (2nd ed.), *Illustrating Computer Documentation*, *Secrets of User-Seductive Documents*, *The Icon Book* (available in 4 languages), *The Web Page Design Cookbook* with CD-ROM, and the newly published *Designing Web-Based Training*.

Goals for biographies

In writing biographies of staff members, keep in mind your goals. You are not a publicity agent or resume service. Biographies within courses should be designed to:

▶ **Humanize the course.** Let learners put a face and a persona with the names of staff.

▶ **Establish the authority** and credibility of the staff and hence the course.

▶ **Capitalize on the fame** or reputation of an authority associated with the course.

Checklist of what to include in the biography

▶ **Name.** Include an informal name if this is how the learner should address this staff member.

▶ **Picture.** Make sure the instructor posts a *friendly* picture. Most photographs of instructors look like driver's license photographs at best and police mug shots at worst. Here's a tip, but use it quickly before it becomes a cliché: Pose the instructor in front of a computer screen displaying the home or title page of the course.

▶ **Title** or job position.

▶ **Personal welcome and greeting.** Include a brief text message, voice recording, or video clip that demonstrates the person's warmth, enthusiasm, and sincerity.

▶ **Description of the person.** Briefly list the staff member's credentials, philosophy, and personal interests. Make clear the affiliation. For whom does he or she work? Whose interests does the person represent? Link to a personal Web page for more details, a resume, or a complete biography.

▶ **Contact information.** Tell how to contact this person. List their e-mail address; telephone, fax, beeper, and mobile numbers; postal address; and personal Web page address.

▶ **Authority** What makes this person credible and worthy of respect? What awards and degrees has the person won? What offices has he or she held? What books, papers, and articles has the person written?

▶ **Office hours.** When will this person be available to meet with learners in person or electronically?

▶ **Humanizing details.** Optionally include a few personal items, such as a favorite poem, book, music, sports, movies, or quotation.

This is a long list. You do not need to include everything on it. Only tell what would make the learner sign up for the course and give the instructor/author credibility with learners.

Terms and Conditions page

Most courses require learners to agree to a short statement of the terms and conditions of the course. This approval may be part of the registration form or a separate page the learner must pass before beginning the course. Here is an example:

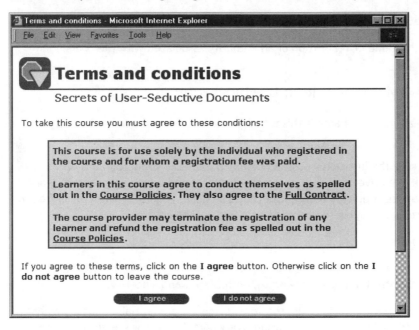

The Terms and Conditions page typically contains a short form of the contract, including an agreement to be bound by the full contract and the policies of the course. It also includes links directly to those referenced documents.

> Education. That which discloses to the wise and disguises from the foolish their lack of understanding.
>
> — Ambrose Bierce, *The Devil's Dictionary*

Course policies

Policies are long, boring, and utterly essential. These "rules by schools" set clear expectations, limit legal liability, and ensure that all learners are treated equally. It is the bedrock of your agreement with learners.

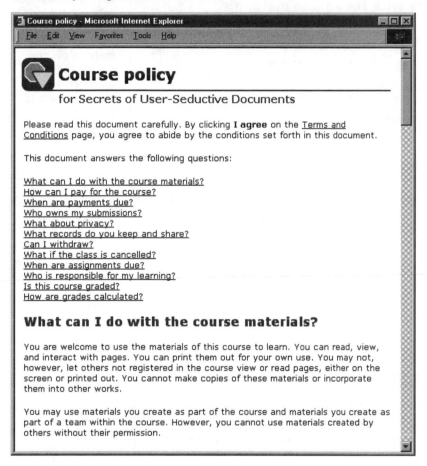

The Course policy is typically a long document that provides details only summarized or mentioned in the Course description. The policy is a complex document that will require involvement of course authors, instructors, administrators, attorneys, and managers. Let's look at some of the issues addressed in policy statements.

What can learners do with the course?

Learners can take the course. But what else can they do? What rights do they have to use the materials of the course in other ways?

What can I do with the course materials?

You are welcome to use the materials of this course to learn. You can read, view, and interact with pages. You can print them out for your own use. You may not, however, let others not registered in the course view or read pages, either on the screen or printed out. You cannot make copies of these materials or incorporate them into other works.

You may use materials you create as part of the course and materials you create as part of a team within the course. However, you cannot use materials created by others without their permission.

Here's an example policy that spells out what learners can do with the materials in the course and with materials they create as part of the course.

Payment methods

Specify how learners can pay for registration to the course. If payment is limited to credit cards, you may just want to put that information on the registration form. However, you may want to provide more options.

How can I pay for the course?

You can pay for your course registration in several ways.

Credit cards. We take Visa, MasterCard, and American Express.

Account number. If your organization is taking several courses, you can set up an account ahead of time and charge courses to it. E-mail us for details.

Purchase order. Approved companies can charge course registrations to a purchase order number. Contact us to set up an account.

Business check. We accept business checks. Allow one week for U.S. and Canadian checks to clear and two weeks for checks from other countries.

Wire transfer. You can wire us your registration fee. E-mail us to get the destination number.

Cash. Do **not** send cash. We would just lose it.

This example lists several ways learners can pay course fees.

Billing policy

Spell out when payments are due. For example:

When are payments due?

In general, you must pay before beginning a course. Your credit card will be charged at the time of registration. Customers with accounts will be billed monthly and are expected to pay within 30 days.

Withdrawal and guarantee policy

Spell out your withdrawal or cancellation policy. Make clear how late a learner can withdraw and how much of the fee will be refunded. Also tell learners what their grade will be if they withdraw after the course has started. Specify what a learner must do to withdraw. For example:

> ### Can I withdraw?
>
> You can withdraw from a class at any time. If you have opted for a grade, a grade of *incomplete* will be recorded. If you withdraw during the first week, 100% of your fee will be refunded. Between the first and third weeks, you can withdraw and have 50% of your fee refunded. After the third week, no refunds will be made.
>
> To withdraw, fill in the form at:
> www.ergoglyphics.com/registration?action=withdraw.
> You do not have to give any reason for withdrawing.

If you offer a money-back guarantee, mention it. Spell out conditions under which students can withdraw from the course and receive a full refund.

Cancellation of course or enrollment

Under what conditions can the provider cancel a class or remove a student from a class? What refund will be made in this case?

> ### What if the class is cancelled?
>
> We reserve the right to cancel *any* class at *any* time. If we do cancel a class, you will receive a full refund.
>
> We also reserve the right to cancel the enrollment of any learner without reason. If we cancel an enrollment, the student will receive a full refund.

Ownership and use of learners' work

Make clear who owns work produced by the learner within the course: the student, the course provider, or the student's sponsor? Works by learners include class assignments submitted to the instructor, postings to class forums, and comments in chat sessions and other collaborative events.

> ### Who owns my submissions?
>
> You retain copyright to any work you create within this course and may use it as you see fit. We will not use any of your work for purposes other than your learning without getting your permission first. If we use your material, we will credit your work if you so desire.

You may also want to make clear in what ways work contributed by a learner can be used, for instance, as an example in future courses, in other course-related ways, or outside the course. If the learner's material is used, will the learner receive a credit line or be anonymous?

Privacy

Clearly state who will have access to what information, especially information about learners and information contributed by learners.

What about privacy?

Except for information you share with your instructor and with other learners enrolled in this class, your contributions are private.

Your grades, scores on tests, submitted materials, and comments in discussion groups are confidential to the class. They will not be released without your permission. If your employer needs a copy of your grades, you must give permission first.

In interacting with your instructor and fellow learners, you are expected to use your real name, unless you are in the witness relocation program. Only staff and other learners will have access to your name and e-mail address.

In your privacy policy, set clear rules for:

▶ **What information is available to outsiders.** Also spell out what information about learners will be made available to instructors and administrators, other learners, the learners' employers, and outside parties.

▶ **Use of pseudonyms.** Set a policy on the use of aliases or pseudonyms in collaborative activities.

▶ **Privacy of e-mail addresses.** Define a clear policy of who will have access to the e-mail addresses of learners. One solution is to assign learners a special class-only e-mail address, which is the only one revealed to classmates and which expires a few weeks after the class ends.

What is monitored and recorded

Spell out what data about the learner is monitored and recorded. For example:

What records do you keep and share?

Since this course is not normally graded, we do not record grades or scores. We do not keep submissions more than a few weeks after the class ends. If you have requested a grade, we do record a grade and keep it forever or at least until we forget where we put it.

Spell out:

▶ Which activities are tracked?

▶ What is recorded about each activity?

▶ How are learners identified? By anonymous ID or by actual name?

▶ How long are records retained?

▶ Are specific results retained or just statistical summaries?

▶ Who can have access to the results and summaries: instructor, administrators, others?

When assignments are due

Remove any ambiguity about when assignments are due or when events occur. Such ambiguity can occur when learners are in different time zones on either side of the International Date Line. "Well, it's still Tuesday here!"

> ### When are assignments due?
>
> We operate on international time. We define our day by the UTC or GMT clock (London time). That means, if we say an assignment is due on 12 June, we mean it is due **before** Midnight (00:00 hours) 13 June in London, 1:00 AM (01:00 hours) 13 June in Berlin, and 7:00 PM (19:00 hours) 12 June in New York.

Student responsible for learning

Require learners to take responsibility for their own learning. Let them know that they are responsible for participating in activities, completing work on time, and contacting the instructor or other staff members when they need help.

> ### Who is responsible for my learning?
>
> You are. It is your responsibility to learn the material in this course to your desired level of knowledge. It is not the facilitator's duty to teach you. Your facilitator and perhaps classmates can help you, but only you can learn.

Make clear that technical problems are not an excuse for failing to complete the work. Students are responsible for identifying problems and seeking help.

Grading method

When it comes to grading, learners want to know everything. Those within organizations and institutions that use grades as credentials can become quite anxious on the subject of grading. Keep no secrets; tell them all.

What kind of grade is assigned?

Tell learners if the course is graded and what kind of grade they can expect to receive.

> ### Is this course graded?
>
> We do not normally assign grades. However, at the time of registration, you may request a grade. You must do so in an e-mail message to the instructor. We will even let you decide the style of grade you want to receive: pass/fail, letter grade, or number (95 of 100). Just tell us what form you want. If you opt for pass/fail, you must obtain the equivalent of a C letter grade to pass.

Formula for calculating the grade

If learners receive a grade in the course, spell out how that grade will be determined. Tell learners what activities and events count toward the final grade and how much each one counts. To the extent possible, specify the scoring criteria and grading formula.

How are grades calculated?

No grades are assigned, but to complete this course you must accumulate at least 150 points. Points are awarded as follows:

Component of the course	How many?	Points each	Maximum points for this component
Activities and exercises	10	5	50
Lesson tests	5	10	50
Participation in discussions	10	5	50
Final exam	1	100	100

Use these questions as a checklist as you write your grading policy:

▶ What does the grade attempt to measure? Level of knowledge, improvement, attitudes?

▶ What parts of the course contribute to the grade and how much does each contribute? Tests, exercises, collaborations, projects?

▶ Who scores the activities? The instructor, the learner, the computer, fellow learners?

▶ Deadlines. What happens if required items are submitted late?

▶ How are incomplete assignments graded?

▶ How must tests be taken? Are tests proctored?

▶ How are collaborative activities evaluated? Quantity of interaction? Quality of interaction? Help given fellow students?

If active participation contributes to the final grade, state exactly how you define participation and how it will be scored. In a new medium like WBT, learners may have a different meaning for participation than you do.

Copyright page

To preserve your ownership of your course and all its many pieces of text, graphics, and multimedia, state your copyright ownership clearly. Place with a brief notice on each page linked to a Copyright page that spells out intellectual property rights and privileges.

In your copyright statement and policy, include these items:

▶ Copyright statement

▶ Trademarks and service marks used in the course

▶ Material included by permission from others

▶ Usage or licensing policy. Who can link to the material? Who can reproduce it? Who can grant permission?

Have the page reviewed and approved by your attorney.

TechnoTip: To produce the copyright symbol © in HTML, use "©".

If the copyright of the artwork is different from that of the page on which it appears, include a copyright notice in the border of the picture as part of the artwork. Make the notice as small as is still legible.

Legal Contract page

The legal contract states the agreement with the learner and anyone else licensing the course.

Contract with the learner

The contract with the individual learner states exactly what the learner can and cannot do with the course and what rights the learner has and which the learner waives.

Here is a brief checklist of items you may need to include in your contract.

- ▶ Limitations of liability.
- ▶ What the learner can do with course materials.
- ▶ Who can take the course?
- ▶ Right to change the course without warning. What notice will be given?
- ▶ Statement that there is no other contract.
- ▶ Who can speak for the company?
- ▶ Legal name and address of the company.

Contract with the organization licensing the course

Sometimes an organization may license a course for use by some or all of its workforce. This type of contract is different from the one with the individual learner. Such a contract may need to cover additional points:

- ▶ On how many servers may the course be installed?
- ▶ How many users may access the course? Simultaneously? Total with access?
- ▶ What groups may access the course? All employees? Members of a department? All employees at a particular site?
- ▶ Access restrictions. Intranet only, not on the Internet?
- ▶ Prices. Per course, per student-enrollment, per student-completion, per server, per user?
- ▶ Limitations on reselling or reusing material.
- ▶ Responsibility for disruption of service.

REGISTER LEARNERS EFFICIENTLY

Create a simple, streamlined process for signing up for a course. In most cases, this will involve a registration form followed by an e-mail acceptance.

Simplify registration forms

If learners must fill in a registration form to take your course, make sure they do not need a course on how to fill in the form.

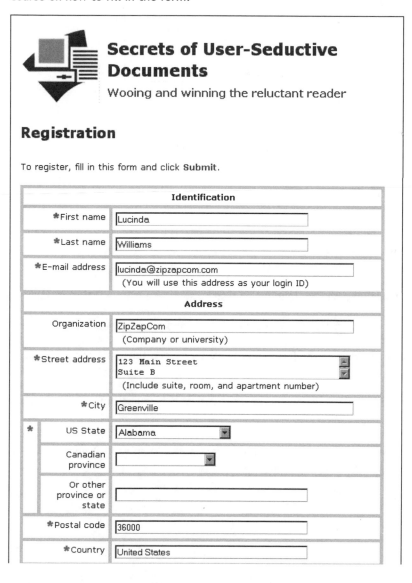

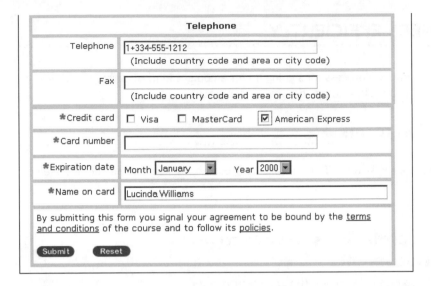

Here are some tips for better registration forms:

▶ Keep the form short. Do not ask for more information than you really need.

▶ Label each item clearly. If a short label is not sufficient, add a line of text just below the input area to provide additional details.

▶ Flag required items clearly.

▶ Fill in values with best guesses as defaults. Avoid reverse-patriotism. If most learners come from your country, make it the default.

▶ Minimize typing. Where possible, let learners choose by selecting from a list of options.

▶ Design the form to accommodate international addresses and phone numbers.

▶ Group items to show the logic of the form and to give learners a sense of accomplishment as they complete each section.

▶ Require learners to consent to the contract and policies of the course before submitting the form.

Administrative tip: I like to use the learner's e-mail address as a login ID. It is guaranteed to be unique and learners are not likely to forget it.

Confirm registration by e-mail

To acknowledge registration and to motivate learners, welcome them individually with an e-mail message.

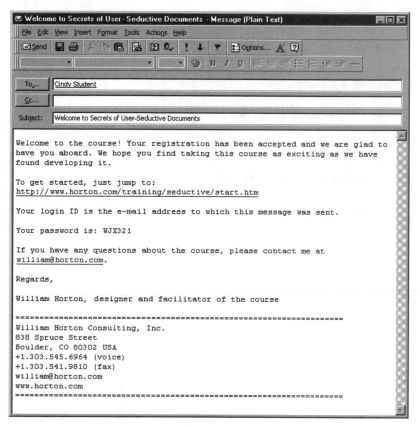

In the welcoming e-mail message, provide:

▶ Enthusiastic and sincere greeting.

▶ Clear confirmation that the registration was accepted.

▶ URL for the course home or welcome page.

▶ Login ID and password. (Note: sending both ID and password in one e-mail message may pose a security risk. As an alternative, send each one in a separate message or tell learners how to obtain them.)

▶ Reminder of the first course deadline, if the course is not self-paced.

▶ Invitation to contact the instructor or other staff members for help.

▶ Signature showing the real name of a human being, not just the name of an organization.

RUN THE COURSE SMOOTHLY

Certain parts of the course shell are used continually as the course proceeds.

Welcome page

The Welcome page greets learners as they first enter the course. It makes them feel at home and eager to get on with the course. Here is an example:

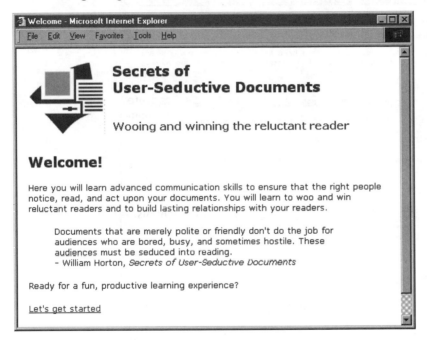

The Welcome page is not a substitute for the (detailed) Course Description (p 80) or Syllabus page (p 400). In the Welcome page (p 108), include just the content necessary to orient learners and motivate them to start the course.

▶ **Course title**. Just so learners know that they are in the right course.

▶ **Welcoming greeting**. Make learners feel at ease and appreciated. Let them know this will be an enjoyable experience.

▶ **Brief statement of what the course is about**. Remind learners of why they signed up for the course. Include a 1-3 sentence statement of what they will experience moving through the course. Emphasize what the learner will do and be able to do.

▶ **Attractive graphic**. Include a tasteful and interesting graphic. You can use the course emblem, a montage of images related to the subject, or a photo of the instructor. If you include a picture of the instructor, make sure it is clear, friendly, and inviting.

▶ **Inspiration.** You may want to include something that adds an extra bit of motivation, such as a welcome from an authority or the instructor, or an inspiring quotation.

Biographies of learners

Some courses require learners to post brief biographies to the course Web site or discussion group. Others do not. Some make biographies optional.

Whether to include biographies

Posting biographies is a genuinely controversial and cantankerous issue among WBT designers.

Reasons *to* post biographies	Reasons *not to* post biographies
▶ Learners more quickly get to know and trust their peers. ▶ Collaborative activities advance more rapidly. ▶ Learners discover and pursue common interests. ▶ Learners feel less isolated and find learning warmer and less sterile.	▶ Some learners prefer to keep personal details private. Some are shy or self-conscious. ▶ Biographies may reveal details that trigger racial, gender, or age bias. ▶ Many learners are embarrassed by a bad photograph, or their own relative lack of credentials.

More and more organizations are making biographies optional and letting learners omit any details they do not want to share.

Suggest what to include in the biography

You may want to provide learners a template or a checklist prompting them to include useful details about themselves. Here is such a checklist:

▶ Name (as they want to be addressed by others in the course)

▶ E-mail address

▶ Photograph

▶ Goals for education

▶ Job position and employer, or school and department

▶ Personal information, such as hometown, tastes in music and film, hobbies, and pets

Remind learners not to include intimate details (such as a home address or home phone number), special ID numbers, or other facts that could be used to harm them.

Roster page

The class roster lists the names and electronic contact information for staff and learners. The purpose of the roster is to enable learners, instructor, and other staff members to communicate with one another. Here is an example:

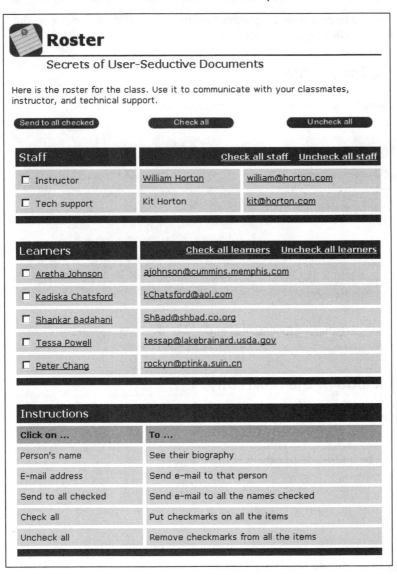

Course Home page

The Course Home page is the default location when restarting a course. Use it for announcements about the course. Here is an example:

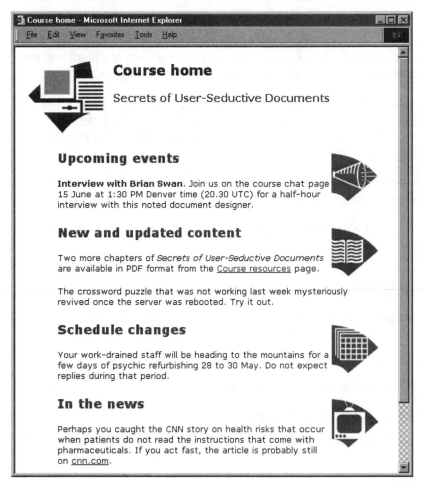

What to include

On the home page, inform learners of:

▶ Upcoming events, activities, tests

▶ Changes to the original schedule

▶ New content, especially related to material already covered

▶ News events in the subject area

Such announcements may motivate learners to frequently revisit the course, taking lessons in smaller chunks.

Design tips

Make the home page an efficient and welcoming place for learners.

▶ **Design it like the cover of a magazine.** Catch attention in news stories. List intriguing content.

▶ **Do not clutter it with one-time information.** People will come to your home page repeatedly. Do not clutter it with information learners will read only the first time. Put background and introductory information on a Course Description page (p 80).

▶ **Keep announcements concise.** Keep the course home page concisely focused on the issues of most interest to learners. Few learners consider the instructor's detailed biography and instructional philosophy essential [88]. Put these items on a separate Instructor's Biography page (p 94).

▶ **Link to more detailed information.** If an announcement is long by nature, summarize it here and link to a separate page containing the full announcement.

▶ **Encourage learners to bookmark the home page.** On startup, invite the learner to add a bookmark to the course home page.

Consider alternatives

Instead of putting announcements on the course home page, you may want to consider one of these other ways of delivering such messages:

▶ Put announcements into a special thread of the course discussion group.

▶ Make announcements in a course e-mail newsletter.

▶ Post announcements to a Learner Home page (p 112).

▶ Use a Special Announcements or What's New page.

Learner Home page

Some WBT tools, especially those used by universities, display a home page customized to the individual student. It provides pertinent details, announcements, and reminders for all the courses the learner is taking. With such a page, the learner does not have to visit the individual home pages for each course in which the learner is enrolled.

Consider using a Learner Home page if learners are typically enrolled in more than one or two courses at a time or if you are using a WBT tool that automatically creates and maintains Learner Home pages.

Syllabus page (for virtual classroom courses)

The syllabus is the core of instructor-led WBT courses. It lays out the schedule of the course and links to all the activities, presentations, readings, staff members, and external resources of the course. Because it is such an essential element of instructor-led WBT, we have included a description of the Syllabus page (p 400).

Teacher's guides

For courses to be taught or facilitated by local teachers, provide a teacher's guide. Include topics that the local teacher will need to lead, participate in, or just support.

▶ **Strategy**. What does the course aim to teach and how does it work?

▶ **Overview**. What does the course contain? Summarize the content.

▶ **Requirements for the teacher**. What must teachers do to get ready?

▶ **Special challenges**. What problems have previous teachers reported?

▶ **Teaching in the classroom**. Tell teachers what materials are available and how to get them. Suggest ways to introduce WBT materials in the classroom.

PROVIDE NEEDED RESOURCES

Some pages of the course framework help learners find the learning materials they need throughout the course. Some of these resources are internal to the course and others reside on the wider Internet. Resources pages include links to high-priority resources, searching devices, descriptions of textbooks, and details of class projects that span individual lessons.

Course Resources page

The Course Resources page presents the learner with a list of resources of value throughout the course—rather than in a single lesson. These include resources that are a part of the course and some available elsewhere on the Internet.

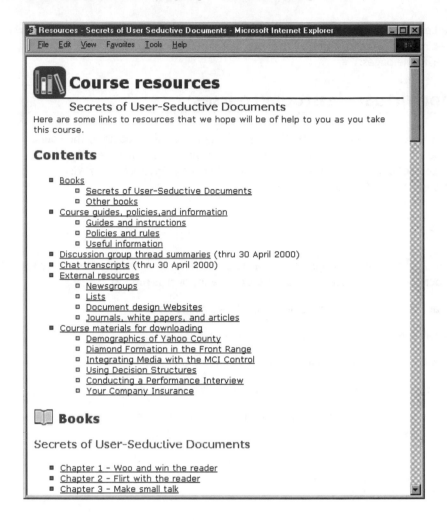

List useful course resources

Make it easy for learners to find and re-find resources within the course. Make the list complete. Here are some resources you may want to include and link to:

▶ Syllabus, agenda, timetable

▶ Past exams, projects, discussion-group threads

▶ Tutorial on the learning system

▶ Documentation for required course software

▶ Technical support for the course

▶ How to Study guide

Include external resources, too

Provide links to other real-world resources:

▶ Other web sites on the same subject as this course

▶ Newsgroups on the subject

▶ FAQs on the subject

▶ Forms used in a process being taught

▶ Reports, specifications, data sheets, and white papers on the subject of the course

▶ Computer programs used for tasks taught in the course.

Add value with commentary

For resource jump pages, add value by grouping, labeling, and describing what is important to the user about each link. Give its name and say who owns it. Comment on its quality. How relevant, objective, accurate, and timely is it? Does downloading and playing the resource pose any performance problems?

Search-the-net page

Include a page for triggering searches with the most popular search engines. Let learners select both external (Internet) and internal (within the firewall on the local intranet) search engines.

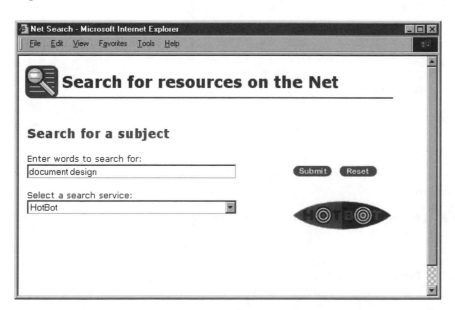

Textbook description

If the course uses a paper textbook (and many should), include a description of the book. Provide enough detail for learners to obtain the book. If the book is optional, include details necessary for learners to decide whether to buy it.

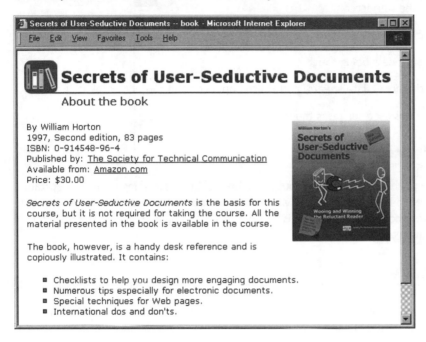

For a textbook description include:

▶ Title

▶ Author's name

▶ Edition and date published

▶ ISBN number

▶ Publisher's name

▶ URL and instructions for obtaining the book from the publisher, a local bookstore, or an Internet bookstore

▶ Description – why this book is necessary or recommended

▶ Price

▶ Photograph of the cover

Class project

If students must complete a substantial project, provide complete instructions.

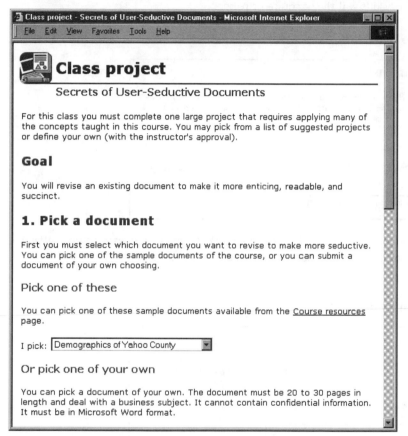

What to include

Goals

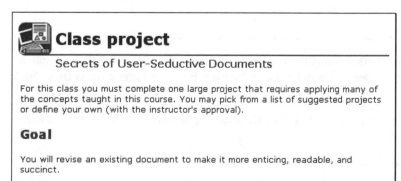

Spell out the objectives of the exercise. What will learners gain by doing the project?

▶ Will they produce something of value itself, such as a plan, analysis, or report?

▶ What knowledge or skills will they acquire or refine?

List of projects to pick from

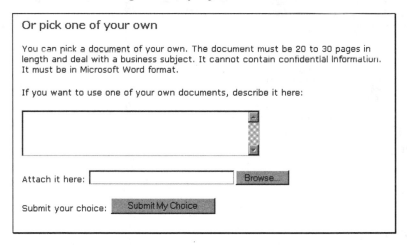

Give learners some ideas for projects, and let them pick the ones they want to do. Letting learners pick a project gives them greater ownership of the tasks and motivates them to complete it.

Process for defining custom projects

You may want to let learners design their own projects. If you do, give the learners explicit directions and criteria for devising a project of their own. Here are some criteria they should use:

▶ **Complexity.** The project must pose authentic problems to solve and should reflect the intricacy of real life.

▶ **Required elements.** List specific components or size of the project.

▶ **Format.** Must sample data or a sample document be in a particular format?

▶ **Subject of the course.** Require learners to state how their project contributes directly to the goals of the course.

▶ **Required tools.** Must the problem be one that requires use of certain computer programs, specialized equipment, or analysis techniques?

▶ **Examples.** You may want to link to examples of approved project proposals from earlier offerings of the class.

Assignment instructions

---

2. Revise the document

Your assignment is to redesign the whole document to ensure that it is noticed, read, understood, and acted upon. You must also explain the changes you made and why you made them.

When you have completed the project, you must submit two documents below (Microsoft Word or HTML format).

Attach the revised document:

[_____] Browse..

Attach a 5-10 page explanation of the changes you made in your revision:

[_____] Browse..

Submit your documents: [Submit My Documents]

Clearly explain what the learner is to do. Tell them:

▶ **Deliverables.** What documents or other materials must learners submit?

▶ **Tools.** What tools must they demonstrate use of?

Make the submission process as easy as possible.

How judged

How the project will be graded

The facilitator will assign your grade based equally on the improvements in the sample document and on your justifications of them. Criteria will include the degree to which all opportunities to improve the document were taken, whether the right seductive techniques were applied, how well they were applied, and whether they were applied for the right reasons.

Tell learners how their results will be scored and graded. What characteristics must their solution possess? Will results be evaluated according to a checklist, a definite procedure, or a formula?

ACKNOWLEDGE SUCCESS

Leave learners with a warm feeling and a sweet taste upon successfully completing the course.

Congratulations page

At the end of the course, clearly signal the end and motivate learners to continue learning. Congratulate them and let them print out a diploma.

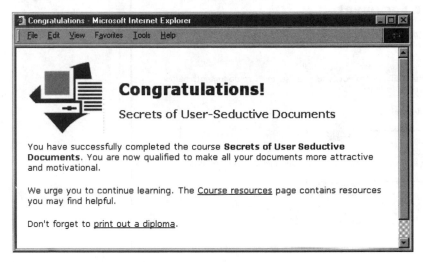

In your page of congratulations:

▶ Congratulate the learner.

▶ Confirm successful completion.

▶ Refer the student to post-class resources or activities.

▶ Invite the student to join the electronic alumni association.

▶ Invite the learner to print out a diploma.

> Socrates gave no diplomas or degrees, and would have subjected any disciple who demanded one to a disconcerting catechism on the nature of true knowledge.
>
> — G. M. Trevelyan

Diploma

At the end of the course, let the learner display and print out a diploma or certificate of completion. Style it something like this.

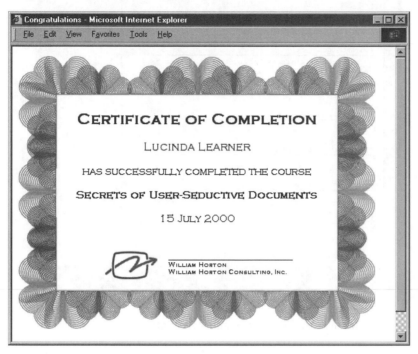

Be careful not to imply that this diploma has more value as an educational credential than it does.

GATHER FEEDBACK

If you want to make your course better, listen to learners. Use every opportunity to learn about them and to solicit their opinions and suggestions.

Welcome feedback

Welcome feedback. Throughout your course, sprinkle links or buttons to let learners offer feedback, point out errors, and make suggestions. Do not make them wait until the end of the course. Make offering a comment as simple as a mouse click.

> If you notice anything wrong or missing, please <u>let us know</u>.

One way to make this easy is to provide a general-purpose comment mechanism that learners can pop up any time they have something to say to you.

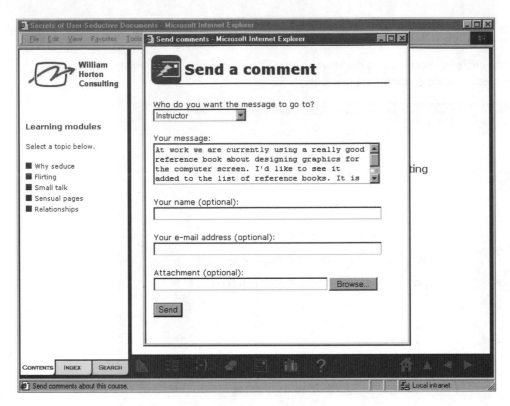

Allow anonymous feedback. Make names and e-mail addresses optional.

Post-Class Feedback page

Post-class feedback questionnaires, sometimes called "smiley sheets" or "bingo cards," are an educational cliché. You finish the course. You fill in a form. WBT has just moved the form to the screen.

Though clichés, post-class feedback questionnaires are valuable—when well designed. They let learners express opinions, make suggestions, and vent pent-up emotions. Here is a typical example:

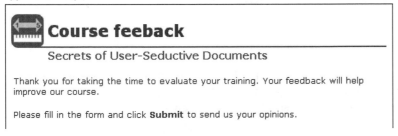

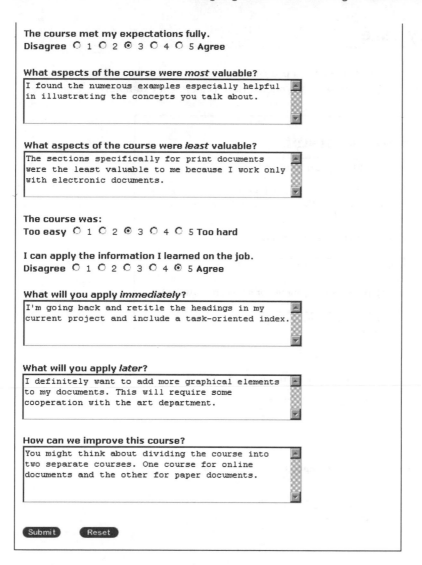

Questionnaires make it easy to gather statistics. But remember that learners may like a course and still fail to successfully apply what the course taught. You can compare results from earlier questionnaires for the same course to detect improvement. Be sure to include questions about what knowledge learners will apply and how they will apply it.

For best results, gather feedback six weeks or even six months after the class. By then learners can tell you whether they have applied what they learned in class or not. Just post the questionnaire on your Web site and send an e-mail message to course graduates asking them to fill in the questionnaires.

Pre-Course Survey page

You may want to begin your course with a pre-course survey to learn more about learners and to more precisely target their learning needs. Here is a typical example:

Tell us about yourself

Secrets of User-Seductive Documents

Thank you for taking the time to fill in this questionnaire. Your answers will help us tailor the course to your needs. Please read the Course Policy if you have any concerns about what we do with this information.

When you have completed the questionnaire, click **Submit**.

Your e-mail address: lucinda@ergoglyphics.com

Tell us what you do at your job, or specify your major if you are a student:

> I write and edit online documents, including help, reference, and support.

What do you hope to be able to do after taking this course?

> To make my documents more enticing and easier to read.

Have you had any training in designing paper, online, or Web-based documents?

> I've had no formal training in this area. All I have is on-the-job experience.

The following questions concern the hardware and software you have. Your answers will help us determine the kinds of collaborative activities we can include in this course.

What computer platform are you using?

○ Macintosh PowerPC ○ Pentium II ◉ Pentium III
○ Other [   ] (Explain)

What is the approximate speed (in MHz) of your computer? [500 ▼]

How comfortable are you with using Web technology?

I am: **Not comfortable** ○ 1 ○ 2 ○ 3 ○ 4 ◉ 5 **Very comfortable**

Have you ever used videoconferencing software? ⦿ Yes   ○ No
If so, what kind: `NetMeeting and CUSeeMe`

Have you ever used chat software? ⦿ Yes   ○ No
If so, what kind: `NetMeeting and CUSeeMe`

Do you have a video camera connected to your computer? ⦿ Yes   ○ No

What wordprocessing software do you use (include the version number)?

`Word 2000`

What drawing or illustration program do you use (include the version number)?

`Freehand 8`

[Submit]   [Reset]

You can use a survey to prescribe just what modules the learner should take. For example, give learners a survey of issues to which they agree or disagree. Based on which items the learner agrees to, recommend detailed study, quick review, or no study.

ADD ACCESS MECHANISMS

Few WBT designers think they can force-march a whole class of learners down a narrow path of the designer's devising. Most freely acknowledge the need to let at least some learners find their own way. Hence, WBT courses are sprouting the same access mechanisms common in online Help and multimedia CD-ROMs.

Menu and tables of contents

The menu is a hierarchical organization of the Web pages that make up a course. A menu is sometimes called the Table of Contents or just Contents, especially in courses organized as a book.

What does the menu do for learners?

The menu lets learners click their way to any individual page. Learners accustomed to navigating the hierarchical file systems in Windows and Macintosh systems readily adapt to such drill-down menus within WBT courses.

The menu previews the contents of the course. It shows what the course or lesson covers, reveals how it is organized, and suggests how much time it will require. Good menus organize the entire course into a few levels with a few choices at each level. They thus simplify the task of finding individual pages.

Several kinds of menus are possible

Designers of WBT courses can choose from a variety of different menu types.

Menus as layered pages of subtopics

For handcrafted courses, the menus often consist of a top page listing sub-menus. Clicking on an entry jumps to another Web page listing either another layer of sub-menus or the actual pages themselves. For example:

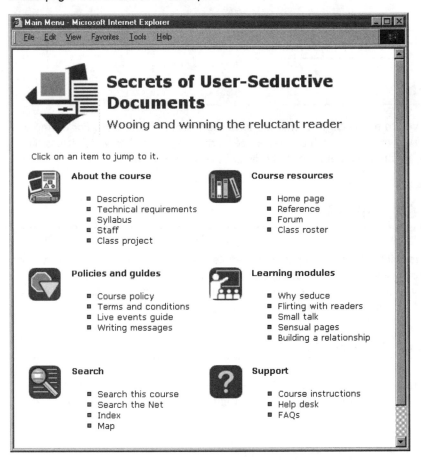

Sidebar of linked topics

A second, slightly more sophisticated menu displays the layered lists of subtopics in one frame of a multi-frame frameset. Thus the menu remains visible as the learner uses it to access pages, which appear in an adjoining frame.

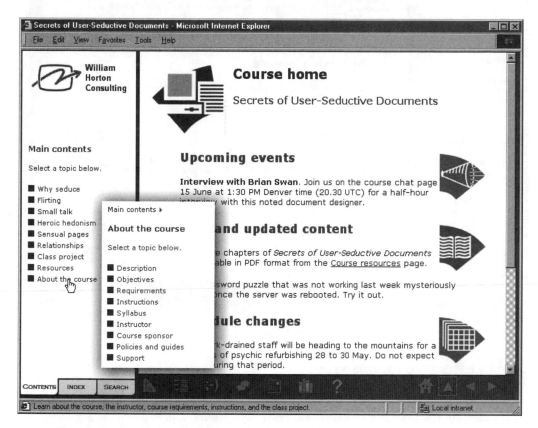

Expanding-outline menu

An even more sophisticated approach displays the entire list of topics as an expanding outline like the Windows Explorer or Macintosh Finder hierarchical views. Clicking on a menu item displays sub-items indented under it.

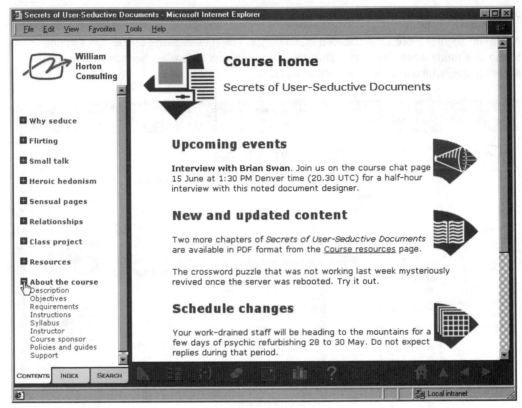

This example requires Internet Explorer 4.0 or Netscape Navigator 4.5.

Design effective menus

Regardless of what style of menu you select or what technology you use to implement it, you still must make it simple and logical for learners. Here are some tips.

Keep entries short. Keep menu entries short. They may have to fit in a narrow window. Do not waste words with "Module 1: . . .".

Divide if the list is long. For more than 10 items, divide the menu into a few main groups, each with a label or graphical emblem.

Pick meaningful categories. When grouping menu items, pick categories that are distinct, are familiar to learners, and have understandable labels.

Fit in one scrolling zone. Fit the whole menu into one scrolling zone if possible. If the menu is too long, break it into multiple levels of linked menus.

Suggest sequence. The order in the table of contents should suggest the order in which learners take lessons.

Display only one or two levels at a time. In the menu, display no more than 2 levels of entries per page. If the menu is an expanding outline, start with just the top level being expanded.

Limit the number of levels. If the table of contents displays only one level at a time, use no more than two or three levels.

Announce the destination. If items in the menu require jumping to a lower level, make items tell or clearly imply what the lower level contains. Phrase the label clearly. Use scripting to display a full title of the menu item in the browser's status bar. Or put a graphic before each item, such as a bullet, and make the ALT text attribute of its tag provide a more detailed explanation.

Distinguish different kinds of targets. In the menu, distinguish among folders (groups of lower-level items), presentation pages, tests, activities, feedback forms, and so forth. Include a distinctive icon in the label to reflect the type of item.

Do not number menu items. Do not number items in a menu. The numbers take up space and distract from the headings. Do not say, "1.2.4 Test: Measuring exposure value", just "Test: Measuring exposure value."

Prompt learners to click. If the menu entries are not obvious links (underlined), add a prompt like, "Click on an item to jump to it."

Orient learners on lower-level menus. If learners can link to a sub-menu, provide the same welcome and orienting information on it as on the main menu—just not so prominently. Provide you-are-here information. On the submenu, make clear that this is a submenu and display the path from the top-most menu down to this one.

Make menus dynamic. Update menus dynamically (perhaps with Dynamic HTML) to keep learners up to date. Highlight the current location. As learners navigate, update the menu. When a learner resumes the course, have it appear the way the learner left it.

Training is everything. The peach was once a bitter almond; cauliflower is nothing but cabbage with a college education.

— Mark Twain, *Pudd'nhead Wilson*

The chief wonder of education is that it does not ruin everybody concerned in it, teachers and taught.

— Henry Adams, *Education of Henry Adams*

Index

The index is an alphabetical list of terms assigned by human indexers. With an index, learners do not have to recall the exact term or spell it correctly. An index can contain synonyms to terms in the text. An index can also use terms not contained in the course itself. Here is an example of an index:

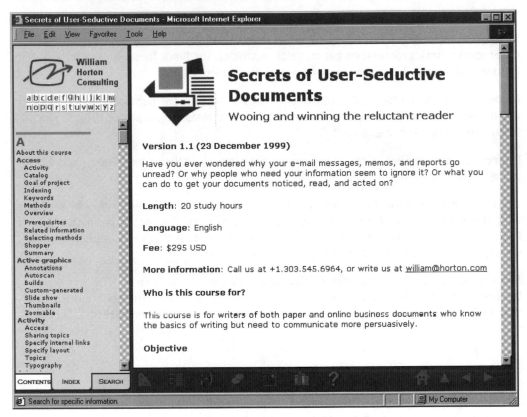

Some tips on formatting indexes:

▶ Format the index so it is similar to an index in a book. Use a hypertext link rather than a page number.

▶ Include up to two levels of entries in the index.

▶ Keep index entries short, especially if the index must fit into a narrow window or frame.

▶ Make the entry clearly imply what will be found at the destination.

▶ Test the index. If learners cannot find something, add or reword index entries until they can.

Map

Include a clickable map if the organization is not strictly linear. A map places a mental model in the mind of the learner. It shows how the subject can be divided into subtopics. It shows which ideas are especially important and how topics are related.

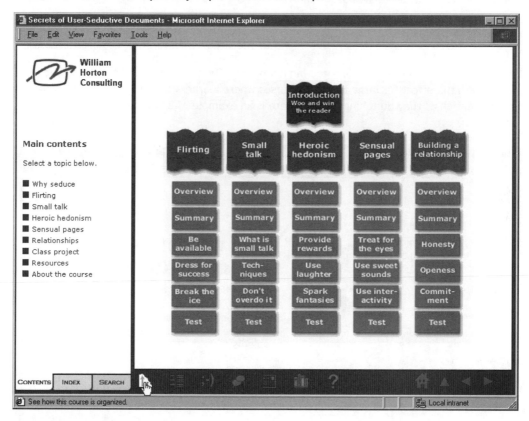

A good course map:

▶ Shows the main categories and subcategories.

▶ Links to categories and subcategories.

▶ Reveals and reinforces the organizing metaphor (chapters, rooms, buildings, etc.).

▶ Is visually attractive.

Should the course map show the organization of the course or the conceptual relationships among its topics? In general, an organizational map is best for aiding immediate navigation within the course, and a conceptual map is better for helping people learn relationships implicit in the material [89].

Search

Some large courses contain a text-search mechanism similar to the **find** command in wordprocessors or Internet search services.

Include a search mechanism

Including a search mechanism—and getting it working effectively—is a difficult task, but often worth the effort for large complex courses where learners spend as much time looking for information as they do taking lessons. Here is an example of a course with a search mechanism.

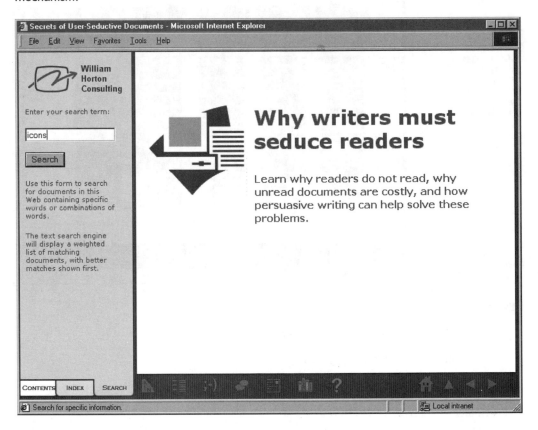

The choice and setup of a search mechanism is a highly technical task. We will not go into the details here but will explain some things you can do to make automated and manual searches more effective.

Problems with search engines

Search engines frequently disappoint searchers. They sometimes miss useful information while finding much that seems of little value. Most search mechanisms cannot distinguish a concept mentioned versus ones where it is really discussed. Sentences like these make fools of some pretty smart search engines:

> This topic is **not** about elephants.

> If you want to learn about elephants, click <u>here</u>.

Most search engines do not distinguish the various senses or meanings of a word. An excellent example is provided by Jutta Degener:

> Once the WebCrawler has visited your essay about the naked incomprehension greeting a women's group's demand for censorship of pornographic newsgroups, the vast majority of its visitors will have been searching for "porn," " naked," and "women" [90].

Search engines are fast but literal-minded.

Make your pages more findable

To increase the reliability of whatever search engine you incorporate, take steps to ensure that the search engine can accurately catalogue pages.

▶ Give each page a descriptive title (the text within <title> tags). This text is what search engines display for matches and it is often given high priority in searches.

▶ Include a keyword meta tag (<meta name="keywords" content="put keywords here">). Choose keywords that learners would use to search for the information on this page.

▶ Include a description meta tag (<meta name="description" content="Describe the page here">). The description should be a concise summary of the page or a description of what it contains.

▶ Put scripts in an external file. Words within JavaScript or VBScript passages can mislead some search engines.

Make it easy to manually find information

One of the most common user complaints is the difficulty of finding a topic visited some days earlier. To fix this problem:

▶ Do not reorganize or rename files too often. Grow the structure by grafting new content to the lower levels of the existing menu.

▶ Encourage learners to bookmark topics of interest.

▶ Do not change the titles or keywords unless the content changes.

▶ Keep the graphic design stable. To freshen the look a bit, change decorative elements, such as color and style of icons, but not the general layout.

▶ Index the course.

HELP LEARNERS OVER HURDLES

Support pages include helpful material such as the Course Tutorial (p 509), Help (p 506), and a FAQ (frequently asked questions) page (p 508). Because these are usually dedicated to overcoming technical hurdles, they are described in Chapter 12.

IN CONCLUSION ...

Summary

▶ There is more to a successful course than lessons. A successful course requires a superstructure of Web pages and forms so that learners can:

  Learn about the course, what it offers, and what it requires

  Register for the course

  Navigate and search the course

  Keep up with changes to the course

  Contact fellow learners, the instructor, or other course staff

  Receive congratulations and a diploma

▶ Many of these "shell" elements are provided by course-delivery systems.

▶ Once you have created a course shell containing these elements, you can share them among multiple courses. Such framework elements are good candidates for templates.

For more ...

Now that you have the course framework, why not fill it with lessons (Chapter 5), activities (Chapter 6), tests (Chapter 7), and other content?

Before you start handcrafting a course framework, you may want to examine the ones provided by vendors of integrated course management and delivery systems, such as TopClass and Docent.

Many of the examples shown in this book are on exhibit at:

  www.horton.com/DesigningWBT/

5

Organize learning sequences

Putting the pieces together

A course is just a sequence of learning experiences enabled by a designer and pursued by learners. Some courses allow but one sequence for all learners, while others let each learner follow a unique path. In this chapter we consider what designers must do so that learners find exactly the sequence of experiences that lets them accomplish their learning goals. First we look at some common ways of sequencing experiences in lessons. Then we look at pieces you are likely to need in your learning sequences. Finally, we present principles and guidelines for sequencing topics in new ways.

PICK FROM COMMON LESSON STRUCTURES

A lesson is a collection of activities and presentations that accomplish one of the sub-goals of the course. Each lesson is larger than an individual page and smaller than the whole course. Learners progress through a lesson along paths determined by the designer or choices by the learner. In many ways, a lesson is a miniature course requiring its own objectives, introductions, assessments, and feedback.

Over the years, designers of distance learning, CBT, and WBT courses have evolved several common lesson structures. These have the advantage of much experimentation and refinement. WBT developers have also begun to experiment with new structures that may deliver training more effectively and efficiently.

Before you start to design your own lesson structures, take a few minutes to consider some of the models presented below. These models are not meant to be solutions to your problems. Use them as a starting point for your own solutions.

Classic tutorials

The classic tutorial, and its many variants, serves as the model for most current WBT lessons. It is a WBT implementation of the way teachers have taught for 50,000 years.

Architecture of classic tutorials

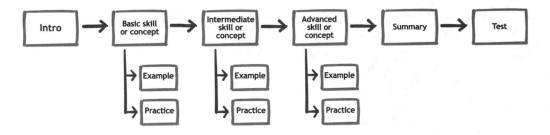

In the classic tutorial, the learners start with an introduction to the lesson and then proceed through a series of pages teaching progressively more advanced skills or concepts. At the end of the sequence, learners encounter a summary or review of the concepts and a test or other activity to measure whether they accomplished the objectives of the lesson.

For each skill or concept taught, the learner has the opportunity to see an example of it in action or to practice applying it. These examples and practice pages are optional.

When to use the classic tutorial structure

The classic tutorial structure is the safe, reliable choice. Use it when you can't think of something better. It is familiar to learners, especially to those who have taken conventional

CBT lessons. Learners seldom get lost in such a simple structure. It is flexible enough to adapt to many purposes yet simple enough to create largely from templates. It fits in well with many of the currently popular structured design methodologies and instructional design formulas. With this structure, novice instructional designers cannot make mistakes so big that a little testing will not detect them.

Variations of the classic tutorial structure

There are hundreds of variations on the theme of the unstructured tutorial. Here are a few of the ways I have bent and twisted the classic tutorial structure to fit specific objectives.

▶ I find that many American and Canadian learners, upon first entering the lesson, experience an immediate itch to jump to the Test to see if they already know what the lesson teaches. For them, I put a button on each page to let them jump directly to the test at any time.

▶ Some learners, who are returning to the course as a refresher, will want to jump directly to the Summary—hence another button.

▶ I have also observed what I call "page flipping" behavior in this structure. Learners skip through the pages of the main sequence without reading them in detail, just scanning to see what they contain. Only after they get a few pages down that road do they decide to actually take the lesson. For them, I include a button to jump back to the Introduction where they can begin the lesson in earnest.

▶ In the classic tutorial diagram, the examples and practices are separate pages and are off the main path. If examples and practices are short and simple, you may want to incorporate them onto the page of the skill or concept they demonstrate.

Tips and guidelines

The classic tutorial structure works well most of the time. As long as you keep it simple—and test to detect and correct problems—you should be able to use it for much of what you teach. When you use the classic tutorial, keep these two tips in mind:

▶ **Do not try to teach too much**. Limit each sequence to no more than 7 to 10 simple skills or concepts.

▶ **Do not omit the practice pages**. Let people apply what they learn as soon as they learn it. Otherwise the main sequence turns into a boring page-turner.

Activity-centered lessons

Some complex and rich activities (Chapter 6) are almost lessons in themselves. Almost. To turn them into lessons you must wrap them in a context and integrate them into your overall course structure.

Architecture of activity-centered lessons

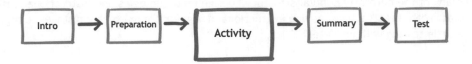

The activity-centered lesson is built on a single, primary activity. After a brief introduction, the learner prepares for the activity. The Preparation page provides any necessary knowledge or motivation not provided by the activity itself. After the activity, the learner encounters the Summary page, which recaps and articulates what the learner should have gotten out of the activity. Finally, the learner takes a test to verify mastery.

When to use the activity-centered lesson

Use an activity-centered lesson for complex concepts, emotional subjects, or subtle knowledge best taught by engaging learners in a rich activity. Use this structure when the activity is incomplete in itself.

Variations on the activity-centered lesson structure

The activity-centered lesson structure is as varied as the activities on which it is centered. Pick the activity, fine-tune it to your purposes, and then fit this lesson structure around it.

Link to alternative materials. One common variation is to link to other learning and reference materials on the subject of the lesson. Include these links in the Introduction, Preparation, or Summary.

Add a practice session. If the Activity is not truly interactive, you may want to graft on a practice page before the test so that learners get a chance to practice what they have learned before being tested.

Test by other means. You can replace the concluding test with any activity that lets learners confirm their mastery of the material taught in the activity.

Tips and guidelines for activity-centered lessons

Obviously you need to pay attention to the quality of the activity. It is the heart of the lesson. Test its effectiveness with actual learners before you add the other components of the lesson.

One component deserves special attention. That is the **Preparation** page. It must concisely provide everything necessary to integrate the activity into your course. It must also supply anything missing or unclear in the activity itself. Here is a checklist of things you may need to include in the Preparation page.

▶ Goals of the activity

▶ How this activity fits into the course

▶ What learners must know before beginning the activity

▶ Rules of behavior in the activity

▶ Instructions for performing the activity

▶ Links to needed information, software, or other resources

Keep the Preparation page short. Include only items that are not provided by the activity itself.

Learner-customized tutorials

In learner-customized tutorials, the lesson branches according to the knowledge or desires of the individual learner. Each learner gets a learning experience shaped to his or her needs.

Architecture of learner-customized tutorials

Like many other lesson structures, the learner-customized one begins with an Introduction page and ends with a Summary and Test. The roles of these pages are the same as in other structures.

Between the beginning and end, the structure alternates Branch pages and regular content pages. The Branch page determines which set of content pages the learner sees. The Branch page may present the learner with a list of paths to choose from, or it may test the user and automatically branch based on the results.

Or the learner may skip the content pages altogether. After completing a set of content pages, the learner may branch again. This pattern of branching to a subset of the available content continues to the end of the lesson.

When to use learner-customized tutorials

Such a structure, though complex to develop and test, can make training much more efficient and effective by helping learners adapt standard materials to their immediate needs. Use this structure when you must train learners with widely varying needs, interests, and initial levels of knowledge.

Although flexible, the learner-customized structure has its drawbacks. Training can be inconsistent. The learning experience is different for each learner and different each time a learner retakes the lesson. Learners find it hard to look up things later. They cannot compare notes.

Variations on learner-customized tutorials

The learner-customized tutorial structure can itself be customized. We can vary how the branching is performed, how long the branch paths are, and how many times the path branches within a lesson. We can also give learners more flexibility to explore multiple paths.

Vary the branching mechanism

To vary the tutorial structure, you can change how the learner's path is chosen. Some are manual and some automatic. Paths can be determined by:

▶ Choices made from a list presented to the learner on each Branch page.

▶ Results of tests on the Branch pages. The test may be scored by the computer or by the learner.

▶ Preferences set by the learner before beginning the lesson. One learner might prefer a more visual presentation while another wants to see all the grizzly mathematical formulas.

▶ Preferences set by the instructor as learning prescriptions for individual learners.

▶ Results of a test taken before beginning the lesson, typically at the start of the course.

Vary the length of branch paths

After branching, the learner encounters a sequence of Web pages before branching again. This sequence may be a single page or several pages. You can vary the number of pages within each path to suit the patience of the learner and the complexity of the subject matter. Keep in mind that the lengths of branch paths need not be equal. One path may require five pages while another gets by with a single page.

Vary the number of branchings

Some lessons consist of just a single Branch page. Other lessons branch and rejoin several times before reaching the end. The choice depends on the needs of learners and on the size of modules for each subject.

Provide more navigational possibilities

Sometimes learners cannot decide between two branches. Or they may decide they are on the wrong one. If learners are experienced in navigating within WBT courses, add navigational links to let learners jump back to the most recent branching pages so they can make another choice.

Tips and guidelines for learner-customized tutorials

Provide explicit instructions on how to take a learner-customized tutorial. Explain what is expected of the learner.

Clarify expectations. If you give learners choices, tell them whether they are expected to learn material on all the choices, or only one, or none. Otherwise, they will miss important information or worry that they are missing information.

Explain the branching scheme. Tell learners how the system determines what material to show them. Explain how their answers to quizzes or questionnaires affect what information they are shown.

Test and refine. This structure is quite complex and can seem unpredictable to learners unless it is so well designed that the flow seems natural and the choices logical. Plan to spend 30 to 40% of your development time testing and refining prototypes.

Alternatives and related structures

Using learner-customized tutorials is not the only way to adapt learning to the needs of individual learners. The knowledge-paced structure (p 141) is a simpler structure that lets learners skip ahead to their current level of knowledge. Generated lessons (p 146), a more technically advanced method, custom crafts an entire lesson to the needs of an individual learner.

Knowledge-paced tutorials

In the knowledge-paced tutorial, learners skip over as much of the lesson as they already know. They dive into the tutorial at their threshold of ignorance and proceed to the end, or until they satisfy their needs.

Architecture of knowledge-paced tutorials

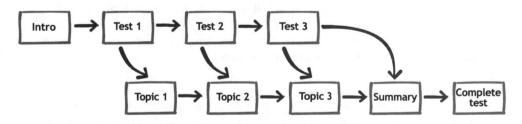

The knowledge-paced tutorial lets learners skip over the content topics on knowledge or skills they already possess. After an introduction, the learner begins a gauntlet of tests. The tests are progressively more difficult. That is, each one tests more advanced levels of knowledge or skills than those before. Learners continue down the test series until they fail to pass a test. At that point, they are directed into a parallel sequence of content topics. Thus each learner enters the sequence at the upper limit of his or her abilities. At the end of the content sequence, learners encounter a brief summary and a test on the entire content of the lesson.

When to use the knowledge-paced tutorial

Use the knowledge-paced structure to handle learners with different initial levels of knowledge or skill. Often, learners are too impatient to endure training on subjects they have already mastered. This structure lets advanced learners skip the parts that are too basic for their needs.

This structure works well **only** if the subject has a definite progression in levels of skill or knowledge. Otherwise, learners will encounter content they already know.

Variations on the knowledge-paced tutorial

The knowledge-paced tutorial is a simple structure that you can easily adapt to your needs. Here are a few variations you may want to consider.

Let learners quit as soon as they meet their goals. This structure lets learners dive in at the level of knowledge they possess. You can also let them exit when they reach the level they desire. Let learners know that they can quit the lesson when they feel they have learned all they need.

Vary the kinds of tests. The test sequence can contain more than traditional true/false, multiple-choice, and short-answer questions. You can use any self- or computer-scored activity to decide where learners should jump into the content path. No one likes taking a long series of tests, so add variety with different types of questions and throw in some games, too.

Make the test gauntlet more sophisticated. Use a more flexible and sensitive testing scheme. Give learners a graduated series of problems to solve. Each time learners get a problem right, they skip ahead five questions. If they get one wrong, they go ahead one. If they get three wrong answers in a row, they go directly to a topic at that level of difficulty.

Return to test stream. If it is not so easy to tell what knowledge is basic and what is advanced, you can simply return learners to the test stream once they complete a content topic. It is probably best to return them to another version of the test they failed so they can confirm that they have indeed learned the material.

Alternatives and related structures

The knowledge-paced tutorial is a simple attempt to customize learning to the current abilities of the learner. Two more sophisticated structures may work better for your situation. The learner-customized structure (p 139) lets learners zigzag their way through material, hitting just the topics they need. Generated lessons (p 146) create a custom sequence of content topics based on an initial test or questionnaire.

Exploratory tutorials

In an exploratory tutorial, learners find knowledge on their own. They are given goals and an electronic collection of knowledge, which they must explore in order to achieve these goals. Learners may be given navigating tools to help in the task. Such structures are sometimes called *unsequenced tutorials* or *knowledge landscapes*.

Architecture of exploratory tutorials

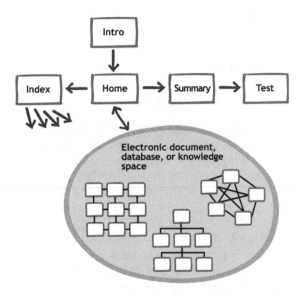

After a brief introduction, learners proceed to the Home page for exploration. From here learners can foray into the linked document, database, or knowledge space to find answers that accomplish the stated goal. Learners may rely on an Index page to launch them to specific destinations. After accomplishing their goals, learners view and take the lesson test.

When to use an exploratory tutorial

Use exploratory tutorials to teach learners to learn on their own. Use them to help learners:

▶ Meet their individual learning goals

▶ Learn to navigate a complex Web site, electronic document, or online database

▶ Develop and hone general online navigation skills

▶ Look up information (just-in-time training rather just-in-case training)

Exploratory learning is best for experienced learners who are comfortable navigating Web documents and who already understand the basics of the field of study.

Variations of the exploratory tutorial

Many variations are possible based on the documents being explored and on the style of interaction.

Vary the kind of document the learner must explore

Some candidates for exploration include:

▶ Electronic reference documents, such as reports, white papers, specifications, brochures, manuals, and books.

▶ Web sites dedicated to the subject of the lesson.

▶ Databases that can be accessed through the Web.

▶ Newsgroups, forums, chat archives, e-mail repositories.

Vary the organization of the document the learner must explore

Some organizations are easier to explore than others. A sequential structure is common among online versions of paper books. Many online documents are organized as a hierarchy of topics and subtopics. Much tabular information is organized in a grid. Many loose collections are linked in a very free-form structure.

Vary the tone

Several years ago, a popular computer game, *Where in the World is Carmen Sandiego?*, required players to look up information in an included paper reference book in order to track down the elusive international criminal. That is exactly the same task as in this lesson structure. All of which suggests making this structure into a game or puzzle.

Tips and guidelines for exploratory tutorials

Provide *structured* support for such unstructured tutorials. Include:

▶ A concise summary of all the material, with links to topics covering individual concepts.

▶ An index. Otherwise learners may have trouble finding specific material.

▶ A test covering all the essential material. In test feedback, provide links to the material learners may have missed.

Provide explicit instructions on how to take an exploratory tutorial and what is expected of learners. Tell learners what to learn, how long to spend learning it, and what will be on the test.

Each page in the exploratory tutorial should have a set of navigation controls allowing the student to return to the Home topic of the lesson. For collections with a regular structure, you can include a navigation control panel to help learners move through the structure in predictable directions.

Here is an example that lets learners graze from a grid of information. The grid, consisting of three columns by seven rows, contains information on various types of content modules for electronic documents. The window is divided into two panels. Across the top on a dark background is the navigation panel. At the bottom is the display of the currently selected page from the grid.

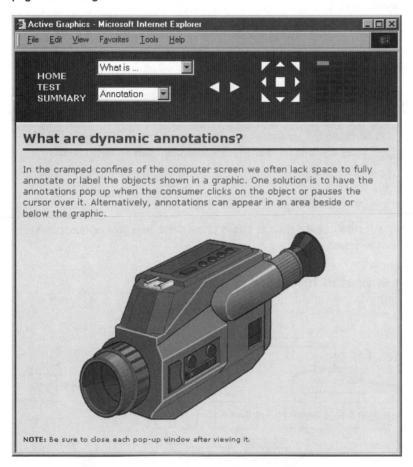

The navigation panel provides controls for navigating among the related topics in the grid. But it is a wee bit complex. So let's take it apart and see what each part does.

 The three text buttons link directly to the Home, Test, and Summary topics.

The select lists let the learner go to a particular row and column by picking their names, like specifying a city address by the nearest street intersection.

 These familiar buttons let the learner step through the grid page by page, across the rows and down the columns.

 The rosette of buttons lets learners navigate up, down, left, right, and along any diagonal of the grid. The square block in the center takes the learner to the Home topic.

The grid map shows the location of the currently displayed page within the grid. Clicking on one of the other boxes causes the page at that location to be displayed.

Alternatives and related structures

The exploratory tutorial is an extended version of the Scavenger Hunt (p 204) and Guided Research (p 207) activities. They are simpler and smaller in scope than an entire lesson.

Generated lessons

Generated lessons tailor a lesson to each learner based on answers to a test or questionnaire presented at the start of the lesson.

Architecture of generated lessons

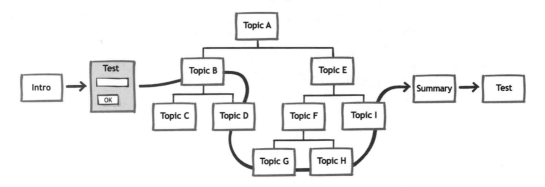

After a brief introduction, the learner takes a test or fills in a questionnaire. The test analyzes the learner's answers and threads a sequence of topics that exactly meets the needs of the individual learner. The lesson concludes with a summary and test.

When to use generated lessons

Generated lessons are useful in custom tailoring learning to individual learners. Use it when you have to train a varied group of impatient people with different needs, varying desires, and different levels of experience. Also use it to provide a targeted review of skills and knowledge. Generated lessons are difficult to construct but worth the effort. You can save learners a lot of time by letting them study just what they need to learn.

Variations of generated lessons

Most of the variations on this structure are compromises on the way a custom lesson is assembled. Creating a custom lesson from a pool of available topics while making sure the next and previous buttons do not generate page-not-found errors is no small task.

Programming generated lessons requires a little programming talent and a lot of hard work. You can use JavaScript or a server scripting language to program the lesson generation, but this programming does take a lot of time to get it working just right. A lot of times when I consider this structure I realize that it will take more time to develop than the total amount of time it will save learners. Then I look for a shortcut. Here are some "elegant kludges" that reduce the programming effort. Instead of threading the topics together, just:

▶ Generate a custom menu and let learners navigate using this menu.

▶ In the complete menu, flag which topics are required, which are recommended, and which are not needed. You can do this in Version 4.0 or higher-level browsers by swapping out a graphic displayed beside each menu item.

▶ Display a list of recommended topics which the learner can print out and use to navigate manually through the standard lesson.

Tips and guidelines for generated lessons

Generated lessons are pedagogically and technically difficult to construct. Do not attempt them unless you have on board (or are yourself) an experienced instructional designer and a competent programmer. A good generated lesson dwells in the fringes of artificial intelligence.

Topics (the content pages) from which the lesson is constructed must be written in a completely modular fashion so that they can be taken independently (p 172).

Alternatives and related structures

If a generated lesson looks like too much work, consider two other lesson structures that customize learning to the learner: knowledge-paced tutorials (p 141) and learner-customized tutorials (p 139).

Review of common kinds of lessons

Let's briefly recap the lesson types and where to use them.

Structure	Description	When to use it
Classic tutorials (p 136)	After an introduction, learners proceed through a series of pages, each teaching a more difficult concept or skill. At the end of the sequence are a summary and a test. Linked to the pages teaching skills and concepts are pages providing examples and practice.	To teach basic knowledge and skills in a safe, reliable, and unexciting way.
Activity-centered lessons (p 137)	The lesson centers on a major activity. After an introduction and preparation, the learner participates in the activity. Afterwards, the learner reviews a summary of what the activity taught and takes a test to prove mastery.	To teach complex concepts, emotional subjects, or subtle knowledge that requires rich interaction with the computer or other learners.
Learner-customized tutorials (p 139)	The lesson branches based on the knowledge or choices of individual learners. After a brief introduction, the lesson branches down a specific path. The path may rejoin and branch again before the summary and test, which cover all topics, regardless of the branches taken.	To let learners customize training to their individual needs. Especially suits learners with widely varying needs, interests, and levels of knowledge.
Knowledge-paced tutorials (p 141)	After an introduction, learners proceed through a series of tests until they reach the limits of their current knowledge. Then they are transferred into the main flow of a conventional tutorial, which ends with a summary and test.	To let impatient learners skip over topics on which they are already knowledgeable.
Exploratory tutorials (p 143)	Learners find knowledge on their own. Learners navigate an electronic document, database, or Web site in which they accomplish specific learning goals. To aid in this task, they may use a special index and navigation mechanisms. Once learners have accomplished their goal, they view a summary and take a test.	To teach learners to learn on their own by developing their skills of navigating complex electronic information sources.
Generated lessons (p 146)	The lesson tailors a learning sequence based on the learner's answers to questions on a test or questionnaire at the start of the lesson. After the custom sequence of topics, learners view a conventional summary and take a test.	To customize learning for those who have very specific needs and not much time or patience to complete topics they have already learned.

CREATE BUILDING BLOCKS FOR LESSONS

As you begin constructing lessons, you will find yourself creating some of the same kinds of pages over and over again. These are the pages you use to welcome learners, introduce the lesson, show examples, and get feedback. Such pages deserve special attention and are candidates for standards and templates.

Welcome page

The Welcome page greets the learner at the start of the lesson. It tells what the lesson is about, why it is important, and what the learner will gain by taking the lesson.

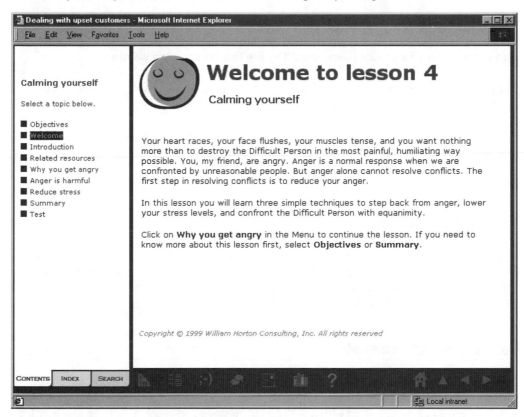

When to use a Welcome page

Use a Welcome page to begin most lessons if a full Introduction page might overwhelm and dishearten prospective learners. The Welcome page's function is primarily motivational. It removes doubt and confusion, and it inspires learners to dig into the lesson. It lets learners confirm that they have selected the right lesson.

Contents of the Welcome page

In a Welcome page, include just enough to orient and motivate the learner. Here are the ingredients of a common Welcome page:

Welcoming title. Begin by telling learners where they are and that you are glad they came. Do this with the title of the lesson, sometimes preceded with a phrase of greetings:

> Welcome to ... The Natural Regeneration Method of Forestry.

> Ready to **Develop Your Financial Plan?**

Graphic emblem. Consider an attractive yet relevant graphic that pleases the eye and arouses curiosity about what may be taught in the lesson.

What the lesson offers. Tell learners what they will gain by taking it. This is not a formal statement of objectives, just a sentence or two promising useful results. You might start with a statement of a problem experienced by the learner and promise to solve it.

Links to more information about the lesson. If the lesson contains an Introduction page (p 151), Summary page (p 156), Objectives page (p 90), or test (Chapter 7), link to them.

Invitation to continue. Encourage the learner to continue. If it is not obvious how to continue, make a suggestion.

> To get started, click **Overview**.

Tips and guidelines

Think of the Welcome page as a cover page to a magazine. Its goal is to entice and preview. But the cover page does not mention everything beneath the cover, just the most substantial and most attractive items. Answer these questions about the subject of the lesson: What is it? Why is it important? What will I gain by taking this lesson? Then stop.

Variations and alternatives

Often the duties of the Welcome page are combined with those of the Introduction page (p 155). The combined page appears at the start of the lesson and is usually called Introduction. Begin such a page with a welcoming message and graphic. Let the less inviting introductory details drape into subsequent scrolling zones.

In a short lesson, the Welcome page does the duties of an Introduction page (p 151), a Summary page (p 156), and an Objectives page (p 90), as well. In longer, more complex lessons, you may need to include all four. In that case, the Welcome merely greets and orients the learner.

Introduction page

The Introduction page establishes the subject of the lesson and prepares the learner to participate in it.

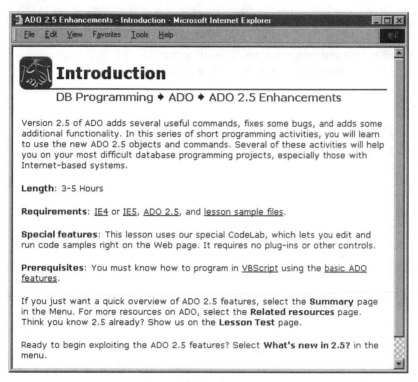

When to use an Introduction page

Use an Introduction page when you need more than a brief welcome. In longer lessons you may need more commitment from learners before sending them down the long road through the lesson's activities and presentations. You may need to set the context of the lesson by showing how it fits into the scheme of the course and how its goals further those of the learner. Often you will need the Introduction page to prepare learners for the content of the lesson.

Contents of the Introduction page

The contents of the Introduction page depends on the contents of the lesson it introduces.

Complete title

Identify the lesson clearly. This is especially important if that task has not been already accomplished by a separate Welcome page (p 149). Repeat the title and subtitle of the lesson and the lesson emblem, if any.

Context

Explain where the lesson fits within the course and how its subject matter logically relates to that of other lessons and the course as a whole.

If lessons are organized in a hierarchy, show the path from the top of the menu down to this lesson.

In a short paragraph or a simple diagram, show how the subject matter of this lesson relates to that of other lessons the learner may have taken or may want to take later.

Goals

Tell learners what they will gain by taking this lesson. You generally do not need a formal objectives statement, just a few statements about what learners will learn and why the lesson is important to them.

Requirements

If the lesson has any hard prerequisites or other requirements, flag them clearly.

Also tell learners how much time the lesson will require. Give a range of times from the quickest normal completion to the maximum amount of time any person should spend on the lesson.

Preparation

Prepare learners to take the lesson. The Introduction should preview what learners will experience in the lesson if there is anything difficult or unexpected about navigating the lesson—or if the lesson offers special pleasures. Preparation can include:

▶ **Suggested path through the lesson**. If the lesson has many options and branches, suggest a default path or at least a starting path.

▶ **List of special features**. Does the lesson offer hidden treasures? Take-away job aids? Learning games?

▶ **Rules that apply in the lesson**. If learners must behave in a special way, say so in the introduction. If the lesson consists of an extended game or role-playing exercise, spell out the rules.

▶ **Prerequisite knowledge**. What do learners need to know before they dive into the content of the lesson? Here is one last chance to provide that information. Or link to it.

Contents of the lesson

If the lesson does not have a separately displayed menu, you may want to include an outline of the lesson. Link each item in the outline to its page, and you have a lesson menu.

Links to related topics

Link to other pages that provide information about the lesson, for example, the Summary page (p 156), Related Resources page (p 154), and the Welcome page (p 149). You may also want to link to the lesson test so that learners can see if they already know what they need to about the course.

Invitation to continue

At the end, nudge the learner to continue into the lesson. Suggest a next action:

> Ready? Click the **Next Page** button to begin.

Variations and alternatives for the Introduction page

Introduction pages vary as much as the lessons they introduce. Simple lessons require a simple introduction—or none at all. Complex lessons require a more thorough introduction.

One common variation is in the coverage of the Introduction page. If a lesson has separate Objectives (p 90), Welcome (p 149), and Related Resources pages (p 154), the Introduction page can be quite concise. If the course itself has an introduction, you may need less introduction for each lesson.

Another variation concerns the motivational duties of the Introduction page. Is the goal of the page merely to report the content of the lesson or is it to inspire learners to complete the lesson?

Simple, short lessons typically have a Welcome page (p 149) but not an Introduction page. A moderately complex lesson might have an Introduction page but not a Welcome page. A very complex lesson might have both an Introduction page and a Welcome page—along with an Objectives page, Related Resources pages (p 154), and a Summary page (p 156).

Related Resources page

Most lessons need to point learners to information outside the lesson itself. A Related Resources page consolidates all such references into one organized display.

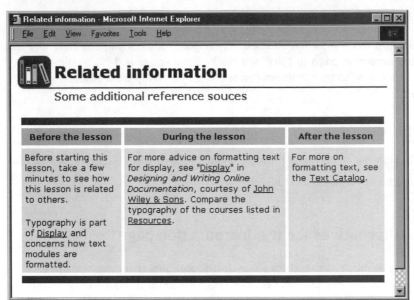

This example lists additional learning resources for a lesson. It divides them into resources needed before taking the lesson, while taking the lesson, and after taking the lesson.

When to use a Related Information page

Include a Related Information page to help learners find all the resources they need to fully learn the subject of the lesson. Use a Related Information page to point to prerequisite knowledge that some learners may lack upon starting the lesson. Such a page can encourage learners to continue studying after the end of the lesson. Use it to accommodate learners who have special interests or who just want to learn more about the subject.

Contents of a Related Information page

Include links and references to materials needed before, during, and after the lesson. Here are some suggestions of the types of information to include:

Before the course	During the course	After the course
▶ Background concepts ▶ Fundamentals of the field ▶ Assessments of knowledge levels	▶ More details to satisfy curiosity and special interests ▶ Glossary to define unknown terms ▶ Complete real-world examples ▶ Calculators, checklists, and other learning aids useful in activities	▶ Practical applications of the subject ▶ Products and services ▶ More detailed and in-depth treatments ▶ Opinions on controversial issues ▶ Theory behind practical techniques

Tips and guidelines

Accommodate different learning needs. List everything that any of your learners might need. Then subtract what the lesson itself provides. Everything left over is candidate for inclusion on the Related Resources page.

The Related Resources page is no place to show off your library search skills. Craft a short list of resources that meets the needs. Vet each source for accuracy, timeliness, and clarity.

Prefer real-world resources used by busy practicing professionals in the field, especially the resources that learners will continue to use after they complete the course.

If the list of resources is quite extensive, you may need to include separate Prerequisite and Follow-up pages for the resources needed before and after the course.

Summary page

The Summary page recaps all the critical points made in the lesson.

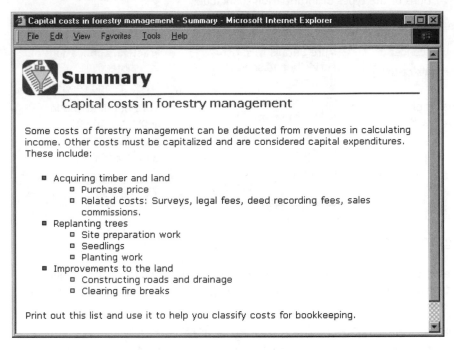

When to use a Summary page

For each lesson or major sequence, include a concise textual summary for impatient learners, those refreshing their memories, and those with low bandwidth connections.

Contents of the Summary page

A summary contains just what its name implies. It should list or display all the main points learners should take away from the lesson.

Condense rather than describe knowledge

Repeat in concise form the facts that learners should remember. Do not just list areas of knowledge. Say, "You learned that ...", not "You learned about ...". In summaries, tell people what they should remember, not what they "saw."

Summarize with quick tips

Summarize the contents of a practical lesson or course with a list of tips for applying the contents of the course. These tips can take several forms:

▶ Instructions to the learner to act

▶ Affirmations to begin the day with

▶ Mantras for the learner to chant

▶ Slogans to print out and thumbtack to cubicle walls

▶ Mnemonics to make key points memorable

Tips and guidelines

Design for printing out. Design the summary so that learners can print it out and use it as a job aid. Encourage them to do so.

Format text for scanning. Format textual summaries as lists rather than as block paragraphs. Use bold type and color to emphasize the organization of the list and to highlight important items.

Summarize in graphics. Use a diagram, chart, table, or other graphical format if it is the best way to summarize content.

Link to information summarized. For each item in the summary, include a link to the page where the learner can get full details on the item.

Variations and alternatives

Put the summary at the beginning, not the end. For those with moderate knowledge already, the summary may be all they need. You can save those learners from having to take the whole lesson. For those with less knowledge, the summary serves as a preview and advance organizer. It alerts those learners to what ideas are important.

When you put the summary at the beginning, consider renaming it *Overview*.

Featured Example page

The Featured Example page presents a single example along with commentary about it. It is sometimes called simply *Example page* or *Case Study page*.

When to use a Featured Example page

We often need to show examples of what we are talking about. Most of the time, we can present examples in line with the material they illustrate. Some examples, however, defy this treatment. Some are too complex or too large. Others need detailed commentary. Other examples need special treatment to show that they are examples and not part of the commentary. These special cases require building a page around the example.

Contents of a Featured Example page

In the Featured Example page, introduce, present, and describe the example. Include answers to these questions:

▶ What does the example show?

▶ Why is it important?

▶ How typical is it?

▶ What should I notice in the example?

▶ How can I learn more about what the example shows?

Tips and guidelines

Distinguish example and commentary. Clearly delineate what is example and what is commentary. If you present the actual example on the Featured example page, put a border around the example, put it on a background of a different color, or in some other way distinguish it from everything else on the page.

Show how abstract concepts apply to the learners. Use examples that help learners see how abstract concepts apply to them as individuals. The more abstract the subject, the more you need to show a concrete example, especially for software. For example, to introduce a computer screen, show a simple version with typical data the learner can appreciate.

Avoid off-target examples. Forego controversial examples, especially ones with political implications. I once saw a lesson page that used a US Presidential candidate as a humorous example. His supporters were not amused—or educated. Avoid examples with regional or national limitations.

Variations and alternatives

One of the most common variations is to present the example in a separate window. Normally popping up a new window is an unnecessary distraction, but in a few cases, it prevents confusion. If you are discussing Web pages, electronic documents, or other online media, you may need to display the example in a separate window to make clear what is example and what is commentary about the example. Here is a windowed example from a course on designing electronic courses:

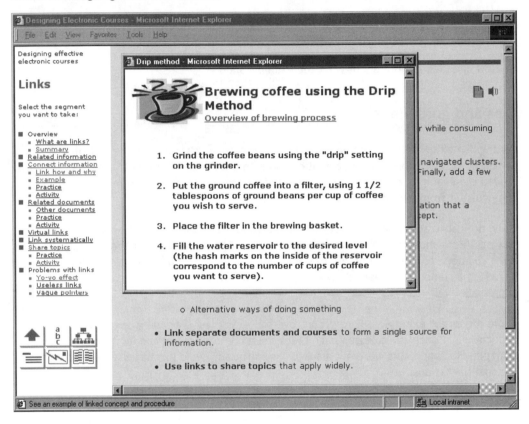

The lesson is not about coffee. It is about displaying procedures. But to see the example realistically required putting it in its own window the way it would appear in real life.

There are other ways of presenting examples. Case Study activities (p 226) require learners to actively examine an example. Guided Tours and Field Trips both examine several aspects of a single subject. A Gallery presents a well-organized and labeled collection of examples.

> Rules make the learner's path long, examples make it short and successful.
>
> — Seneca

Code Sample page

A Code Sample page is a special kind of example. It shows a fragment of a computer program or script.

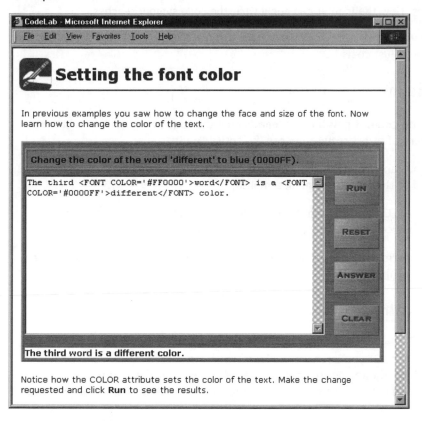

This example teaches HTML commands for formatting text. Learners edit the code sample in the text area. When they click **Run**, the results are displayed in the area below the code sample.

When to use a Code Sample page

Codes samples are essential when teaching computer languages, including scripting languages (JavaScript), formatting languages (HTML, CSS, XSL), and document structuring languages (XML).

Contents of the Code Sample page

When teaching programming, use a series of ever more ambitious code fragments. For each code sample include:

▶ **Transition**. How does this fragment relate to the previous one in the sequence? What does it add? What is the motive for including it or using it?

▶ **Code sample**. The actual code itself. It should be clearly delineated, perhaps color-coded in a monospaced font, and appropriately commented. It should be clear whether this is a complete sample or just a fragment from a larger whole.

▶ **Instructions**. How to execute the code. Must the learner copy and paste the code sample into another file? Then what? Or can the learner just click on a button to run the sample?

▶ **What to notice**. What is different from the previous example and why it is important?

▶ **How to apply it**. How the learner can apply what the code sample teaches.

▶ **How to try on your own**. Variations the learner can try. Start with specific code changes and conclude with just goals.

Tips and guidelines

Simplify running the code. If possible, let learners run the code at the click of a button. Minimize the amount of effort required to see the actual results.

Show results. If you cannot run the code directly, include a graphic to show the results. Or explain in detail what the sample would accomplish.

Keep learners active. Encourage them to try out variations in the sample until they are comfortable that they could write the sample on their own.

Link to language information. Link to a detailed language dictionary for the programming language you are teaching.

Variations and alternatives

You can vary how active the learner is in examining the code samples. You can just present the code and narrate it. Or you can have the learner run the code sample to see what it does. Better still, have the learner try making small then larger alterations to the code to see the effects. For an especially ambitious code sample, have the learner write the sample from scratch.

The Code sample page is a specialized form of the Featured Example page (p 158). You may want to consider using a Featured Example page instead.

> Example is the best precept.
>
> — Aesop

> What does education often do? It makes a straight-cut ditch of a free, meandering brook.
>
> — Henry David Thoreau, *Journals*

Event Playback page

The Event Playback page lets learners play a previously recorded event, such as a video lecture, an audioconference, or a chat session.

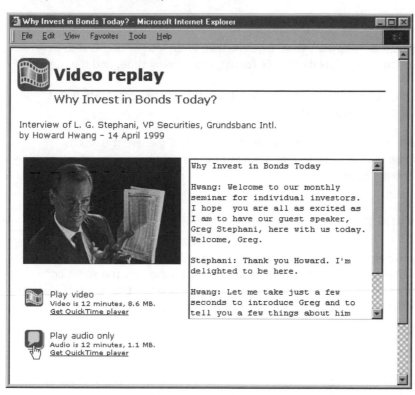

This example lets learners replay a previously recorded videoconference. It includes the video and audio version as well as a text transcript.

When to use it

The Event replay page lets learners review and replay previously recorded live events. It is especially useful when:

▶ Events are rich with detail, and learners may need to experience them multiple times to get all they offer.

▶ Learners cannot participate in a live event. The recorded version lets them make up for what they missed.

▶ Libraries of prerecorded events exist and have valuable educational content.

Contents of the Event Playback page

In the Event Playback page, include information the learner needs to decide whether to play back the event. Also include the buttons and knobs to control how the recording plays. Here's a checklist for what to include:

▶ **Event title**. Include a subtitle if necessary to immediately communicate what the event offers.

▶ **Presenter**. Give the name, title, and organization of the speaker or leader of the event.

▶ **Photograph** of the presenter.

▶ **Trigger to download or play the event**. Give the learner an icon or text link to begin playing the recorded event. Specify the file format, the running time, and the file size.

▶ **Transcript**. If possible, include a complete text transcript of the presentation that learners can read as they listen and watch.

▶ **Summary**. Include a concise recap to help learners decide if the event is worth replaying. For some learners, the summary may suffice. A quotation or two from the transcript may make a good summary.

Tips and guidelines

▶ **Do not start the download or playing of media automatically**. Let learners look at the page to decide whether they want to play the media. Often the text transcript or summary may be enough. Initially, display the photograph and the transcript. If learners decide to play video, have the video playback control replace the photograph.

▶ **Expose playback controls** so that learners can start, pause, resume, and restart the playback.

▶ **Include a transcript if possible**. Showing the text is necessary for those with connections too slow to download the media, for those with hearing disabilities, and for those who have trouble understanding the spoken words as the media play back.

▶ **Keep the event short**. If it is more than 15 to 20 minutes, consider breaking it into separate events.

Variations and alternatives

You can vary this basic design to accommodate many different kinds of events. You can include the mix of media (text, audio, video) required by each event. Some may require only a text transcript while others demand a full range of media.

Include multiple versions of the event so that learners can pick the one that fits their connection speed and patience. You can provide larger and smaller video windows and supplement video with an audio-only version. Unless a speaker is demonstrating something visual, the audio version will work just fine.

Choice page

A Choice page presents alternatives and invites learners to pick one. Each choice takes the learner down a different path through the course.

When to use a Choice page

Insert a Choice page whenever you want learners to decide where to go next. You can stack Choice pages to form a menu system (p 125). You can use them to let learners select just the learning paths that meet their needs (p 139). Use choice pages in simulations and other interactive activities (p 253). Choice pages are essential in diagnostic procedures.

Contents of a Choice page

Keep choices simple and clear. Focus the learner's attention on making the best possible decision. On the Choice page, include just what learners need to make a choice:

▶ **Title**. Name the page with the question learners must answer.

▶ **Introduction**. Frame the question. Prepare learners to answer the question. Provide any necessary background information.

▶ **Question**. Ask the question. Or begin a sentence that each alternative could complete.

▶ **Choices**. Make each choice distinct and clear.

Tips and guidelines

Keep Choice pages simple. Require learners to make only one decision per page and limit the number of choices to just a few. Phrase the question and answers as simply as possible. Forgo any distracting graphics or irrelevant navigation buttons.

Do not make choices final. Let learners change their minds. Tell learners that they can change their mind later. Remind them that they can just back up to get to the Choice page and make another decision.

Make choices easy to read and select. Let learners click on the alternative to choose it. When you make each alternative a link, the default HTML formatting underlines it, which can make it hard to read. Here are a few remedies:

▶ Use a style for links that does not underline the text. Be sure to tell learners to click on their choice.

▶ Put buttons beside choices.

▶ Front load the choices and make the first word of each line into a link. This remedy has the effect of emphasizing important words.

Procedure page

Procedure pages help put the "act" in active learning. They provide clear instructions for someone to do something.

 How to retrieve data with ADO

For many of your Web-based database projects you will need to use ADO to pluck a few values from a database.

If you want to run the example shown here, you will need the SampleData.mdb database. Plus, you will need to create an ODBC connection to the database.

Here's how to use ADO to retrieve data from a database:

1. **Set up the connection object.**

   Create the object and open the connection using the ODBC name.

   ```
   Set myConnection = CreateObject("ADODB.Connection")
   MyConnection.Open "theODBCNameOfTheDatabase"
   ```

2. **Set up the command object.**

   Create the command object and set up its connection.

   ```
   Set myCommand = CreateObject("ADODB.Command")
   Set myCommand.ActiveConnection = myConnection
   ```

---

3. **Create the command and set its parameters.**

   Set the query to retrieve records and set other parameters to the command.

   ```
   Set myCommand.CommandText =
   "SELECT * FROM theTable WHERE fieldA = 'XYZ';"
   Set myCommand.CommandType = 1
   ```

4. **Create a recordset containing the needed records.**

   Create a recordset to hold the retrieved data and retrieve the records.

   ```
   Set myRecordset = CreateObject("ADODB.Recordset")
   myRecordset.Open myCommand, , 0, 1
   ```

5. **Use data from the recordset.**

   ```
   LocalVariable = myRecordset("FieldA")
   ```

6. **Close the recordset and connection.**

   ```
   myRecordset.Close
   myConnection.Close

   Dispose of the objects.
   Set myRecordset = nothing
   Set myCommand = nothing
   Set myConnection= nothing
   ```

This procedure will form the basis for many of the examples in this course. Take a few minutes to learn these steps.

 **Troubleshooting**

If you have trouble, compare your code with that in the `SampleRetrieval.asp` file. Try running that page. If it also fails, you probably do not have a good ODBC connection to the database. Try deleting the existing connection and redefining it.

When to use Procedure pages

Use Procedure pages whenever you need to guide someone in performing a step-by-step procedure.

Contents of a Procedure page

Provide everything learners need to perform the procedure and to recover from common problems.

▶ **Title.** Title the page so it clearly announces what the procedure accomplishes.

▶ **Goal.** Tell learners exactly what the procedure will accomplish.

▶ **Prerequisites.** If learners must know something, have something, or do something before they begin the procedure, say so.

► **Steps.** List the steps in a one- or two-level numbered list.

► **Confirmation.** If it is not obvious whether the procedure succeeded, tell learners how to verify their success.

► **Troubleshooting.** Tell learners what to do if the procedure does not succeed.

Tips and guidelines

If the procedure requires looking away from the computer screen, encourage learners to print out the page. Also encourage them to print out the page if the procedure is one they can use as a job aid.

In each step, include only one main action. Feature that action by making it the first word of the step or by visually highlighting it.

Clearly distinguish actions from responses, commentary, and alternatives.

Variations and alternatives

You can enrich many step-by-step procedures by using graphics and multimedia to lead learners through difficult procedures. Add photographs or drawings to show critical steps in the procedure. Use animation or video to show complex motions. Use audio so learners can perform the procedure while looking away from the computer screen.

Lesson Feedback form

The Lesson Feedback form gathers comments and suggestions about the lesson while it is still fresh in the learner's mind.

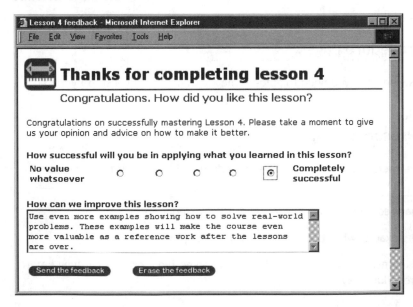

This example uses a custom Active Server Pages script and component on the server to format the form's contents and e-mail it to the instructor.

When to use a Lesson Feedback form

Use the Lesson Feedback form at the end of each lesson to let learners comment on the lesson and to make suggestions for improving it. Get feedback when learners are energized. Get feedback in small doses. Such feedback is more focused and immediate than that you will gather by a course feedback form displayed at the end of the entire course.

Contents

The secret of getting good feedback is keeping the form simple and short—no more than a single scrolling zone. Include:

▶ Congratulations on completing the lesson.

▶ Invitation to give feedback.

▶ One point-on-scale question for rating the effectiveness of the course.

▶ One text-entry area for making a suggestion.

▶ Buttons to submit the feedback.

Tips and guidelines

Phrase the question to ask more than "Did you like the lesson?" Learners may like our lessons and still learn nothing from them. Instead, probe whether learners met their goals in taking the lesson or whether they feel confident they can now apply what they learned.

Variations and alternatives

You have at least two other ways to get feedback on a lesson. In the Course Feedback page (p 122) you can ask questions relating to individual lessons. Throughout the course you can include buttons linked to a general-purpose feedback form (p 121).

Review of building blocks

Let's briefly recap the kinds of pages commonly used in constructing lessons.

Ingredient	Function	When to use it
Welcome page (p 149)	Greets the learner, tells what the lesson is about, and makes clear why the learner should take it.	For every lesson, unless its duties are performed by an Introduction page.

Ingredient	Function	When to use it
Introduction page (p 151)	Establishes the subject and characteristics of the lesson and prepares the learner to begin the activities of the lesson.	When the learner needs more than a brief welcome, for example, when learners need background information or extra motivation.
Related Resources page (p 154)	Provides pointers to information the learner may need before, during, and after taking the lesson.	The subject is complex and the lesson cannot contain everything every learner needs on the subject.
Summary page (p 156)	Recaps the important ideas of the entire lesson so that all learners see all the ideas regardless of the path they took through the lesson.	For all lessons having more than a few pages or activities.
Featured Example page (p 158)	Presents a single example or case study along with commentary about it.	For complex, rich, life-like examples that require detailed commentary or some special treatment.
Code Sample page (p 161)	Demonstrates a unit in a computer programming or scripting language.	To teach computer languages, including scripting languages (JavaScript), formatting languages (HTML, CSS), and document structuring languages (XML).
Event Playback page (p 163)	Lets learners review a previously recorded live event, such as a video lecture or chat session.	When not all learners can participate in live events or when some will need to review the event afterwards.
Choice page (p 165)	Lets learners pick from alternatives, typically when choosing a path in a lesson.	Whenever you want learners to decide where to go next, for example, in a branching structure or a menu system.
Procedure page (p 166)	Provides clear instructions on how to do something.	To guide learners through a moderately complex procedure by providing step-by-step instructions.
Lesson Feedback form (p 168)	Invites learners to evaluate the effectiveness of the lesson and to suggest improvements.	To get immediate, fresh feedback on the lesson.

DESIGN YOUR OWN LEARNING SEQUENCES

You can design a lot of courses using only common lesson structures presented earlier in this chapter. But a familiarity with the principles of combining, linking, and sequencing pages to shape learning experiences qualifies you to do more. You can then design lessons and courses that exactly fit the needs of your learners. This section discusses some of the principles for structuring learning sequences.

Design an orderly organization

The lack of architectural discipline leads to ill-structured WBT lessons and courses, which in turn lead to confused, disoriented, and frustrated learners. Unless a course is clearly and logically organized, learners may feel overwhelmed or lost. Such feelings of disorientation can seriously reduce their ability to learn [83].

> [Learners] prefer clearly defined learning outcomes, or tasks, and recommended sequencing, from which they can orient themselves at any time [91].

Fairly extensive research has established the dangers of disorientation for those navigating complexly linked hypertext structures [92].

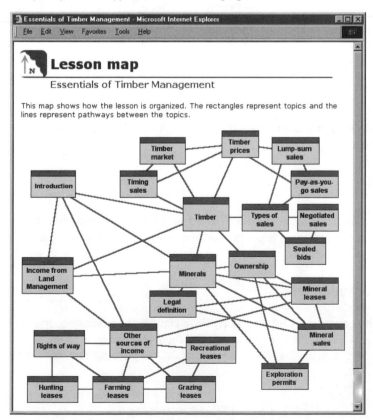

Here is an example without clear organization. This lesson appears disorganized with no clear learning path and no guidance for selecting paths and topics.

The lesson is not as disorganized as this diagram makes it appear. But the learner cannot know this.

Here is another version of the same lesson. Notice how the organization is simple, regular, and predictable. Learners navigate more reliably and comfortably with such a hierarchical structure [89].

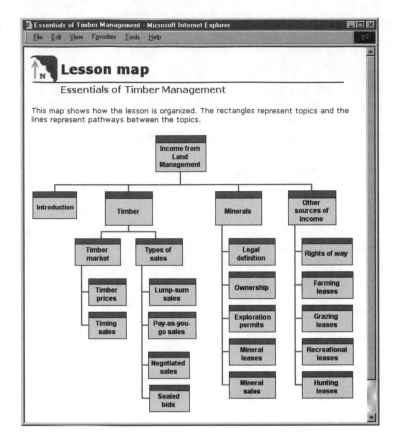

Such a structure need not be restrictive. Within individual topics, you can include cross-references to related topics and take shortcuts. It is just this balance that designers must strike. The structure must be easy to understand and navigate yet flexible enough to accommodate everyone's needs.

Design reusable modules

Modularity is the password of WBT. Designers praise it, vendors promise it, and standards committees are working on recipes to serve it up. But while it is a worthwhile goal, it is not without problems and costs of its own.

The ideal of reusable modules

Developing training would be easier and a lot less costly if we could just assemble courses from off-the-shelf components. Need a lesson on background theory? Aisle seven, shelf four. Tests? They're in the back next to activities. Feedback forms? On the discount rack near the checkout counter.

This dream contrasts with the nightmare reality of different groups simultaneously developing training modules that accomplish the same purposes. I once uncovered three projects within a corporation each producing courses that were 90% identical. The WBT business looks like the pre-industrial age before interchangeable parts.

The quite reasonable goal is to enable designers to assemble much of their courses from modules that have already been designed, developed, and thoroughly tested.

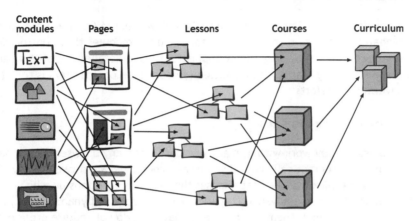

Program designers can assemble a curriculum from proven courses. Course designers can put together a course by integrating existing lessons or mini-courses. Lessons can be assembled by pre-defined topics or Web pages, which in turn can be constructed from a library of standardized animations, video clips, sound recordings, graphics, and boilerplate text.

Problems with a naïve view of modularity

Modularity is a beautiful goal and has great benefits in practice, but designers must honestly admit the challenges it poses.

▶ **Real-world knowledge is highly interrelated, and skills are interdependent**. Concepts that make good blocks in a schematic diagram sprawl and slither all over the place when you try to corral them into modules.

▶ **Technical incompatibilities thwart reuse**. A module created with WebWonker cannot be integrated into a course managed with PathGrinder and displayed in the NoChoice browser on the Zebra operating system. Standards groups are working to define standards, and vendors are starting to support them, but promises outnumber results.

▶ **Learners feel they have entered the land of a thousand user interfaces**. On one page buttons are at the top, on the next they squat on the bottom. Tranquil earth tones abruptly shift to pulsing neon. Text-only pages alternate with multimedia extravaganzas. Unless developers follow common standards for the user interface, visual appearance, and media usage, learners are in for a bumpy ride.

Start modularizing now

You do not have to wait for technological solutions to emerge or for everyone else to modularize their materials. You can start reusing your own materials. Here are some approaches to follow.

Follow standards

As standards develop and are implemented in tools, follow them. AICC (www.aicc.org) has published standards for course management systems and the modules they control. IMS (www.imsproject.com) is developing a more sophisticated and detailed set of standards. The IEEE's Learning Technology Standards Committee (grouper.ieee.org/p1484/) is trying to coordinate several such efforts.

Design cross-everything modules

Design your courses so they work with as many versions of as many browsers on as many operating systems as you practically can. If you have a choice between two equally effective solutions to a problem, pick the one that imposes the fewest restrictions on who will be able to take your course. Do not use advanced browser features, such as Dynamic HTML, if you can do the same thing without them. Prefer file formats that do not require proprietary plug-ins or that have plug-ins available for all operating systems.

Modularize at all levels

Design independent, self-contained modules at all levels. Minimize dependences between courses. Make lessons more self-sufficient. Make sure each page is complete in itself. Design multimedia modules so they can be dropped on a page without a complex integration procedure. Do not make modularity a crusade, just the routine way you solve problems for all the components of the course.

Limit free-form linking

If we include a module that contains links to other modules, we must include those modules as well. Or else we must repair a lot of broken links. Eliminating links entirely would solve this problem but would hide crucial relationships and remove valuable navigational pathways. One partial solution is to reduce the amount of navigation done by handcrafted, hard-coded links in the body of Web pages. Here are some solutions:

▶ **Enrich the navigational mechanisms.** Add a menu, index, and search facility so that learners have more ways to find related topics.

▶ **Display the menu in a separate frame.** That way, learners can navigate to related topics there rather than by links within the body of Web pages. Revising the organization of the course requires changing just the Menu, not dozens of individual pages.

▶ **Automate sequential navigation.** Have the Next and Previous buttons calculate where to go based on an easily maintained list of topics rather than by hard-coded links on each page.

Summarize rather than link to small bits of information

If a piece of information can be expressed concisely, consider including it right where it is needed, rather than linking to it elsewhere. This will entail some duplication, but the duplication may outweigh the risk of broken links or disoriented learners.

Sequence modules

A course is a sequence. It may be a sequence of class meetings and homework assignments. Or, it may be a sequence of Web pages. I like to think of it as a sequence of experiences encountered by learners.

That definition begs a very good question. Who determines the sequence? The course author? The instructor? The learner? A random number generator? Fate? We can step back from the philosophical abyss by acknowledging that two approaches are more commonly used than others. In one approach, the course unfolds in a linear sequence decided by the course designer. In the other approach the selection and order of learning experiences are controlled by the individual learners moment by moment as they navigate the course. In this second design approach, designers make the learners' navigation easier by layering material. This layered approach is discussed in a later section (p 177). Here we discuss principles for designing linear sequences of experiences.

Use sequences to train novices

Sequential learning paths are utterly simple. You can go forward. Perhaps you can go back. It's hard to get lost in hyperspace with so few choices. And with such a simple sequence, there are few distractions to draw learners away from the material being presented.

If you are an expert and you know from having explained a subject many times that a certain sequence works best—then use that sequence. A test comparing a linear, sequential structure with a web-like, hypertext structure for teaching engineering concepts found that the sequential structure worked better, especially for learners already having more trouble mastering the material [87].

Put learning events in the right order

The best sequence for teaching something is not always obvious. Often the best order for teaching steps in a procedure is not the exact order in which the steps are performed. For some concepts, the logical order is not the best order for explaining the concept. In training:

▶ Teach simple skills before complex ones.

▶ Introduce concepts necessary for understanding other ideas.

▶ Teach skills the learner can immediately apply and recognize the value of.

For example, in teaching learners to use a computer program, many training programs begin by teaching the learner to install the program. Unfortunately, this is one of the most complex tasks the learner must perform and one without any immediate benefits.

An alternative approach has learners start out on properly configured computers. It first teaches how to perform common, simple tasks with the program and only later deals with installing and setting up the program. By then, the learner is comfortable with basic features, motivated to install the product, and confident in the training [93].

Consider standard teaching sequences

Over the years, instructional designers have researched and tested many sequences for teaching various kinds of material. Though they quibble over the details, most advocate a sequence something like this:

1. Motivate the learner.

2. Preview the sequence.

3. Have the learner recall prior knowledge.

4. Present new ideas.

5. Provide feedback.

6. Test understanding.

7. Enrich learning.

Such standard sequences form a blueprint that designers can use to organize their learning activities.

Overcome problems with sequences

Sequential learning paths are simple and reliable. They let the designer control the order of experiences encountered by the learner. But they are not without problems. Here are some of the common complaints about sequential learning paths along with simple remedies for them.

Problem	Solution
Long sequences can be tedious. Some learners lose heart and give up.	▶ Keep sequences short. Recommendations vary from five minutes to one hour. Aetna used 15-minute lessons to keep interest high [27].
	▶ Interleave presentations with activities.
	▶ Let learners see where they are in the sequence, how much progress they have made, and how much more they have to go.

Problem	Solution
Some learners may already know the material in early parts of the sequence.	▶ Let learners skip through pages. Do not require them to scroll to the bottom of the page to find the Next button. ▶ Let learners jump ahead to the Summary or Test page so they can see if they already know the material in the sequence.
Some learners may need only part of what is covered in the sequence.	▶ Let learners jump to individual topics within any sequence longer than 6 or 7 pages. List these topics in a lesson menu.

Layer modules

If the designer or instructor does not determine the sequence of learning experiences, then who does? Why, individual learners of course. And there lies a problem. How do learners, who by definition do not know the material they are studying, know enough to consume it in sequences that let them learn what they need to know as efficiently as possible?

To help learners find their own way, designers can arrange the course in layers that learners explore in logical, systematic ways.

How is layering different from sequencing?

In sequential presentations, we typically start with the background information, proceed to the main idea, and conclude by adding some interesting details.

All learners who proceed down the sequence are exposed to all the same material in exactly the same order. Everybody gets the theoretical background before being exposed to the main idea.

Everybody has to go through the theoretical background to get to the main idea. Learners have few choices.

Layering turns that organization on its side. With a layered presentation, the learner starts with the main idea. The learner may then choose to learn about the theoretical background or to see additional details. These are choices left to the learner. The learner may quit after learning the main idea. Or the learner may pursue one or both of the deeper topics.

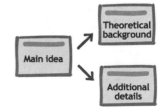

What are layers of knowledge?

In layered designs, the learner starts on the first layer and then selects links to jump to progressively deeper layers as necessary.

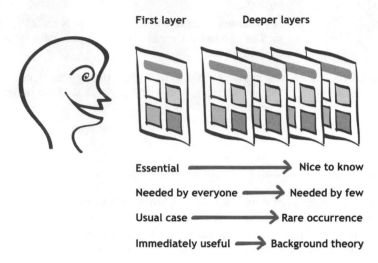

On the surface are skills and knowledge that all learners need all the time. On deeper layers are things that only a few learners occasionally need.

Use layering to put learners in control

Layered structures put learners in control but not without providing them the navigational aids they need to find just the training they need. A layered structure works well when there is simply too much material for all learners to learn it ahead of time (just-in-case learning), or when the specific needs of individual learners vary widely. Layered approaches are the core of self-guided, just-in-time, and just-what-you-need training applications. Layering is popular in electronic documents [2] and electronic performance support systems.

Example of a layered structure

Let's take a look at an example of a layered approach. It shows a module from a geography course for professionals who travel internationally on business.

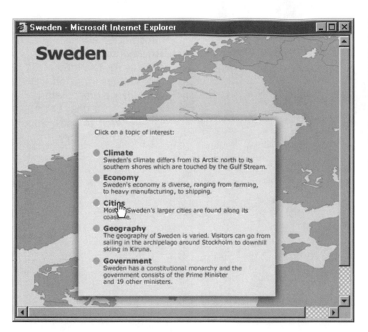

We start with a unit on Sweden. It provides us with some high-level information on Sweden and invites us to probe deeper for more details or more specific information. We ask for information on cities.

Clicking on **Cities** ...

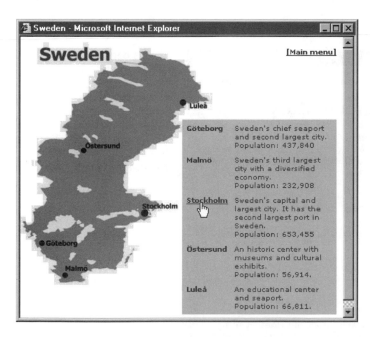

... reveals this map listing the main cities and providing basic information about each. For more details about a particular city, we can click on its name. We select **Stockholm**.

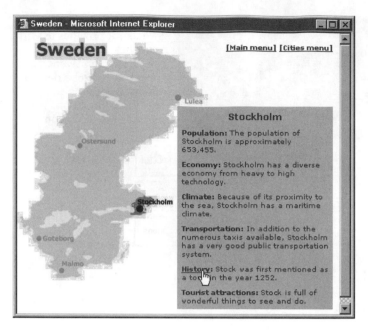

Now we see a summary of information about Stockholm along with choices for the kind of detailed information we want. If we want details we click on a link. Let's say we want to know about Stockholm's **History**.

At this deepest level, we get a detailed recap of the history of the city of Stockholm. Since there is no deeper information, there are no links downward, but there are links to take us back to shallower layers.

Schematically, the layered course that we traversed has an architecture something like this:

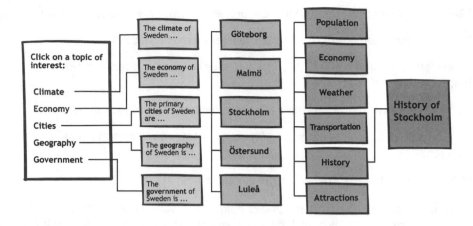

Layer course content

From the beginning, classify the content of your course by its location in the layering scheme.

Top layer   Preview, overview, summary, quick-reference aids.

Middle layer   Complete developments of main, high-priority ideas.

Bottom layer   Rarely needed subjects. Common reference documents. Links to standards, specifications, and external reports.

Overcome common architectural problems

Some common ways of combining and linking Web pages lead to problems for learners navigating the resulting structures. Let's take a look at these problems and see how to avoid them.

The as-shown-above syndrome

The as-shown-above syndrome is the tendency of designers to assume that everybody takes the course in exactly the sequence the designer intended. You see it in phrases and instances like these:

▶ "As shown above" and "As shown below" (Where the items mentioned are not on the current screen.)

▶ "Earlier you read that ..."

- ▶ "By now you have learned how to ..."

- ▶ "Repeat the preceding steps" (When the preceding steps have scrolled off the screen.)

- ▶ "... will be explained later" (But will the learner be reading later?)

- ▶ Abbreviations spelled out only the first time they are used and terms defined only the first time they are used

- ▶ Warnings, cautions, notes, and conventions in the beginning of the course

- ▶ "The next step in the process is ...." (Where the learner arrived at this topic directly from a search)

- ▶ Links labeled <u>Return to X</u> (when we did not come from X)

The solution is to make no hard assumptions about which path learners will follow. If understanding one idea requires understanding another, state the other idea, or link to it, or at least signal the requirement. Make it easy for learners to find needed information out of sequence. Here's where an index pays for itself. As does a good menu and a search facility.

The yo-yo effect

The yo-yo effect occurs when learners have to repeatedly return to a higher-level page before examining the next item in what seems like a logical sequence to them.

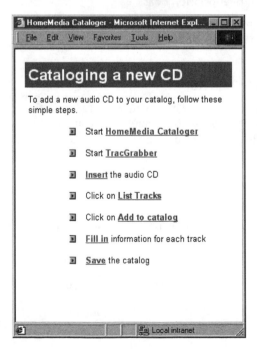

Here is an example that suffers from the yo-yo effect. This example teaches how to use a product to catalog audio CDs.

To get more details on how to perform a step, the learner must click on one of the steps.

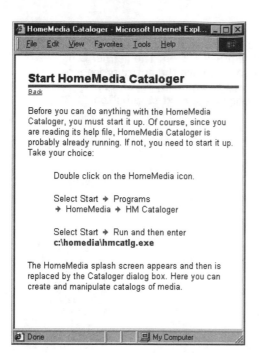

Once the learner completes studying how to perform step 1, he or she has to go back to the overview and manually select the second step.

To fix the yo-yo effect we just lay down a browsing trail through the entire sequence of detailed steps.

Notice that the top-level procedure now contains a link labeled **Next step**, which the learner can select to go to the first step in the procedure.

And on the page about performing the step is a link to the next step and a link to the previous step. The learner can navigate through the entire procedure one step at a time by repeatedly clicking on the **Next step** button.

As our example shows, the solution for the yo-yo effect is supplementing the links between the overview and detailed topics with a trail of links through each of them in sequence.

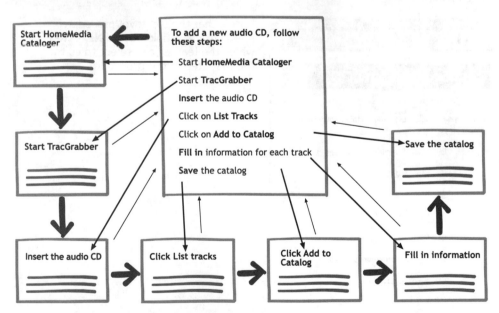

Construction signs and dead ends

Do not link to pages containing just an *Under Construction* sign. It is OK to mention planned improvements but do not force users to click or search to find out that you have not provided them yet. Inform learners before they jump or click that the destination is not available. For example:

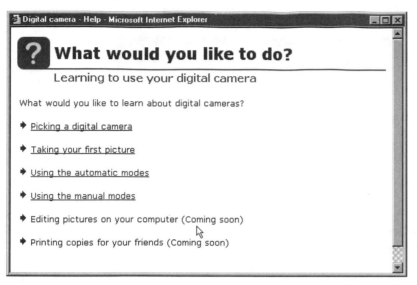

Likewise, avoid dead-end topics on which the only choice is the browser's Back button.

Integrate foreign modules

Sometimes the best way to build your course is to include pages and lessons developed by others. Technically, you can do so just by linking to these "foreign" modules. However, modules developed by someone else following different standards may look different, use a different approach, and further different goals than your modules. Foreign modules may not fit the framework of your course.

Craft a docking module

The solution is to craft a "docking module" to integrate these foreign modules into your course.

Example of a docking module

Here is an example of a module designed for one course but appearing within another.

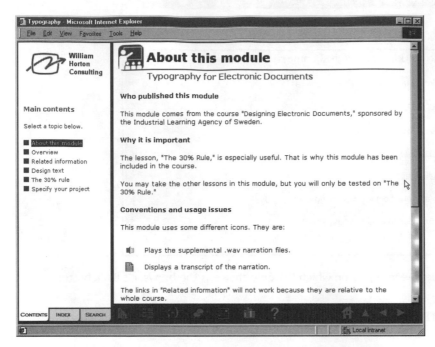

Notice the brief introduction to the module. It tells the learner where the module comes from.

It also provides some guidance to the learner by telling which lesson is important.

The page also tells the learner what file formats are used and what the different icons mean.

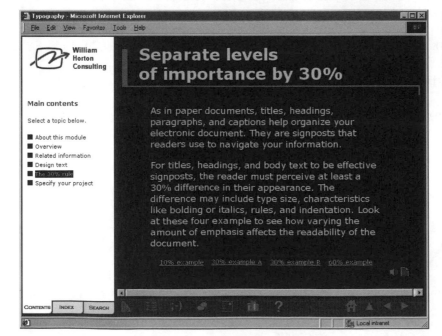

Here is the foreign module shown within the standard course frameset.

What to include in a docking module

A docking module consists of all the things you do to make the foreign module meet the needs of your learners. Some of the components of a docking module are:

A special window to display it. If the foreign module is of a different shape or size than your modules, you may need to craft a special frameset. You can also display it in a separate window alongside the window for the main part of your course.

Introduction. You may need to create a preview, introduction, abstract, overview, or description of the module to tell learners what to make of the foreign module.

Cautions about it. Let learners know any limitations of the module that are different from those for native modules. What conventions does it follow? How accurate and relevant are its materials? Who owns it and how is its use restricted?

Aids in accessing the content. Give learners any help they may need in accessing the foreign module and displaying its content. Provide:

▶ Instructions on taking the module.

▶ A special menu and index linked to its content.

▶ Help obtaining any plug-ins or fonts it requires.

▶ Glossary to define different terminology used in the module.

Certification test. The foreign module may not provide a test, or its test may not measure what is important to you. Add your own test to measure what learners got from the module.

Make navigation practical

Here are some practical tips to ensure that learners can navigate your course confidently and accurately.

Suggest a path. At every point, tell people what to do next. Give them a default action.

> To continue, click **Next**.

> You have completed module 7. Pick another module from the table of contents.

Do not compel learners to take these choices, just suggest them.

Help learners return from digressions. If you let or encourage learners to deviate from a recommended sequence, tell them how to resume. Make clear how to get back to where they left off in the course. And how to get to the login screen directly.

At the end of any planned digression, include a button to return the user to the main sequence or most recent menu. Or bookmark the point of digression and let learners resume by pressing a **Resume** button.

Put additional readings only at end. Provide links to "more interesting information" only at the end of an activity that requires the learner's full attention. Do not let such links distract the learner from a difficult task.

Add a few cross-links. For quicker navigation, consider adding a few cross-references between related topics so learners do not have to go up and down the hierarchy to move between related topics [89].

Build shortcuts to popular destinations. Ensure that all users can quickly, simply, and reliably find their way from any page to the: home page, page they entered from, table of contents, index, search, and previous page.

Build for expansion. Design your structure for 20% to 50% growth, or the amount of expansion you would expect within about six months.

IN CLOSING ...

Summary

- ▶ Lessons consist of sequences of logically linked Web pages that together create rich learning experiences.

- ▶ The classic tutorial structure is the most common, safest, and least efficient of common lesson structures.

  Other structures customize learning paths to meet the needs of learners.

- ▶ Certain components are common in many types of lessons. These include the following pages: Welcome, Related resources, Introduction, Summary, Event playback, Lesson feedback, Branching, Procedures, and the Featured example.

- ▶ Orderly, predictable organizations outperform chaotic, mysterious ones.

- ▶ To organize lessons and courses, analyze dependencies among concepts and the learner's current level of knowledge.

▶ Strive for complete self-contained modules that can be combined to teach complex subjects.

▶ Instead of sequential structures, consider layered ones, especially for self-guided as-needed learning.

For more ...

For some more ideas structuring learning experiences, consider more sophisticated activities (Chapter 6) or alternatives to conventional courses (Chapter 13). Most lessons contain tests (Chapter 7).

To keep track of standards for modular training, visit the Web sites of organizations involved in these efforts:

▶ Aviation Industry CBT Committee (AICC) at www.aicc.org

▶ IMS at www.imsproject.com

▶ IEEE's Learning Technology Standards Committee at grouper.ieee.org/p1484.

Many of the examples shown in this book are on exhibit at:

www.horton.com/DesigningWBT/

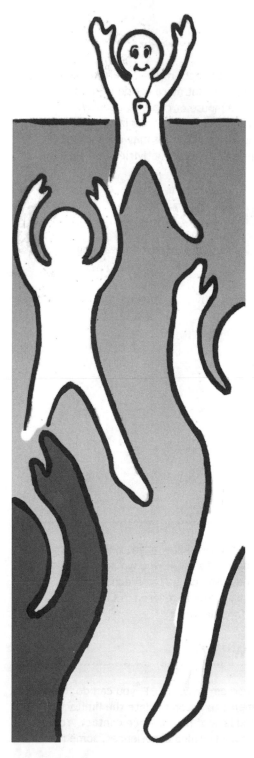

6

Activate learning

Exercises, practice sessions, and projects to ensure an active learning experience

Learning activities are the verbs of learning. They put people in action. They elevate learning from passive reading and watching to active seeking, selecting, and creating knowledge. With well-designed learning activities, WBT can be fun, efficient, and highly effective.

Interactivity boosts learning. People learn faster and develop more positive attitudes when learning is interactive [94]. The adage, "Practice makes perfect" has support from many different studies of learning outcomes [95]. In general, people learn more effectively and efficiently when they decide how much to practice [96], especially learners with already high levels of knowledge [95].

WHAT ARE LEARNING ACTIVITIES?

Learning activities, or just *activities* for short, are coordinated actions that exercise basic intellectual skills, thought processes, and analysis techniques. But mere action is not a learning activity. People learn little by merely clicking the mouse or chatting about vacation plans. People learn by considering, researching, analyzing, evaluating, organizing, synthesizing, discussing, testing, deciding, and applying ideas. Activities may use mouse clicks and chat sessions, but their goal is to provoke the exact mental activities that lead to learning.

What are the components of learning activities?

Most learning activities have three phases, each of which may involve several learning actions.

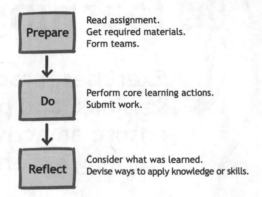

Prepare — Read assignment. Get required materials. Form teams.

Do — Perform core learning actions. Submit work.

Reflect — Consider what was learned. Devise ways to apply knowledge or skills.

When should you use learning activities?

Learning activities can be used to teach, to exercise, and to test knowledge, skills, and beliefs. Activities cater to those who learn best by doing and to those who would rather discover a fact for themselves than be told about it. They can also be the mechanisms whereby we evaluate the learning of students. Their use as tests is covered in Chapter 7. Here we concentrate on their uses to teach and to reinforce learning.

What kinds of activities are possible in WBT?

Any kind of activity is possible. If you can do it in a classroom or with CBT, you can do it in a WBT course. Of course, you may have to make adjustments to accommodate the limitations of WBT technology, mainly the restricted bandwidth and lack of face-to-face contact. You can compensate by using new Web technologies to produce learning experiences, some not possible in the classroom or with traditional CBT.

Do activities require a class?

Some activities are performed by a class as a whole. Some activities require multiple teams. Others require just one learner to perform the activity and one instructor to provide feedback. Still others use the computer to provide feedback and hence are suitable for the solo learner. Most activities can be adapted for any size group, even a group of one.

USE COMMON LEARNING ACTIVITIES

In this section we survey formats for learning activities. These techniques are proven and flexible. When well designed and appropriately deployed, they work well. These activities can be adapted to work with any subject matter. Many can be used with the class as a whole, by small teams, by individuals monitored by the instructor, and by learners working alone. Here is a summary of the activities we will be discussing in this chapter:

Activity	Description	When to use it
Webcasts (p 195)	Many distributed learners participate fully in a conventional training event transmitted by a network.	To teach material best taught by traditional classroom activities, especially ones that require extensive interaction between the instructor and learners.
Presentation sequences (p 199)	Learners read, listen to, and watch carefully crafted explanations in a Web browser.	To provide a consistent high-quality explanation to all learners.
Drill-and-practice activities (p 202)	Learners repeatedly practice applying specific knowledge or a well-defined skill.	To help learners memorize facts that they must be able to recall without hesitation.
Scavenger hunts (p 204)	Learners find reliable sources of information on the Internet or their corporate intranet.	To make learners more self-reliant by having them locate reliable sources of information on the subject they are studying.
Guided research (p 207)	Learners gather, analyze, and report on information.	To teach learners to conduct informal research on a subject. This activity is especially valuable for learners who will have to conduct informal research as part of their job.

Activity	Description	When to use it
Guided analysis (p 211)	Learners analyze data to evaluate its validity, spot trends, and infer principles.	To teach a formal analysis technique or to guide learners to discover trends and principles for themselves.
Team design (p 219)	Learners work as coordinated teams to produce a single design or to solve a complex problem.	To teach design skills that are applied as part of a team or to teach basic teamwork skills.
Brainstorming (p 223)	Distributed learners work together to generate creative solutions to a problem or to accomplish some other goal.	To teach brainstorming in its own right or as part of a course involving problem solving, creative thinking, or team design.
Case studies (p 226)	Learners study a meaningful, detailed example of a real-world event, process, or system to abstract useful concepts and principles.	To teach complex knowledge that cannot be reduced to a simple formula. To use specific, concrete particulars to teach abstract, general principles.
Role-playing scenarios (p 232)	Learners adopt assigned roles in simulations involving complex interpersonal interaction.	To teach subtle interpersonal skills and to reveal the complexity of many human endeavors.
Group critiques (p 237)	Learners receive and react to the criticisms from their peers. Learners submit a work that others in the class critique.	To teach learners how to use critical comments of others to improve their own work and how to offer helpful criticism of the work of others.
Virtual laboratories (p 242)	Learners conduct experiments with simulated laboratory equipment.	To prepare learners to operate real laboratory equipment or to guide them to discover principles and trends on their own.
Hands-on activities (p 246)	Learners perform a real task outside the lesson.	To teach hands-on tasks and to show learners how to apply abstract knowledge gained in other activities.
Learning games (p 251)	People learn by playing. Learning games are computer simulations that let learners practice a highly interactive task.	To give learners experience performing a task without the risk or cost of the real activity.

Symbols used in the diagrams

Here is a key defining the symbols used in the diagrams of this chapter:

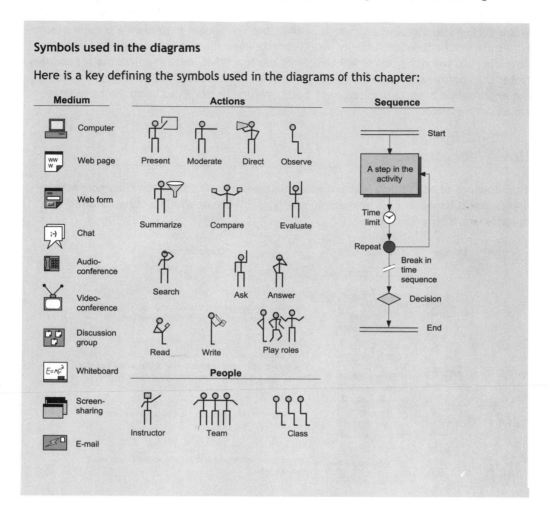

Webcast

Webcasts use the network to transmit a conventional training event so that many distributed learners can participate fully. The most common format is a lecture or speech followed by questions from learners. The presenter and audience are connected by a chat or conferencing system. Participants may also use screen sharing and whiteboard tools during the session.

When to use Webcasts

Use Webcasts to teach any kind of material best taught by traditional classroom activities. Typically these are ones where the material requires extensive interaction between instructor and learners. Such situations occur when it is impossible to anticipate what learners already know and what they need to know. If you cannot predict what questions learners will ask, a Webcast may be the best way to answer their questions.

Webcasts are also useful when there is neither time nor budget to prepare a presentation with sufficient built-in interactivity. Use Webcasts when there is not enough lead time for development, when the course will be offered too few times, or the subject matter changes faster than permanent materials can be revised. Webcasts should not be used just because the organization is too lazy to prepare a better version or merely to avoid having to revise classroom materials.

How Webcasts work

The sequence of actions in a Webcast is largely the same as those in the classroom activity on which it is based. Here is an example of a typical Webcast with a lecture followed by a question-and-answer session.

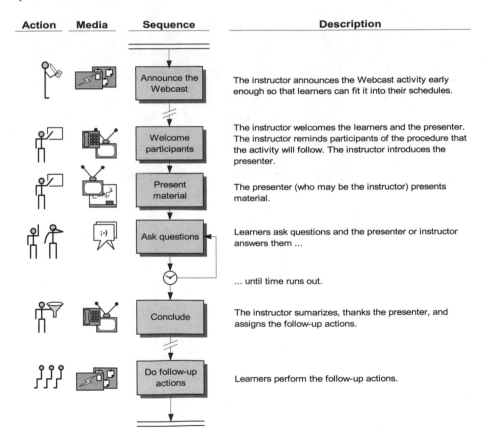

Action	Media	Sequence	Description
		Announce the Webcast	The instructor announces the Webcast activity early enough so that learners can fit it into their schedules.
		Welcome participants	The instructor welcomes the learners and the presenter. The instructor reminds participants of the procedure that the activity will follow. The instructor introduces the presenter.
		Present material	The presenter (who may be the instructor) presents material.
		Ask questions	Learners ask questions and the presenter or instructor answers them ...
			... until time runs out.
		Conclude	The instructor sumarizes, thanks the presenter, and assigns the follow-up actions.
		Do follow-up actions	Learners perform the follow-up actions.

Note: This diagram, and the others like it throughout this chapter, comes from planning forms I use to design such activities. A key defining the symbols used in the diagram is included at the start of this section.

Example of a Webcast

The management of ZipZapCom decided to discontinue floppy-disk drives as standard equipment in their laptop computers. The move perplexed product reviewers, scared potential customers, and discouraged sales representatives and distributors. The sales reps and distributors stopped selling ZipZapCom laptops, saying they could not explain the new design to customers.

To get sales back on track, ZipZapCom has prepared an emergency mini-course on "How to Sell Floppy-Less Laptops" for sales reps and distributors. The course announcement (sent by e-mail to every sales rep and distributor) lays out the plan for the mini-course. Here's a copy of that e-mail announcement.

```
YES YOU CAN SELL FLOPPY-LESS LAPTOPS
====================================

You have told us you need help selling ZipZapCom's line of floppy-less
laptops. Help is on the way in the form of a one-hour mini-course titled:

    How to sell floppy-less laptops

The live, interactive course will explain the decision to discontinue
floppy disk drives in ZipZapCom laptops and help you sell potential buyers
on the change.

When and where
--------------
    18 August 1999
    8:30 AM New York Time (13.30 UTC)
    Server: www.zipzapcc.com/meetings/floppyless.htm
    Password: zipzaprules

Agenda
------
Welcome by R. Howard Finnigan, CEO ZipZapCom (2 min)
Marketing reasons for change by Margaret Mandible, VP Mktg. (5 min)
Engineering reasons for the change by Hector de Castro, Engineering
Director (5 minutes)
How to sell customers on the change by Terry Graves, Product Manager,
Laptops (5 minutes)
Tough questions. Use chat or e-mail to give us your toughest questions.
Pretend you are a customer and voice your concerns. Our management team
and your peers will help you figure out an effective answer to every
concern. (40 minutes)
Continuing education by Terry Graves. How we will use discussion groups
and scheduled chat sessions to share sales techniques and solve problems
as they arise.

Before the class
----------------
E-mail a list of your questions and concerns about floppy-less laptops to
tgraves@zipzapcc.com. These will help us prepare.
Make sure your computer is set up to run NetMeeting (receive both audio
and video). For help go to:

www.zipzapcom.com/internal/training/mediahelp.htm
```

Here is a snapshot of a part of the course. The speaker is answering questions submitted by the audience.

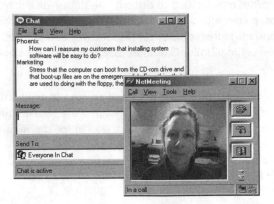

Variations of Webcasts

Although the most common form of this activity is a lecture, there are many more interesting forms. A few include:

Demonstration. Via videoconferencing or screen sharing the instructor shows how to perform a task. Learners are then called on to demonstrate similar tasks to the rest of the class and to the instructor.

Debate. Two authorities (or two learners acting as authorities) argue opposing sides of an issue. The audience can then ask questions of the debaters. Finally, the audience votes on the issue debated.

Interview. The instructor interviews an expert or recognized authority. Learners are also permitted to ask questions or to submit questions in advance.

Q&A. The instructor skips the lecture and participants ask questions of an expert or the instructor. To keep the procedure orderly, the instructor may require learners to submit questions before the Webcast.

Panel discussion. Three or four experts each make a brief presentation on a subject followed by questions from the audience.

Stump the experts. A team of learners research an area of knowledge and then pretend to be experts in the field. The rest of the class asks this team questions. The questions test the team's expertise and the class's ability to recognize when the "experts" are wrong.

Press conference. A learner or team makes a newsworthy announcement on the subject of the course. Class members ask questions. The instructor comments later on the quality of the questions and answers.

Reference desk. A team of learners attempts to quickly find answers to questions posed by the rest of the class.

Impostor test. A real expert and a learner both pose as experts on a subject. The rest of the class asks questions, trying to spot which is the real expert and which is pretending.

Round-robin lecture. The instructor starts lecturing on a subject. After a few minutes, the instructor picks a learner to continue the lecture. After a few more minutes, that learner picks another learner to continue, and so on until all learners have had a chance to participate.

Oral exam. The instructor poses a question to an individual learner. After that learner answers, other learners comment on the answer. This variation reverses the directions of questions and answers.

For additional information ...

Webcasts are a form of live collaboration. You can find detailed advice on designing and conducting effective live events in Chapter 9.

Presentation sequence

Presentation sequences explain things to learners. They are commonly used to convey straightforward information. Learners pass through the sequence individually—each at a different time and at a different pace. While experiencing a presentation sequence, learners are physically passive, but mentally active.

Presentation sequences rely primarily on text and graphics to tell their stories. They may also incorporate sound, animation, and video. Some include interactive media like virtual reality models or small simulations. Presentation sequences usually conclude with interactions that test or reinforce the knowledge learned from the core presentation.

Although presentation sequences may allow some optional topics, the primary pathway is linear. This structure lets the designer control the order of learning experiences. The learner can control the pace of the story and can ask some questions, but the designer remains the storyteller.

When to use presentation sequences

Presentation sequences provide a consistent, high-quality explanation to all learners. They work well for teaching established information in a highly efficient way to many people.

Presentation sequences allow the designer to control the order of learning actions experienced by the learner. Use them where designers really do know the best way to teach certain material. Someone who has taught a course for 10 years may know that certain explanations work better than others and that ideas must be introduced in a particular order to avoid confusion.

Presentation sequences are especially effective for courses that have no class or instructor. These kinds of activities rely solely on the computer to present information and possibly to provide feedback.

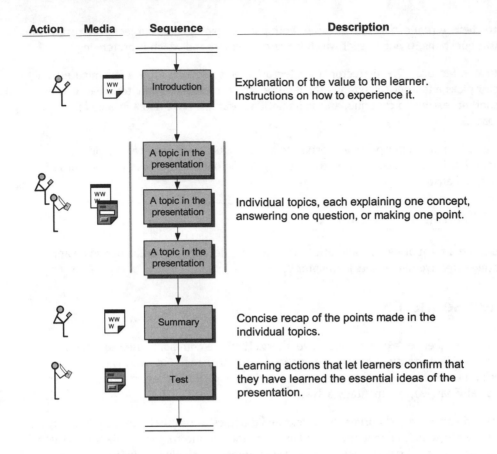

Action	Media	Sequence	Description
	WWW	Introduction	Explanation of the value to the learner. Instructions on how to experience it.
	WWW	A topic in the presentation / A topic in the presentation / A topic in the presentation	Individual topics, each explaining one concept, answering one question, or making one point.
	WWW	Summary	Concise recap of the points made in the individual topics.
		Test	Learning actions that let learners confirm that they have learned the essential ideas of the presentation.

How presentation sequences work

In the presentation sequence solo learners interact with the computer to learn about the activity, experience the individual topics of the presentation, get a summary, and then test the extent of their learning.

> Now, I cannot see that lectures can do so much good as reading the books from which the lectures are taken. I know nothing that can be best taught by lectures, except where experiments are to be shewn. You may teach chymistry by lectures:- You might teach making of shoes by lectures!
>
> — Samuel Johnson

Example of a presentation sequence

Here is an example from the middle of a presentation sequence on calculating heat transfer in mechanical devices.

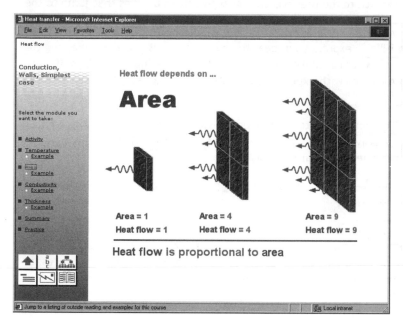

This example explains the relationship between heat flow and area. Voice narration supplements the graphical explanation. The table of contents (to the left) outlines the entire presentation sequence, which includes an introductory activity, examples, a summary, and a practice exercise.

Variations of presentation sequences

Presentation sequences are as varied as designers are clever. You can alter them by your choice and sequencing of topics, by use of different media, and by ways you share control over pacing and branching with the learner. You may also want to model your presentation on one of these familiar forms:

Slide show. Base the presentation on the business slide show. Make each topic resemble a single slide. Put in informative graphics and just enough text to convey the main point. Use voice to narrate the slides. If you cannot use voice, then provide a complete text narrative to accompany each slide. This is the model used for the example you just viewed.

Videotape. Model the core of the presentation on a video sequence. Keep the sequence short (under 5 minutes) or break it into separate sequences. Give learners play, rewind, and fast forward buttons to control the video.

Book. If a book is the best way to present information, use a book, not WBT. But if a segment of a WBT course is best presented as a linear sequence of text, then you can model that sequence on a book. Just make sure the text is legible, and add illustrations to focus attention on key ideas. If learners must read more than 3 - 5 pages of text, let them print out the presentation and read it from paper.

Tips and guidelines for presentation sequences

Here are some suggestions that come from my own experiences designing presentation sequences:

Let learners control the presentation. Give learners buttons or other controls that advance to the next topic or backtrack to the previous one. Also give them buttons that jump to the introduction, summary, or test from anywhere in the presentation.

Pick the best mix of media to express your ideas to your learners. If you are explaining to recent college graduates how things move, animation and video are logical choices. If you are discussing abstract concepts with experienced practitioners in a field, text may be the best choice.

Keep learners active. Combine presentation sequences with interactive Web forms so the learner is not physically passive for too long. Alternate a presentation that teaches a concept with an action that lets the learner apply the concept.

Make reading easy. Let learners print out long reading passages. Not all presentation sequences need be on the screen.

Link rather than write. Excellent presentation sequences on many subjects already exist on the Web. Consider linking to one of these available presentation sequences. Make clear that someone else provides the material. Otherwise learners may be confused by differences in the appearance of the materials. Also make sure the provider of the materials has no objections to your use of the materials.

Drill and practice

Drill-and-practice activities repeatedly exercise a simple or small area of knowledge. They are like the flash cards used to teach multiplication or a foreign language vocabulary.

Drill-and-practice activities build on a simple testing cycle. The system presents a problem, which the learner tries to solve. The system provides feedback on the learner's solution before posing another problem. Then the cycle repeats.

When to use drill and practice

Educational theorists of late have so thoroughly condemned drill and practice that it is easy to believe that this method has no use whatsoever. However, drill and practice is very useful in helping people memorize facts that they must be able to recall reliably without hesitation. Some examples include:

▶ Foreign language vocabulary

▶ Sign language

▶ Symbols, emblems, and signs used in a profession

▶ Spelling, grammar, and punctuation rules

▶ Syntax of a programming language

Use drill and practice to help people learn the simple rules and procedures that they must apply unconsciously as part of higher-level activities.

How drill and practice works

A drill-and-practice activity starts with an introduction that welcomes learners and explains how the activity works. Then learners repeatedly solve problems and receive feedback on their solutions. At the end, learners review what they have learned and try applying it in a more realistic situation.

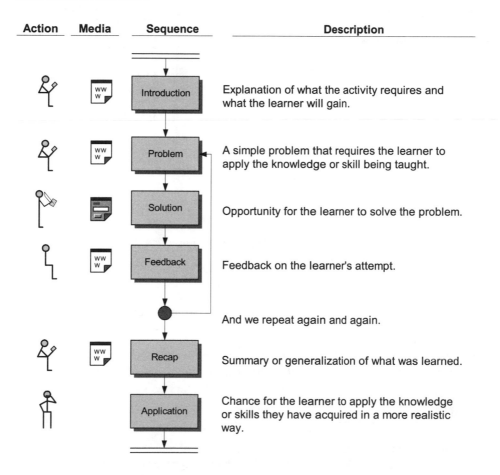

Action	Media	Sequence	Description
	WWW	Introduction	Explanation of what the activity requires and what the learner will gain.
	WWW	Problem	A simple problem that requires the learner to apply the knowledge or skill being taught.
		Solution	Opportunity for the learner to solve the problem.
	WWW	Feedback	Feedback on the learner's attempt.
			And we repeat again and again.
	WWW	Recap	Summary or generalization of what was learned.
		Application	Chance for the learner to apply the knowledge or skills they have acquired in a more realistic way.

Example of drill and practice

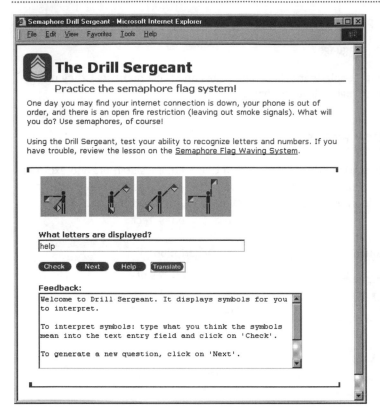

This drill and practice teaches the Semaphore Flag System. This part of the exercise teaches the learner to recognize individual flag positions and associate them with letters of the alphabet. The learner views a grouping of flags and then types in the equivalent letters. The time and accuracy of the learner's response are measured. As the learner's performance improves, the system presents more and more signs at once.

In a related drill and practice, the learner is given words to translate into flags.

Tips and guidelines for drill and practice

Here are some ideas for you to try when designing a drill and practice:

▶ If possible, design the activity so that it can generate an infinite number of new problems. That way the material is always fresh.

▶ Increase the difficulty level as the learner progresses. Give more complex problems or require faster responses.

▶ Drill and practice is seldom sufficient in itself. Combine it with other learning activities to teach how the rote knowledge taught in the drill and practice can be applied.

Scavenger hunt

Scavenger hunts challenge learners to find their own sources of information on the network. In a scavenger hunt, learners gather scattered bits of knowledge from various Internet and intranet sources. To prove that they have found the sought-for item, they provide:

▶ The requested fact or knowledge

▶ A citation of it in a standard work

▶ The URL were it can be found

When to use a scavenger hunt

Use a scavenger hunt to teach learners to find their own sources of reliable information on the Internet or an intranet. This is especially valuable in fields where the best, most up-to-date, most accurate information is found only online. In such fields, knowing where to find information is an essential job skill in its own right.

Use scavenger hunts to teach learners to:

▶ Find information on the Internet or intranet

▶ Navigate a large reference document, such as a specification or technical manual

▶ Retrieve information from a database

Scavenger hunts teach learners to find, evaluate, and select sources of information. In addition to learning how to find sources, as a bonus, learners acquire sources they can rely on in the future.

How a scavenger hunt works

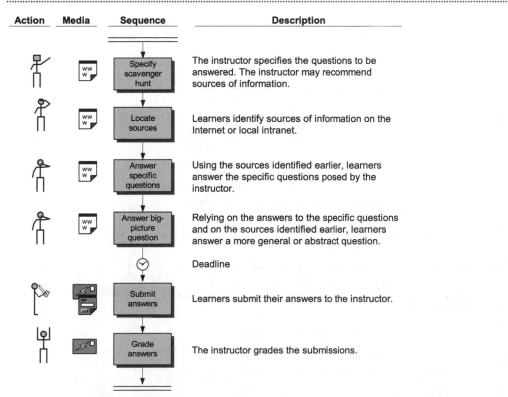

Action	Media	Sequence	Description
	WWW	Specify scavenger hunt	The instructor specifies the questions to be answered. The instructor may recommend sources of information.
	WWW	Locate sources	Learners identify sources of information on the Internet or local intranet.
	WWW	Answer specific questions	Using the sources identified earlier, learners answer the specific questions posed by the instructor.
	WWW	Answer big-picture question	Relying on the answers to the specific questions and on the sources identified earlier, learners answer a more general or abstract question.
			Deadline
		Submit answers	Learners submit their answers to the instructor.
		Grade answers	The instructor grades the submissions.

Example of a scavenger hunt

Learning a rapidly advancing body of knowledge requires learning how to keep current with changes in the field. For instance, programmers must have access to the latest information on a programming language, database technologies, and the various code libraries they use daily in their projects. Such information is quite volatile because producers are frequently releasing new versions of their tools as well as the inevitable patches, bug fixes, and work-arounds. With such volatility, printed documentation and classroom training cannot keep up. The programmer who relies on the tools and documentation that came in the box is left behind.

In this example, future Visual Basic programmers are challenged to locate the latest code, documentation, and technical tips for a programming library used to manipulate databases.

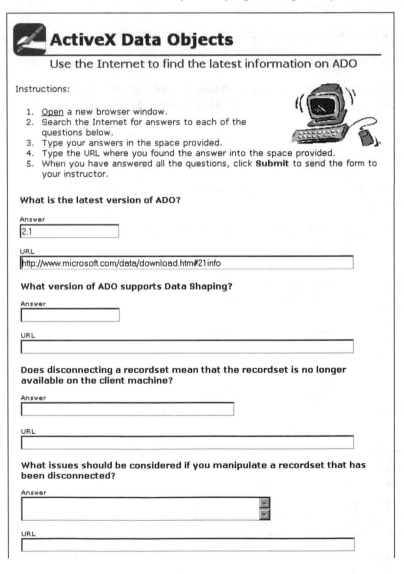

Were there any changes to the PutChunk method between ADO 1.5 and ADO 2.0?

Answer

URL

Submit

Variations of scavenger hunts

To give the scavenger hunt more of a game flavor, add a countdown timer that imposes a visible time limit on searches.

Combine the scavenger hunt with other activities to accomplish more sophisticated learning objectives. For example, combine it with guided research (p 207) or guided analysis (p 211) to teach learners to identify sources of information, to extract facts from them, and to analyze the facts in detail.

Tips and guidelines for scavenger hunts

Scavenger hunts do not have to be complex. They can be as simple as a list of 15-20 short questions that learners can answer by consulting Web resources.

Emphasize that merely answering the question is not enough. The goal of the scavenger hunt is to identify reliable sources of information for use in the future. Require learners to identify the source of their answer and to judge the accuracy of information provided by that source.

To emphasize the importance of data gathered in the scavenger hunt, have learners use that data in calculations or in making decisions.

Guided research

In our complex world, research is a basic skill. Rote memorization of facts will not do in most fields. There is too much to learn and what is true today may not be true tomorrow. Guided research teaches learners to conduct research—how to gather, analyze, and report on information.

In a guided-research activity, learners consult various sources of information on a topic and then assemble a report, jump page, or multimedia scrapbook summarizing the topic.

When to use guided research

Because this type of activity works well with individuals, teams, and entire classes, make it a staple of instructor-led net-based courses. Use it to teach learners how to conduct informal research on a subject, especially if learners will frequently need to prepare reports summarizing their research efforts.

Although locating information and analyzing it are a part of guided research, these activities are not the primary focus. Use guided research when you want to teach learners to evaluate, select, and organize information. To teach just information gathering, use a scavenger hunt (p 204); and to teach analysis, use a guided analysis activity (p 211).

How guided research works

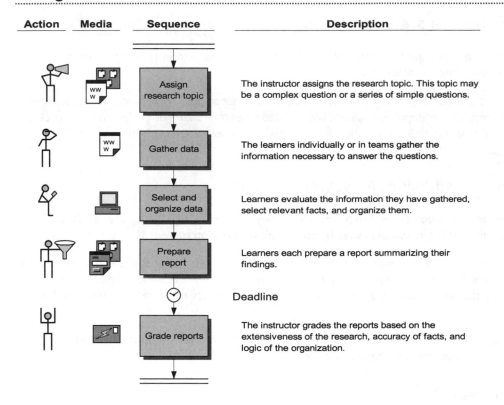

Action	Media	Sequence	Description
		Assign research topic	The instructor assigns the research topic. This topic may be a complex question or a series of simple questions.
		Gather data	The learners individually or in teams gather the information necessary to answer the questions.
		Select and organize data	Learners evaluate the information they have gathered, select relevant facts, and organize them.
		Prepare report	Learners each prepare a report summarizing their findings.
		Deadline	
		Grade reports	The instructor grades the reports based on the extensiveness of the research, accuracy of facts, and logic of the organization.

> **We never stop investigating. We are never satisfied that we know enough to get by. Every question we answer leads on to another question. This has become the greatest survival trick of our species.**
>
> — Desmond Morris, *The Naked Ape*

Example of guided research

The Yellowstone fire 10 years later

Fire management policies for public and private forests

In July of 1988 a series of massive forest fires raged through Yellowstone National Park and the surrounding area. The American pubic watching the nightly reports on the fires' progress were aghast at how the Forest Service could let such a thing happen. Politicians were interviewed on national talk shows about the destruction of the park. Forest Service officials were second-guessing their "let-it-burn" policy.

Using the information links provided (and any you find on your own), answer these questions:

1. How many acres were burned?
2. What percentage of the park does this acreage represent?
3. To what extent have the burned areas regenerated?
4. Have any artificial regeneration techniques been used?
5. What conclusions have the experts reached regarding fire management in Yellowstone? Do they agree?
6. Is Yellowstone a special case? That is, does this park differ significantly from other National forests to the extent that its management policies should be unique?
7. If you were in charge, what policy would you recommend?
8. Would you follow the same policy if you were in charge of a private forest? Why?

About the assignment

Due	Wednesday, December 8, 1999
Format	Microsoft Word 97 or later.
Collaboration?	No. Work on this assignment by yourself.
Send to	Send as an attachment to assignment10@anywhere.com
Questions?	instructor@anywhere.com +1.313.555.1234
Suggested links	Yellowstone Fires and their Legacy Plant and Animal Adaptations in Yellowstone National Park Yellowstone Bounces Back After 1988 Fires Yellowstone Fires of 1988 Map The Yellowstone Fires, National Geographic Radio Expeditions Rebirth evident after '88 fires Scientists: 1988 Fires were Good for Yellowstone Park Yellowstone blooms 10 years after fires World Wildlife Federation: Yellowstone blooms 10 years after fires Wildland Fire The Four-Foot Forest: The Politics of Small Wood

In this course for professional foresters, learners are asked to consider the conclusions that were drawn after the 1988 fires swept through Yellowstone National Park.

6

Activate learning

Variations of guided research

You can adapt guided-research activities for many different kinds of courses and for different class sizes—even classes of one. Here are some ideas on how to adapt guided research to your needs:

Assign each researcher a different perspective

Rather than have each learner perform the same research task, pick a complex subject and assign each learner a different perspective to research. For example, a course on project management could research the case of the Swedish ship, Vasa, which sank on its way out of Stockholm Harbor on its maiden voyage in 1628. Perspectives to research would be:

▶ **Technical**. What was the design flaw that caused the failure?

▶ **Managerial**. What was the management process of designing and building the ship?

▶ **Social**. What social pressures contributed to the bad design?

▶ **Legal**. What were the civil and criminal proceedings that followed?

▶ **Historical**. How did Swedish history influence the design of the ship? How did the failure affect events afterwards?

▶ **Aesthetic**. Many features of the ship were decorative. What was the role of aesthetics in design at that time?

▶ **Scientific**. How was the ship recovered and preserved? What did scientists learn by restoring it?

Learners can consider the research of all different perspectives to augment their own.

Scrapbook

One popular form of guided research is the scrapbook. Here learners gather and organize knowledge on a subject. They create a scrapbook by cutting and pasting (not linking) resources. Learners can later post their scrapbooks to a forum for others to comment on.

Give learners instructions such as these:

> Visit the resources listed below. Collect text, pictures, statistics, bits of multimedia, and quotations important to your role and assignment. Assemble the pieces into a scrapbook, annotated with brief explanations of what they mean and why you selected them. Prepare a table of contents showing the logical organization of the materials you have collected.

Day in the life of ...

Have learners research a real, historical, or fictional character and then write about what this person experiences on a typical day. Pick a person who has contributed to the subject matter of the course or who is an exemplary practitioner in the field.

Ongoing research

For a research project, require learners to keep and periodically submit logs of their research activities. The instructor can identify additional sources, suggest more efficient techniques, and challenge questionable resources. Once a week, require the team to submit a brief summary of their findings.

Tips and guidelines for guided research

Emphasize the importance of evaluating, selecting, and organizing facts. Without proper guidance, many learners may just gather and repeat facts. This is why the activity is called *guided* research.

Guided analysis

Guided analysis steps learners through the process of analyzing data. Guided analysis answers one of the most important questions ever asked: "So what?" Guided analysis helps learners to separate useful from useless information and to infer general principles and conclusions from separate, confusing, concrete instances. It teaches learners how to turn data into information and even knowledge.

When to use guided analysis

You can use guided analysis activities in two ways. The primary use is in teaching formal analysis techniques. The technique may involve calculating or estimating mathematical values. Or it may involve sorting, classifying, or ranking items according to defined procedures.

A secondary use is teaching principles *revealed* by the analysis of data. In this case, the guided analysis is just a means to the end. Guided analysis exposes a trend or pattern that the learner might not otherwise notice or believe.

How guided analysis works

In guided analysis, the learner follows the procedure specified by the instructor to gather and analyze data. After several cycles of gathering and analyzing, the learner abstracts a principle revealed by the analysis and tests it by analyzing new data. The learner may have to revise the principle until it reliably predicts results. Once the principle is successfully formulated, the learner summarizes what he or she has learned.

Action	Media	Sequence	Description
		Assign analysis activity	The instructor assigns the analysis task and provides access to the data and instructions on how to perform the analysis.
		Gather data	The learner gathers data for the analysis. The learner may have to search for the data on the Internet or it may be provided by the instructor.
		Apply analysis	The learner applies the analysis technique as specified by the instructor.
			Repeated for different sets of data.
		Abstract a principle	The learner abstracts a trend, pattern, or law revealed by the analysis.
		Test principle	The learner tests the principle by seeing whether it predicts results for new data.
			If the results were not as predicted by the principle, the learner must revise the principle.
		Report	The learner briefly summarizes the principle or analysis technique learned.

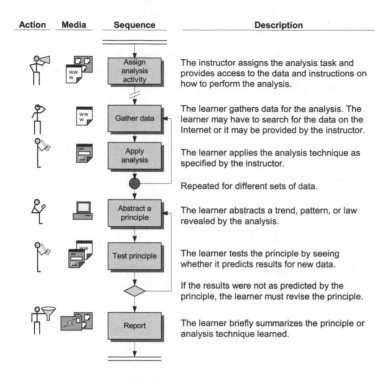

Example of guided analysis

Analyze soil texture

Learn to use the soil texture analysis chart

Soil texture refers to the relative proportions of sand, silt, and clay particles which make up the soil mass. Soil texture can be determined exactly in a laboratory analysis. It can also be adequately classified in the field, after some experience, by sight, feel, and the use of the chart shown below.

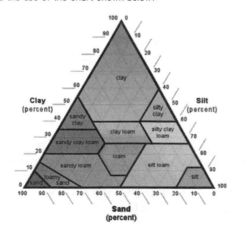

This example guides forestry professionals in classifying soil textures based on the proportions of sand, loam, and silt in the soil.

To practice using the chart, classify the soil texture for each of these samples:

40% silt, 20% clay, 40% sand	sandy loam ▾
20% clay, 23% sand, 57% silt	silt ▾
50% clay, 50% sand	clay ▾

Variations of guided analysis

Guided analysis can be used with or without a class and as an individual or group activity. Here are some ways you can vary the activity to suit your needs:

No instructor. If the course has no instructor, just present instructions clearly on a Web page.

Instructor demonstrates technique. If the technique is complex, the instructor may demonstrate the technique using screen-sharing or whiteboard collaboration tools. After the demonstration, learners can ask questions to make sure they understand the technique.

Team analysis. If the analysis is complex or requires many steps, assign teams to perform the analysis. Teams can divide the work among members, and members can help each other master the analysis technique.

> I profess both to learn and teach anatomy, not from books but from dissections; not from positions of philosophers but from the fabric of nature.
>
> — William Harvey

Ways to guide analysis

One way to guide analysis is to have the learner apply a specific formula or procedure. Here are a few more methods of analysis. Each focuses attention and thought on a different aspect of the data.

Summarize

One of the simplest and most universally applicable analysis techniques is summarizing an area of knowledge. To summarize, learners must decide what is true, select what is important, and express ideas in their own words.

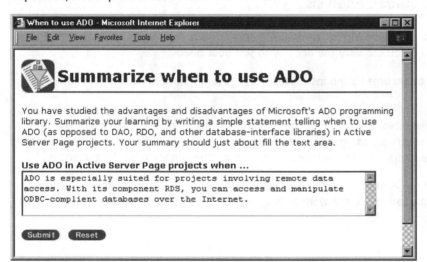

Here is a guided analysis example from a programming course. It asks an open-ended question but gives the learner only a limited amount of space in which to answer. Notice the prompt for the text area.

A blank text area is not always the best way for learners to express a summary. For some subjects, you may want to have learners draw a picture and submit it by e-mail or discussion-group posting. For other subjects, you may want to structure the form of the summary. For instance, you could let learners construct a summary by clicking checkboxes to indicate which of several statements apply, by putting the steps of a procedure in sequential order, or by assigning priorities to statements in a list.

Compare and contrast

Evaluating complex data is ... well, complex. One way of simplifying it is to guide learners in comparing two alternatives. The easiest way to do this in WBT is to have learners complete a Web form creating a side-by-side comparison. For instance, in the following example, learners compare two major indexes of the stock markets in the United States.

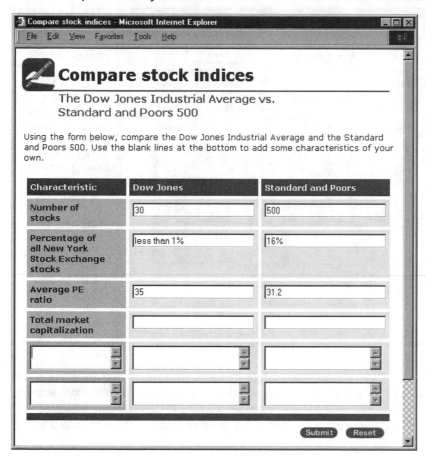

The form draws attention to critical differences between the two indexes. It requires learners to juxtapose contrasting facts so differences are inescapable.

To encourage independent thought, the form includes blank rows where learners can compare the two indexes according to characteristics the learners select.

Plot data

Over the decades, learners have consumed forests of grid paper drawing charts and graphs to detect trends and patterns in numerical data. With Dynamic HTML or plug-ins, learners can plot data right in their Web browser.

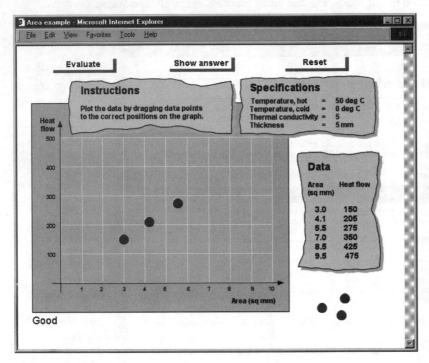

Good

This example of guided analysis provides measurement data and allows the learner to plot it by dragging dots into place on the virtual graph paper. Doing so reveals a simple relationship between area and heat flow, which makes even the most dull-witted learner shout "Eureka!"

This example requires Macromedia's Shockwave plug-in.

Plotting data points is tedious and teaches nothing by itself. So, why not just show the graph with the points already plotted? The act of plotting the data forces learners to more actively process it and more active processing leads to deeper learning [94]. Just make sure that learners discover the relationship hidden in the data. Provide a hint or draw the trend on the graph, if necessary.

Classify items

To classify items, learners assigns real-world or net-available objects to established categories. To accomplish this, learners can match items from one list to another, drag an object over another, type code numbers into text boxes, or answer a series of multiple-choice or select-list questions.

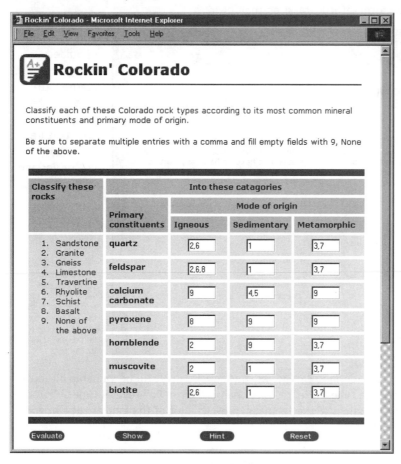

In this example of guided analysis learners classify some common rock types by their primary mineral constituents and mode of origin.

To classify one of the rocks listed on the left, the learner types its number into the box in the appropriate rows and column. For instance, basalt (8) is an igneous rock and its primary constituents are feldspar and pyroxene. So, the number 8 is entered in the 2nd and 4th rows of the igneous column.

6

Activate learning

Outline items

Most technical and business fields rely on hierarchical organization. Having learners outline items requires them to put individual items into a hierarchical scheme. This kind of guided analysis teaches general organizing skills as well as particular organizational schemes. The ability to organize separate facts indicates advanced understanding of a subject [97]. It prepares learners to perform difficult tasks on their own.

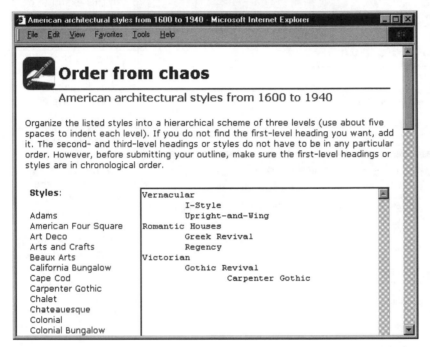

This example of guided analysis asks learners to organize the list of architectural styles by categories and sub-categories.

This example uses a custom Active Server Pages script and component on the server to format the form's contents and e-mail it to the instructor.

In a field without clear, well-defined categories, this activity may still be valuable although quite complex. Allow enough time for learners to change their minds several times. Or make it a team activity. The discussions of the team can provoke a lot of thinking about categories and classification schemes.

Tips and guidelines for guided analysis

Do not forget what you are teaching. If you are teaching the analysis technique, emphasize the technique. Lavish attention on each step. If, however, you are using the analysis to reveal principles that are the real subject, then focus attention on the principles. Keep the analysis simple.

Eliminate unnecessary steps that may distract from what you are teaching. If finding the data is not part of the lesson, provide it or link directly to it. If calculations are complex, provide a calculator.

Team design

The communications capabilities of networks let individuals at separate locations work as a team. Team-design activities use these capabilities so that learners in a class can work as coordinated teams to produce a single design or to solve a single complex problem—no matter where they are.

Ideally, each team must do original research, analysis, and design to complete its part, which yet another team integrates into a common solution. Teams communicate using discussion groups, chat, e-mail, and conferencing tools in order to complete their assigned tasks.

When to use team design

Team design activities are valuable to teach skills that designers apply as part of a team rather than as individuals. Team design activities are also valuable in teaching teamwork skills in their own right. As more and more work requires coordinating with distant colleagues, team design activities will become a more common part of training courses.

Some common team design projects require learners to create:

▶ A financial plan for a new type of business

▶ A report on the feasibility of a new product

▶ Recommendations on the use of a new medical procedure

▶ Proposed laws to cover new technology

> Nothing becomes real till it is experienced—even a proverb is no proverb to you till your life has illustrated it.
>
> — John Keats

How team design works

In team design activities, the instructor assigns a design task and helps learners organize themselves into teams. Teams work independently, producing successively more refined versions of their work, which they submit to the integration team. The integration team merges the work of the other teams and submits the final project to the instructor for grading.

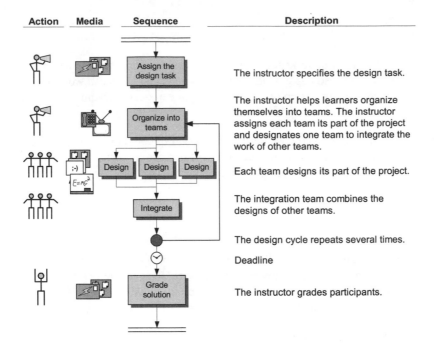

Action	Media	Sequence	Description
		Assign the design task	The instructor specifies the design task.
		Organize into teams	The instructor helps learners organize themselves into teams. The instructor assigns each team its part of the project and designates one team to integrate the work of other teams.
		Design Design Design	Each team designs its part of the project.
		Integrate	The integration team combines the designs of other teams.
			The design cycle repeats several times.
			Deadline
		Grade solution	The instructor grades participants.

Example of team design

In this example, participants are given the task of preparing a business plan for a new venture.

 Develop a business plan

A collaborative assignment

You and your teammates have an idea for a "killer" e-commerce Website. You know there is a tremendous amount of money to be made by selling low-cost virtual vacations. Your company would provide—for a fee, of course—a complete vacation package including photos, itinerary, "stories" for the folks back home, postcards, even fake ticket stubs and receipts.

What you need is money. So, you and your teammates must develop a business plan that will show prospective investors how you plan to make this business a success and convince them that they should invest money.

About the assignment

Deliverables	The class will write a business plan that is sure to entice investors to fund this "unique" business venture. The business plan should include sections on:
	
	■ Services and products
	■ Customer analysis
	■ Competition
	■ Key strategies
	  □ Marketing
	  □ Content
	  □ Licensing
	  □ Pricing
	■ Operation
	■ Risk assessment
	
	In addition, the plan should have an Executive Summary that summarizes the business plan and outlines a plan of action for a potential investor.

Instructions	The class has been divided into teams and the assignments posted in the forum. Each team should select a team leader. The team leaders should then decide how to divide the work necessary to produce a plan meeting the requirements in the scenario. Some suggestions are: ■ Divide the work by section--services and products, customer analysis, etc. ■ Divide the work by research, writing, and editing. Remember, one team needs to be responsible for managing the work flow and preparing the final plan for submission. At the conclusion of this assignment, the management team will post the completed Business Plan and Executive Summary to the forum. Plus, each class member will summarize (approx. 500 words) the duties they performed on their team and what they learned from being part of a team. These summaries should be sent to instructor@horton.com. Use the "Business Plan" thread in the class forum for *all* communication about this assignment. Do not communicate privately.
Required?	Yes
Date due	Tuesday, February 15, 2000
Graded?	Yes
Grading policy	The plan will be graded for completeness and ingenuity. Each class member's grade will be whatever the plan receives. In addition, each class member will be evaluated on the quality of their individual summaries.

Variations of team design

Team design is a broad category that you can adapt for classes of various sizes and for teaching various subjects. Here are a few suggestions:

For a small class. In a small class, each team can be a single individual. The instructor can take a more active role by integrating the parts and giving feedback on the work in progress.

For a large class. In a large class, use parallel design. Divide the class into large teams and assign the same problem to each large team. Each large team must come up with its own solution and post it on the server for other teams to see. After seeing the designs of other teams, a team may revise its own solution. At the end of the activity, each team must pick the best solution submitted by another team and justify its choice.

For language learning. For language learning, create teams of native and non-native speakers to solve a problem together. Teams must work in the language being learned.

Mosaic or Jigsaw model. Take a large book, Web site, or other complex work made up of somewhat independent pieces. Divide the class into teams. Assign each team a part of the whole to review. Each team can further subdivide the work by assigning parts to individuals, or all the members of the team can work on the team's assignment. Then:

▶ Each team prepares a summary of its part and a critical review of it.

▶ An über-team assembles the pieces and writes a review of the whole.

▶ Individual members comment on the consolidated review, and the über-team revises it.

Tips and guidelines for team design

Make clear the grading criteria. Will grades be awarded to the class as a whole, to separate teams, or to individuals? Some learners may feel uncomfortable that largely unseen colleagues determine their grade.

Provide a suggested timeline for progress on the project. Lacking face-to-face contact, learners may not feel fully obligated to complete their share of work on time.

The goal of a design activity must be appropriately challenging—not too difficult and not too easy. If learners have not worked in virtual teams before, they will require about twice as much time to complete a team activity as they would working together in a classroom.

> One thorn of experience is worth a whole wilderness of warning.
>
> — James Russell Lowell

Brainstorming

Brainstorming is the process of generating lots of new ideas. In a brainstorming session the leader poses a problem for which participants suggest solutions. The goal is to produce as many ideas as possible. In brainstorming, no ideas are rejected or criticized.

Brainstorming is a common part of most courses that involve creative design. The communications capabilities of the Web allow brainstorming sessions with participants from around the globe.

When to use brainstorming

Brainstorming can be taught as a valuable skill in its own right. It is an important aspect of courses in team design, problem solving, and creative thinking. Brainstorming can also be useful as part of any course that requires learners to solve problems in an original way.

How brainstorming works

The brainstorming session starts with the instructor's posting a question or issue for discussion. Participants offer ideas as quickly as possible. The session usually begins using a real-time medium such as chat or conferencing. When the flow of ideas slows, the instructor may move the session to a discussion group (p 348).

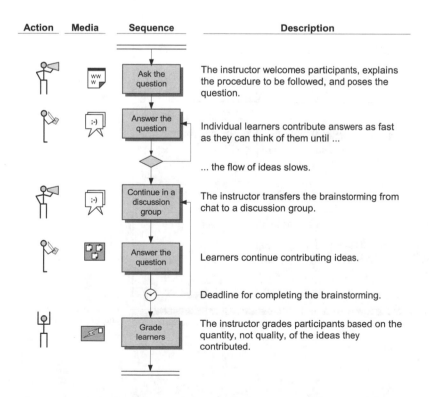

Action	Media	Sequence	Description
	WWW	Ask the question	The instructor welcomes participants, explains the procedure to be followed, and poses the question.
	;-)	Answer the question	Individual learners contribute answers as fast as they can think of them until ...
			... the flow of ideas slows.
	;-)	Continue in a discussion group	The instructor transfers the brainstorming from chat to a discussion group.
		Answer the question	Learners continue contributing ideas.
			Deadline for completing the brainstorming.
		Grade learners	The instructor grades participants based on the quantity, not quality, of the ideas they contributed.

Example of brainstorming

The following example of brainstorming is from a class for architects and building contractors on how to remodel homes. The purpose of the session is to show learners how creative thinking can help them work within a tight budget.

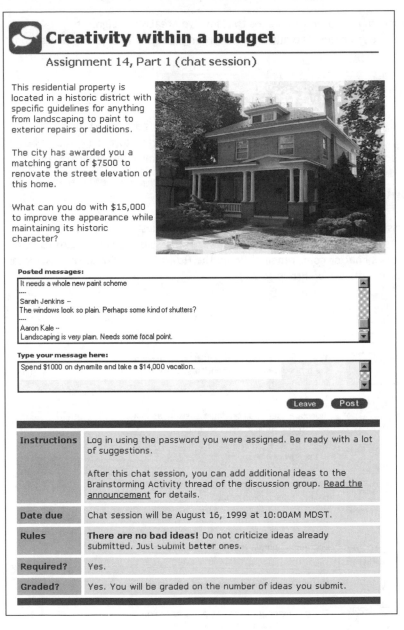

The session starts with a chat session where learners rapidly suggest ideas.

This example uses Macromedia's MultiuserServer and Shockwave plug-in.

Creativity within a budget

Assignment 14, Part 2 (discussion session)

This residential property is located in a historic district with specific guidelines for anything from landscaping to paint to exterior repairs or additions.

The city has awarded you a matching grant of $7500 to renovate the street elevation of this home.

What can you do with $15,000 to improve the appearance while maintaining the historic character?

Instructions	This is a continuation of Assignment 14. Please read the chat transcript posted in the "Brainstorming Activity" thread of the discussion group. During this week, add more ideas to the thread. Post as many ideas as you can—the more ideas the better. However, don't repeat ideas entered by others.
Date due	Contribute during the week of August 16, 1999.
Required?	Yes
Rules	**There are no bad ideas!** Do not criticize ideas already submitted. Just submit better ones.
Graded?	Yes. You will be graded on the number of ideas you submit.

After the chat session slows, the brainstorming session shifts to a discussion thread. Here we see the announcement and description of the thread.

:-) **Remodeling homes**

Working within a budget

/ WBT Forums

Forums [Remodeling homes ▾]

✎ Post New Topic

Show activity for last: [This year ▾]

Expanded Topics · 🗀 Compress

📂 **Introduction to our forum** 8/1/99 by *Instructor*
📂 **Course summary** 8/1/99 by *Instructor*
📂 **Administrative support** 8/1/99 by *Forum administrator*
　└ NetMeeting problems 8/1/99 by *Sarah*
　　└ re: NetMeeting 8/1/99 by *Forum administrator*
📂 **General comments** 8/1/99 by *Instructor*
　└ File naming conventions 8/1/99 by *Instructor*
📂 **Assignment 1** 8/27/99 by *Instructor*
　└ From Kit Horton 8/28/99 by *Kit Horton*
📂 **Brainstorming Activity** 8/16/99 by *Instructor*
　└ Paint 8/16/99 by *Sarah*
　└ Landscaping 8/18/99 by *Ken*
　└ Windows 8/19/99 by *Jerrod*
　└ Chat session transcript 🖻 8/16/99 by *Instructor*

Here we see the top level of the discussion group showing a number of threads, including the Brainstorming Activity thread and the responses posted to it.

Variations of brainstorming

To adapt brainstorming to your needs, consider using a different mix of collaboration mechanisms or setting a theme for the brainstorming activity.

Use more media. If you have the capability, use other media. Audioconferencing is a good investment, as many people find typing slows their production of ideas. If you use audio, remember to record the session and post a typed transcript or summary to the discussion group.

A shared whiteboard lets learners contribute ideas by sketching or pasting in their drawings or clip art. For visual subjects, a whiteboard is especially valuable.

Skip the chat. If learners are familiar with brainstorming, you may want to conduct the whole brainstorming session as a discussion group. This is a good alternative if it is difficult to get all learners together at the same time. Some brainstorming participants find it hard to be creative when it is four hours past their bedtime.

Set in context. You can give the brainstorming a more realistic flavor by situating it in a life-like situation. Set a scene. Tell a story of a real problem. Ask learners to pretend they are characters in the story. Have them offer solutions from the perspective of their characters.

Tips and guidelines for brainstorming

Enforce the prime rule of brainstorming. Make sure all participants understand the one and only rule of brainstorming: **There are no bad ideas**.

Emphasize that participants cannot criticize ideas submitted so far but can add better ideas. Remind participants that they score points for the number (not quality!) of ideas.

Ask thought-provoking questions. Ask open-ended questions that can have many answers. For example: What if X? How do we make X better? Why should we do Y?

Keep ideas flowing. Prime the pump with a few ideas of your own. Periodically restate the question in a new way. Reverse the question. For example, after asking how to make X better, ask how to make it worse.

Case study

Schools have used case studies since—well since there were schools. Case studies give relevant, meaningful experiences from which learners can abstract useful concepts and principles.

In a case study, learners are given a comprehensive example to study. The case can be a real world event, process, or system. The learner is also given materials that describe or perhaps even simulate the case. After working with these materials, the learner attempts to answer questions about the case or to generalize the principles revealed by the case.

WBT case studies differ from classroom case studies in the variety of material available through the Internet, in the use of interactive multimedia presentation, and in the multiple perspectives possible through collaboration. WBT case studies can include a richer mix of materials for the learner to examine and can more realistically mimic real world cases.

When to use case studies

Case studies teach abstract, general principles from specific, concrete particulars. As such, they mimic the way most people learn most of what they know: by observing and analyzing their own experiences. Case studies are good for teaching complex knowledge that cannot be reduced to a simple formula. They are especially good for teaching the judgment skills necessary to deal with complex, contradictory situations common in real life.

How case studies work

The instructor assigns and explains the case to study. Learners then work to answer questions provided by the instructor, posting their answers to a discussion group for critique by classmates. Finally, learners send the instructor a list of the principles they inferred from the study.

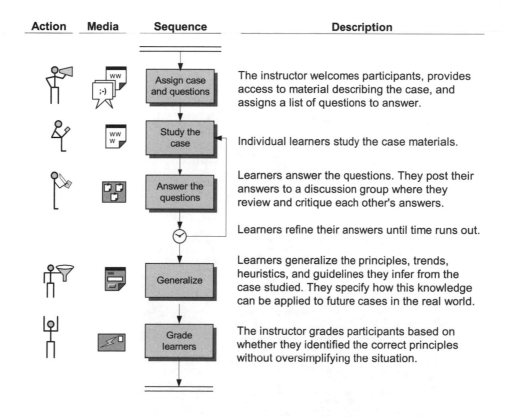

Action	Media	Sequence	Description
		Assign case and questions	The instructor welcomes participants, provides access to material describing the case, and assigns a list of questions to answer.
		Study the case	Individual learners study the case materials.
		Answer the questions	Learners answer the questions. They post their answers to a discussion group where they review and critique each other's answers.
			Learners refine their answers until time runs out.
		Generalize	Learners generalize the principles, trends, heuristics, and guidelines they infer from the case studied. They specify how this knowledge can be applied to future cases in the real world.
		Grade learners	The instructor grades participants based on whether they identified the correct principles without oversimplifying the situation.

Example of a case study

In this example learners are asked to analyze a failed attempt to provide technical support for customers using a software product. Here you see the assignment and an overview of what happened.

 The Case of the Vengeful Customer

How ZipZapCom barely survived in the court of public opinion

Please review the facts surrounding this incident and answer the questions listed at the end of this page.

Synopsis

In 1997 ZipZapCom Software Corporation, makers of WordSoWrite, received some very unflattering press in the large computer trade magazines about their poor technical support. In fact, these articles about ZipZapCom sparked several diatribes by the technology pundits of the day regarding the state of support in the software sector—ZipZapCom was mentioned frequently. As a result some consumer action groups started lobbying for stricter consumer protection laws for software products!

As you can imagine, this was a management nightmare for ZipZapCom. Not only did the company's reputation suffer, but its sales plummeted, its stock price fell, and the CEO was forced to resign. All this because of one customer support call that was poorly handled.

Fortunately, the incident that sparked this disastrous chain of events was well documented. Below is a chronicle of those events. In the right-hand column are source materials that support each of the events documented. Click on them to review the source information.

Chronicle of events

Date	Time EST	Customer's actions	Technical Support actions	Supporting material
6/24/97	10.00	Calls reporting a print driver conflict with WordSoWrite, version 3.5.	Tech273--Advises customer that there is a software patch available for WordSoWrite 3.5 that will fix the conflict. Gives customer the URL for this patch. Does not give customer a case number.	Knowledge base article about upgrade patch Transcript of conversation Recording of conversation
	13.15	Calls back stating that there is still a conflict with the print driver and WordSoWrite. And yes, the upgrade patch for version 3.5 has been installed.	Tech360--Questions customer about the printer brand and model. Asks about the version of the print driver. While the customer holds, technician determines that there is a more up-to-date driver available. Tells customer to download and install this updated driver. The problem should be fixed. Tells customer the case number--RS624315	Transcript of conversation Recording of conversation URL of print driver update
	14.00	Calls back [very frustrated]. States that the updated print driver does not fix the problem. States that everything else works "just fine" with this driver, even the other modules of the ZipZapCom office suite.	Tech254--Advises customer that there have been no other reports of a similar problem. However, says that the problem will be escalated to a level-two technician who will call the customer back by 16.30 this date.	Transcript of conversation Recording of conversation

[The chronicle continues for several more scrolling zones.]

Assignment

Premise	You are the consultant that was called in to evaluate the incident.
Instructions	You are to: 1. Investigate the incident, reading the supporting materials. 2. Prepare a report outlining the main factors contributing to the escalation of this incident and what actions or attitudes could have diffused the situation. 3. Draw a Kipling diagram showing how support information should flow throughout the company and to the end user. 4. Post your report and diagram to the class forum under the Case Study thread.
Date due	Monday, May 8, 2000
Required?	Yes
Graded?	Yes. It will count as 20% of your grade in this course.
Questions?	E-mail instructor@horton.com or call +1.313.555.1245

Variations of case studies

Case studies can take many forms. Here are some of our favorites:

Virtual field trips

Virtual field trips (p 559) take learners out into the real world to observe how the subject of the course is applied. A virtual field trip lets learners observe how concepts that are taught in their simple, pure form in the classroom are applied or misapplied in the real world.

Observe-and-comment activities

Learners observe a video or animation sequence (or just read a narrative) of people interacting. They can view the sequence as many times as they wish. Then they comment about what they have seen, answering such questions as:

▶ **What happened?** What did the people do? What did they think? How did they feel? What did the people gain or lose? What did they learn?

▶ **What does it mean?** What does the experience mean to you? How does it apply to your real-world experiences?

▶ **What will you do?** What have you learned? How will you think or act differently in the future? How will you apply what you have learned?

Prompted examples

Send learners off to analyze examples available on the Web. For each example, tell them:

- **What the example shows.** Do not be too specific. Just explain how the example relates to the subject under discussion.

- **What to notice.** What are the important features? Where should the learner focus attention?

- **Questions to answer.** The answers form the deliverable for the activity.

- **What to think about.** Ask questions that guide the learner to think about how this example relates to others or to the subject of the course.

Mini-case studies

You can provide realistic, real-world experience by presenting a series of concise case studies. The formula is simple: Start with a statement of the situation. Introduce any characters, objects, or organizations of importance. Spell out crucial relationships among them. Then alternate questions and answers about the situation. Questions should require the learner to carefully examine the situation, infer facts not stated, apply principles, and deduce conclusions.

As a follow-up, pose additional questions to learners. Have them submit their answers to a discussion group. Or challenge learners to make up their own case studies and submit them to a discussion group for use and critique by other learners.

Reaction papers

Have learners express their reactions after carefully examining a work in the field of study. The work can be a simple example, a case study, or a physical artifact. To structure the activity, give learners a form to fill in. Include areas for them to enter:

- **Personal goals.** What do you hope to gain by examining the work?

- **Summary.** What does the work say? What does it mean to all those who come in contact with it?

- **Reaction.** What is significant about the work for you? What does your own background and experience tell you about it?

- **Utility.** How can you apply what you learned in this activity to your own work?

> The knowledge of the world is only to be acquired in the world and not in a closet.
>
> — Lord Chesterfield

Tips and guidelines for case studies

Provide a rich mixture of case materials

Traditionally, case studies have used just paper memos, transcripts of interviews, and sometimes videotapes. Today case studies can include a much wider variety of materials. Because these materials can be downloaded over the network, there is no extra cost for printing multiple copies. Some of the materials you can use include these:

▶ Conventional business documents, such as reports, specifications, instruction manuals, memos, and letters

▶ Blueprints and drawings

▶ Spreadsheets of numerical data

▶ Charts and graphs

▶ Video or audio interviews

▶ Simulators of the actual system

▶ E-mail addresses of experts for learners to interview

Where possible, include live documents, such as word processing and spreadsheet files, that the learner can experiment with.

Require concise analysis

One of the best tests of whether someone understands something is asking him or her to summarize it in a new form. Some forms for the summary include:

▶ Press release

▶ Advertisement

▶ Poster

▶ Block diagram or organization chart

▶ Executive summary

▶ Book jacket and blurb

▶ Headline and first few paragraphs of a newspaper story

▶ Storyboard for a 60-second TV news spot

▶ 20-second sound bite

▶ Review or synopsis

Role-playing scenario

Children learn much adult behavior by playing at being an adult. Likewise, adults can learn much by playing the role of someone else.

In a role-playing scenario, the instructor states a goal and assigns learners roles in achieving that goal. Learners research their roles. They then collaborate via chat, conferencing, discussion, or multi-user domains to play out their roles to achieve the goal.

When to use role-playing scenarios

Role-playing is a valuable way to teach subtle, interpersonal skills and to reveal the hidden complexity of many human endeavors. Here are some common uses of role-playing activities:

▶ Force someone to view events from a different perspective. Give an environmental activist the role of a real-estate developer.

▶ Allow someone to experience events online that they would not experience in real life. For example, let a man experience sexual harassment as a woman.

▶ Demonstrate the many perspectives necessary for a complex undertaking. Have a management team guide a project from initial idea to successful product.

▶ Teach interpersonal skills. Hold a committee meeting to find an effective compromise among competing ideas, groups, and individuals.

How role-playing scenarios work

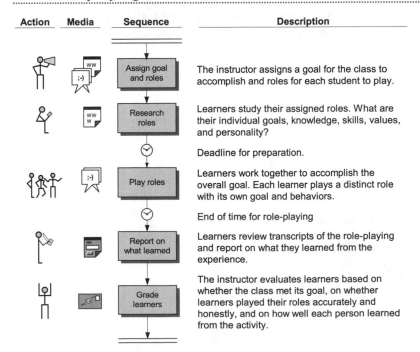

Action	Media	Sequence	Description
		Assign goal and roles	The instructor assigns a goal for the class to accomplish and roles for each student to play.
		Research roles	Learners study their assigned roles. What are their individual goals, knowledge, skills, values, and personality?
			Deadline for preparation.
		Play roles	Learners work together to accomplish the overall goal. Each learner plays a distinct role with its own goal and behaviors.
			End of time for role-playing
		Report on what learned	Learners review transcripts of the role-playing and report on what they learned from the experience.
		Grade learners	The instructor evaluates learners based on whether the class met its goal, on whether learners played their roles accurately and honestly, and on how well each person learned from the activity.

Example of a role-playing scenario

In the following example, participants simulate the meeting of the town Architectural Review Committee to consider proposed renovations to a home in a historic district.

 Clash of the Bureaucrats

A role-playing activity

Before any modifications can be made to the exterior of a home in the city's historic district, the Architectural Review Committee must review the plans and issue a Landmark Alteration Certificate. This certificate is required in order to obtain a building permit for the project.

The owner of this single-story residence within the historic district wishes to increase the living area of the home from 1350 sq. ft. to 2800 sq. ft. Due to various zoning restrictions regarding increasing the "footprint" of the existing residence, the only alternative is to build up, adding a second story and an attic. A meeting with the Review Committee to approve the homeowner's plan is scheduled.

The roles: Each student has been assigned one of the roles described below. (Check the Committee Meeting thread in the forum for the assignments and e-mail addresses of class members.)

Architectural Review Committee

Chairman—Appointed by the mayor. Main interest is in keeping the peace.

City Architect—University professor of architecture. Has no experience working in the real world.

City Attorney—A real hairsplitter. Main interest is the letter of the law.

City Historian—Authenticity, authenticity, authenticity. Wants all renovations to move the structure closer to its original state. Failing that, wants to ensure "sympathetic" alterations.

Homeowner's team

Architect—26 years old and just starting out. Really wants this commission and the recognition it will provide.

Contractor—Pragmatic. Knows that using historic construction techniques and restoration materials will be expensive. Wants the job but thinks homeowner will baulk at the additional expense involved in being "historically correct."

Homeowner—Has a growing family. Needs the space. Knows that his home is a good investment and any improvements will pay off in the long run. Wants to help maintain the character of the neighborhood—within reason. Funds are limited.

Interested parties

Eastside neighbors—Concerned that a second story will block their view of the mountains.

	Westside neighbors—Believe any renovations will add to their property's worth. You have a week to research your role and prepare arguments and collateral material for the "Architectural Review Committee" meetings.
Reference material	Use the following material to help prepare for the meeting: ■ <u>Map</u> of the historic neighborhood ■ Renovation <u>guidelines</u> by the Landmark Alteration Committee ■ Architectural <u>rendering</u> of the street-side elevation ■ Gallery of <u>photographs</u> of the other homes on the block ■ Gallery of 1875 to 1914 <u>photographs</u> of the neighborhood ■ <u>Sun-study</u> of the eastside neighbor's property
Deliverables and deadlines	Complete researching roles by Monday, **July 17, 2000**. Review committee posts its evaluation of the proposed renovation by Thursday, **July 20, 2000**. [Should be posted as one response to the Committee Meeting thread in the <u>forum</u>. Committee members will need to correspond via the thread to arrive at a consensus.] The homeowner's team and the Interested Parties should post their responses by Monday, **July 24, 2000**. [The responses should be posted to the Committee Meeting thread in the <u>forum</u>. Homeowner's team will need to correspond via the thread to arrive at a consensus. Same with the Interested Parties] If there is still disagreement among the participants, the Review committee must post its final decision by Wednesday, **July 26, 2000**. The homeowner's team, working with the Interested Parties, will post its final decision whether to go ahead with the renovation by Friday, **July 28, 2000**. All students should review the entire Committee Meeting thread in the <u>forum</u> and submit a report [Word 97 attachment to the <u>instructor</u>] on what this exercise taught you about collaboration and compromise by Monday, **July 31, 2000**. List guidelines you could use in a similar situation.
Required?	Yes.
Graded?	Yes. Students will be evaluated based on whether: ■ The class, as a whole, met the goal. ■ Each student participated fully and honestly.
Questions?	Contact the <u>instructor</u>.

Variations of role-playing scenarios

Role-playing scenarios can be used to mimic all the different situations that bring individuals into contact and possibly conflict. Here are some forms that make good learning activities:

Behavior critique. To teach learners the correct behavior for a particular situation, model and critique bad behavior. Assign someone the role of demonstrating inappropriate behavior. Assign the rest of the class the role of reacting to the bad behavior.

Court trial. Put a concept, historical figure, or organization on trial. Assign roles of judge, accused, prosecutor, defense attorney, witnesses, and jury.

Board meeting. Simulate a meeting of the board of directors of a corporation, university, hospital, or other organization. Assign each participant specific goals, attitudes, and personality. Spell out known and secret relationships among those at the meeting. Give the meeting an agenda and a time limit.

Murder mystery. To teach investigative skills of any kind, have learners play roles in a murder investigation. Each member receives a role. For each role there are publicly known facts that everyone has access to and privately known facts that only the role-player knows. Role-players can be asked or tricked into revealing these hidden facts. Each role-player also has secret motivations. Role-players are either suspects or investigators. Investigators must solve the mystery by interviewing the suspects, examining artifacts, and exchanging notes.

If a murder mystery does not fit your situation, substitute one of these investigations:

▶ Finding hidden treasure

▶ Learning the cause of an airplane crash

▶ Discovering the cure for a disease

▶ Locating a missing person

Who am I? Each learner picks and researches a different well-known person from the field of study. Learners then write a speech from this person's viewpoint and in this person's style. Learners post their speeches to a discussion group. Learners comment on each other's speeches. Comments are from the perspective of the person being impersonated. Learners defend the positions taken by their characters. At the end, each learner must guess the identity of the other impersonated characters.

Tips and guidelines for role-playing scenarios

Introduce the scenario fully. Spell out the details of the scenario. What is the general situation and what problem does it pose for the learner? What role must the learner play? For each role, what are the motivations and behaviors? How is success defined and how will the activity be scored?

Assign roles carefully. Emphasize positive, creative roles rather than negative, critical roles. Be especially careful whom you assign to power positions, such as Manager, Judge, and Critic. Consider the personality of learners. Do they have the right mix of humility and assertiveness? Can they handle the power? Are their social skills adequate?

Assign roles related to the subject

In team assignments give learners roles that relate to the subject or metaphor of the assignment. For example, an activity involving estate planning might have the following roles:

The deceased	(As a ghost) Comments on how well the proceedings accomplish the goals of the Will.
Executor	Tries to carry out the Will of the deceased while paying as little in taxes as possible.
Estate attorney	Represents the legal interests of the estate.
Property appraiser	Establishes a value of the property bequeathed by the deceased.
Tax agent	Must approve the proposed estate tax return or else settle the dispute in court.
Estate accountant	Prepares the estate-tax return.
Tax court judge	Rules if the executor and tax agent do not agree on the amount of taxes due.
Banker	Holds the cash, securities, mortgages, and deeds that make up the bulk of the value of the estate.

Otherwise use generic roles

If you cannot use roles associated with the subject of the activity, you can always use some of these generic roles. These are all roles that learners should find familiar.

Presenter	Initially offers content. May present material developed by a team.
Journalist	At end of the activity and phases of it, writes a brief recap. Writes an interesting summary for the outside world.
Researcher	Tracks down facts. Resolves factual disputes.
Judge	Rules on the relevance and appropriateness of material.
Editor	Edits, enhances, polishes the work of others.
Brainstormer	Suggests new ideas and new areas for research.
Devil's advocate	Argues unpopular positions and ones not suggested by the evidence. Asks questions that the external audience might ask.
Annotator	Adds secondary and meta information.
Mediator	Helps resolve disputes before appeal to Judge.

Critic	Evaluates in an unbiased and positive way the work of others.
Lawyer	Identifies and comments on legal issues raised by activities.
Censor	Points out issues that may unnecessarily offend some in the audience.
Manager	Coordinates the activities of all other participants in a team activity. Sequences activities and reminds others of commitments.
Moderator	Controls who speaks when in chat sessions and debates. Reminds team of original intent whenever the discussion strays.

Have learners use their role name in messages

For class activities, have participants in chats and discussion groups post their messages using the name of their role (Instructor, Tech Support, Juror 4) rather than their personal name.

Kick off action in role-playing activities

In role-playing activities, it is not unusual to wait for minutes or hours for action to begin because everyone is waiting for someone else to take the lead. In a new environment like a computer-mediated game, people may hesitate to take action. To overcome this reluctance, start the game with a specific trigger event that requires a response from a specific character.

Group critique

Often people learn more from the comments of their peers than from the lectures of instructors. Group critiques have learners help other learners to refine their work. Group-critique activities take advantage of discussion groups to help learners learn from other learners. In the simplest form of group critique, a learner prepares an individual answer to a question, posts it for other to critique, and then revises it before submitting the final version.

When to use group critiques

Group critiques teach learners to give and accept criticism. Use group critiques to:

▶ Teach learners to refine their work by incorporating the ideas of others.

▶ Condition learners to accept and filter the criticism of their peers.

▶ Teach learners to offer helpful criticism.

▶ Offload from the instructor much of the work of evaluating and critiquing learners.

How group critiques work

Learners research and write answers to questions posed by the instructor. They then post their answers to a discussion group where other learners critique the answers. Learners can revise their answers any time before the deadline, after which the instructor grades their answers.

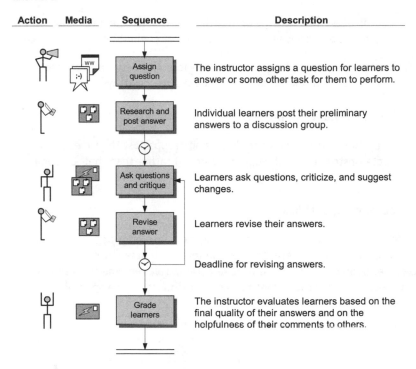

Action	Media	Sequence	Description
		Assign question	The instructor assigns a question for learners to answer or some other task for them to perform.
		Research and post answer	Individual learners post their preliminary answers to a discussion group.
		Ask questions and critique	Learners ask questions, criticize, and suggest changes.
		Revise answer	Learners revise their answers.
			Deadline for revising answers.
		Grade learners	The instructor evaluates learners based on the final quality of their answers and on the helpfulness of their comments to others.

Example of a group critique

This example shows the assignment for a group critique activity. Learners are asked to select their best picture, submit it to the discussion group, view the photographs of other learners, critique these photographs, and finally to submit a better version of their original photograph.

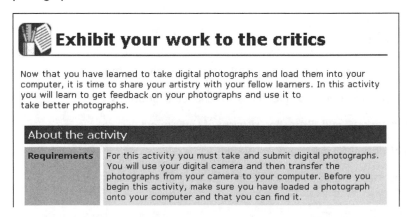

Exhibit your work to the critics

Now that you have learned to take digital photographs and load them into your computer, it is time to share your artistry with your fellow learners. In this activity you will learn to get feedback on your photographs and use it to take better photographs.

About the activity

Requirements	For this activity you must take and submit digital photographs. You will use your digital camera and then transfer the photographs from your camera to your computer. Before you begin this activity, make sure you have loaded a photograph onto your computer and that you can find it.

Useful information	For this activity you will want to pick your best photograph. For some help deciding which to submit, consult one of these guides from Kodak: <u>Guide to Better Pictures</u> and <u>Remedies for Problem Pictures</u>.
What you must do	1. **Pick one of your best digital photographs**. Your photograph must be in JPEG (.jpg) format and no larger than one megabyte. It should show a scene or objects other learners will recognize. 2. **Submit the photograph**. To submit the photograph, fill in the form at the bottom of this page. Specify the photograph as an attachment. To do so, find the field called "File containing the photograph:," click on the Browse button, and locate the file containing the photograph. Then click the Submit button. 3. **Critique the photographs of others**. You will find the photographs in the <u>discussion</u> group under the thread "Photographs to critique." In commenting on the photographs of others play the role of an upbeat art critic who emphasizes the positive aspects of the work. 4. **Take a better photograph**. Read the critiques of your photograph. Then go out and take a better photograph and submit it. Only your last-submitted photograph will be graded.
Rules	You are responsible for taking, loading, and submitting the photograph on time and for accessing the discussion group. Your photograph must be an original photograph that you took with your digital camera. At any time during the process, you can submit a better photograph. Only your last submission will be graded.
Grading criteria	This activity is **required** and **graded**. This activity will count for 5% of your final grade. Your grade on this activity will depend equally on the quality of your photograph (only the last one you submitted) and on your comments about the photographs of others. Both will be evaluated by the instructor, whose judgment is final.
Tip	Print out these instructions so you can refer to them as you fill in the form.

To submit your photograph

Your name:	
Photograph title:	
Why did you take the photograph?	
File containing the photograph:	Browse...
Send the file:	Submit Reset

Variations of group critiques

You can vary the basic group critique by changing how the critique is performed, what is critiqued, and what kinds of comments are solicited:

Use revision features of word processor

If the whole class uses the same word processing program, you can have learners prepare a detailed, precisely formatted document in the word processor. Learners can use the revision features of the word processor to insert their comments into the body of the document.

Serial review

As an alternative to posting the answer to a discussion group where all other learners can critique it at once, you may route the document through learners in sequence so each sees the comments of the previous reviewers. Imagine the class sitting around a circular table. Learners start by passing their own document to the learner on their right. When a learner finishes reviewing a document, he or she passes it to learner on the right. Eventually, each document passes all the way around the table and comes back to its author.

This approach cuts down on duplicated comments because each reviewer sees the comments of those who saw the document earlier. However, reviewers do not see the comments of later reviewers. Also, the process can slow significantly if some reviewers are late.

Critique a specification

Many decisions are complex, involving tens or even hundreds of interconnected choices. Because the individual choices are related, judgment, compromise, and balance are required to render the best decision. To let learners practice such complex decisions, give them a form to fill in. On the form require them to specify all the interconnected choices of the complex decision.

Criticism comes easier than craftsmanship.

— Zeuxis, 400 B. C.

Specify typography

Send in your ideas for review

Part of the planning of an electronic document is deciding what typeface, size and color to use for the different kinds of text. This kind of planning is important to ensure consistency throughout a project.

Background color: FFFFFF
(Use hexadecimal numbers)

Font families: Verdana, Arial, Helvetica
(Specify all)

	Size (pts)	Color	Style		
Title (at top of topic)	18	003366	☑ Bold	☐ Italic	☐ Underline
Body text	10	000000	☐ Bold	☐ Italic	☐ Underline
2nd Level Heading	14	336699	☑ Bold	☐ Italic	☐ Underline
3rd Level Heading	13	666666	☑ Bold	☐ Italic	☐ Underline
List Items	10	000000	☐ Bold	☐ Italic	☐ Underline

Submit   Reset

This example of a group critique has learners specify the typography of a Web page.

The Web form provides a checklist of choices and makes relationships among these choices visible. It can control the amount of guidance given the learner.

Tips and guidelines for group critiques

The value of group critiques depends on the quality of the comments offered by the group. For best results, guide participants in offering practical, encouraging comments.

Monitor and moderate critiques

The instructor should monitor and moderate the critiquing. Be prepared to jump in if the comments degenerate into personal attacks. Remind reviewers that part of their grade depends on the helpfulness of their comments.

Offer helpful comments

The instructor can promote helpful comments by offering some as an example. If learners seem reluctant to criticize the work of others, the instructor can start the process and establish a pattern of helpful comments.

Specify criteria for self- and peer-critiques

Provide objective criteria for critics to use. Focus the critique on the work, not the person who created it. Make clear that personal criticisms are not helpful. You may want to go so far as to provide a form to structure the critique.

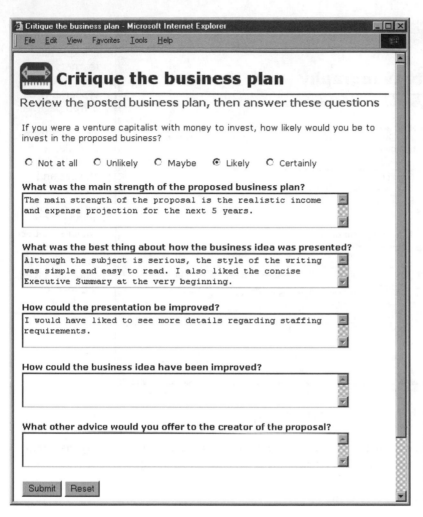

Here is the form eliciting a critique of a business plan.

This example uses a custom Active Server Pages script and component on the server to format the form's contents and e-mail it to the instructor.

Virtual laboratory

A virtual laboratory provides an on-screen simulator or calculator that learners can use to test ideas and observe results.

When to use virtual laboratories

In a virtual laboratory, learners can try all kinds of experiments without risk of damaging equipment or injuring themselves, fellow learners, or lab technicians. They can also conduct experiments not possible in even the most generously funded real laboratory. Use virtual laboratories:

▶ **To prepare learners to use real laboratories**. Virtual laboratories prepare learners for efficient work in real labs [98]. Virtual labs can start as simple, limited representations of the real lab. As learners master simple experiments, the lab can reveal more controls and variables so that in the end the virtual lab has the same richness and range of experimentation as the real laboratory.

▶ **Instead of real laboratories**. You can also use virtual laboratories to replace real laboratories. Once built, virtual laboratories have no additional costs for supplies, maintenance of equipment, or replacement of broken parts. Learners do not have to drive (or fly?) to the laboratory. Virtual laboratories are never crowded, never closed, and never broken. They never blow up.

▶ **For abstract experiments**. Virtual laboratories are not limited to simulating real laboratories. With a virtual laboratory, learners can swap the orbits of planets, tinker with the global economy, or create a hybrid of a peanut and a panda. Use virtual laboratories to let learners experiment with concepts of any scale and any level of abstraction.

▶ **To discover principles**. Virtual laboratories guide learners to discover principles, trends, and relationships for themselves. Many learners give more credibility to concepts they discover for themselves and tend to remember them longer.

How virtual laboratories work

The learner gets the assignment, learns to operate the laboratory equipment, and then embarks on a series of experiments, carefully recording the results of each. After the last experiment, the learner generalizes what he or she has learned.

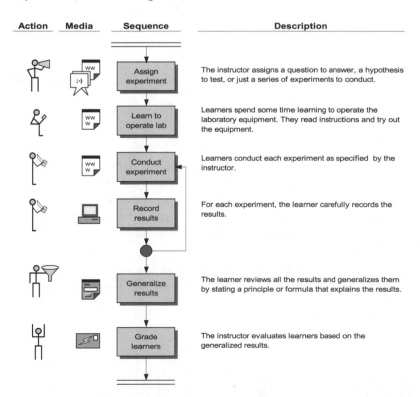

Example of a virtual laboratory

In this example, mechanical designers conduct experiments to learn how heat flows through a surface. This activity appears early in the lesson to get learners thinking about all the factors (area, temperature, and thermal conductivity) and how they are related.

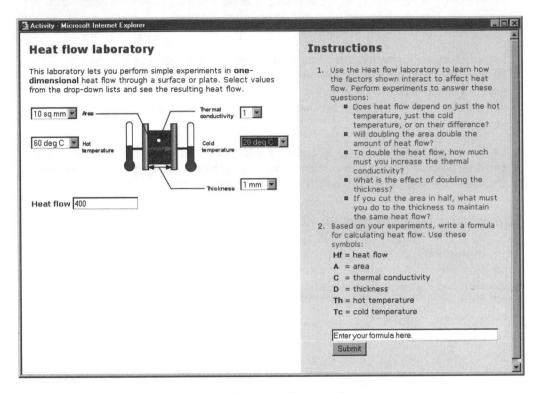

Notice how the instructions remain visible during the experiments.

> Argument is conclusive … but … it does not remove doubt, so that the mind may rest in the sure knowledge of the truth, unless it finds it by the method of experiment. … For if any man who never saw fire proved by satisfactory arguments that fire burns … his hearer's mind would never be satisfied, nor would he avoid the fire until he put his hand in it … that he might learn by experiment what argument taught.
>
> — Roger Bacon, *Opus Maius*

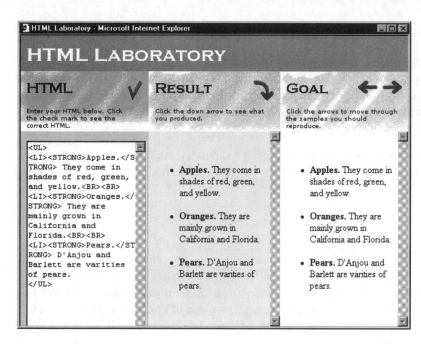

Here is another virtual laboratory used to teach HTML. It consists of three panels. On the right is a goal. The arrows in the upper-right let the learner advance through a series of progressively more challenging goals. In the left column is a text-entry area where the learner can type in the HTML necessary to create the goal. Clicking the downward curving arrow over the center panel processes the learner's HTML and shows what it produces. The learner can compare the result to the goal and adjust accordingly. Learners, who are stumped, can click the check mark above the HTML area to see the solution for the currently displayed goal.

Variations of virtual laboratories

To get the most from a virtual laboratory activity, you can vary how the laboratory operates and how it is used to test the learner's hypotheses.

Virtual laboratories can simulate results produced under various conditions. For instance, allow learners to alter settings to see the effects of:

▶ Different magnifications of a microscope or telescope

▶ Different wavelengths of light or color filters

▶ Eyesight of different species

▶ Different film-speeds, focal lengths, f/stops, and shutter speeds in a camera

Have learners state their perceptions or beliefs. Then have them conduct an experiment to learn how their ideas compare to reality.

Tips and guidelines for virtual laboratories

Focus your efforts on what you are teaching. Do not let operating laboratory equipment get in the way of learning. If the purpose of the activity is to teach someone to use real laboratory equipment, then make the simulation richly detailed. If the purpose is to teach concepts that the experiments can reveal, simplify the laboratory equipment so attention flows to the pattern revealed in the results.

Use the laboratory in multiple courses. Developing a simulated laboratory is a lot of work. Consider whether you can use the same laboratory in multiple activities or even in multiple courses.

Hands-on activity

Hands-on activities give learners real work to perform. In a hands-on activity the learner completes a task outside the lesson, such as performing a calculation with an on-screen calculator, designing something on paper, or operating a piece of machinery. The hands-on activity guides learners through the real-life task, provides feedback on their success, and may test what they learned.

When to use hands-on activities

Use hands-on activities to teach hands-on tasks. Hands-on activities give learners a chance to practice what they are learning. They are powerful stimuli for learning practical skills.

Hands-on activities, though not especially effective in teaching abstract knowledge, can provide a pleasant descent from the stratospheric heights of conceptual thought common in such courses.

How hands-on activities work

The instructor assigns a task and gives detailed instructions. The learner performs the procedure, checking each step as performed. After a review of the procedure, the learner repeatedly performs the task on his or her own.

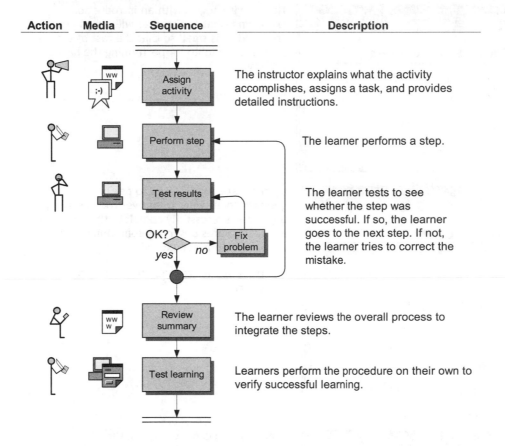

Action	Media	Sequence	Description
		Assign activity	The instructor explains what the activity accomplishes, assigns a task, and provides detailed instructions.
		Perform step	The learner performs a step.
		Test results / OK? yes / no Fix problem	The learner tests to see whether the step was successful. If so, the learner goes to the next step. If not, the learner tries to correct the mistake.
		Review summary	The learner reviews the overall process to integrate the steps.
		Test learning	Learners perform the procedure on their own to verify successful learning.

Example of a hands-on activity

The following example teaches use of the Windows system calculator to convert decimal numbers to their hexadecimal and octal equivalents.

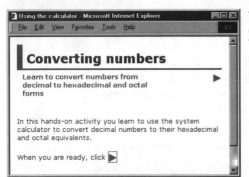

The activity begins with an introduction explaining what the learner will accomplish. The window is small so that the rest of the screen is available for performing the hands-on activity.

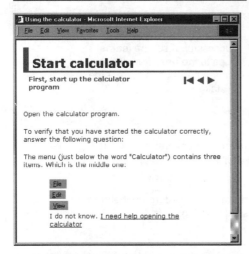

Learners are given a step to perform and a question to answer. To answer the question, they must successfully complete the step. The answer requires observing something not visible until the step is completed.

A correct answer reveals the next step in the procedure.

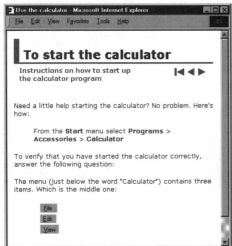

Learners who cannot perform the step successfully can click "I need help opening the calculator" to get more detailed instructions.

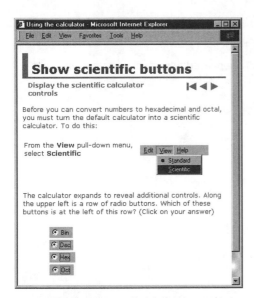

If learners make a mistake, they receive help getting back on track. For example, learners who click on **Dec** rather than the correct answer **Hex**, see the next page.

Here, learners have three choices: to try again, to go back a step, or to start from the beginning.

For simple steps, where errors occur almost exclusively from inattention and carelessness, let learners go back and try again.

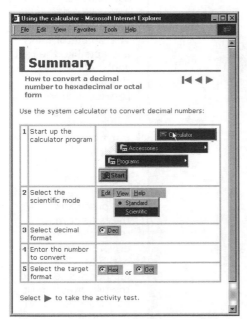

After completing the activity, learners see a summary. It serves as a review as well as a job aid.

Suggest saving, bookmarking, or printing the summary. Make sure the summary is compact enough to print to a single page of paper. Or provide a button to jump to a special printable version.

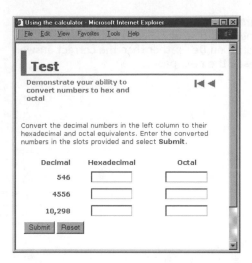

Finally, learners test their ability to perform the procedure on their own.

Require repeated applications to confirm and lock in the skills.

Variations of hands-on activities

If operating an actual system is too dangerous or daunting to the learner, provide a simulator that mimics the look and feel of the real system.

The following is an example of a simulator of the control panel for defining connections between the operating system and various databases.

This simulator lets learners practice setting up connections without any risk of damaging data or the system. The simulator looks and acts like the real control panel—except the simulator restricts learners to the task being taught and provides instructions if needed.

Here the simulator is near the beginning of the procedure. Here the learner must select the correct driver for the database. The learner has selected the driver and must now click on **Finish** to continue.

Simulators are not limited to computer activities. A simulator could mimic the reactions of other members of a team in a project-planning lesson or play the role of a customer in a sales simulation.

Tips and guidelines for hands-on activities

Print out instructions. If people must perform the activity away from the computer, let them print out the instructions and any other materials they may need. If they must record data, give them a paper form on which to write the data.

Submit snapshot. One way to monitor learning of computer skills is to require the learner to perform an activity and to e-mail a screen snapshot of the resulting screen. The learner can likewise submit a digital photograph of the result of any hands-on activity that produces visible results.

Use gatekeeper observations. To control advancement to the next step, use questions about things the learner can only observe by successfully performing the current step. Such questions can focus attention on those parts of the scene that will be important in the next step.

Learning game

Learning games let people learn by playing. Learning games are computer simulations that allow learners to practice a highly interactive task. They provide a model of a real-world system. By repeatedly playing the game, the learner spots and infers principles.

When to use learning games

Use learning games to let learners gain experience performing an activity without the risk or cost of the real activity.

▶ **The real activity takes too long.** Example: making genetic modifications to plants

▶ **The real activity is too dangerous.** Example: operating a nuclear power plant

▶ **Training on real systems is too expensive.** Example: learning to fly the Space Shuttle

▶ **Failures are expensive.** Example: investing in crop futures

▶ **Failures are embarrassing.** Example: triggering a false alarm in a security system that may summon the police

▶ **The subject is too boring.** Example: planning meals using government nutritional data (p 256)

Learning games are expensive and time-consuming to develop—typically 100 times the cost of a simple multiple-choice text question. Often they are worth the expense, but not always.

How learning games work

In learning games, learners act to achieve a goal. Games begin with instruction on the goal and basic rules of the game. Learners are then given the goal and put into a situation. To achieve the goal, learners must repeatedly react to change the situation.

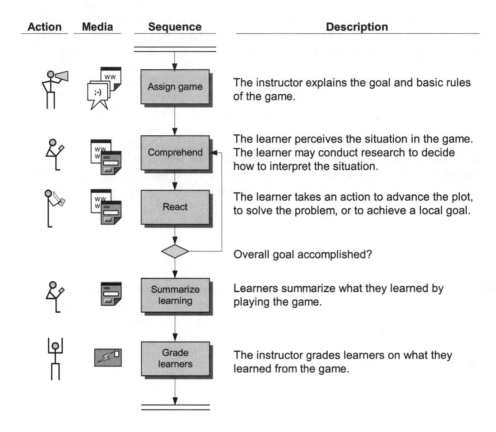

Action	Media	Sequence	Description
		Assign game	The instructor explains the goal and basic rules of the game.
		Comprehend	The learner perceives the situation in the game. The learner may conduct research to decide how to interpret the situation.
		React	The learner takes an action to advance the plot, to solve the problem, or to achieve a local goal.
			Overall goal accomplished?
		Summarize learning	Learners summarize what they learned by playing the game.
		Grade learners	The instructor grades learners on what they learned from the game.

We learn geology the morning after the earthquake.

— Ralph Waldo Emerson

Example of a learning game

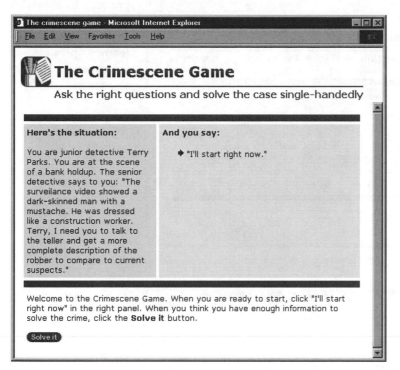

This game teaches interviewing skills in the context of a police investigation. Learners are assigned the task of interviewing a witness to a bank robbery to elicit clues to the identity of the robber.

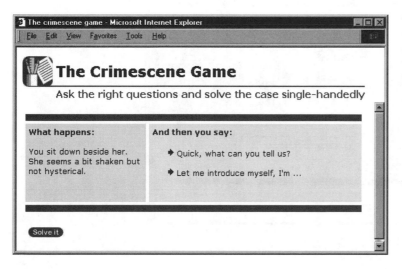

The game provides the learner with choices that affect the course of the game.

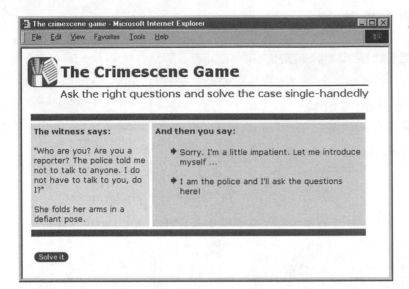

Most feedback is provided by events in the game. Events reveal whether the learner's previous action was appropriate.

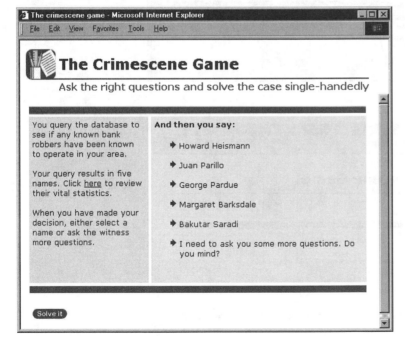

At any point learners can try to solve the mystery.

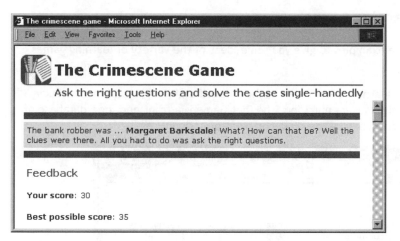

Learners receive a score based on the efficiency with which they solved the mystery.

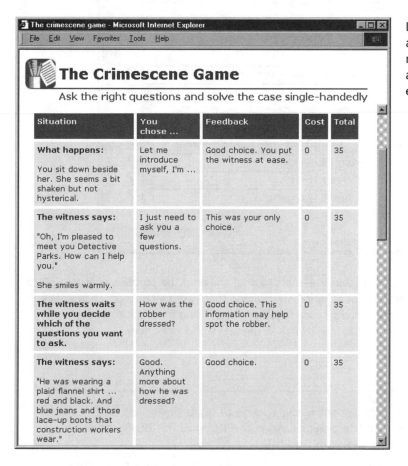

Learners also receive a critique that recaps their actions and comments on each of the actions.

Variations of learning games

Here are a couple more examples to give you some ideas of the variety of learning games you can use in WBT.

In the following game, learners order meals to meet specific dietary requirements. They then see how their choices affect nutrition. The Diet Game is a front end for a database of nutrition information published by the US Department of Agriculture.

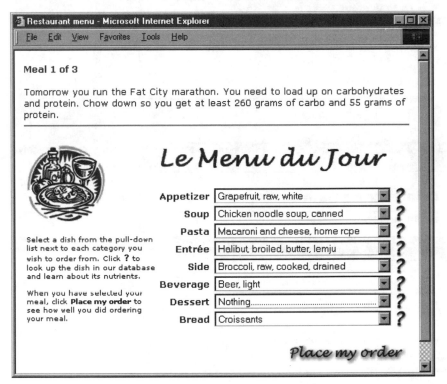

The following jigsaw puzzle requires learners to drag and drop the puzzle pieces into place to configure a network. It is not as simple as it looks. There are more pieces than slots and only compatible components can be used together. There is no fixed solution: any combination of components that would work in the real world work here.

> It is the child in man that is the source of his uniqueness and creativeness, and the playground is the optimal milieu for the unfolding of his capacities and talents.
>
> — Eric Hoffer, *Reflections on the Human Condition*

Though this example used a Macromedia Director Shockwave movie, it could have been implemented in JavaScript and Dynamic HTML within a version 4.0 browser.

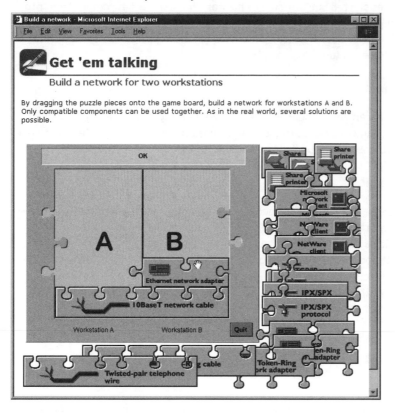

Tips and guidelines for learning games

Explain the game clearly

Explain the goal clearly. Make clear any limitations, such as the amount of time available. Learners may reject any game that imposes arbitrary or unfair rules. And it is learners who decide which rules are unfair.

Emphasize learning, not just acting

▶ Simulate the thought-processes, not just the physical actions. Avoid games that measure only how quickly and accurately the learner can move the mouse, unless that is the skill you are teaching.

▶ Require the learner to make the same kinds of decisions as in the real activity.

▶ Avoid arbitrary limitations on how the learner accomplishes the goal. If there are three ways to do the task in the real world, allow three ways in the simulation.

Challenge learners

Make the game easy to get started but difficult to master. You can design competition into the game so players compete against one another. Or challenge learners to top the best scores of others or their earlier best efforts. As learners get more skill at the game, limit how long they can take for each turn.

Manage competitiveness

Excessive competitiveness can get in the way of effective learning. If learners are highly competitive anyway, the game may not produce the desired outcome. Do your learners need to learn to compete or to cooperate? Design the game accordingly.

Provide meaningful exhibits

To make games more realistic and exciting, incorporate objects from the world of the game. For example: business reports, memos, and e-mail messages, technical manuals and industry standards, company policies and procedures, meeting minutes, and other sources. Where possible, just link to real documents available on the network. Such exhibits provide a low-bandwidth alternative to video and sound. Or, for greater realism, make these exhibits available to learners only after they have taken actions that would make them available in the real world—such as asking for them.

CONVERT CLASSROOM ACTIVITIES

If you have activities that work in the classroom, do not assume they will work as well in the virtual classroom. Instructional designers have learned some hard lessons about dumping classroom courses online. They have also discovered new ways of implementing proven teaching methods. Let's look at how the Web changes what we can do in activities.

What WBT adds to regular classroom activities

What does the Web add to the resources available for classroom activities?

▶ **Source of materials**. The Web contains rich lodes of case studies, papers, examples, and tools. Although their quality may vary and some of them may change or disappear, these resources represent a super cyber-library.

▶ **Communication within the class**. The Internet enables communication among class members scattered over 24 time zones. E-mail, chat, audio- and videoconferencing, discussion groups, and other collaboration tools mean that learners and instructors need not be in the same room or even the same hemisphere to stay in touch.

▶ **Electronic transport**. With the Web, materials can be transmitted electronically rather than transported physically. Learners can download materials as needed. Instructors do not have to make photocopies and hand them out in class. The same goes for assignments. Learners can e-mail or post their work rather than having to drive to class or the instructor's office.

▶ **More media.** Instructors and learners are not limited to text and simple graphics in handouts and submissions. They can use hypertext links to point to related material, multimedia to explain more fully, and interactivity to add interest.

▶ **Automated grading.** Using client- or server-side scripts, designers can automate much of the grading of activities. Learners get immediate feedback. Instructors get more time for other activities.

▶ **Less tedium.** Activities can use on-screen tools for analyzing, calculating, charting, and presenting data. Much of the unproductive work of performing activities is eliminated or at least streamlined.

What WBT subtracts from classroom activities

Some actions are not as easy in WBT as in classroom courses. In conventional WBT, it is difficult to:

▶ **Monitor learners' emotions.** Instructors cannot look learners in the eye. The honesty and mental state of learners are hard to monitor.

▶ **React to body language**, gestures, facial expressions, or tone of voice. Such nonverbal expressions are crucial in teaching subjects like acting, sales skills, motivational speaking, and in dealing face-to-face with angry customers.

▶ **Exercise teamwork** with rapid exchange among team members. The inevitable delays squash spontaneity and slow the pace of team activities.

▶ **Establish the authority of the instructor**. Without face-to-face contact, many learners rely more on themselves and other learners and less on the instructor.

How to convert classroom activities to WBT activities

Here is a checklist of changes to make when converting successful classroom activities for use in WBT.

Write complete, clear instructions. In classroom activities it is easy to ask the instructor to clarify a point. It is not so easy in WBT.

Replace library readings with Web readings. Find equivalent materials on the Web and link to them. Or post them yourself.

Automatically grade simple activities. Learners love the immediate, anonymous feedback. Instructors love not having to grade routine activities.

Use the Web to distribute and collect assignments. To hand out assignments, post them to the server and announce their availability. Have learners submit assignments by e-mail. Or have learners complete assignments by filling in a form whose contents are then e-mailed to the instructor, posted to a special incoming-homework forum, or written into a database. (See page 488 for an example.)

Allow more time for collaborative activities. If learners are new to Web collaboration, first attempts at teamwork will take twice as long as in a classroom setting.

Can the talking head. Convert the non-interactive portions of lectures to presentation sequences that the learner can take at any time (p 199).

Replace face-to-face with electronic collaboration. Reengineer the interactive portions of lectures—say the question-and-answer periods—as Web equivalents. You can schedule weekly electronic class meetings via videoconferencing (p 364) or by chat (p 354). Or you can channel routine interactions through discussion groups (p 348).

Empower learners. Encourage learners to rely more on themselves and on each other and less on the instructor. Make activities as self-sufficient as possible. Design complex tasks as team activities.

Let learners print out lengthy readings. If extensive reading is required, let learners download and print out properly formatted copies of paper documents.

Desynchronize where practical. Since learners in twelve time zones will find it difficult to schedule synchronous meetings (p 55), redesign activities so they can be done asynchronously. Rely more on discussion groups (p 348) and less on chat (p 354) and videoconferencing (p 364).

Activate Web forms. Use Web forms rather than paper forms to structure exercises. Use the interactivity of Web forms to warn of missing information or careless mistakes.

MAKE YOUR ACTIVITIES WORK BETTER

Two instructional designers each create an activity to teach a concept. In both activities the learners perform the same actions. Yet one activity works much better than another. Why? Often the success of an activity depends on more than what actions are assigned to learners. It also depends on how the activity is designed—that is, how clearly it is organized, how it is presented to learners, how their actions are guided, what external resources are used, and how the instructor's workload is managed.

Select appropriate activities

Successful activities precisely target learners and what they need to learn. Before you begin designing an activity, make sure you can answer these questions:

▶ What is the purpose? What exactly are learners to learn? Which learners? All or just a specific group?

▶ How long will learners require to complete the activity?

▶ How open-ended should the response be? Do learners need the scaffolding of a form with specific slots with clear labels? Or should they be left to organize the response themselves?

▶ How will the submissions be evaluated?

▶ Will the responses of one learner be available to others? Only after all are submitted? Or posted as received, awarding bonus points for early postings?

Provide complete, clear instructions

One of the most common complaints of learners is "I didn't understand what I was supposed to do. The instructions were not clear." One of the most common complaints of instructors is, "I spend too much time answering student's questions about how to do an activity."

Here is a checklist and running example for what to include in the instructions for an activity. The example is from the instructions of the group critique example (p 238).

Example

Now that you have learned to take digital photographs and load them into your computer, it is time to share your artistry with your fellow learners.

In this activity you will learn to get feedback on your photographs and use it to take better photographs.

Requirements

Before you begin this activity, make sure you have loaded a photograph onto your computer and that you can find the file.

Checklist

✓ **Put the activity in context**

In activities, point out how the activity fits within the course:

▶ What will you learn, practice, or be tested on?

▶ How is this activity related to other material? Does it depend on, extend, or illustrate the material?

Is this activity related to other activities? Does it complete or continue work begun in an earlier activity?

✓ **List requirements**

At the start of the activity, list everything the activity requires:

▶ Knowledge

▶ Tools

▶ Computer programs

▶ Sample data

Useful information

For this activity you will want to pick your best photograph. For help deciding which to submit, consult one of these guides from Kodak: Guide to Better Pictures and Remedies for Problem Pictures.

1. Pick one of your best digital photographs. Your photograph must be in JPEG (.jpg) format and no larger than 1 megabyte. It should show a scene or objects other learners will recognize.

2. Submit the photograph. To submit the photograph, fill in the form at the bottom of the page. Specify the photograph as an attachment. To do so, find the **Photograph** field, click on the **Browse** button, and find the file containing the photograph. Then click the **Submit** button.

Deadlines

Photographs must be received by: **3 March 2000**, Noon, Eastern Standard Time (17.00 UTC).

Comments can be made until **20 March 2000**, Noon, Eastern Standard Time (17.00 UTC).

You can also submit a replacement photograph at any time up to the second deadline.

✓ **Mention sources of information**

If the activity requires reading or viewing outside information, tell learners how to find this information.

In scenarios, start by telling the learner his or her role. Then describe the goal and the challenge to overcome.

✓ **Tell learners what they must create**

Tell learners exactly what they must do to complete an activity. Specify the content and format of submissions. Name a specific file format or target browser. If precise specifications are not possible, provide examples of acceptable instances along with comments on their strengths and weaknesses.

✓ **Tell learners how to submit work**

Provide complete instructions for submitting an exercise or activity.

Tell users how to interact with the activity. Do they click, tab, type, or enter?

Remind learners that they can paste answers into text-entry fields.

✓ **Flag the due date**

Post the due date in a prominent location formatted conspicuously.

Specify the time and time zone, too. Otherwise you will have excuses like, "Well, it was still the 20th in Hawaii."

Tell learners how much time to spend on an activity lacking a clear stopping point.

Rules

Your photograph must be an original photograph that you took with your digital camera.

At any time during the process, you can submit a better photograph. Only your last submission will be graded.

In commenting on the photographs of others, play the role of an upbeat art critic who emphasizes the positive aspects of the work.

Grading criteria

This activity is **required** and will count for 5% of your final grade.

Your grade on this activity will depend equally on the quality of your photograph (only the last one you submitted) and on your comments on the photographs of others. Both will be evaluated by the instructor, whose judgment is final.

Tip: Print out these instructions so you can refer to them as you fill in the form.

✓ Spell out the rules

Spell out any requirements on how the work is to be done:

▶ Individually, in teams, or as a class.

▶ Can submitted work be revised or replaced?

▶ Types of comments in collaboration.

▶ Roles the learner is to play.

✓ Specify grading criteria

Spell out how activities are graded. Who will grade the activity? What will affect grading and what will not:

▶ Spelling

▶ Formatting

▶ Citations

▶ Following specific formats

▶ Completeness

▶ Numerical accuracy

✓ Encourage printing out instructions

Encourage learners to print out instructions for activities if:

▶ Instructions are complex, long, or involve many steps.

▶ The activity involves interacting with the screen.

Simplify activities

The simpler an activity, the more time learners spend learning and the less time they spend figuring out how to perform the activity. Simplify the parts of the activity that are simple in real life. Focus learners' efforts on the hard real-life decisions built into the activity.

Keep instructions visible

If an activity is complex, leave the instructions displayed throughout. Position instructions so they do not scroll off the screen as the learner performs the activity. If the instructions for an assignment are complex or involve interacting with the screen, format them for paper and encourage learners to print them out.

Make finding resources easy

Unless you are teaching learners to find resources, make resources easy to find. Otherwise learners may spend too much time searching for information and too little time learning from it. Here are some ways to help learners locate materials, arranged from least challenging to most challenging for the learner:

▶ Provide the data for learners. Prune and organize it so that the needed information is easy to extract.

▶ Link to a source that features the needed information. Give learners words they can use to search for the needed content.

▶ Link to an intranet or Web site on which learners find the information themselves.

▶ Link to multiple sources that together provide all the needed information.

▶ Specify a search service and keywords to conduct a search for pages that may contain the information. "Search Yahoo! for 'cabinetmaking tools.'" You can simplify the mechanics by linking to the search service or even triggering the search directly from a link.

▶ Suggest a general search strategy. "Use an Internet search engine to find information on programming add-ins for Word 2000."

> Everything should be made as simple as possible, but not simpler...
> — Albert Einstein

Make downloading materials easy

Simplify the procedure for downloading materials and tools. Do not require a learner to download a sample, download its viewer, download a separate program to decompress the other downloads, learn to operate the decompression program, decompress the downloaded medium and viewer, learn to operate the viewer, view the medium, and them delete all the files when they are through.

Let learners download sample data

If an activity requires sample data or other special files, provide a button or link to download them.

ACTIVITY

To practice formatting a table of contents, you can create your own document with a complete set of headings. Or you can download a <u>sample document</u> (ToCSample.doc, 97K) with a complete set of headings and a table of contents already in place. Just click on the link and specify where you want to save the document. After it downloads, open it in Word 2000.

After learners complete the assignment, let them download the "solution" to the assignment.

Provide complete information

For large files the learner must download—such as data sets, detailed images, databases, video sequences, application programs, or complex documents—provide this information:

▶ Description

▶ File format

▶ Size

▶ Link to download a viewer

▶ Instructions on viewing the example

▶ Tips on what to look for

Make available paper forms and documents

Let learners download and print out any paper forms they need. For example, the following page requires filling in a paper form. It provides a link to download a copy of the blank form in Adobe Acrobat (.PDF) format.

6

Activate learning

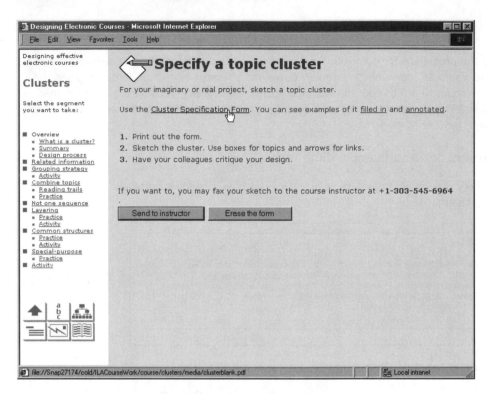

Because the browser has an Acrobat plug-in, the blank form appears right in the browser. The learner can then print out the blank form.

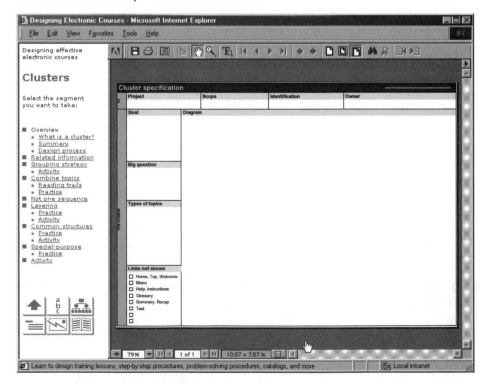

Likewise, if learners must read lengthy passages of text, let them download and print them out.

Supply time-saving utilities

Learners should not waste time taking notes, making calculations, looking up words. Make it easy for learners to start up a word processor or text editor, calculator, and online dictionary.

Web security restrictions make it difficult for a Web page to start a program on the learner's machine. Even if you know how to do this technically, you may run afoul of IT departments that frown on such remote manipulation. To safely provide such utilities:

▶ Implement utilities on the server and deliver them through the browser. A server-based database can hold a glossary. Requests for a particular term can be formatted as plain HTML and sent down the wire to the browser.

▶ Implement (or purchase) utilities as ActiveX controls or Java applets, which can run inside a browser.

▶ Implement utilities in JavaScript or VBScript so they run in the browser. Such scripting languages are simpler and quite adequate for calculators and the like.

▶ Buy a WBT tool that includes Web-based utilities.

▶ Make sure learners know how to start up the utility programs already on their computer.

Give hints

In all complex activities, include hints in case learners get stuck or just need a little boost. Hints can take many forms:

▶ Principles that help turn separate events into a comprehensible pattern.

▶ Cautions about unexpected events, hidden features, exceptions to rules—anything people are not likely to figure out on their own.

▶ List of things to try when stuck.

▶ Suggested order in which to perform activities.

▶ More specific instructions on how to perform the next step.

▶ Background information that the learner may be missing

Notice how this simulation activity includes buttons to provide hints and pinpoint exactly where the learner should click.

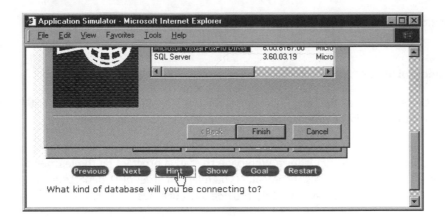

Employ guides

Use an on-screen guide to direct learners while adding a bit of whimsical humor. Guides are icons or animated characters that instruct the learner on how to proceed through an activity. They may speak in speech balloons, with recorded voice, or with synthesized voice [66].

The animated character in this example delivers hints within the Application Simulator. The agent is pointing out some crucial parts of the simulated screen.

This example uses the Microsoft Agent ActiveX control.

For sophisticated activities, you can give learners a choice of guides, each of which provides a different perspective.

Design entry forms to structure thought

Many activities require learners to enter their answers into a Web form. Design the form to streamline the task and help learners think productively about the problem they are solving.

Specify a format for answers

You could let learners submit answers in any format they chose. However, there are good reasons to structure the answer. A structured answer can:

▶ Prompt the learner and guide the analysis.

▶ Focus attention on the idea being taught and not on irrelevant details.

▶ Simplify evaluation by the instructor.

▶ (Perhaps) permit automatic evaluation and scoring by the computer.

Supply the form

The most direct way to structure an answer is to require the learner to fill in a form. For example:

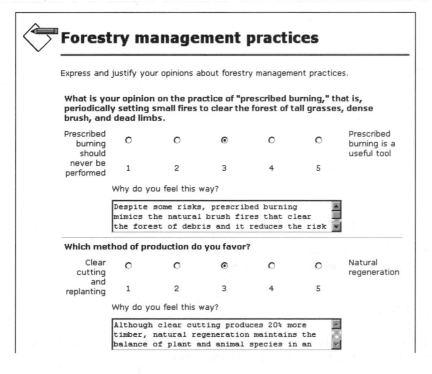

This example uses a custom Active Server Pages script and component on the server to format the form's contents and e-mail it to the instructor.

This form requires the learner to form, express, and defend opinions. It simplifies and focuses the process by defining each issue as a scale between two extreme positions. It simplifies answering by letting the learner pick a point along the scale. It includes five points so learners realize they have a range of responses.

The text area requires learners to defend their positions. Its size strongly encourages them to be brief.

Label to provoke clear answers

Vague prompts lead to vague answers. Text-input areas are especially difficult because they provide few constraints or hints as to the form of the answer. To help learners stay on track, label the field in a way that implies the form of the answer.

Label a text-entry area with an incomplete statement that the learner is to complete.

> This week I learned …
>
> "But we don't do much color printing," says the customer. You say, …
>
> My worst job interview began when …
>
> To better serve customers, I will …

Leave the right amount of room for entries

As a rule, make text response areas about 25 to 50% larger than the size of the response you want. Most people will fill ½ to ¾ of the available area.

One answer per slot

Do not require learners to enter more than one answer in a field or an e-mail. If an activity has three questions, provide three text boxes, one for each question.

Use the Internet as a source of material

The Internet is a vast library of resources for learning. Along with sleazy sex sites and the mail-order emporiums is a treasure of examples, case studies, and catalogued data on every subject imaginable. Much of it is free.

Product literature and documentation

Most high-tech companies provide detailed marketing literature, operating instructions, reference manuals, technical specifications, and other product documentation available. Use these materials in courses that involve selecting, evaluating, or operating such products.

Magazines and trade journals

Established paper-based magazines and trade journals are joining Web-only periodicals in making articles, abstracts, and back issues available over the Web. Some charge for access to complete articles or back issues, but most provide free access to summaries of current articles.

Scientific and engineering data

Increasingly, government agencies, university research laboratories, and professional associations are making their collections of scientific data available over the Internet. For example, NASA makes available 250 years of data about the sun [86].

Although raw data might not seem useful in its own right, it can be used to fuel activities on many subjects. When designers of the Yohkoh Public Outreach Project proposed a Web page showing the current location of the Yohkoh solar-observation satellite, teachers immediately found uses for it in teaching science, math, geography, creative writing, physics, geometry, and social studies [86]

Newsgroups

If more than a thousand people are interested in a subject, you can bet there is an Internet newsgroup on the subject. Newsgroups provide a great resource to introduce learners to subjects as they are practiced in the real world.

Have learners access a newsgroup, lurk for a while, then join in the conversation, and finally report on what they have learned. Have the learners report on what the real function of the group appears to be. For what kinds of questions is it a good source? For which kind is it not an effective source? Is its function primarily scholarly, job-related, or social?

Direct observation sites

Live Webcasts have shown babies being born, hearts being bypassed, and sex being had. But not all Webcasts are so spectacular. Some have solid educational value. David Iadevaia, an astronomer and professor at Prima College in Tucson, Arizona, built an observatory with video cameras throughout [68]. The telescope was equipped with a CCD imager so its images too could be converted to video. This setup let learners see Iadevaia working the control room, observe the equipment being set up and used, and peek through the telescope itself. Learners could even request high-resolution images sent by e-mail. This elaborate setup, which cost about $60,000, gave learners an in-depth glance at what an astronomer really does. (You can find it through www.api-az.com).

Other courses and tutorials

Before you develop a course or lesson on a subject, consider whether you can borrow, lease, or rent someone else's course. For many subjects, competent courses exist. Many course publishers, especially private individuals and universities, will let you link to their course for free or for a nominal licensing fee. Even licensing content from a commercial course vendor may be less expensive than creating it yourself. (For some suggestions on how to incorporate such foreign material into your course, see page 185.)

IN CONCLUSION ...

Summary

▶ Learning activities can teach, test, and exercise knowledge and skills. They give participants an opportunity to learn by doing.

▶ Some types of learning activities are well established. These include Webcasts, drill-and-practice sessions, case studies, role-playing scenarios, and learning games.

▶ Effective activities use the Internet effectively, provide clear instructions, and require deep thinking and reflection.

For more ...

If you cannot find the kind of activity you need in this chapter, see:

▶ Ruth Clark's classic *Developing Technical Training* [99], which is chock full of techniques that you can easily translate to WBT activities.

▶ Chapter 20 of *Web-Based Instruction* [100].

For more ideas for activities, see Chapter 7 on tests and Chapter 13 on alternatives to traditional courses. Tests can be used as activities. Many of the alternatives to courses can be scaled down and reworked as activities.

Many of the examples shown in this book are on exhibit at:

www.horton.com/DesigningWBT/

7

Test and exercise learning

Tests, quizzes, and self-evaluations

Feared by learners, discounted by educational pundits, short-changed by instructional designers, tests are, nevertheless, an essential element of learning. We may call them quizzes, drills, examinations, assessments, competence monitors, or demonstrations of mastery. We may cloak them as games or puzzles. Yet, they remain an essential ingredient for gauging a learner's progress.

273

Feared by learners, discounted by educational pundits, short-changed by instructional designers, tests are, nevertheless, an essential element of learning. We may call them *quizzes, drills, examinations*, assessments, *competence monitors*, or *demonstrations of mastery*. We may cloak them as games or puzzles. Yet, they remain an essential ingredient for gauging a learner's progress.

Tests, along with other kinds of activities, give learners an opportunity to apply the concepts, skills, and attitudes they have learned. Well designed tests provide a reliable way to measure progress objectively.

DO WEB-BASED TESTS WORK?

The Web provides an effective yet inexpensive way to test knowledge, skills, and attitudes. Tests conducted over the Internet obtain the same results as those on paper, and learners in one study strongly preferred the Internet-delivered tests [101]. In a study of 400 vocational-technical learners in Pennsylvania, Internet-conducted tests showed no differences in scores, redesign needed, or any bias due to gender, economic disadvantage, or educational disability relative to the same test on paper. In that test, 75% of the learners said they preferred taking the test over the Internet, even though 68.8% of the learners had no Internet experience. Test administrators said that tests conducted over the Internet took a little less time to prepare and to conduct and a lot less time to analyze data.

Web-based testing eliminates the costs and effort of printing, distributing, and collecting test papers. For many kinds of tests, answers can be scored and results recorded automatically. The cost savings multiply with the number of distributed test-takers. Costs for converting a 100-question paper test to Internet delivery were about $1500 to $2500 USD. Costs for conducting and scoring the test were $2 USD per test-taker [101].

PLAN TESTING CAREFULLY

Before you begin writing a test, take a few minutes for the high-level design decisions that determine the kind of test you create.

> Our plans miscarry because they have no aim. When a man does not know what harbor he is making for, no wind is the right wind.
>
> — Seneca

Why are you testing?

One of your first decisions in designing a test is to list your goals. Here are some reasons for testing. Some are good, and some are not.

Good reasons	Bad reasons
▶ Let learners gauge progress toward their goals.	▶ Fulfill stereotypes and expectations. It's a course; therefore, it must have tests.
▶ Emphasize what is important and thereby motivate learners to focus on it.	▶ Give the instructor power over learners. Pay attention or else.
▶ Let learners apply what they have been learning—and thereby learn it more deeply.	▶ Torture learners. Training is supposed to be painful. Tests can ensure that it is.
▶ Monitor success of parts of the course so that the instructor and designers can improve it.	▶ Prove to management, clients, and customers that the course works. (Proving success of the course is not bad—just using tests to do it.)
▶ Certify that learners have mastered certain knowledge or skills. To meet a legal or licensing requirement.	

Consider testing carefully. Contradictions lurk within these lists. What learners want to learn may not square with what instructors want to teach. Knowledge required for certification may not be sufficient to actually do the job.

Once you have decided why you are testing and what you hope to measure, you can make tactical decisions on what kind of test to use. Some of these decisions will require balancing your lofty objectives against the stark limitations of your authoring tools and the reality of your budget and schedule. Let's look closer at the decisions you must make.

What do you want to measure?

Review the learning objectives you set for the segment of material being tested. What were you teaching: knowledge, skills, or attitudes? And exactly what were the facts, understanding, abilities, and beliefs learners were to acquire?

Watch out for the "as shown above syndrome." Learners do not always start at the beginning of the course and proceed straight through to the end. Learners may jump into the middle of a topic in the middle of a lesson in the middle of the course. Many consider this their right. They will consider you unfair if you test them on material not found in the section supposedly covered by the test—or in a clearly identified prerequisite section.

Will the test be graded?

Will the learner receive a grade on this test? And will that grade be permanently recorded? The answers to these questions depend on your overall grading strategy. That is, how do individual tests factor into calculating the final grade? The answers can also depend on your assumptions about how well motivated learners are. Do professionals taking the course on their own need grades to motivate them? Are there more effective ways than tests to measure performance? Only your knowledge of the learners and their motivations can provide an answer.

When teaching adults, my preference is to **not** record scores unless required to certify performance of learners. In general, treating adult learners as responsible, conscientious beings yields better results. It also avoids the complexity and record keeping that often distract instructors from the task of teaching.

How will the test be graded?

Who grades the test? When designing a test, you must consider what happens after learners fill in the answers or complete the task. How is their performance evaluated? What feedback are they given? Here are some possibilities, with their advantages and disadvantages:

Technique	Advantages	Disadvantages
Answers are evaluated by a script or program on the learner's computer.	Evaluation is immediate. No network connection is required. Works for courses on CD-ROM or hard disk. The computer is nonjudgmental. Learners do not fear human criticism.	Limited to simple forms of evaluation. Instructor cannot monitor learner's progress.
Answers are transmitted to a remote computer, which analyzes them and generates a response.	Instructor can monitor learner's progress. Evaluation is quick. The computer is nonjudgmental.	Requires network connection. Limited to simple forms of evaluation.

Technique	Advantages	Disadvantages
Answers are e-mailed to the instructor, who grades them and writes back with an evaluation.	No limit to the kinds of questions. Instructors can spot learners' subtle misconceptions. Instructor will have knowledge necessary to evaluate learners.	Quality of evaluation depends on the knowledge of the instructor. Learners have to wait for a response. Requires extra work by instructors. Learners may feel reluctant to expose their ignorance to the critical gaze of the all-powerful instructor.
Learners have a co-worker or on-site advisor examine their answers and comment on them.	Coworkers can show how something applies to the learner's real-world work activities.	The co-worker may not be available. The learner may have to print out the screen. Co-workers may lack knowledge and expertise necessary.
Learners evaluate their own work using a procedure spelled out by the instructor.	Having the learner find the answers in the preceding material provides a second learning opportunity.	The answers are not easy to find. Learners will consider searching for answers a waste of their time.
Other learners evaluate the work.	Peer evaluations help learners develop judgment skills. They can also foster a sense of teamwork.	Learners may lack the necessary knowledge. Some learners are not mature enough to politely and objectively evaluate their peers, with whom they feel they are competing.

Activities graded by humans are traditionally called exercises. See Chapter 6 for more ideas on human-evaluated activities.

When will feedback be delivered?

When will you tell learners how they scored on the test? Sooner is better, but sometimes delays are necessary even with automatic scoring. You can deliver feedback automatically after each question or after the whole test. Or you can deliver feedback after evaluation by a human being. This section discusses the merits of each approach.

After each question

Scoring each question as the learner answers it provides immediate feedback but can interrupt the flow of the test. In general, I prefer this approach. It makes tests more fun and prevents misconceptions.

Architecture

Although many variations are possible, most tests with feedback after each question stem from a design such as this:

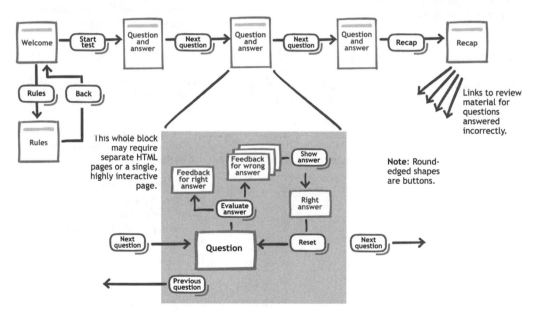

The test starts with a Welcome or Introduction topic, proceeds through questions and answers, and ends with a Recap or Summary topic. The Welcome may link to detailed instructions or rules. The Recap may supply links to more material for incorrect answers. Most of the feedback, though, centers on each question. After answering a question, learners receive feedback on their answers—whether right or wrong. Learners are also shown the correct answer.

Advantages and disadvantages

Immediate feedback is a powerful motivational force. It fits learners' expectations for computer-based media. Click-boom, it's there! Immediate feedback makes tests seem a bit more like games and less like interrogations.

Immediate feedback corrects misconceptions before they have a chance to sink in. If feedback comes only after answering the whole series of questions, the learners will have transferred the answers (right and wrong) from short-term to long-term memory before being confirmed or corrected.

Immediate feedback also keeps the learner from missing several related questions because of a single, simple misunderstanding.

Getting feedback piecemeal, however, can make the test take longer and prove frustrating to impatient learners, especially ones with a high level of knowledge who get few questions wrong. Immediate feedback can also make it harder for learners to answer a series of closely related questions. Interruptions for feedback break the continuity of the test.

Design guidelines

If you do choose to provide feedback after each answer:

▶ Make each question complete in itself. After reading the feedback, learners are unlikely to remember details of the preceding question.

▶ Let learners skip over lengthy feedback for correct answers. Make the feedback brief and let learners click a button to advance to the next question.

▶ Do not reveal too much. In the feedback to one question, do not give away the answer to another question.

▶ Do not require immediate remediation. If learners get a question wrong, you can display links to let them restudy the material, but do not require them to follow those links. Let them move on to the next question.

▶ At the end of the test, provide a recap with links to let learners review material for questions they got wrong.

▶ If the test is timed, stop the timer while the learner is getting feedback and restart it only when the learner advances to the next question. Make sure learners understand that they can take all the time they want to read feedback.

After test is complete

Postponing evaluation until learners have answered all questions is more efficient and more economical but less fun.

Architecture

Tests that postpone feedback to the end share many of the features of tests with immediate feedback, except that feedback occurs only in the Recap.

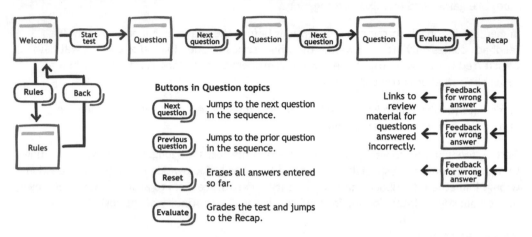

The Recap summarizes results and links to detailed feedback on the main areas of misunderstanding. These detailed feedback topics are typically linked to the original material or to remedial material.

Advantages and disadvantages

By evaluating answers only at the end of the test, you reduce the number of screens the learner must view and the time required to take the test. The learner can quickly navigate back and forth among the questions, answering them at will.

By evaluating at the end, your feedback can be more targeted. If several questions test the same concept, learners see the feedback just once, not over and over again. A sophisticated evaluation procedure can identify patterns of mistakes and provide feedback at a higher level than for individual questions.

However, postponing evaluation can prove frustrating to some learners. Misunderstanding one question can cause them to miss other questions. Guess whom they blame!

Design guidelines

If you do design tests with evaluation only at the end of the test, follow these common-sense guidelines:

▶ Make questions independent and self-contained. Misunderstanding one question should not lessen chances of getting other questions right.

▶ Keep tests short. Learners should be able to complete the whole test in 5 to 10 minutes.

▶ At the end, provide clear feedback on questions the learner got wrong with links to the original material or to new material on the subject.

After a delay for human evaluation

If a test question is complex and its answer must be carefully considered by the instructor or fellow learners, immediate feedback is not possible. The answer must be transmitted to an evaluator who scores it and sends back a reply.

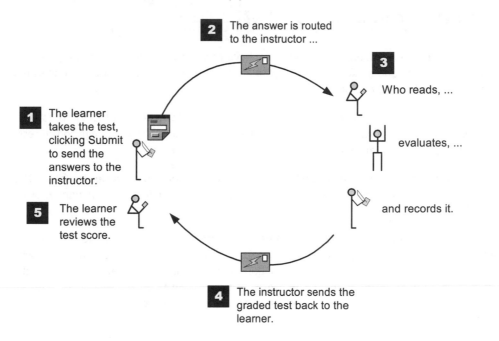

For evaluation, the answer must be electronically routed to the person doing the evaluation, who must read and consider it, compose and perhaps edit a reply, and send the reply, which the learner must retrieve and read. Throw in time zones, weekends, holidays, and work priorities, and the delay can be several days.

For tests with delayed evaluation, use the strengths of human evaluation to offset the problems caused by the delay.

▶ Give priority to scoring tests. Guarantee 48-hour turnaround if you can do so without compromising the quality of evaluations. If instructors will be unavailable, they should find stand-ins.

▶ Let the learner proceed with the course, even if a passing grade is normally required before beginning the next segment.

▶ Motivate evaluators to respond quickly. If the evaluators are learners, consider basing part of the final grade on the promptness and quality of their evaluations.

▶ Schedule tests so that the evaluator will be able to respond immediately. Make a habit of scheduling tests on a day when instructors will be available on immediately following days. Some instructors like to schedule tests on Friday so that they can grade them during the quiet time over the weekend.

> ▸ Warn learners about potential delays. If learners decide when to take tests, publish a calendar indicating when the instructor will be available to grade tests. One course had this policy: "You will receive your grade within two business days at the office of the instructor."

How much time can learners take?

Should you limit the amount of time learners have to complete the test? Limiting the time can add challenge and make cheating a little harder. It can also intimidate some learners and may unfairly handicap others.

Time limits can help measure how quickly learners can perform certain tasks and how quickly they can recall facts. The ticking clock can add a game-like challenge to the test. It can also ensure that learners use their time efficiently in the test.

With a limited amount of time available, learners have fewer opportunities to cheat. They have less time to look up information in other sources, to call friends on the phone, or to consult past tests.

Time limits put a lot of pressure on learners. The pressure can cause some learners to perform below their real level of knowledge. Time limits may unfairly penalize those who read slowly, who have a slow network connection, or who are connected to an overloaded server. Time limits definitely handicap those with reading difficulties, such as second-language speakers who may have to consult dictionaries and glossaries to interpret the questions.

Consult your legal department. Someone could argue that timed tests discriminate against second-language speakers and those with reading disabilities.

To help you decide whether to time the test, ask yourself this:

> In the real world, when learners have to apply what they have learned, how quickly must they respond?

If you are teaching how to shut down a nuclear reactor in an emergency, the answer is **Yes**, speed matters. If you are teaching attorneys how to write a contract, the answer is **No**. It is more important to get the contract exactly right than to finish it ten minutes faster.

Can learners retake the test?

Do learners get one chance to take the test or many? Letting learners retake the test gives them a second chance to demonstrate mastery of the material but requires you to create multiple tests and can complicate grading.

Letting learners retake a test gives them a second (or third or fourth) opportunity to gauge their mastery of the material. It is a kindhearted thing to do. It is the necessary thing to do if you require a passing grade before the learner can advance to the next segment.

However, to let the learner retake the test, you must have a second set of test questions. Merely redisplaying the original questions would not accurately measure the learner's knowledge.

If learners can take the test over, how do you calculate their grades? Which grades are recorded? Here are some choices and recommendations on when to pick them:

Which score is recorded?	When to use this approach
Only the first attempt	Learners try hard on the first attempt because they know they cannot improve their grade. Subsequent attempts are still helpful to let learners know whether they have mastered the material before they advance to subsequent lessons.
Only the most recent attempt	Learners have an incentive to restudy material after an unsatisfactory test score. Some, however, may just take the test repeatedly hoping for a better score. It is best to limit retries to one or two.
Only the best attempt	Learners can keep studying and taking the test until they achieve satisfactory scores. Because retaking the test entails no risk, some learners may just take it repeatedly. It is best to limit retries to one or two.
An average of all attempts	Learners can improve their grade, but each attempt has less and less effect. Thus learners have incentive to score well on the first or second attempt.

What to do in case of technical problems?

What happens if a learner cannot take a test because of technical problems at the system level? The network balks, the server stalls, or the database crashes. Publish a procedure for learners to follow to report problems. This procedure must work even if the server and network are down. Have a make-up test ready—or some other activity the learner can perform.

What if the learner's computer or network connection fails? How can the instructor know if the learner's excuse is valid or the electronic equivalent of "The dog ate my homework"? One solution is to allow each learner one or two such excuses—no questions asked.

SELECT THE RIGHT TYPE OF QUESTION

You can use a variety of test questions. This section introduces the most popular types. It is weighted heavily toward simple ones that do not require the latest technology, high-bandwidth connections, or lots of plug-ins. It also features ones that can be evaluated by the computer.

True/False questions

True/false questions require learners to decide between two alternatives, typically saying whether a statement is true or false.

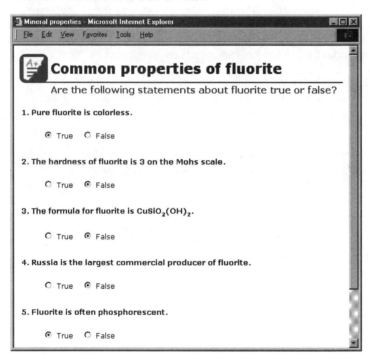

Here are examples of true/false questions from a course on identifying minerals.

When to use true/false questions

Use true-false choices to test learners' abilities to make definite judgments. True-false questions require learners to make a binary decision:

▶ Is a statement right or wrong?

▶ Will a procedure work or not?

▶ Is a procedure safe or unsafe?

▶ Does an example comply with standards?

▶ Should you approve or reject a proposal?

▶ Which of two alternatives should I pick?

Before using a true/false question, consider other types of questions as well. True/false questions are restricted to simple cases and may encourage guessing:

However, a well-designed true-false question that requires the same thought processes as the real world activity is more accurate and valuable than a three-dimensional, immersive simulation that invokes only the decision-making skills of the video-game parlor.

How to design true/false questions

To make true/false tests effective, design them so they require more thought than guessing.

▶ Ask more than one true/false question on a subject. The odds of getting them all right by guessing diminish with each additional question.

▶ For each subject, phrase true/false questions in different ways so that sometimes the right answer is false and other times it is true.

▶ Phrase the question in neutral terms so you do not imply an answer.

▶ Provide clear hints or explanations for incorrect answers.

Phrase the question to fit the answers

Make the question simple and straightforward. Do not ask what the learner thinks or feels or believes unless that is what you are testing.

 No   **Yes**

Do you think that the following   Is the following statement true or
statement is true or false?   false?

Often a statement followed by true/false radio buttons provides sufficient instructions.

> **InStr() returns 0 to indicate that the string was not found.**
>
> ○ True
> ◉ False

In true/false questions, phrase the question and answers so that the answers match the form of the question. Do not ask a yes/no question and label the answers true/false.

☹ **No**　　　　　　　　☺ **Yes**

Does cuprite contain copper?	Does cuprite contain copper?
○ True ○ False	○ Yes ○ No

Cuprite contains copper.	Cuprite contains copper.
○ Yes ○ No	○ True ○ False

Use true/false questions for any binary choice

Questions need not have yes/no or true/false answers. Any binary opposites will do. Phrase the answer as a binary choice if that is more natural.

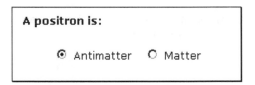

A positron is:

◉ Antimatter　　○ Matter

Watch out for cases where the choices are not mutually exclusive or where there really are more than two choices possible. Here is such a case:

U.S. Senator Foghorn is a:

○ Republican　　◉ Democrat

The Honorable Senator could be an independent or a member of a third party. Or the senator could switch party affiliations next week. Such questions may work better as multiple-choice questions with a "none of the above" choice.

Discourage guessing

Many learners guess on a true/false question, figuring they have a 50-50 chance of being right. Unless you are teaching a course in probability or gambling, you should discourage such behavior.

You can discourage guessing in several ways:

▶ **Penalize guessing**. In scoring true/false questions give 1 point for right answers, 0 points for unanswered questions, and –1 point for wrong answers. Thus guessing is no better or worse than not answering.

▶ **Require higher scores**. Statistics to the rescue! The odds of getting 5 of 10 true/false questions right by guessing are 50%. But the odds of getting 80% correct are only about 5%.

▶ **Ask more questions**. Increase the number of true/false questions to 20 and the odds of getting 80% right by guessing drop to less than 1%.

Alternative forms for true/false questions

Most true/false questions are formatted as a pair of radio or option buttons, but any form that clearly implies a choice between opposites or between just two alternatives will do. Here are some graphical alternatives that have been used for true/false questions:

▶ On-off switch.

▶ Fork in the road.

▶ Pair of doors

▶ A one and a zero (for computer scientists)

▶ Smiling face vs. frowning face

Multiple-choice questions

Multiple-choice questions display a list of answers for learners to choose from. Multiple-choice questions are easy to construct and easy to understand, but they do tempt some learners to guess rather than think.

There are two main types of multiple-choice questions: *pick-one* and *pick-multiple*. Pick-one questions ask the learner to pick just one item from a list. Pick-one questions are what most people think of as a multiple-choice question. The second type, called *pick-multiple*, lets the learner answer by picking one, some, all, or none of the alternatives.

Pick-one questions

Pick-one questions require learners to answer by picking a single answer from a list of possible answers. Only one answer is correct.

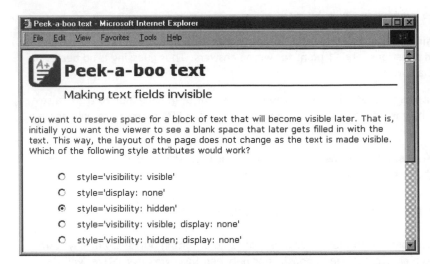

In this example from a course on Dynamic HTML, learners are given a desired goal and asked to select the one combination of style attributes that accomplishes the goal.

Use pick-one tests for questions that have one right answer. They work well for activities that require people to assign items to well-defined categories.

▶ **Assigning numerical ratings.** Example: ranking loan applications by degree of risk.

▶ **Learning to recognize members of specific classes.** Example: identifying the species of a particular plant.

▶ **Recognizing one of several causes of a problem.** Example: diagnosing the cause of a headache.

▶ **Picking superlatives:** the best, worst, greatest, least, highest, or lowest member of a group.

Pick-multiple questions

Pick-multiple questions let the learner pick one or more answers from a list of possible answers.

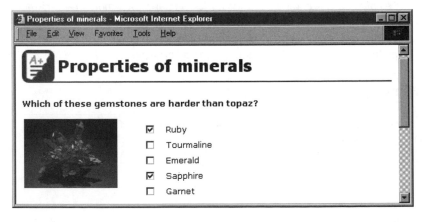

In this example, the learner can pick all the answers that are correct.

Use multiple-answer tests for asking questions with more than one right answer. Multiple-answer tests allow more sophisticated questions than are possible with single-answer or true-false tests. They require making a series of related judgments. For instance:

▶ Picking items that meet a criterion

▶ Deciding where a rule applies

▶ Making a quick series of yes-no decisions

▶ Picking examples or non-examples of a principle

Alternative forms for multiple-choice questions

Traditionally, multiple-choice questions present their options using radio buttons for pick-one questions and checkboxes for pick-multiple questions. Even if you need variety, do not reverse these forms. That would confuse learners. Instead, consider an alternative form.

Use selection lists for multiple multiple-choice questions

If you want to ask several multiple-choice questions about a subject or if space is tight on the page, consider using a series of selection lists. Here is an example:

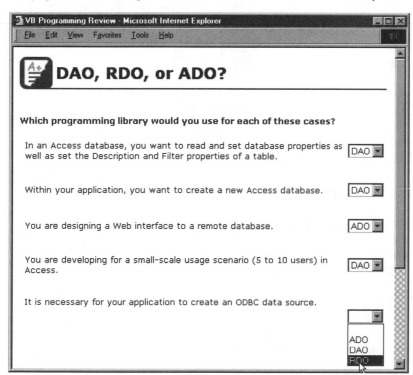

This form works especially well if all the questions have the same set of possible answers.

It does, however, mean that learners must know how to make a choice in a selection list. Most people figure out checkboxes and radio buttons on their own. Operating a selection list should be a problem only for the novices at filling in Web forms.

Use click-in-picture questions for visual choices

If you want to let learners select among visual alternatives, you can present the choices as pictures and have learners indicate their choices by pointing and clicking. Because such questions are used primarily for visual subjects, they are treated as a separate type of question called a "click-in-picture" question (p 293).

Text-input questions

Text-input questions require the learner to type in the answer to a question. Typically, these are short answers to very specific questions.

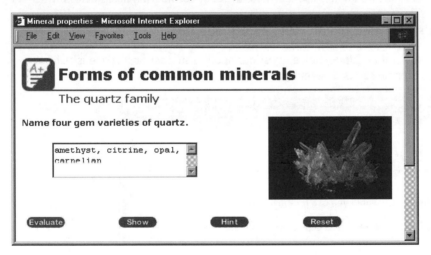

In this example, learners type in the names of semi-precious stones of the quartz family.

When to use text-input questions

Use text-input tests to verify that learners have truly learned the names of things. Use them to test recall of:

▶ Technical or business terms

▶ Part numbers

▶ Abbreviations

▶ Commands and statements in a programming language

▶ Vocabulary in a foreign language

How to design text-input questions

The most difficult aspect of designing text-input tests is phrasing the question so that the computer can evaluate the answer.

▶ Phrase the question to limit the number of correct answers.

▶ Phrase it so that the answer can be evaluated based on the presence or absence of specific words or phrases but not on the exact order or syntax of the answer.

▶ Accept synonyms (other words with the same meaning), grammatical variants, and common misspellings.

▶ Tell learners how to phrase their answers. Give an example of a properly phrased answer. Make clear whether the answer is to be text or numbers or mixed.

▶ If the question is complex, break it into separate questions, each with a simple answer. Do not ask two questions to be answered in one input box.

▶ Tell the learner the length, format, required parts, and other constraints on a free-form input. If you do not state a length, most learners will assume they can fill the input box.

Although automatic scoring of free-form text is not practical in most cases, you can write your question so that the completeness can be evaluated. For example, if you ask learners to compare various gemstones, the system could scan the learner's answer for the names of gemstones ("ruby," "diamond," "opal," and so forth) and for characteristics ("color," "hardness," and so forth).

Where possible, validate the form of the input right on the page before evaluating whether it is the correct answer or not. By "validate" I mean check for small mistakes that do not indicate subject-matter knowledge. For example, suppose you ask for a number. An engineer would probably not enter "One hundred ten" but you cannot be sure. A validation check examines the input to determine whether it is a number or text. If the input is not a number, the validation check throws up a caution and invites the leaner to correct the form of the input.

TechnoTip. Server scripting languages, like Perl, include commands for recognizing complex patterns in text. Such capabilities are called *regular expression processing*. Recent versions of JavaScript and VBScript have brought these capabilities to the browser. If you are willing to do a bit of programming, you can make your tests more flexible in how they evaluate answers.

Matching-list questions

Matching-list questions require learners to specify which items in one list correspond to items in another.

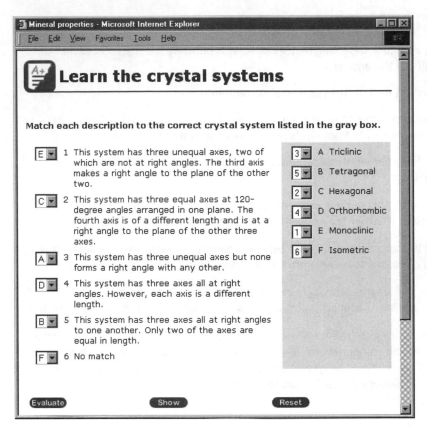

In this example, drop-down lists let the learner choose answers keyed to a list of available choices. The learner can select from the list on the left or the one on the right. The two lists are synchronized. Setting an item on the left sets the selected item on the right and vice versa.

When to use matching-list questions

Use matching-list questions to measure knowledge of the relationships among concepts, objects, and components [97].

Use them to match:	With:
Terms	Definitions
Pictures	Captions
People	Titles or accomplishments
Tools	Their uses
Diseases	Symptoms or cures
Items	Their opposites
Question	Answer
Part of one whole	Another part of that same whole

How to design matching-list questions

Make matching easy so that learners can focus their attention on the relationships between items in the two lists.

▶ **Write list items clearly.** Use familiar terms or provide a glossary for the learner to look up terms.

▶ **Keep the lists short so that they both fit in the same display.** If they do not fit, give the learner a button to jump back and forth.

▶ **Let learners indicate matches simply.** Rather than having them type the letter or number of the matching item, let them select it from a list of choices, drag and drop items on one another, or draw lines between items.

▶ **Eliminate the "process-of-elimination" effect** by including more items in one list than the other or by letting learners choose "None" if an item has no match in the opposite list.

Alternative forms for matching-list questions

Lists are not restricted to text items. One or both lists can be graphics. Graphical matches can be expressed by dragging an icon or object over another and dropping it there. Because drag-and-drop is used for more than matching, it is treated as a separate question type (p 295).

Click-in-picture questions

Click-in-picture questions ask the learner to select an object or area in a picture by pointing to it with the mouse and clicking the mouse button.

In this example, learners are taught to decypher the identification badges used at a secure facility. Learners answer the question by clicking on the correct area of the badge.

When to use click-in-picture questions

Use click-in-picture tests to test visual recognition of objects or parts of a system. Use them to ask questions such as these:

Which of the tools pictured are necessary to repair breaks in optical-fiber cables?

In which cities on the map does our company have research laboratories?

Which button on this dialog box darkens the displayed image?

Where along this scale of pH values would you rate acetic acid?

Click on the flags of the countries in which French is the primary language.

Which button on the control panel would you select to trigger an emergency shutdown of the nuclear reactor?

Where would you plug in the external microphone?

Use click-in-picture tests instead of text multiple-choice questions when it is more important that learners know where something is or what it looks like than what it is called.

Use click-in-picture tests to avoid awkward eye and hand movements.

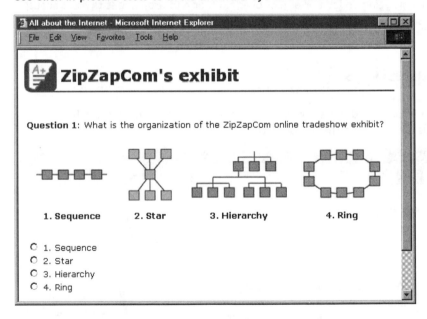

Do not do this! Here the learner must locate an area in a picture and then indicate a choice by clicking in a separate list of radio buttons.

How to design click-in-picture questions

For pick-in-picture questions use clear images and write clear instructions.

▶ **Explain exactly what learners are to select.** An area? An object? A point on a scale?

▶ **Make targets visually distinct.** Make them visually separate objects or areas with distinct borders.

▶ **Make targets large enough** so that learners with only average eye-hand coordination can quickly select them, say 20 by 20 pixels as a minimum size.

▶ **Show the scene the way it would appear in the real world,** if simulating real-world activities, such as pushing buttons on a control panel.

▶ **Design the picture so it downloads quickly.**

Drag-and-drop questions

Drag-and-drop questions require learners to move icons or images to specific locations on the screen. Drag-and-drop questions test the ability to assign items to the correct category or to arrange the parts of a system into a whole. Drag-and-drop questions are used in several kinds of activities (pp 216, 217, 242).

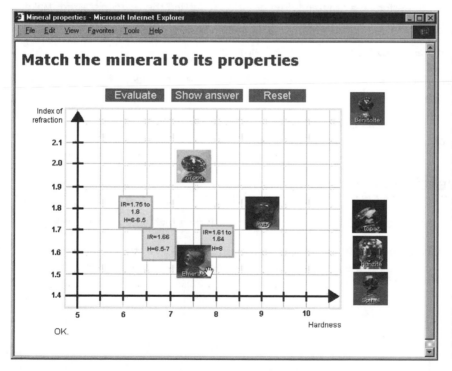

In this example, learners must drag pictures of gemstones onto slots that correctly show each gem's index of refraction and hardness.

This example uses a Macromedia Director shockwave movie.

Before 4.0-level browsers, drag-and-drop questions required special software, typically a Java applet, a Shockwave movie, or an ActiveX component. With the Dynamic HTML provided by 4.0-level browsers, a drag-and-drop question can be implemented directly in the browser window.

When to use drag-and-drop questions

Use drag-and-drop questions to test the learner's ability to classify items into categories or put parts together into a system. Use them to test the learner's ability to:

▶ Name things by dragging names onto them.

▶ Classify things by dragging them into boxes representing the categories.

▶ Rank things by dragging them into position along a scale.

▶ Assemble the pieces of a whole by dragging them into correct positions relative to one another.

▶ Show subtle relationships among a family of objects. Learners position objects so their proximity to other objects shows how closely they are related.

How to design drag-and-drop questions

The hardest part of designing a drag-and-drop question is getting the learner started. Make sure learners know what they are supposed to do.

▶ **Prompt the learner** to drag the pieces to their slots.

▶ **Make clear which pieces the learner can move.** Describe the objects in text. Give them a distinctive graphical style, such as shaping them like pieces of a jigsaw puzzle.

▶ **Make the slots or targets clear.** Make them visually distinct. Show them as boxes or indentations.

Simulation questions

Simulation questions use a simulation to let learners perform a highly interactive task.

Simulations can be used as tests, as learning activities (p 251), and even as the core of an entire course (p 567). Here, though, we consider just their use to **test** knowledge and skills.

> Experience keeps a dear school, but fools will learn in no other.
>
> — Benjamin Franklin

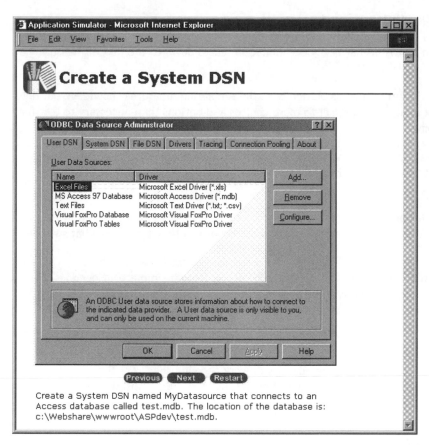

Here is an example of a simulation test. It uses the Application Simulator. The simulator page is missing the **Feedback**, **Hint**, and **Show answer** buttons that are present when the simulator is used to demonstrate or teach a procedure.

Simulations test learners' abilities to perform complex activities. If learners accomplish the assigned task with the simulator, they pass the test and can presumably perform the real activity.

Simulations are expensive and time-consuming to develop—typically 100 times the cost of a simple multiple-choice text question. Often they are worth the expense, but not always.

When to use simulations as tests

Use simulations for tests when:

▶ You are testing the ability to perform a procedure rather than abstract knowledge about a subject.

▶ The procedure is complex, requiring learners to make decisions, not merely follow a sequence of steps.

▶ The speed of performing the task is important to its success.

▶ You are qualifying people to perform a task in the real world.

How to design simulation tests

A good simulation test is primarily a good simulation scaled down to the task of measuring a single objective.

Simplify the simulation. In the simulation test, the simulation measures knowledge but does not teach. Do not expose the learner to more choices and options than necessary to test for the target objective.

State the goal clearly. Tell learners exactly what they must accomplish to pass the test. Spell out any restrictions. Must they accomplish the goal using a particular method or feature? How long can they take?

Explain the simulation. Make sure learners know what the simulation does and how they can interact with it. What buttons can they press, what knobs can they turn, and what switches can they flip?

Reveal the limits. No simulation is a perfect copy of the thing it simulates. How does the simulation differ from the real system? What are the limits on actions learners can take? What dangerous aspects of the real system are harmless in the simulator? What features and capabilities are turned off?

Spell out scoring rules. If the test is not graded pass/fail, spell out the criteria for awarding points. Are learners rewarded for the quantity of work accomplished? Are they penalized for the amount of time they took, the number of actions used, or minor mistakes made along the way?

Fill-in-the-blanks questions

Fill-in-the-blanks questions require learners to supply missing words in a paragraph of text or missing items in a table. Fill-in-the-blanks questions are also called *cloze* questions. Such questions have been used for hundreds of years and are a staple of education.

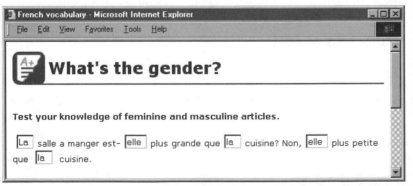

Here is a classic example used to test knowledge of French grammar, syntax, and spelling.

Fill-in-the-blanks questions work just like the paper workbooks into which for hundreds of years students have penned answers. With the WBT version, learners fill in their answers by typing or by picking from selection lists.

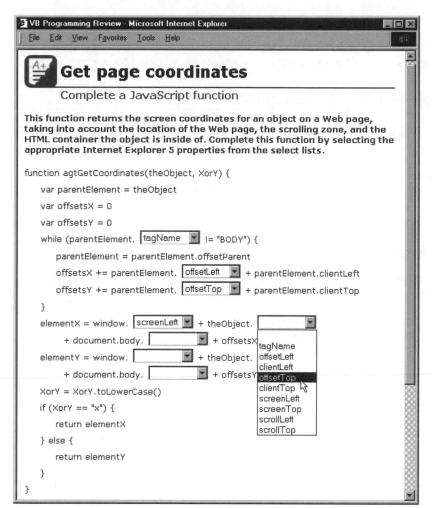

This example uses selection lists from which learners pick words in a programming language to complete a function.

As you can see, a fill-in-the-blanks question is really just a tightly integrated series of text-input or multiple-choice questions.

When to use fill-in-the-blanks-tests

Use fill-in-the-blanks questions to measure the learner's ability to "apply knowledge within a contextual matrix." That just means that learners use a partial answer to figure out the complete answer. Use fill-in-the-blanks questions:

▶ **To test incremental knowledge.** Learners know part of a subject and apply what they know to infer answers.

▶ **Where context matters.** Learners infer the correct answer from surrounding text or code.

▶ **To measure ability to apply verbal knowledge in context.** Learners guess the right words from the words that come before it and the words that follow it.

▶ **To ask complex questions.** Learners answer questions with multiple interrelated parts.

▶ **To provide scaffolding.** The context provides the support learners need early in learning a subject. Learners need not have mastered the knowledge supplied by the context.

How to design fill-in-the-blanks questions

Make fill-in-the-blanks questions simple and predictable so learners focus on answering the question.

▶ **Introduce the context**. Explain where the incomplete sample comes from and what it attempts to accomplish. For example, "Here is a paragraph from a Russian tour guide suggesting sights to see in your first day in St. Petersburg."

▶ **Explain the goal**. Tell learners what criteria they should use to fill in the blanks. For example, "Pick words that turn the paragraph into a concise summary of …."

▶ **Use a selection list to let learners pick among several plausible alternatives** if there are too many possible right answers.

▶ **Make sure the context provides enough clues** so that the learner can enter or pick the correct alternative. Test your questions.

EXPLAIN THE TEST

One of the most common complaints about tests is that the rules were unclear or that the procedures were not explained fully. If learners do not understand the "rules" of a test, they may not score well and will blame the creator of the test. Taking tests on the computer may be a new experience for many. The novelty, mixed with equal parts of anxiety and ignorance, can lead to a lot of silly mistakes. Take the time to tell learners how to take the test.

Explain tests thoroughly

Learners are curious beings, especially when it comes to tests. They want to know all the rules and regulations and restrictions—before they begin the test. But no one wants to read a bunch of boring rules. So keep the rules as simple as possible, express them concisely, and encourage learners to know the rules before they begin the test.

Here is a comprehensive list of the kinds of questions learners ask.

▶ **Is the test graded?** What effect will this test have on the overall grade? What is a passing grade? What grade should the learner achieve before going on to the next lesson?

▶ **What does the test cover?** Just the current lesson? All lessons up to this point?

▶ **Is the test timed?** How much time is available? What is the penalty for taking too much time?

▶ **When must the test be taken?** Before a deadline? During a specific period? At a certain hour and day? Before advancing to the next lesson?

▶ **How long is the test?** How many questions are on the test? (Especially important if the questions scroll off the bottom of the screen or are on subsequent pages).

▶ **How are answers scored?** How many points are awarded for each question? What are the penalties for incorrect answers, incomplete answers, and unanswered questions?

▶ **How accurate must my answers be?** Do spelling, capitalization, and grammar count? How precise must calculations be? Does the order of entries matter?

▶ **What form does the test take?** What kinds of questions are used: multiple-choice, true/false, fill-in-the-blanks, or others? Does everyone get the same questions or are questions picked at random?

▶ **Can I take the test later?** If so, how do I skip the test? How do I take the test later?

▶ **Can I retake the test for a better grade later?** How many times? Which score is recorded: the first one, the last one, the best one, or an average of all attempts?

▶ **What resources can I use to take the test?** Calculators, computer programs, books, Web sites, or other sources of information?

▶ **How realistic are the questions?** Are drawings to scale? Are numbers realistic?

▶ **How will the test be graded?** Who will grade the test: the computer, my instructor, my peers, or myself? When will I receive my grade?

▶ **Must questions be answered in sequence?** Does advancing to the next question automatically trigger scoring the current question?

▶ **What if I experience a computer failure?** What if the computer, network, or the testing program crashes during the test? What effect will this have on my score? How do I restart or resume the test?

That's a long checklist. It is too long to put all of it in one place and expect many learners to read it. The following sections suggest ways to deliver this information.

Separate instructions from questions

Because learners need a lot of information about tests, a single set of instructions might be too long for impatient learners to read. One common approach is to put different kinds of instructions in different places, depending on how broadly the instructions apply:

For instructions that apply to:	Put them here:	And:
All tests in a course.	A general "Rules for Tests" page that explains all the features, procedures, and assumptions common to all tests.	Link to these instructions from the introduction to each test.
A particular test.	The "Welcome" or "Introduction" for that test.	Link to the "Rules for Tests" page.
A particular question within a test.	Just before the question itself.	If the instructions are complex, stop the timer while the learner reads the instructions.
Problems that occur after the course is created but before it can be revised.	Frequently asked questions file for the course.	Add these points to other instructions the next time the course is revised.

> Examinations, sir, are pure humbug from beginning to end. If a man is a gentleman, he knows quite enough, and if he is not a gentleman, whatever he knows is bad for him.
>
> — Oscar Wilde

Welcome the test-taker

The Welcome to the Test page introduces the test and provides the information the learner needs to begin the test. This page covers the rules specific to the individual test and refers learners to the Rules for Tests page for general rules that apply to all tests.

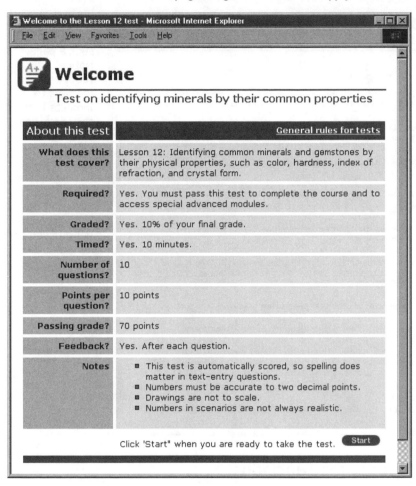

Here is an example of such a Welcome to the Test page. It prepares learners for a critical test.

Within the browser window:

Welcome

Test on identifying minerals by their common properties

About this test	General rules for tests
What does this test cover?	Lesson 12: Identifying common minerals and gemstones by their physical properties, such as color, hardness, index of refraction, and crystal form.
Required?	Yes. You must pass this test to complete the course and to access special advanced modules.
Graded?	Yes. 10% of your final grade.
Timed?	Yes. 10 minutes.
Number of questions?	10
Points per question?	10 points
Passing grade?	70 points
Feedback?	Yes. After each question.
Notes	■ This test is automatically scored, so spelling does matter in text-entry questions. ■ Numbers must be accurate to two decimal points. ■ Drawings are not to scale. ■ Numbers in scenarios are not always realistic.

Click 'Start' when you are ready to take the test. **Start**

Spell out the rules

The Rules for Tests page tells learners the rules and conditions that apply to all tests. It ensures that all learners have an equal chance to score well on the test. It prevents erroneous assumptions from handicapping learners with less experience.

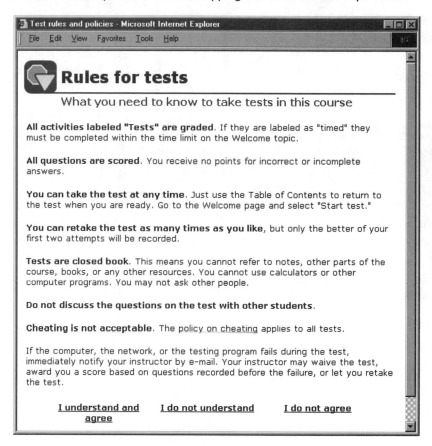

Here is an example of such a page. Notice that it requires learners to indicate that they have read the page and understand what it says.

Learners who click on **I do not agree** are not allowed to continue the course.

Guard against computer malfunctions

Few things produce more terror, frustration, and panic than a computer failure during a timed test. Although you cannot absolutely prevent such incidents, you can take steps to lessen their frequency and impact.

▶ **Test, test, test.** Before using a test in your course, put the test through thorough testing of its own. Verify that the test works under these conditions:

The minimum hardware configuration.

The server under maximum load.

Learners doing "absurd things that no one would ever really do."

▶ **Tell learners what to do if the server crashes during a timed test.** Give them a procedure to follow, and suggest they print it out.

▶ **Time and score each question individually.**

Keep the test-taker in control

We want learners to feel in control as they take tests. That way they focus on the content of the test. The key to control is information and having appropriate choices.

▶ **Explain before starting the timer.** Explain the test before it begins. Give all the instructions for a test before starting the timer. After presenting the instructions, require learners to select a "Start test" button to actually begin the test, especially if the test is timed.

▶ **Speak in a positive tone.** Strike a balance between being intimidating and reassuring. Encourage learners to succeed but not to fear failure.

▶ **Minimize methodological mumblings.** Keep your pet theories to yourself. Learners want to know the subject you are teaching, not the "ism" you are following. Few learners care whether you are a constructivist or a destructivist. They just want to get on with the test.

▶ **Let learners skip optional tests.** If tests are optional, let learners skip them. Make this easy with explicit buttons.

▶ **Make status clear.** Let learners know how much they have done and how much they have left to do. Some systems display a console showing the time and number of questions:

Test 14: Using ADO 2	
Questions answered	**Time remaining**
4 of 10	5:36 of 10:00

DESIGN EFFECTIVE QUESTIONS

Phrase questions precisely and clearly

Unless learners can understand the question, they cannot answer it. The difference between a clear and unclear question may be just a single word or punctuation mark. Take a little extra time to make sure your questions ask what you want them to.

Word questions and answers clearly

Tests should measure learners' knowledge of the subject matter, not their ability to unravel tricky questions or to parse complex writing. Give clear directions and make answers easy to interpret and select.

▶ Make the answers complete enough that their meaning is clear. Avoid pronouns.

▶ Phrase the question to tell learners how many answers they can pick. Otherwise, they may select too few or waste time trying to select more than one.

A native speaker of English should have little problem figuring out in the following example that the first "It" means the Model 329/X and not the more recent 329. However, someone with English as a second language or someone reading in a hurry or someone feeling a bit of test anxiety could easily misinterpret the reference.

> **Why should a customer select the Model 329/X over the 329?**
>
> ☐   The 329/X has a longer battery life than the 329.
> ☐   It weighs 10 kg more.
> ☐   It can scan 12-14 frequencies simultaneously.
> ☐   It costs about the same.

Notice also that the only clue that more than one item can be selected is the use of checkboxes rather than radio buttons. A nervous test-taker could overlook that subtle cue. Here is an improved version of the question:

> **Select all the reasons why a customer should select the Model 329/x over the Model 329.**
>
> ☐   The 329/X has a longer battery life than the 329.
> ☐   The 329/X weighs 10 kg more.
> ☐   The 329/X can scan 12-14 frequencies simultaneously.
> ☐   The 329/X costs no more than the 329.

KISS—Keep It Simple for Students

The challenge in a test should be answering the questions, not interpreting them. Tricky wording is a special problem for anxious and impatient readers—especially ones reading in a second language.

▶ Stick to simple sentences. Avoid complex sentences with embedded clauses.

▶ Use complete and standard punctuation.

▶ Use common terms.

▶ Provide a glossary for any technical terms you must use.

▶ In negative test questions, emphasize the word **NOT** or its equivalent.

Ask just one question at a time

Phrase questions so that only one answer is required. Do not ask or imply a second question, as does this shameful example:

> A customer approaches your trade show booth and says, "I've got a phone, a fax, an answering machine, and a Caller-ID box. I'm running out of space. Do you have something that can help me?" Which features of MessageMunger would you demonstrate?
>
> ☐ Caller IDeal
> ☐ Faxtopia
> ☐ Foreward Hot
> ☐ Telly Ho!
> ☐ AnswerVault

This example asks two questions. The first question is from the customer and asks about a product. The second is from the test itself and asks about features.

Rephrase the question to something like this:

> A customer approaches your trade-show booth and says, "I've got a phone, a fax, an answering machine, and a Caller-ID box. I'm running out of space. I hear your MessageMunger can help." Which features would you demo for this customer?
>
> ☐ Caller IDeal
> ☐ Faxtopia
> ☐ Foreward Ho!
> ☐ Telly Ho!
> ☐ AnswerVault

Now the example asks a single question.

Ask job-related questions

Phrase your questions so that they resemble the kinds of decisions learners will have to make when applying the knowledge and skills you are teaching. Phrase questions so they re-create what would actually occur on the job. Set a scenario and word questions as if coming from a customer, the boss, a subordinate, an angry co-worker, or someone you are training.

 No

 Yes

What are the three methods of peer mediation identified by Professor Morty Cerebrum?

John, a co-worker, bursts into your office. He collapses into your guest chair and mutters, "I'm either going to quit or throw my simpering weasel of a boss out the window!"

How do you respond?

If you cannot imagine the question being asked on the job, then why are you asking it in a test?

Avoid obsolescence

Avoid questions whose answers may change over time. In rapidly changing fields, new developments or a new version of software can change the answer to such questions.

☹ **No**   ☺ **Yes**

What companies have always paid a stock dividend?

Through 1999, what companies had always paid a stock dividend?

What is the maximum disk size under the current version of Microsoft Windows?

When Windows 98 was released in June of 1998, what was the maximum disk size supported?

Be careful when asking absolute questions:

Absolute questions assume rigid categories with razor-sharp boundaries. Beware questions of these forms:

Are _____ ever _____?

Is _____ always _____?

Are all _____ _____?

A single exception changes the answer. Learners can be quite clever in tracking down that one obscure, minor, nearly unknown exception you forgot about.

Emphasize important words

In phrasing questions, emphasize small crucial words on which the meaning of the question depends—words that could cause the learner to misinterpret the question if not read correctly. Here is an example:

Which of these items is **not** an example of romdibulation?

Usually the most critical words are reversing or constraining words: *not, only, just, one, first, last,* and so forth. Emphasize the word, but not by underlining it, as learners are likely to interpret underlined words as hypertext links.

Make all choices plausible

Multiple-choice tests are simple to construct but may encourage learners to guess rather than think about the answer. Also, by listing incorrect answers, multiple-choice tests may cause learners to remember the wrong answers rather than the right ones. To avoid these problems, design the questions to encourage learners to think carefully about their answers. Here are some guidelines:

Keep all answers about the same length

Make all answers approximately the same length. Or at least make sure that the longest answer is not always the right one. Guess which of these answers is right:

> **A caller immediately asks to be transferred to a specialist. You say:**
>
> ○ No, I have to talk with you first.
> ○ Are you sure that is what you want?
> ○ I can do that if you wish, but why don't you let me get the information I need to transfer you to the specialist who can best deal with your problem?
> ○ Sure, I'm transferring you now.

Make all choices grammatically equivalent

Make all choices grammatically similar. More importantly, make sure that each is compatible with the question, especially if the answers are offered as potential completions of a lead-in phrase. Can you spot the not-too-subtle hint in the following example?

> **A customer who wants forward load-balancing should select the Model 329/X because it includes an ...**
>
> ☐ Bi-frequency filter.
> ☐ Gizmoidial redial reduction gear.
> ☐ External voltage monitor.
> ☐ Reversal charger module.

The lead-in makes clear that only one answer is correct and that it begins with a vowel. Rephrase the question something like this:

> **A customer who wants forward load-balancing needs which of these Model 329/X features?**
>
> ☐ Bi-frequency filter.
> ☐ Gizmoidial redial reduction gear.
> ☐ External voltage monitor.
> ☐ Reversal charger module.

Make choices parallel

Phrase all answers at the same level of abstraction, generality, and degree of common usage. Can you guess the right answer to this question?

What are the colors of the control panel on the Model 329/X?

    ○   Tan and black.

    ○   Modesto Blue and Remington Red.

    ○   Gray and blue.

    ○   Beige and brown.

All the colors are common ones—except those in the second answer.

Challenge test-takers

Many questions do not appropriately challenge learners. Perhaps some designers fear scaring or offending voluntary learners. Or through carelessness designers give away the answer to the question. The best questions are those that require learners to think deeply about the subject matter in order to arrive at an answer.

Keep questions challenging

▶ Supply enough plausible choices so the answers are not too easy to pick out. Provide at least three plausible alternatives similar enough that the learner has to read them carefully and think deeply.

▶ Avoid give-away words like *poor*, *inadequate*, *all*, or *any*.

▶ Include "none of the above" and "all of the above" when appropriate.

▶ If you can't think of five plausible alternatives, throw in a couple of humorous ones.

If you can only think of three alternatives for a pick-one question, add two more, like this:

    ○   The first real choice

    ○   The second real choice

    ○   The third real choice

    ○   All of the above

    ○   None of the above

It is crucial that the last two appear at the end and in this order since "none of the above" can include "all of the above" but not the other way around.

Do not make questions too easy

In a too-easy test, little subject knowledge is required to pass the test, just a keen eye, a logical mind, and a bit of luck. Let's take a look at a too-easy test.

In the next example, notice that the first and fourth questions can be answered by looking at the picture. The second compares the mineral to the one other mineral whose hardness most people are familiar with. Most people could answer the third question by recalling that June is the month when many people get married and diamonds are used for engagement rings. The last question can be answered by connecting *Fluorite* to the similar word *fluorescent*, which is close in meaning to *phosphorescent*.

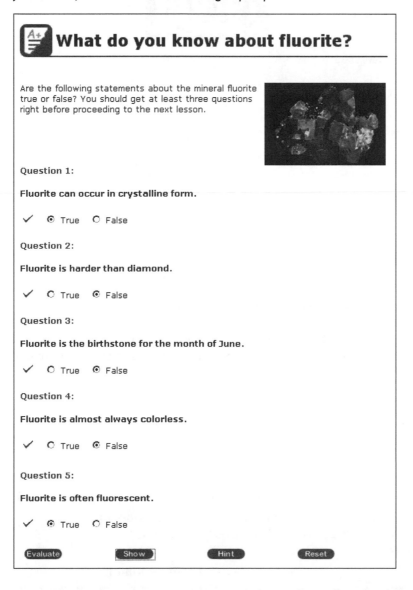

Because only three correct answers are required, learners need little more than luck and cleverness to pass the test. The next example shows a test that actually requires knowledge of the subject matter.

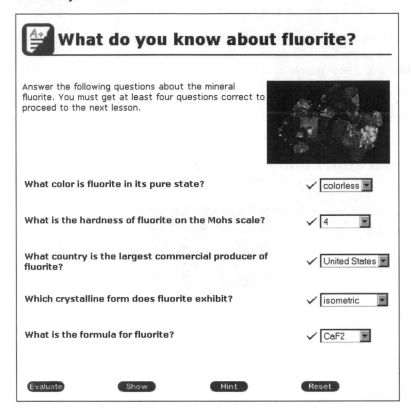

Here the questions are harder. There are more choices per question. And the passing score eliminates guessing as a reasonable strategy.

Make sure one question does not answer another

In a series of test questions, one question may ask about a subject mentioned in another. Often one of the questions provides unintended information that indicates the answer to the other. Can you guess the answers to the following two questions?

> Tests are most often used to humiliate and humble students— thereby distracting them from what a poor job we are doing training them.
>
> — Thorndon Killibit

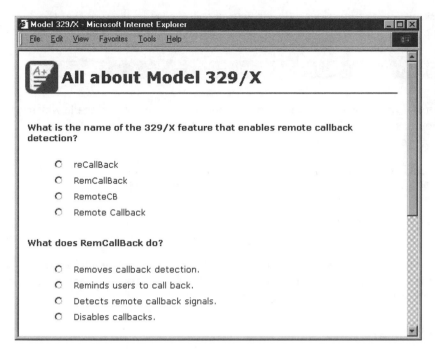

Notice how the first question provides a clue for the second question, which provides a clue for the first question.

Do not ask slanted questions.

Do not ask questions where one answer is strongly implied by the tone or nature of the question. Can you guess the intended answer of the following question?

> **Our Model 329/X is superior to the competition's model.**
>
> ○ True   ○ False

Of course, if you are a sneaky and devious designer, you may want to throw in a few such questions with answers the opposite of the bias.

Do not reveal the answer

Do not reveal the answer in a window title, file name, message, or URL. If tests involve scripts or external files, make sure that the URL or file name, which may be displayed in the browser's status bar, does not give away the answer. Suppose the learner points to a potential answer and the status bar shows this message:

Or

http://www.wbt/tests/internet/rightanswer.html

If the question asks which picture shows a Gothic Revival style house, make sure that the title of the pop-up window is not:

Likewise, be careful if the answers are evaluated by scripts in the same Web page in which learners enter their answers. Technically astute learners could view the source of the file and read the scripts to see which answer is right.

TechnoTip: Make such source-snooping harder by including the scripts in separate files that you include by reference, something like: `<script src='myscript.js'></script>`.

Streamline test questions

Design your tests so learners can take them at maximum efficiency. Do not require learners to waste time reading lengthy questions and awkwardly typing in answers. Such wasted time adds to the frustration and anxiety of test-takers unnecessarily.

Simplify selecting answers

Reduce the effort required to indicate the correct answer. Minimize the amount of typing and the degree of eye-hand coordination required.

▶ Let learners choose the answers in multiple-choice tests by clicking on items. Let learners select a text item by clicking on the text. Clicking on the text should have the same effect as clicking on the associated radio button or checkbox. Do not underline these links. (**TechnoTip**: In 4.0 browsers you can do this by defining the link's style thus: `<a style='text-decoration:none' … >`)

▶ If multiple-choice answers are presented visually, let learners answer by clicking on the pictures.

Keep choices concise

Do not repeat words in each answer that could be put in the question. Notice how much text is repeated in each question here:

What are some differences between hornblende and biotite?

☐ Although both biotite and hornblende can be black in color and both occur in granite, only hornblende contains sodium.

☐ Although both biotite and hornblende can be black in color and both occur in granite, hornblende crystals are triclinic and those of biotite are monoclinic.

☐ Although both biotite and hornblende can be black in color and both occur in granite, hornblende is harder than biotite.

☐ Although both biotite and hornblende can be black in color and both occur in granite, biotite cleaves in one dimension while hornblende cleaves in two dimensions.

Now notice how much easier it is to compare the answers when the repeated information is moved to the question:

> **Both biotite and hornblende can be black in color, and both occur in granite. What are some differences between hornblende and biotite?**
>
> ☐ Only hornblende contains sodium.
>
> ☐ Hornblende crystals are triclinic. Those of biotite are monoclinic.
>
> ☐ Hornblende is harder than biotite.
>
> ☐ Biotite cleaves in one dimension while hornblende cleaves in two dimensions.

SEQUENCE TEST QUESTIONS EFFECTIVELY

Most tests consist of a sequence of questions. Consider how separate questions are best combined for a comprehensive test.

Ask multiple questions about one scenario. For complex subjects, create a series of test questions based on the same situation, scenario, or description.

Make it easy for the learner to refer to the original explanation:

▶ Link back to the original explanation from each question.

▶ Repeat salient facts in each question.

▶ Display the scenario in a separate frame or window from the questions.

Ramp up the difficulty. Vary the difficulty of test questions so that no one completely fails yet few get a perfect score. Start with the simpler questions. That way learners taste success and are motivated to continue trying. Learners who cannot answer any of the first three questions are likely to despair and not sincerely try later ones. Or they may spend so much of their time on the initial difficult questions that they do not get to the easy ones within the time limit of the test.

Keep the sequence short. Few people like long tests. Four or five questions make a nice pop quiz. A dozen are enough for almost any sequence. A test containing more than 15 questions is a police interrogation.

If you feel these limits are too restrictive, break your test into multiple short tests and sprinkle them among the presentation of material.

Enable navigation. If practical, let learners skip back and forth among the questions, answering the ones they can and skipping over the ones they cannot. Either put all the questions onto the same Web page or include navigation buttons to skip among the pages of a test. Make clear that skipping over a question does not lock in an answer until the time limit expires.

Make questions independent. Answering one question should not affect a learner's ability to answer subsequent questions. Make sure that the wording of one question and its answers do not imply the answers to subsequent questions.

Vary the form of questions and answers. To keep a series of questions from becoming monotonous, vary the way questions and answers are phrased.

- ▶ **Mix different forms of questions:** true/false, multiple-choice, text-entry, drag-and-drop, and click-in-picture.

- ▶ **Design each question to test for a different common misconception.** Ask different kinds of questions, such as what, when, why, where, and how.

- ▶ **Vary the form of questions.** Ask learners to pick the right answer. Then the one wrong answer. Then the best answer. Ask which of a list of statements do apply, then which do not apply.

- ▶ **Vary the position of the correct answer** in multiple-choice lists. However, if several questions have the same list of answers, do not vary the order of the answers.

GIVE MEANINGFUL FEEDBACK

After learners answer a question, they crave feedback. Did I get the right answer? No? Why not? What's wrong with my answer? What did I misunderstand? How can I correct my misunderstanding? Provide such feedback. And, if necessary, include links back to the original material.

Provide complete information

Tests can teach too. Feedback on test questions helps learners correct misunderstandings and augment knowledge. Feedback that merely says "Right" or "Wrong" does little to motivate or instruct learners [94]. For each answer, consider including:

- ▶ **The question.** Repeat or redisplay the question. If questions are numbered, include the question number.

- ▶ **Right/wrong flag.** Avoid vagueness. Do not say "Almost" or "Not quite" but simply "Wrong" or "Incorrect."

- ▶ **The correct answer.**

- ▶ **The learner's answer.** Learners may not have entered what they thought they did.

- ▶ **Why the correct answer is right** (and, if necessary, why the learner's answer is wrong).

- ▶ **Link to the original presentation** or a remedial one on this subject. Also include instructions on how to resume after reviewing the material.

Here is a simple example of helpful feedback. It annotates the learner's answer to provide the necessary feedback.

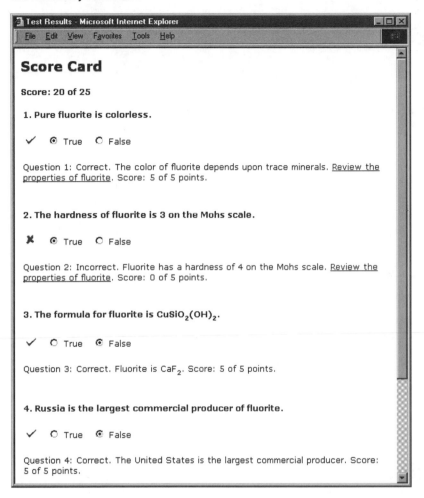

For right answers ...

For a correct answer, be brief. Tell learners they were right and state the main reason why (they might have guessed the answer). Be enthusiastic, but do not be effusive. For positive feedback, just say "Correct," "Right," or "Yes."

For right answers, challenge the learner to think about how they got the right answer and to consider other methods.

> Right. How did you get your answer? Did you already know? Or did you look it up on a Web site or get it through a newsgroup? Or was some paper document the source?

The feedback for a correct answer can teach additional information. You already have the attention of a happy, receptive learner. Use it. Notice how the following example adds related information.

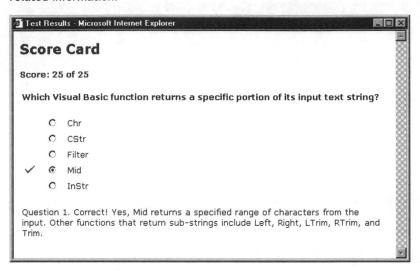

> Praise out of season, or tactlessly bestowed, can freeze the
> heart as much as blame.
>
> — Pearl S. Buck

For wrong answers ...

For an incorrect answer, gently but clearly point out the problem.

Use a neutral term

For negative feedback, use a neutral term, such as "incorrect" without any exclamation points, please. You can also use "sorry" or "not quite," though these may seem a bit patronizing. Do not say, "Wrong!!!" or "Gotcha" or "I don't think so."

Do not embarrass or insult the learner

Do not shout at people if they get something wrong—no flashing headlines or embarrassing noises.

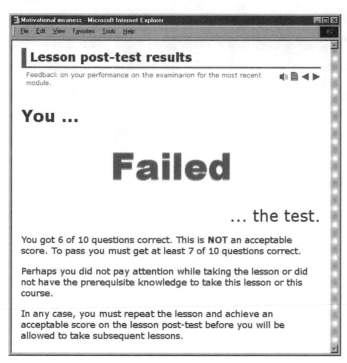

How would you like to receive this feedback? The word *Failed* appears in a blood red color and jiggles on the screen, accompanied by a chorus of boos. Also notice the condescending tone.

Acknowledge partial success

Give learners credit for the questions they got right. Encourage learners to try again. Give them choices so they feel in control. Notice how this feedback acknowledges an almost-passing score and suggests alternatives for how the learner should proceed.

Since your score was close to a passing score, you may want to quickly review the lesson summary and then retake this test. (You will see a new set of questions.)

If you feel you understand the material well enough, you may go on to the next lesson.

You can always return and take this test later.

Hint first

Instead of giving the correct answer as feedback to an incorrect guess, consider displaying a hint and challenging the learner to try again. Or include a **Hint** button to let learners request a little help answering the question.

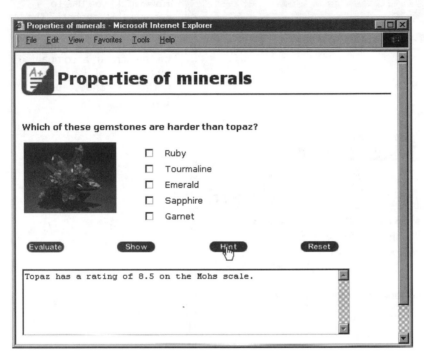

Notice how clicking on the **Hint** button reveals a fact that makes answering the question easier.

If many right answers are possible ...

If a question can have several right answers, say so in the feedback. Provide one such answer with comments on why it is right. Or list all the answers and describe when each is the best answer. For example:

> Incorrect. There are several ways to move backward to the end of a recordset, depending on the type of recordset you created. The most direct is the .MoveFirst method, which works for all recordsets that allow moving backward and forward in the recordset. Moving to an absolute record number is another alternative, for recordsets that support it, because it repeatedly uses the .MovePrevious method until .BOF tests true. For recordsets opened for forward-only movement, you must reopen the recordset.

This example corrects misunderstandings that programmers may have about how to navigate within data they have retrieved.

Tell why other answers are wrong

If many learners give the same wrong answers, consider providing feedback on why these answers are wrong. For pick multiple questions, make clear why other choices are wrong.

> The correct answers are Doyle and Scribner.
>
> Doyle and Scribner are both common methods of measuring the lumber volume of trees. Cordage is a measure of the volume of cut wood and is used for pulpwood. IDN and Wocon are just made-up terms and have nothing to do with forestry.

Avoid wimpy feedback

Compared to the computer games that players love, much electronic training gives timid feedback.

> … the feedback given the learner is too dull, too politically correct, and a tad too worried about the possibility of hurting the feelings of the person taking the course. Often feedback consists of telling the user she answered a question incorrectly and inviting her sweetly to review the lesson again so she can get it right—Bob Filipczak, *Training Magazine* [102].

In a game, you always know exactly how well you are doing. If you fail to perform, the game mocks you or your character dies. I am not suggesting we abuse or decimate our learners; just consider a bit more direct approach. Avoid weak and vague feedback messages like these:

> Good try, but you could have done better.
>
> We're sorry but that is not the best answer.
>
> Almost. Would you like to try another guess?
>
> Close, oh so very, very close.
>
> Oh, too bad.
>
> Bummer!

Simply say "Right" or "Wrong" and explain why the answer was right or wrong.

Include a show-answer button

If the feedback does not reveal the correct answer, consider including a **Show Answer** button. The **Show Answer** button lets learners at least see an acceptable answer before moving on—thus ensuring they are not left remembering their last incorrect attempt. It also prevents frustration from rising to the point that it interferes with learning.

True, a **Show Answer** button can be abused by learners unwilling to try to answer the question for themselves. In practice, it is seldom a problem. Most learners select it only after they have tried to answer the question on their own. To force learners to answer the question before selecting **Show Answer**, hide or disable the **Show Answer** button until the learner answers.

IMPROVE TESTING

Few tests are perfect the first time out. With careful monitoring and revision, however, you can eliminate the most common problems.

Monitor results

One of the best ways to improve a course is to examine the log files after a reasonable number of learners have taken tests. Look for the symptoms of easily corrected problems, such as these:

Questions with higher or lower than normal success rates	These questions may be too easy or too hard.
Questions that many learners skip.	Learners may not understand these questions, they may take too long to read, or they may be too difficult to answer.
Large number of questions left unanswered on timed tests.	If learners leave more than a few questions unanswered, you may need to increase the time or decrease the number of questions.

Solicit feedback from learners

Invite learners to comment on the tests. Request feedback from learners about a test, but only after the test has been graded. This delay gives learners time to calm down so their responses are more reasoned and less emotional. And learners respond based on the actual grade rather than the anticipated one. Learners can point out unclear or unfair questions.

Make tests fair to all learners

Sometimes learners may feel tests are unfair. They believe that tests ask improper questions or do not give all learners an equal chance to answer questions correctly. Common complaints include:

▶ Questions not within the scope of stated objectives.

▶ Questions that depend on irrelevant skills or on knowledge not mentioned in prerequisites.

▶ Culturally biased questions that rely on knowledge that one culture might possess but another might not

▶ Questions on information not in the current unit of study—the as-shown-above-syndrome

▶ Complex, tricky language that is especially difficult for second-language readers

▶ Unfamiliar terminology

▶ Unreasonable time limits

As a check on course design, make each test question pass a test itself. This test has three questions:

▶ Which objective does this question test?

▶ Where was the material presented?

▶ Can someone with minimal reading skills interpret the question and answers accurately and swiftly?

Test early and often

As soon as you teach learners something, give them an opportunity to apply that knowledge in order to lock it into memory and demonstrate competence and to proceed with material that is more difficult. Asking questions about knowledge learners have just acquired helps them consolidate and integrate the knowledge [94].

Include more short tests rather than just a few long ones. In a large course, include several exams evenly spaced throughout the course—not just one big exam at the end.

Many courses present a series of concepts and then test on them all. By the time learners reach the test, they have forgotten what they learned about the earlier concepts. Also, the big test can seem intimidating.

Instead of one big test at the end, sprinkle small tests throughout the material. Thus learners do not proceed without learning. Because these tests are small, they are less intimidating. After the final concept, present a brief review and a short test on all the concepts.

Design the smaller tests so they accurately predict performance on the larger tests.

Define a scale of grades

Rather than a pass-fail threshold, give learners ranges of scores along with recommendations of how to proceed. For example:

---

100 points Perfect! Feel free to skip ahead. You may want go directly to the test for the next lesson.

90-99 points Great! You have a firm grasp of the basics. Skim the next lesson before taking its test.

75-89 points Good! You understand the basics. You can continue with the next lesson now.

50-74 points Your score should be better before you proceed to the next lesson. Please review the summary and take the test again.

0-49 points You need to spend some more time working on the basics. We suggest you take the lesson again, paying special attention to the practices and activities. Then when you feel you have mastered the material, take the test again.

Vary test and practice forms

Vary the types of test questions you ask. As a rule, do not use the same type of test questions more than three times in a row. For example, to test knowledge of the vocabulary of a programming language, you can use all of these forms:

▶ Pick one definition from a list.

Use InStrRev to:

- ○ Compare two strings.
- ○ Convert a string to uppercase or lowercase.
- ○ Reverse a string that is passed to it.
- ⊙ Return the first place within a string that another string occurs, from the end of the string.
- ○ Return the first place within a string that another string occurs.

▶ Pick one term from a list.

Which Visual Basic function returns a specific portion of its input text string?

▶ Match terms and their definitions.

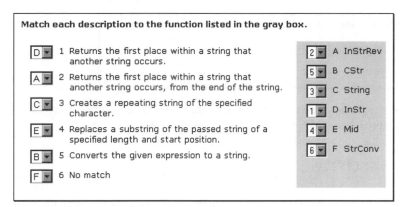

Match each description to the function listed in the gray box.

D ▼ 1 Returns the first place within a string that another string occurs.

A ▼ 2 Returns the first place within a string that another string occurs, from the end of the string.

C ▼ 3 Creates a repeating string of the specified character.

E ▼ 4 Replaces a substring of the passed string of a specified length and start position.

B ▼ 5 Converts the given expression to a string.

F ▼ 6 No match

2 ▼ A InStrRev
5 ▼ B CStr
3 ▼ C String
1 ▼ D InStr
4 ▼ E Mid
6 ▼ F StrConv

▶ Crossword puzzle.

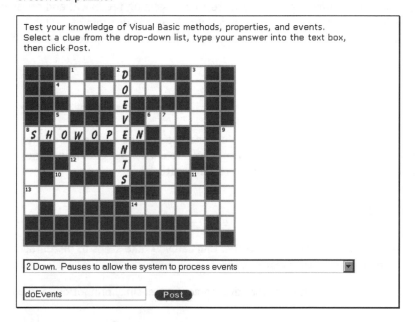

Test your knowledge of Visual Basic methods, properties, and events. Select a clue from the drop-down list, type your answer into the text box, then click Post.

2 Down. Pauses to allow the system to process events ▼

doEvents   Post

▶ Type a term to match a definition.

In the Common Dialog control, which property limits the file types shown in the Open File dialog box?   Filter

▶ Type a term into context.

```
Complete this code to create an instance of Microsoft Word.

Dim x as Object

set x     = CreateObject("word.basic")
```

Such variety can make training more interesting—and more effective. Learners exercise different skills and solve different kinds of problems, just as in the real world.

Do not score every activity

Give learners lots of practice activities and just a few recorded tests. Tracking the learner's every attempt and recording every score discourages quick, spontaneous action. The rapid cycle of assessing a situation, forming a hypothesis, testing it, getting feedback, and revising the hypothesis is a valuable learning event in its own right. Give learners lots of opportunities to practice without the fear that their every mistake is being recorded in ink.

PREVENT CHEATING

Alas, some people will cheat—even highly paid professionals taking the course under their own initiative. Sometimes even people who know the answers cheat. But cheating denies learners a chance to see how well they have mastered the material.

Why do learners cheat?

Only when you understand why learners may be cheating can you take steps to discourage cheating. What are some of the reasons learners cheat?

▶ Test scores affect the learners' chances for advancement, licensing, promotion, and pay increases.

▶ Learners fear the embarrassment of a low test score.

▶ Learners are angry with the instructor, the organization offering the course, or their own organization.

▶ Learners find cheating more challenging and fun than taking the test.

▶ Some cultures do not view cheating as wrong but as a sanctioned part of the adversarial relationship with the instructor whereby learners demonstrate their cleverness.

How can I detect cheating?

Before you assume you have a problem with cheating—and always before you accuse anyone of cheating—check to see if there is any evidence of widespread cheating. Compare test results to other activities, such as participation in discussions. Compare results on new and old questions. Compare proctored and unproctored results.

Inconsistent results warrant closer examination. Are the differences caused by differences in the difficulty of various ways of monitoring performance? Or are they evidence of cheating?

How do learners cheat?

Cheating takes many forms. Here are a few of the common ways that WBT learners cheat:

▶ Get others to take the test for them (the impersonation problem).

▶ Use extra resources, such as books, notes, calculators.

▶ Ask other learners what is on the test.

▶ Create multiple accounts and take the test more than once.

▶ Examine the JavaScript or VBScript used to score answers.

Reduce cheating

You probably cannot eliminate cheating, but you can reduce it to a minimum. There are three main strategies for dealing with cheating. One approach, called the *Trust* method, aims at reducing the incentives for cheating. It trusts learners to obey the rules. The second approach, sometimes called the *Fence* method, tries to make cheating impossible. The third method, the *Threat* method, threatens learners with punishments if they are caught cheating. You may choose one or more of these approaches or combine elements from them, depending on your situation.

Trust approach

In the Trust approach, you remove unnecessary incentives for cheating and then trust learners not to cheat. The core of the Trust approach is to remind learners that they are responsible for their own learning, that they only cheat themselves, and that you trust them. Here is such a statement:

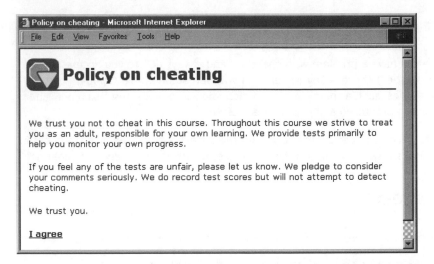

After posting a similar reminder, take steps to reduce the incentive to cheat. Where you can do so without reducing the educational effectiveness, lessen the importance of tests and allow activities that would otherwise be considered cheating:

▶ **Make tests easier**. Add a few easy questions so that no one gets zero correct.

▶ **Reduce the importance of grades**. Does your organization really need to record a grade?

▶ **Use tests for only a small percentage of the total grade**. Consider the learner's participation in discussions, team activities, and other evidence of performance.

▶ **Allow "open-Web" tests** in which learners can consult all available resources.

▶ **Let learners challenge questions they consider unfair**, and let other learners decide whether the question was unfair or not.

Fence approach

In the Fence approach, you try to make cheating impossible. You build a fence between appropriate and inappropriate behavior. You may not succeed totally, but you can make cheating harder than studying. At the very least, you can plug the biggest security holes in your testing procedures:

▶ Create new test questions for each test.

▶ Randomly select questions from a list.

▶ Randomly order multiple-choice answers.

▶ Put the evaluation script for a test in a separate file and call it by reference.

▶ Require proctored paper final exams.

▶ Perform evaluation only on the server, not within the test itself.

Threat approach

In the Threat approach, you threaten punishment to those caught cheating. Such an approach requires authority over the learner. Thus it is usually instigated and enforced by the learner's employer rather than just the course provider.

The essence of the threat is a clear, strongly worded policy stating that cheating will not be tolerated and will be punished. Because penalties may include demotion, suspension, or dismissal, the organization drafting the policy must do so deliberately and carefully. Typically, such a policy is proposed by the human resources department and drafted by the legal department. A policy should include statements such as these:

► Cheating is defined as taking unfair advantage on tests and other graded activities.

► Cheating is wrong and will not be tolerated.

► The testing organization will attempt to detect cheating.

► Learners caught cheating will be punished. Punishments range from mild warning for a first occurrence to termination of employment for repeated incidents.

► Those who help another cheat are treated as cheaters.

► Those who fail to report cheating by others are treated as cheaters.

► Accusations of cheating are treated as confidential. Knowledge of the incident will be limited to the legal department, the human resources department, the person accused, and that person's immediate supervisor.

► Those accused of cheating may appeal. (Spell out the process.)

The policy on cheating can be integrated into the "contract" that the learner must agree to before beginning the test. In fact, you may want to make agreeing to the no-cheating policy a condition for enrolling in the course. The Threat approach is drastic and can make honorable learners feel untrusted. I suggest reserving it for cases in which learners are immature or the pressures to cheat are high.

Validate test-takers

WBT testing suffers from one big concern: How do we ensure that the person taking the test plays by the rules?

► Is the person taking the test who they say they are?

► Are they alone?

► Are they using only permitted tools, reference works, and other resources?

► Did they know ahead of time what the questions would be?

These are the same concerns that have confounded those in the distance-learning field from its inception, and, to some extent, all large classes where instructors cannot know and observe each test-taker individually.

Proctor tests

The most common method to authenticate test-takers is to have the test proctored by a school official, librarian, or corporate manager at a site near the learner. Some schools require the learner to take the test on campus [61].

Identify by background

Another method to authenticate test-takers is to gather details about the background of the learner. Use these details to ensure that the same person participates throughout the course:

1. At the beginning of the course, ask learners to describe their job and how the subject of the course relates to that job. Require specific details.

2. Verify the description independently.

3. As a "final exam" have learners write a detailed plan for how they will apply what they have learned in the course to their jobs. Require a specific action plan.

4. Grade on the specifics and plausibility of their plan. Ensure that the plan is consistent with the learner's job and learning goals as described in Step 1.

Observe by video?

One possible solution is to use videoconferencing facilities to observe learners as they take a test. In some environments, videoconferencing is technically feasible but must overcome some tough problems. Some organizations may not want to allocate network bandwidth to such purposes. Some learners may lack the technical skills or support needed to get video cameras working. Learners may object to being spied on. And there are definite limits on how much an instructor can observe through video.

CONSIDER ALTERNATIVES TO TESTS

Testing in WBT obviously has limitations and is not always the best way to evaluate the progress of learners. Testing is certainly not the only way. Before you start designing tests, take a few minutes to consider alternatives to tests.

Use more than formal, graded tests

Not all assessments need to be formal, graded tests. Use a mixture of different forms of assessment:

- ▶ Formal graded tests
- ▶ Open-book tests
- ▶ Self-graded tests
- ▶ Ungraded tests
- ▶ Activities
- ▶ Games
- ▶ Puzzles
- ▶ Research projects
- ▶ Tests taken by teams instead of individuals

Measure performance in the workplace

To verify that learning is transferred to the workplace, conduct a simulation or role-playing exercise in the workplace. To see how well managers at the Response Marketing Services division of Moore Corporation in Green Bay, Wisconsin, had mastered interviewing skills taught by a CD-ROM course, the company had managers conduct mock interviews with interviewers from outside the company [103].

The Mortgage Bankers Association of America phoned learners at their desks, asking them to quote the current rate for fixed-rate mortgages [58]. The phone call tested whether they had mastered the material of the course they had just completed.

Help learners build portfolios

Instead of testing on knowledge, have learners create tangible evidence of their learning. Base grading on a work-ready portfolio the learner assembles during the class [104]. The portfolio can consist of samples of a variety of work products or the completion of a single, complex plan or report.

For those already working in the field of the course, the portfolio can consist of materials that can be used immediately on the job. For those preparing for a new field, the portfolio can consist of samples that demonstrate competence to practice in the field.

Have learners collect tokens

Rather than requiring learners to pass a series of tests, challenge them to collect tokens that represent completion of activities. Each test and activity is worth a certain number of tokens in proportion to the scope and value of the knowledge it requires. For "tokens" pick objects related to the subject matter or the prevailing metaphor of the user interface.

IN CLOSING ...

Summary

- ▶ Use tests to let learners gauge their progress and administrators measure the effectiveness of the course.

- ▶ Use a variety of text forms—from simple true/false and multiple-choice questions to matching-list, click-in-picture, fill-in-the-blanks, and simulation questions.

- ▶ Write test questions so they measure skills and knowledge, not the ability to decipher tricky phrases or to make lucky guesses.

- ▶ For simple questions, provide feedback immediately so misconceptions are identified and corrected before they take root.

- ▶ Consider alternatives to automatically scored tests for grading: on-job simulations, portfolios, and instructor-scored tests.

- ▶ Test early and often. Use unrecorded tests for frequent practice. Make tests more like challenging games and less like school examinations.

For more ...

For more sophisticated tests, consider using learning activities (Chapter 6). Most will, however, require grading by the instructor.

Search the Web for **online testing** or **Web-based testing**.

Before buying a tool for authoring and delivering WBT, try out the types of tests it provides and investigate how you can add tests of your own design.

Simulations integrate teaching and testing. Consider a learning game (p 251) or whole simulation course (p 567).

Many of the examples shown in this book are on exhibit at:

www.horton.com/DesigningWBT/

8

Promote collaboration

E-mail, chat, discussion groups, screen sharing, conferencing, and more

In WBT courses, distributed learners and instructors can use the Internet to communicate fully and freely. Learners and instructors can use e-mail, discussion groups, chat, virtual response pads, and conferencing to exchange messages as part of formal learning activities (Chapter 6) or just to ask a question. The Web makes collaboration easy.

DECIDE WHETHER TO USE COLLABORATION

Collaboration can energize learners, promote deeper learning, and make learners more self-reliant—but not without some costs and risks.

Collaboration works

Adding discussion groups, chats, and e-mail to courses motivates learners, increases participation in projects, and enlivens discussion. Learners are more willing to participate in online discussions and other activities than in traditional ones [60]. With collaboration, learners "feel more empowered. They are daring and confrontational regarding the expression of ideas" [60].

Virtual teams can be as effective as face-to-face teams [105]. And, for motivated adult learners, collaborative learning can be more interactive and effective than traditional classroom learning [106]. In one controlled experiment, learners who worked together but who lacked face-to-face contact with the instructor scored 20% higher than those in a traditional classroom course [55].

Collaboration mechanisms simplify communications. Internet collaboration tools promote full and spontaneous communication among learners, instructors, and others. No one has to look up an address on a smudged, out-of-date address list, find a stamp, decipher someone else's handwriting, or file away copies for future reference. Because communication is easier, participants communicate more often and more freely.

Communication is more complete. Once learners become accustomed to the ease of electronic collaboration, they communicate more freely. This leads to more lively conversations, which in turn spur even more collaboration [107]. Fewer questions go unasked. Fewer ideas are held back.

Learners are treated equally. Because learners are anonymous, they are free of bias and stereotyping. Race, gender, age, background, appearance, and disabilities matter less than knowledge and creativity. Anonymity empowers people to participate more fully and confidently in collaboration [108].

Learners become more self-reliant. Learners, in the absence of face-to-face contact with the instructor, compensate in two ways. First, they are forced to seek out their own sources of information, learn to evaluate them critically, and monitor their own learning. Secondly, they rely more on fellow learners. They form study groups, participate more actively in discussions, and take more responsibility and authority for themselves [55].

Instructors can monitor the performance and behavior of learners in an unobtrusive manner. Instructors can lurk in discussion groups and chat sessions. They can request that learners copy them (using the CC: feature in their e-mail program) on all course-related e-mail exchanges.

Learners share knowledge and the burden of learning. The ability of collaborators to share thoughts on the same issue enables collaborative learning [74]. Benefits include:

▶ Learners can harvest the knowledge of the entire community.

▶ Learners draw inspiration from the wealth of viewpoints contributed.

▶ Instructors have ample feedback to improve basic learning materials.

▶ Instructors are freed from having to repeatedly answer the same question.

▶ Instructors do not have to comment on submissions one by one.

▶ The instructor is not the only evaluator. More eyes are more likely to spot more problems—and offer more creative insights.

But collaboration is not easy

Proponents of collaboration in WBT (and vendors of collaboration tools) rhapsodize on the bountiful blessings of collaboration in WBT. This romantic myth is often repeated:

> In a collaborative learning environment, learners are exposed to many people's opinions and interpretations of objects and events. The learner's own ideas and conceptions are valued and are debated by the learning community. Since learners' misconceptions are challenged they have occasion to modify their knowledge structures—Christian Pantel, *A Framework for Comparing Web-Based Learning Environments* [109].

In reality, the process is often brutalizing, inefficient, and demoralizing. Exchanges are peppered with flames, slurs, and slams. Discussions can meander worse than a rudderless ship with a drunken captain on a stormy night.

Without good design, some learners are penalized. Poorly designed group learning activities "can stigmatize low achievers, exacerbate status differences, and create dysfunctional interactions among learners" [110]. Collaborative activities may not be suited to those anxious about interacting with other learners [111].

Not everyone can participate. Some people will not be able to participate in synchronous events due to illness, travel, business engagements, or family duties. Unfortunately, these people are often the busy go-getters who want and need training most.

Instructors must work harder. Lacking face-to-face contact with the instructor, learners demand more virtual contact with the instructor through e-mail, chat, and discussion groups [68]. As one instructor put it, "I used to answer a question once in class. Now I answer it twenty times by e-mail."

Conversations are awkward. In face-to-face meetings we rely on the gestures and tone of voice of others to alert us that they are wrapping up a point and that we should prepare to respond [112]. In Web collaboration, these cues may be missing, and awkward silences may result. Bob, after several seconds of silence, suddenly realizes he did not listen to Mary's last question and must ask her to repeat it.

DETERMINE THE KINDS OF COLLABORATION MECHANISMS

This section provides you with general guidance in picking collaboration mechanisms to weave into your course. First, decide what kind of person-to-person interaction best furthers the objectives of your course. Then, implement this interaction in the form and technology appropriate for your situation.

Consider all the issues

To decide which collaboration mechanisms to incorporate into your course, answer each of the questions in this section. Each question helps you zero in on your specific requirements. Armed with these requirements, you can decide how to implement the needed capabilities.

Do you really need a collaborative event?

Collaborative activities are too complex and expensive to use when a simple Web page would work just as well. The first question to ask yourself is "Do I really need a collaborative event?" If information is simple, you can just present it in a well-designed Web page. If all you need is interactivity, consider whether the computer can provide that interactivity. For any proposed collaborative activity, specify the essential roles of the instructor and learners.

Which media do you really need?

Make a list of the media learners must use to communicate in collaborative events: text, voice, body language, static pictures, moving pictures, interactive drawings or computer programs, and so forth.

The choice of collaboration mechanisms limits the vocabulary of signs and signals used in meetings [112]. These limitations have real effects on learners' abilities to communicate fully. If you are teaching basic writing skills, text will do fine. If you are teaching interviewing skills, voice and body language are necessary.

Consider also any materials you already have prepared: slides, papers, videotapes, speeches, photographs, and so forth. Although these materials may not be ideal, you may need to use them until you have time to prepare better materials. What collaboration mechanisms can best handle these materials?

How do you need to route messages?

Who will send messages to whom? What message routing schemes (topologies) do you need?

One to one   ☐ ⟶ ☐   In one-to-one or private messaging, only the sender and the receiver have access to the message. This scheme is like a telephone conversation (two-way) or a private letter (one-way).

Broadcast

Broadcast messaging enables one person to send a message to everyone else. Typically this scheme is used by the instructor for making announcements to all learners in the course.

Some-to-some

In a some-to-some routing scheme everyone can send messages and everyone can select which messages they receive. This is like a bulletin board where everyone can post notes but no one need read more than catch their eyes.

All to all

In all-to-all messaging everybody receives every message sent by everybody. This is like a roundtable meeting where everybody hears everything said by everybody else.

These routings are just the simplest and most common forms. Most real activities combine several modes. For example, a question-and-answer session begins with a broadcast requesting a question. This is followed by the transmission of the question in a one-to-one mode, which is finally followed by broadcast of the question and its answer.

Which mechanisms can learners use effectively?

You should match the capabilities of collaboration media to the needs and capabilities of your learners. There is no use in selecting a mechanism that learners cannot operate successfully. Consider the skills and expertise of learners:

Language fluency. Some collaborations requires greater language skills than others. Unless learners are all fluent in a language, real-time collaboration mechanisms like chat, audioconferencing, and videoconferencing may frustrate those who would prefer e-mail or discussion groups, which allow more time to carefully compose and revise a response.

Accents. Internet audio quality can exacerbate difficulties in understanding speakers with a distinct accent. I took part in one international audioconference conducted in English in which the Swedes could not understand the Pakistanis, who could not understand the Texan, who could understand everybody except the British, who thought all the Americans "sounded like a bad Hollywood movie."

Typing skill. Chat is a spontaneous medium—for touch typists. Unfortunately, many learners are not proficient typists.

Technical expertise. Some learners have been chatting on the net for years. Others are still trying to master the double-click. You need to consider how comfortable learners are with computer and Internet technology. How much must they extend themselves to master collaboration tools? If learners already know how to use a whiteboard, then screen sharing is not much of a stretch. If they have just learned to use e-mail, expecting them to master chat, whiteboard, and videoconferencing is probably too much.

Also consider what technical support you can offer. If learners must master collaboration tools on their own, they may become discouraged. If you (or the tool's vendor) provide tutorials and phone support, the task is less daunting.

Which tools will learners prefer?

You should also consider which collaboration mechanisms learners would prefer to use. Few learners have much experience with collaboration tools. We are still in the first act and nobody's died or fallen in love yet. But we can notice some trends.

Learners like to control their online persona

With asynchronous, non-visual media we have greater control over our persona. We can choose our words carefully. We never have to respond in anger or without time to think. We can edit out our negative traits. We can filter our responses according to how we want others to perceive us. Many learners, citing reasons such as these, have told me they like discussion groups better than other mechanisms.

What tools do people really use?

Reliable statistics are hard to come by. Often learners have little choice: Either use the tool or drop the class. In one Web-conducted geography course at Western Michigan University, learners used various tools as follows [53]:

Web pages	100%
Online meetings (with NetMeeting)	100%
Whiteboard	83%
Screen sharing	57%
Chat	30%

Although the use of chat may seem low, my experience is that this figure is actually quite high. Almost none of the 1000 learners who took a pilot Web-based course on coaching skills used the available chat rooms [57].

How large and widely distributed is the class?

Collaboration requires people with common interests. For real-time collaboration, it helps if most of them are awake. So consider the size of your class and from which time zones learners will be taking it. Consider these cases:

Class of one. Some courses are not structured as a class. Learners proceed at their own pace on their own schedule. Normally no two students are at the same place in the material at the same time. In such a case, real-time activities are not practical. In fact, collaboration may be difficult indeed (p 392). Emphasize self-guided activities.

Small class. In a small class, say 5 to 10 learners, collaboration works well. You can use all-to-all routings without overloading participants. You may not have enough people for team activities though.

Large class. In large classes, over a dozen or so, all-to-all routings are not practical. You must rely more on broadcast and some-to-some routings. Collaboration activities require more supervision and control.

Time-zone spread. If more than a few time zones separate learners, live events become difficult. If learners are in many different countries with different political, business, and religious holidays, live events may be impossible to schedule.

What will collaboration mechanisms cost?

Collaboration mechanisms can be expensive. The costs of equipping all employees' computers with video inputs, upgrading the intranet to T3, and site-licensing collaboration software can shove some collaboration mechanisms out of the reach of cost-obsessed companies.

Consider what hardware and software your organization has in place. Take an inventory:

▶ What is the capacity of your organization's network? How much additional traffic can it carry?

▶ What built-in multimedia capabilities do the PCs have? Sound output? Sound input? Video input?

▶ What collaboration tools are already licensed as part of the operating system, of an e-mail system, or of a dedicated collaboration package?

Do learners have high-speed connections?

Learners may have a fast network—in theory—but have slow individual connections to that network. What speed modem and dial-up connections are available for mobile learners? A T3 network is no good to the hotel-bound learner whose laptop sports a mere 14.4 Kbps modem.

What will be the real speed of the network by the time you release your courses?

To the right is a rough scale of what real speed most media require.

1 Mbps	Videoconferencing (2-way)
256 Kbps	Videoconferencing (1-way)
128 Kbps	Audioconferencing
56 Kbps	Screen sharing
28.8 Kbps	Whiteboard, chat
14.4 Kbps	Discussion groups, e-mail, keypad

TechnoTip: Do not depend on a fast Internet connection

Your learners around the globe are all connected to the Internet with high-speed connections. Why then does the sound stutter and video skip? The problem may be what is termed "Internet latency." Internet latency is a flashy term bandied about to explain why the actual speed of the Internet is far short of its theoretical speed.

First, the speed of a connection between point A and point B is no faster than the slowest link between A and B. An individual packet of information may travel through thousands of different cables, routers, and gateways—any one of which can add a hairpin curve to the expressway. And each packet may take a different route with different impediments. Not until all the packets have wandered in can the message be reassembled and displayed or played.

Second, the packets of your videoconference can run into a traffic jam. Those packets must travel over the same links used by twenty million Internet users trying to download the latest bug fix for their browser and the fan club of the latest pop singer swapping pirated recordings of their idol.

Third, the speed of the connection does not matter if the server is even slower. Pumping out large video and audio files can slow even the fastest server. If the server delivering your course has other duties to perform, it may occasionally be slower than promised.

Pick an approach

Before you start picking specific brands of collaboration tools, you should decide on a strategy to provide collaboration mechanisms. Some strategies emphasize ease-of-use; others emphasize advanced capabilities. Some are more expensive than others. The three most common approaches are (1) letting learners use any tool that meets industry standards, (2) using already-implemented collaboration tools, and (3) buying a WBT package with built-in collaboration tools.

Specify standards, not tools

One solution is to leave open the choice of tools and instead specify the industry standard protocol you will use for each capability. You then implement servers that use these industry-standard protocols (IRC, POP3, NNTP). And you let learners pick the tools they prefer for each capability. Just require that the tools can all communicate using the standard protocol. Some common standard protocols include these:

Capability	Protocol	Name
E-Mail	POP3	Post Office Protocol, Version 3
	SMTP	Simple Mail Transfer Protocol
	IMAP	Internet Message Access Protocol
Chat	IRC	Internet Relay Chat
Discussion	NNTP	Network News Transfer Protocol
File download	FTP	File Transfer Protocol
Audioconferencing and videoconferencing	ITU H323	International Telecommunications Union H323
Screen sharing, whiteboard	ITU T120	International Telecommunications Union T120
Directory services	LDAP	Lightweight Directory Access Protocol

8

Promote collaboration

Use the organization's collaboration tools

Many companies and universities have already installed collaboration and conferencing tools, such as Microsoft's Exchange and Windows NetMeeting or IBM's Lotus Notes. Most Web-server packages include e-mail, news, and chat servers. The tools already in place may provide most of the capabilities you need in your course.

Using the corporate tools not only demonstrates an enterprise solidarity that can win favor with the IT department, it also makes the course more a part of everyday business. Obviously, costs are less as there is less software to buy and the wires are already strung. Learners are already familiar with these tools, so there is little additional training required.

Established tools, however, may not be ideal for your course. With a little creativity, though, you can probably make them work—at least until you can justify a more costly solution.

To use such tools, link to them where possible. Otherwise, provide simple, clear instructions on how to start up and use each tool for a particular event.

If your organization's basic conferencing tools are not adequate, you may want to upgrade to a more powerful product. A dedicated conferencing package offers advanced and convenience features that may prove important if your course relies heavily on interpersonal communications.

Some of the organizational collaboration systems come with add-ons or companion products that add features needed for WBT. For example, IBM would be happy to enhance your Lotus Notes installation to include Lotus Learning Space, a complete suite of tools for delivering training over an intranet. Which brings us to our next option ....

Buy an integrated WBT package

Several vendors offer server-based packages for delivering WBT. Such packages range from virtual classrooms that support mostly synchronous events to course-management systems that supply infrastructure for mostly asynchronous courses. Many of these packages include or are built around collaboration and communications tools. A few of the better-known WBT and collaboration packages are:

▶ WebCT (www.webct.com)

▶ TopClass (www.wbtsystems.com)

▶ Lotus Learning Space (www.lotus.com/home.nsf/welcome/learnspace)

▶ Generation21 (www.generation21.com)

▶ Centra (www.centra.com)

▶ Docent Enterprise (www.docent.com)

Such packages often provide more than collaboration tools, so choose one based on more than your needs for collaboration. These tools can be a bit expensive, so make sure your choice matches your current and future needs well.

> Those things for which the most money is demanded are never the things which the student most wants. Tuition, for instance, is an important item in the term bill, while for the far more valuable education which he gets by associating with the most cultivated of his contemporaries no charge is made.
>
> — Henry David Thoreau, *Walden*

IMPLEMENT COLLABORATION POLICIES

Electronic collaboration is a new world sparkling with potential for effective learning experiences, but harboring a few social and legal pitfalls. To realize the potential while protecting learners and your organization, you need effective policies spelling out what is and is not appropriate behavior. You may choose to include these policies as part of the general course policies (p 97) or as a separate policy.

Your collaboration policies should govern learners, instructors, and staff alike. But I suggest writing them to learners. The following section includes a sample policy along with comments. It may not fit your situation, but use it as a start toward developing your own policy. Make sure your legal department and management team approve the policy before you release it.

Our policy on collaborative activities

This course contains activities that involve collaborating with fellow learners, your instructor, and others. Such activities are a valuable part of learning, and we want you to get the most from them. To ensure effective collaboration, this policy spells out acceptable and unacceptable practices.

You are expected to follow this policy completely. If you violate this policy, you may be removed from the course.

Messages

OWNERSHIP Submitted messages become the property of ZipZapCom Training Department.

PERMISSIONS Before you submit anyone else's work, make sure you have their permission in writing. Clearly identify the owner and source of the material. It is OK to quote something submitted by another learner, provided you credit the source.

PRIVACY Assume that all messages you post are available to the rest of the class and the general public. Do not write something you want to keep secret from anyone: your boss, your mother, or your children.

PROPRIETARY OR CONFIDENTIAL INFORMATION Do not post or reveal proprietary, classified, secret, or otherwise restricted information.

RESPONSIBILITY The comments of learners represent their opinions, not necessarily those of their organizations or anyone else.

Behavior

WELCOME EVERYONE Make people of all backgrounds, ages, races, religions, national origins, genders, sexual orientations, and beliefs feel welcome. Refrain from statements of hatred, bigotry, and racism—even in jest. Make no defamatory statements or any that infringe the rights of others.

Specify what actions will be taken against those who violate the policy or whose postings violate company policies or laws.

Alternate ownership statement: Messages are the property of the sender. You may not republish any message without the sender's permission.

Alternate privacy statement: Postings to the group are private to members of the course. Do not reveal them to anyone outside the course.

Note: The discussion group moderator should reject inappropriate messages; remind senders of these policies (p 387).

DISRUPTING LEARNERS AND LEARNING Avoid any behavior that makes learning harder for others: Sending provoking, distracting, or misleading messages is forbidden. Messages designed to provoke angry or irrelevant responses are not allowed.

Send only messages that help others, further a conversation, or resolve an issue. Avoid messages that are:

> Irrelevant to the topic under discussion
>
> Unclear or misleading
>
> Repeats of an earlier posting
>
> Vulgar or suggestive
>
> Rants, diatribes, or temper tantrums

Though not forbidden, such messages may be removed by the moderator.

SPOOFING AND FORGERY Never pretend to be someone else in your interactions with other learners. (Role-playing activities are an exception.) Never alter documents of others. Never post documents under someone else's name.

PROFANITY Behave the way you would in a classroom or boardroom. Avoid obscene and profane language.

PORNOGRAPHY Send no pornographic materials.

Disputes

DISAGREEMENTS You may disagree with someone's idea. In fact, you are encouraged to question and challenge ideas. You are not, however, to attack persons. No libelous statements. No flames, verbal abuse, or harassing language.

REMEDIES If you experience what you consider inappropriate behavior on the part of another learner, or if a conflict with another learner prevents you from learning, it is your responsibility to confront the other learner and attempt to resolve the problem. If you cannot resolve the problem on your own, contact the instructor.

Alternative: If you experience what you consider inappropriate behavior on the part of another learner or if a conflict with another learner prevents your learning, contact your instructor immediately.

Personal security

DO NOT REVEAL SENSITIVE INFORMATION Do not reveal sensitive personal information to other learners. Notify the instructor immediately if anyone requests information such as this:

Home address

Phone number

Government ID numbers, Social Security number (or equivalent), or driver's license number

Credit card numbers

Accounts and passwords

Do not request this kind of information from others.

Attachments

VIRUS SCAN Scan any files you submit for viruses. You are responsible for any damage caused by files you upload.

FILE FORMATS For your submissions and attachments, select file formats that display correctly in the course's standard browser and environment. See technical requirements for details. Do not submit files that require nonstandard plug-ins or viewing programs.

Advertising

SALES OR SELF-PROMOTION Do not use the course to promote yourself, your organization, your company, or its products. It is OK to mention your own experiences and products that may be relevant to the course discussion. The mention should be objective and low-key. Sales pitches, chain letters, advertisements, or commercial activities are forbidden.

PICK SPECIFIC COLLABORATION MECHANISMS

Web technologies provide a wide range of collaboration mechanisms: e-mail, discussion groups, chat, whiteboard, screen sharing, response-pads, audioconferencing, and videoconferencing. This chapter guides you in selecting among these collaboration mechanisms. It helps you see what each offers and how its use in training may differ from its use elsewhere.

E-mail

E-mail is the most common method of collaboration in WBT. E-mail includes private messages sent one-to-one, say from a learner to ask a question of the instructor. Or they can be broadcast from the instructor to the class. (E-mail lists are considered as a kind of discussion group and are discussed on Page 348.)

Use private e-mail for immediacy, intimacy, and impact

Use one-to-one e-mail messages to ask and answer individual questions, but not for questions of general interest.

Do not use e-mail for routine messages that do not require special attention from the recipient. If a response is optional and the subject is not critical, post the message to a discussion group. If an immediate answer is crucial, use the telephone.

Perceived urgency

High

Personal visit

Telephone call

Private e-mail

Broadcast e-mail

discussion group posting

Low

Use private e-mail for intimacy and privacy. With e-mail exchanges learners feel more privacy (and more loneliness) than they do on discussion groups and chats [38]. Use e-mail for responses that might embarrass the recipient if posted in a public discussion group.

Use e-mail broadcasts for urgent class announcements

Use e-mail for announcements and reminders of approaching tests, imminent deadlines, upcoming events, schedule changes, guest speakers, and other newsworthy items.

TechnoTip: So that addresses are not revealed to the entire class and do not take up too much space in broadcast e-mail messages, put your address in the **To:** slot. Put the recipient list in the **bcc:** slot.

Only the instructor should broadcast messages

In general, only the instructor should broadcast messages to the entire class. Learners wishing to communicate with all others should post messages to a discussion group.

And only in special cases

Do not broadcast e-mail messages to the whole class except in special cases:

▶ At the beginning of the class to test learners' ability to receive and reply to e-mail.

▶ To announce critical changes, reschedule required events, and schedule tests.

▶ To correct a serious problem or widespread misconception.

Keep broadcast messages short

Keep broadcast e-mail messages short. Make them concise announcements. Direct readers to a Web page or discussion-group message for complete details.

Consider alternatives for course announcements

There are two other ways to make class announcements besides e-mail broadcasts:

▶ **Course home page.** If all learners stop at the Home page on their way into the course, put headlines of announcements there. Link the headlines to detailed explanations.

▶ **Announcement discussion group.** If learners regularly check discussion groups, you can set up a specific discussion group for class announcements and post announcements there.

However, if an announcement is critical, you may still want to send it by e-mail.

Use e-mail effectively

Here are just a few points that become important when using e-mail within a course.

Set reasonable expectations. Set reasonable expectations for response to e-mail, say 24 to 48 hours. That is, respond within two days and do not send a message that requires a response sooner than that.

Respond promptly. If you cannot respond quickly, send a short message acknowledging the message and promising a full reply later. Say when. If you will be out of your office for several days, use the auto-reply function of your e-mail system to notify senders when you will respond.

Introduce yourself when sending unsolicited e-mail. Begin by explaining who you are and your interest in the recipient. Explain why you are writing to this particular individual. Begin with a neutral greeting, such as "Dear colleague:" or "Greetings:".

Require delivery receipts only in special cases. Require delivery receipts for e-mail only where necessary. Some consider receipt requests a form of snooping. Do require delivery receipts if delivering a warning to a learner. You may need to document when the message was delivered.

Discussion groups

Discussion groups provide an opportunity for ongoing electronic conversations among a group of people. One person posts a question or an opinion. Others read it and attach replies. Then still others add comments on the replies. The sequence of commentary can go on indefinitely.

What are discussion groups?

Unfortunately, the names *e-mail list*, *mailing list*, *bulletin board*, *news server*, *newsgroup*, *net news*, *forum*, *discussion group*, and *list server* are used somewhat interchangeably to describe different forms of message exchange. I cannot remedy that linguistic overlap, but I can tell you how I use terms in this book. I divide discussion groups into three main categories: e-mail lists, newsgroups, and forums.

E-mail lists

E-mail lists let members of the list broadcast e-mail messages to all other members of the list. (E-mail lists are often called *list servers*, *listservs*, or just *mailing lists*.) An e-mail list server maintains the list of subscribers to the list, in WBT typically the members of a class. When a message arrives, a copy is dispatched to every member of the list.

Most course designers tell me they are phasing out e-mail lists in favor of threaded forums or newsgroups.

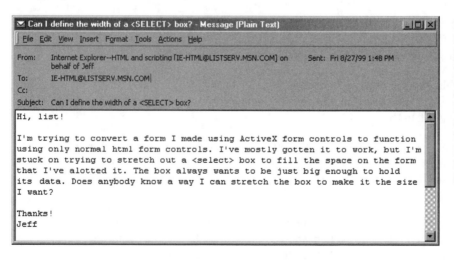

Here is a message posted to an e-mail list that discusses HTML issues affecting the Internet Explorer browser.

The main advantage and disadvantage of e-mail lists are that learners access them using their e-mail software. Learners do not have to learn any new software. However, if the list is very active, their e-mail inboxes are inundated with messages.

Newsgroups

Internet newsgroups are sites where people post messages relevant to the subject of the newsgroup. Newsgroups are also known as *net news* or *news servers*. Newsgroups rely on a standardized protocol so that many different programs (called a *newsreader*) can be used to read and write messages to a newsgroup.

There are several brands of newsreaders. Although they can all access the same newsgroups, the way they look and work can differ somewhat. For example, here is the group news.announce.newusers displayed in Netscape's newsreader.

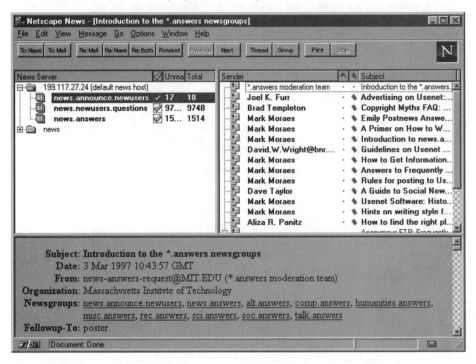

The newsgroup address is listed in the left pane, postings are listed in the right pane, and the text of postings appears in the bottom pane.

Tens of thousands of newsgroups are publicly accessible on the Internet. You can also set up private groups on your intranet just for use by your classes.

Newsgroups provide threaded discussion at the cost of some complexity. One advantage of newsgroups is that they are well established. The protocols for reading and writing messages are standardized and well documented. Hence, there are plenty of newsreader programs available to pick from, and many users are familiar with using them.

Another advantage is that messages can be threaded. That is, replies are displayed indented under the original message. Threading makes following a strand of the conversation much easier.

The main disadvantage of newsgroups is that they can be a bit intimidating to those unfamiliar with them.

Forums

The term forum is used, in this book at least, to refer to discussion groups that offer more features than standard newsgroups or that can be integrated more smoothly into the user-interface of the course. Many such forums depend on proprietary software. Here is an example built using aspForum from Blindside Software Design (www.blindsidesoftware.com).

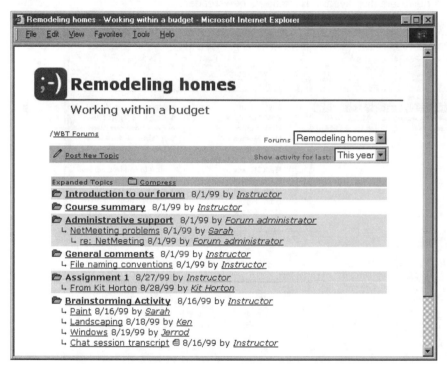

I have found one compelling reason to use forums instead of newsgroups: You can build a forum right into the Web page so that learners do not have to learn to use a separate newsreader. By integrating the forum into the Web page, you eliminate much of the difficulty of navigating and posting forum messages.

The main disadvantage of forums is that the designer must learn the forum's particulars and must design it into the course.

To find vendors of forum software, search the Web for **Web forum software**.

Use existing discussion groups

A link to an existing discussion group provides access to outside experts and their expertise.

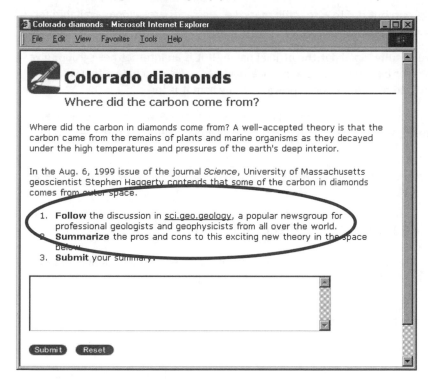

This example contains a link to a geology newsgroup.

Why use an existing discussion group?

Why would you want to refer learners to an existing newsgroup? Here are some good reasons.

▶ To provide access to immediate information in a rapidly changing field.

▶ To let them ask questions of experts and others like them.

▶ To provide a source to answer questions beyond the scope of your course.

▶ To expose learners to practitioners in a field they are studying.

▶ To have learners conduct research by "interviewing" others on the newsgroup.

How to refer learners to discussion groups

Here are a few tips on linking to newsgroups.

- ▶ **Link to a newsgroup but not to a specific message.** Messages are seldom available for more than a couple of weeks.

- ▶ **Identify the group fully.** Spell out the official name. If it is an Internet newsgroup, give its Usenet name, for example, "news.announce.newusers". Also, include a few words explaining what kind of information it provides and whom it is for.

- ▶ **Pick the right group.** In any field there may be several active newsgroups. Some deal with general issues, while others focus on esoteric interests. Refer your learners to the right group.

- ▶ **Or link to search services** that can find newsgroup messages. Try www.deja.com for a starter.

Consider setting up your own discussion group

The reasons for setting up a new discussion group for just your learners are similar to those for using an existing newsgroup. There are some additional benefits as well. Course-specific discussion groups:

- ▶ Let learners interact with each other even though they may be 12 time zones apart.

- ▶ Let learners answer each other's questions.

- ▶ Continue discussions as long as necessary. Conversations do not have to stop at the classroom door. Discussion groups keep learners and the instructor talking between scheduled class events.

- ▶ Give everyone a chance to join in, even those who might not contribute in class: shy people too polite to interrupt others, those with limited language skills, those with a speech impediment or dyslexia, those sitting in the back row, those with soft voices, those put off by loud voices, and those whose schedules rule out class meetings.

- ▶ Provide second-language learners a chance to practice their language skills. Such learners can take time to interpret messages, using a dictionary if necessary, and to compose and check replies.

- ▶ Discuss every topic of interest to every learner. In a classroom, the class cannot waste time dealing with issues of interest to only a few. In a discussion group, it takes only two learners interested in the subject to start a productive discussion.

Consider replacing chat and e-mail

Discussion groups offer some important advantages over chat and e-mail. Chat is usually restricted to hectic exchange of small ideas, immediate reactions, and emotional responses among only a few individuals. By the time someone can compose a thoughtful response, the topic of conversation has changed several times. A discussion in e-mail lists lacks continuity and organization.

Threaded discussion groups, however, allow time to compose responses, maintain separate threads for ongoing subjects, let everyone talk at once, and can manage discussions among hundreds of participants.

Discussion groups work

If there is an unsung hero in WBT, it is the humble discussion group. Learners, designers, and instructors continually cite the discussion group as the best thing about a course.

Learners think so. One research project found that 50% of learners felt that their participation in the class discussion group made them write more coherently, participate more outside normal work hours, and think more carefully before responding to questions [39].

Learners want to continue discussions. At the end of a California Lutheran University class that used a discussion group, learners asked the professor to leave it open after the class so that they could continue to communicate with one another [39].

Learners feel connected to the instructor. After one WBT experience, 94% of learners said they felt as well connected to the instructor as in face-to-face classes [60].

Learners feel closer to other learners. At the end of a class that featured electronic discussion, learners reported they had "developed a feeling of closeness never before experienced in an academic setting" [39].

Learners are more self-reliant. One research project found that 13 percent of learners said they were less likely to answer a question from the instructor than in the classroom [39]. This may indicate that in discussion groups learners rely more on other learners and less on the instructor.

Chat

Chat enables real-time conversations among a group of people over a low-speed Internet connection. Chat (or *text-conferencing*) lets learners swap typed-in messages over a network. Each member of the conference sees all the messages typed by the others. Chat sessions are like an instantaneous discussion group.

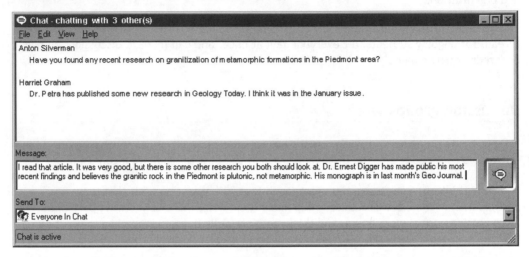

The use of chat sessions in learning is different from their use for social purposes. Learners and instructional designers familiar with the social examples may have to adjust their thinking to use chats effectively in learning.

In WBT, most chat sessions have clear goals and are scheduled in advance. They have definite starting times and typically last for 20 minutes to 90 minutes. Or they may continue until participants run out of ideas or energy.

Chat can be conducted in a tool outside the browser. Thus, the way a chat session looks and works depends on that tool. Or the chat activity can be embedded into a Web page by using a Chat control or applet.

> There is no pleasure to me without communication: there is not so much as a sprightly thought comes into my mind that it does not grieve me to have produced alone, and that I have no one to tell it to.
>
> — Michel de Montaigne

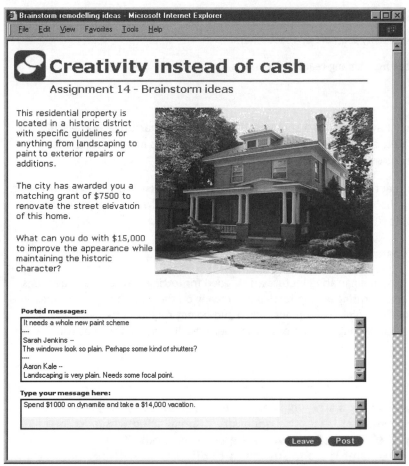

Notice that the chat control is embedded at the bottom of the page rather than in a separate window.

This example includes a Macromedia Director Shockwave object. It communicates with the Macromedia MultiuserServer component.

In a typical chat session, everybody sees all the messages. However, some chat tools allow private messages—ones sent from one person in the chat session to another person in the session. Such messages are seen by the recipient but not by the others in the session.

Use chat for fast-paced exchanges

Use chat to let people at different locations on a network carry on a conversation. Use it when e-mail exchanges are too slow.

Common uses

Some examples of common uses for chat include:

▶ Real-time question and answer sessions.

▶ Brainstorming, troubleshooting, and problem-solving sessions.

▶ Instructors holding "office hours" during which learners can ask questions.

- ▶ "Oral" examinations in a training course.

- ▶ Interviews of experts by learners or researchers.

- ▶ "Study group meetings" among teams of learners.

Not for lectures

Nothing is worse than having to read a sporadically scrolling text narrative—awkwardly composed, inaccurately typed, and saying nothing a textbook does not say better. Do not ever use chat for lectures, OK?

Using chat to narrate actions in a screen sharing or whiteboard session can also be awkward. Having to stop using the visual application to go to the chat window and type a comment or instructions interrupts the flow of the task being demonstrated.

Good for a back channel during demonstrations

Though chat is not good for narrating lectures, it is good for letting learners ask questions while someone is demonstrating an application or drawing on the whiteboard. The questions do not disrupt the person doing the demonstration and do not require a two-way audio channel. The person conducting the demonstration periodically checks the chat window for messages.

> In a tête-à-tête there is a still worse inconvenience; that is, the necessity of talking perpetually, at least, the necessity of answering when spoken to, and keeping up the conversation when the other is silent. This insupportable constraint is alone sufficient to disgust me with society, for I cannot form an idea of a greater torment than being obliged to speak continually without time for recollection.
>
> — Jean-Jacques Rousseau, *Confessions*

Advantages and disadvantages of chat

Chat works well in some circumstances and not at all in others. Consider carefully how well chat can meet the needs of your course. Keep these characteristics of chat in mind:

- ▶ **Nearly immediate**. Chat provides nearly immediate feedback. For complex questions that require follow-up or clarification, a chat session can accomplish in minutes what would take days with e-mail or a discussion group.

- ▶ **Leaves a transcript**. Chat leaves a written transcript. However, it may seem crude when read later. Some participants may object to seeing their off-the-cuff remarks on display. Warn them ahead of time and ensure that providing transcripts does not inhibit discussion.

▶ **Requires a small group**. Chat can seem painfully slow if only two are chatting. If more than five or seven are chatting, however, it can be difficult to keep up, especially if you are a slow typist. By the time you have responded, the conversation has moved on to another topic.

▶ **Requires typing skills**. Chat is spontaneous only for those with good touch-typing skills. Hunt-and-peck typists find it frustrating.

▶ **Often ignored by learners**. Chat, though popular for social exchanges, is not the most popular feature in many WBT courses. In one Western Michigan University geography course, only 30% of learners used the available chat facility, though 57% used screen sharing and 83% used the whiteboard [53]. In another project almost none of the 1000 learners who took a coaching skills class used the available chat rooms [57].

Use chat effectively

Make sure that learners and instructors use chat in ways that advance learning. Even those who have used chat for years socially may not draw analogies to using it for learning. Here are some ways to use chat for learning:

▶ **Pass notes in class.** Use private chat to communicate to another learner or two, perhaps to suggest to teammates how the idea being discussed could be implemented in their class project. Use private chat for messages not of general interest or that might embarrass the recipient.

▶ **Whisper to the teacher**. Use private chat to ask a question or make a comment without interrupting the whole class. Or to remain anonymous from the rest of the class.

▶ **Take it out in the hall**. Use chats to continue conversations started in class meetings, especially ones of intense interest to just a few learners.

▶ **Chat around the clock**. Use chat for other than whole-class meetings. Use it for study groups, team meetings, tutoring sessions, and private meetings with the instructor. Provide a procedure for reserving time slots on the class chat server or for setting up a private chat room.

▶ **Prepare spontaneous comments ahead of time**. If you know what questions you will ask or what answers you will give, you can prepare them in a separate text-editor window. At the appropriate moment you can just cut and paste to the text-conferencing window. Some ingenious souls have even used macros to inject standard comments at the press of a key.

▶ **Listen up**. Keep sessions small and short. Limit chat sessions to seven or fewer persons and keep sessions to 20 or 30 minutes in length.

▶ **Put it in a letter**. Chat is for spontaneous thoughts. If the ideas are deeper than that, or if you require time to find just the right words, send the ideas as e-mail or discussion-group messages.

Whiteboard

Whiteboard tools provide the equivalent of the whiteboards or chalkboards at the front of most every classroom and on the walls of most business offices around the world. In WBT, a whiteboard is a shared drawing area. Participants can take turns drawing on the whiteboard. All participants immediately see everything drawn on the whiteboard. Most often, whiteboards are provided by a program outside the browser. Thus, the way the whiteboard looks and works will depend on that program.

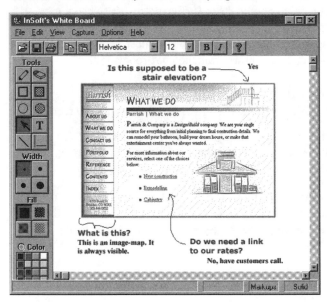

This example shows a captured session that uses InSoft's Whiteboard tool, part of Netscape's CookTalk program. In this session two designers are discussing a Web page layout.

Use a whiteboard for visual learning

Whiteboards let instructors and learners sketch ideas they cannot express in words. Whiteboards are especially important for courses in science, engineering, mathematics, and other subjects that mix graphics and text. Whiteboards are also important for those with limited English language skills and those who express themselves well visually. Whiteboards work well for discussions too complex for chat. Some common uses include discussing:

▶ **Computer screen displays**. Participants can paste screen snapshots of dialog boxes and windows into the shared area.

▶ **Visual appearance**. The color, layout, shape, or contents of any visual display.

▶ **Arrangement and organization of components** of a system. Participants can draw and edit a diagram.

▶ **Charts and graphs** showing numerical trends and patterns.

▶ **Visual symbols** that the learner must learn to recognize visually.

Whiteboards are not limited to one-way presentations to passive viewers. With whiteboards, instructors and learners can interact. Learners can complete a drawing started by the instructor. The instructor or learners can critique a graphic by annotating specific parts. Participants can mark up a photograph, chart, or diagram to suggest improvements.

Use whiteboards effectively

The secret to a successful whiteboard session is the same as that for any conference or meeting: careful preparation.

▶ **Prepare drawings and clip-art** you may need during the conference. Put these into a file you keep open on your computer. Include:

Objects you will discuss

Symbols used in your profession

Arrows, boxes, and other generic shapes

▶ **Establish color codes** for drawings and text. Assign each participant a distinct color.

▶ **Set up rules for proper behavior.**

Take turns. Wait for others to finish before you start drawing.

Do not criticize someone else's drawing skill. Redraw the object for them if you can do better.

▶ **Summarize the session.** At the end, clean up the drawing to remove discarded ideas and arrange it to reflect the conclusion of the group. That way each participant saves a copy as a summary of the session.

Screen sharing

Screen sharing lets learners see what is happening on the instructor's computer. The instructor can demonstrate a procedure or piece of software simply by running it on his or her computer. Remote learners on their screens see exactly what is happening on the instructor's screen. Some sessions even let learners share their own screens or control the leader's screen. Most screen-sharing tools let the leader share the entire computer screen, a particular application, or just a single window.

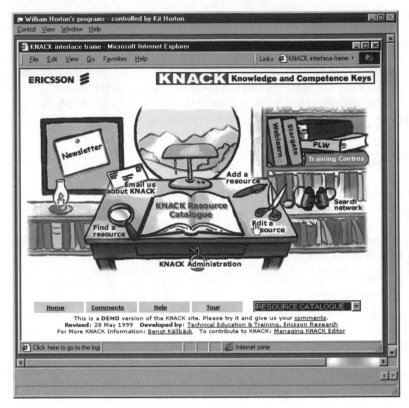

Here is an example of a shared screen. It shows the learner's view as the instructor conducts a tour of a knowledge management system called KNACK. The instructor was in Boulder, Colorado, and the learners were in Stockholm. The item being demonstrated resided on a server in Boulder, across town from the instructor.

Use for screen sharing to demonstrate

Use screen sharing to show computer programs, computer data, pictures, and other material on a computer screen. Use screen-sharing sessions to:

▶ Demonstrate computer programs and teach operations skills.

▶ Let learners view data in applications that are not on the learners' computers.

▶ Show images that cannot be pasted into the whiteboard.

▶ Call on learners to try out skills demonstrated by the instructor. The instructor can take over if learners fail.

Screen sharing is seldom fast enough to show animation or any rapid motions. Use it for demonstrations that require only smooth, simple movements.

Use screen sharing effectively

Screen sharing takes careful preparation and smooth execution for best effect.

▶ **Share just what you need to share.** Share an individual application or window rather than the whole desktop. Share only one program at a time. Do not let other windows cover the application you are sharing.

▶ **Have learners participate in the activity**. Allow learners to control the shared application. Let participants share programs on their computers.

▶ **Use audio to narrate**—if bandwidth permits. Remember that the audio may be delayed and distorted. Speak slowly and clearly. Allow time for learners to listen and understand.

▶ **Keep graphics and backgrounds simple**. Textured backgrounds and intricate graphics take longer to transmit than simple ones.

▶ **Keep security in mind**. If you grant control to others, they can open, modify, and delete files on your system. Do not hand over control and leave the room.

▶ **Quit unnecessary programs**. For better reliability and speed, exit other programs that require computer or network resources. Turn off videoconferencing. You may have to turn off audio temporarily, too.

▶ **Control an application remotely**. Put the application you want to control on another computer rather than on the one from which you conduct the demonstration. That way, you see the same delayed image that others do.

Response pads

Response pads let members of the class make real-time choices or vote on issues. Response pads are on-screen displays that let learners select among alternatives. The choices are tallied and displayed in a composite view. Response pads function like the keypads used by participants in some interactive video courses to indicate their answers to questions posed by the instructor. Web-based response pads, however, require no special hardware.

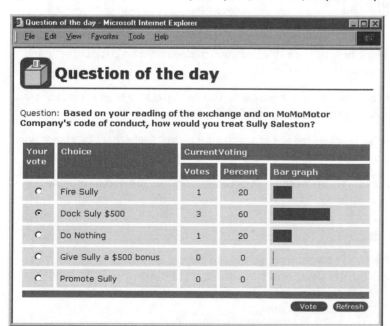

Here is an example of a response pad. After studying the exchange between a customer and a sales representative, learners are asked what action should be taken toward the sales representative. The Voting Machine shows the current voting totals.

8

Promote collaboration

Use response pads to involve learners

One study compared responses from remote sites equipped with a physical keypad responder to those with a telephone. The study found that keypad users responded 80 times more than telephone users. And keypad users asked five times as many questions as telephone users [113]. We should expect similar results with on-screen response pads.

Incorporate response pads into activities

Use on-screen response pads to force choices, administer surveys, and tally votes. Here are some uses for them in WBT:

▶ Conduct a mock trial and have learners vote on the guilt or innocence of the defendant.

▶ Hold a debate and let learners choose the winner.

▶ Survey participants instantly on an issue.

▶ Let the class vote on what subjects to pursue in greater detail.

▶ Get instant feedback on how well learners feel they understand a concept.

▶ Conduct before and after surveys to measure changes of opinion or knowledge.

Use response pads effectively

Use response pads in ways that let learners naturally express choices.

▶ **Collect opinions at the right time**. Record choices at the most revealing times: After an event, during an event, or both before and after an event.

▶ **Make sure learners know how to vote** ("Select your choice and then click **Enter**") and how to refresh their view of others' votes.

▶ **Phrase prompts and choices with extreme care**. Test to make sure learners understand the choices. Explain choices at the beginning of the activity.

▶ **Display vote totals only**. Learners may hesitate to vote if they feel others can learn how they individually voted.

▶ **Log changes of opinion during an ongoing event**. Such logs can provide a valuable source for research.

> The fact that a man is to vote forces him to think. You may preach to a congregation by the year and not affect its thought because it is not called upon for definite action. But throw your subject into a campaign and it becomes a challenge.
>
> — John Jay Chapman, *Practical Agitaion*

Audioconferencing

Audioconferencing uses the network as a telephone. Participants can talk to one another. (Audioconferencing is also called *voice-conferencing* and *net-phone*.)

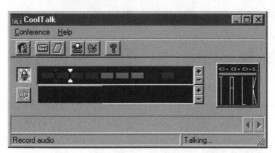

Most often, audioconferencing services are provided by a program outside your browser. Thus, the way audioconferencing looks and works will depend on that program. This example shows a session that uses Netscape's CoolTalk program.

Note: Audioconferencing requires a fast network connection. Unless the connection is as fast as a two-channel ISDN connection (128 Kbps), the sound quality and delays may make the conversation more frustrating than informative.

Use audioconferencing when voice is important

Use audioconferencing when you need to talk to other persons but cannot use the telephone to do so. The first question to answer is: When do you need to use voice or sound? Some answers:

- ▶ **The discussion is complex.** A chat session would require too much typing and have too many delays that break the continuity of the conversation.

- ▶ **Emotions are important.** A tone of voice can tell us if the speaker is angry, excited, sad, or just joking. A text transcript cannot.

- ▶ **Sounds are important.** You want to hear or demonstrate the sound that something makes—a computer disk drive or a healthy human heart, for instance.

- ▶ **Learners lack writing or typing skills** necessary to collaborate fluently by written media. Audioconferencing allows learners who lack writing or typing skills to participate fully [79].

The second question to answer is: Why not just use a telephone? Here good answers are harder to come by.

- ▶ A telephone call would be too expensive.

- ▶ The telephone line is in use or must be kept open for other purposes.

- ▶ You only have one telephone line and it is used for the network connection.

- ▶ Setting up a conference call with more than a few people can be complex.

If you do not need voice or sound, consider using chat, especially if you need a written transcript of the conversation.

Use audioconferencing effectively

Limitations of networking technology make many audioconferences unsatisfactory. Successful audioconferences depend on a mixture of preparation and technique.

▶ **Reduce background noise.** Close the window. Turn off the radio. Turn off unnecessary machinery.

▶ **Speak slowly and distinctly.** The sound quality of audioconferencing software is less than that of the telephone system.

▶ **Put the microphone below and near the mouth.** Keep the microphone out of the breath stream.

▶ **Wait before you talk.** Sound packets can be delayed a second or more. In audioconferencing, silence does not always mean that the other person is waiting for you to talk.

Should you use the telephone instead?

Some companies use plain old telephone networks to provide the audio component of collaboration. MCI WorldCom uses one-way phone links to broadcast lectures and then switches to two-way for questions and answers [33]. Speakerphones are common, and conference calls are not hard to arrange.

When conducting screen-sharing or whiteboard sessions, I prefer to use a telephone connection to provide the audio components. I experience fewer skips, gaps, and delays, and find voices much easier to understand.

Videoconferencing

Videoconferencing lets participants see at least a small video image of the presenter. Some systems allow larger images and two-way views.

Most often videoconferencing services are provided by a program outside the browser. Thus, the way the videoconference looks and works depends on that program. The quality of the video images varies widely and depends on the quality of the connection, the quality of the video camera, and the processor speed of the computers.

The example below shows some frames from a session using Microsoft NetMeeting. A technician is demonstrating how to replace a removable hard disk drive.

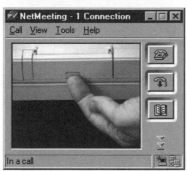

Note: Videoconferences require very fast network connections, typically a 256 Kbps connection. Slower connections produce jittery video that may not convey the idea of motion at all.

Use videoconferencing to show movement

What situations justify the use of videoconferencing? Use videoconferencing when people need to see each other talking and when you need to show moving objects:

▶ **Show moving objects.** Example: explaining how a piece of machinery works, giving instructions on repairing or manipulating equipment, or demonstrating use of a computer program.

▶ **Make people seem real.** Use videoconferencing to introduce the instructor to remote learners and remote learners to the instructor.

▶ **Deliver powerful emotional messages.** Use video to motivate and counsel learners.

▶ **Show off the technology.** People are still impressed by this technology. It suggests that you have invested in the future.

Because videoconferencing requires special software and can clog even high-speed networks, do not use it when a simpler, less expensive alternative works as well. Consider combining whiteboard (to show a series of still pictures) and audioconferencing (to describe them). Or display a still picture of yourself so people can view it as they listen to your voice by audioconferencing.

Plan and prepare for the videoconference

Videoconferencing requires careful presentation. Typically, each hour of video presentation requires 8 to 10 hours of preparation [88].

Keep segments short. No one person should talk for more than five minutes straight. No session should last more than one to two hours.

Prepare graphics beforehand. If you are including existing graphics in a video presentation, make sure you have permission from the copyright holder to transmit the images. Simplify artwork, especially materials designed for printing or for display on a full computer screen. Clean up scanned graphics.

Minimize background distractions. Position the camera so that the background is a blank wall. Or adjust lights so that the background is dark. A noisy background or busy scene takes more work to decode and display and can result in skips in the picture or stuttering in the sound.

Limit to six remote sites. With two-way video, limit yourself to about six remote sites [114]. With more than six remote sites, interaction drops off.

Keep presentations simple. Put details in separate Web pages that learners can read at leisure.

Explain video quality. Explain to learners why the video quality may be lower than they are used to for broadcast television.

Minimize unnecessary movements. Mount the camera firmly. Use a tripod to reduce shake. Point the camera precisely.

Send materials ahead of time. Provide learners with a copy of the slides or other audiovisual aids ahead of time in a format that lets them comfortably follow along with the presenter. This way the slides can use smaller text and more detailed graphics. Perhaps make available a special version of the slides designed for printing in black and white.

Reserve space for picture within picture. If you are using a picture-within-picture effect, decide where the included picture will go on the screen. Leave space for it in the design of slides, other exhibits, and studio layout.

Perform professionally

During the videoconference presentation, the presenter must use the medium efficiently and effectively. Here are a few suggestions.

Keep props at hand. Gather the objects you will show ahead of time. Put them out of camera view but within arm's reach. Practice grabbing and manipulating them.

Hire a sidekick. Have a second on-camera person to interact with the instructor, ask the instructor questions, and take over if the primary instructor runs into a problem.

Hire a director. Have an off-screen director guide all on-screen activities. The director can time and pace the event. Using hand signals or earphones, the director can cue and coach the instructor. The director can also control the position, movements, and switching of cameras. "Lights, camera, action!"

Use a "dead-time" graphic when needed. Have an image to broadcast during the "dead time" while waiting for the class to begin, during any pauses in the class, and immediately after it concludes. Also design one for "We are experiencing technical difficulties."

Vary activities to spark interest. Make videoconferencing sessions as interactive as possible. Periodically pause to answer questions. If no questions are forthcoming, poll the class on an issue or ask questions of individual learners. Play games. Make clear that the session is not a TV program to be watched passively.

Vary camera angle. If one person must talk for more than a minute or so, periodically shift the camera angle. Have the person walk around. Cut away or pan to an object the person is describing. Insert a reaction shot showing the studio audience listening. Use close-ups to show details.

Move smoothly and predictably. Move in slow, smooth, predictable motions. Start and finish movements slowly. Do not inexplicably shift the camera position. Make all movements seem natural and logical. Warn of shifts of locale. "We're now going to the workshop to show how to apply these ideas."

Do not hand write. Avoid hand writing materials on the spot. Such "live write" activity can confuse and frustrate watchers [115]. Viewers may be looking at a one-eighth-screen image of someone hurriedly writing on a large whiteboard. Unless others unanimously agree that you can write very legibly very quickly, type the text onto a blank slide instead. If you must write by hand, print in:

LARGE, THICK, SIMPLE, BLOCK LETTERS

Summary of collaboration mechanisms

This table summarizes the characteristics of various collaboration mechanisms. Review it when you get ready to incorporate collaboration into your course.

Mechanism	Conveys					Bandwidth	Routing				Received		Technical difficulty	Synchronous
	Text	Images	Choices	Sound	Motion		One-to-one	Broadcast	Some-to-some	All-to-all	Automatically	Voluntarily		
E-mail	Y					Low	Y	Y			Y		Low	
E-mail list	Y					Low		Y		Y	Y		Medium	
Newsgroup	Y					Low			Y			Y	Medium	
Forum	Y					Low			Y			Y	Medium	
Chat	Y					Low	Y			Y		Y	Medium	Y
Response pad			Y			Low				Y		Y	Medium	Y
Whiteboard		Y				Medium	Y	Y				Y	Medium	Y
Screen sharing		Y				Medium	Y	Y				Y	Medium	Y
Audioconferencing				Y		Medium	Y	Y		Y		Y	High	Y
Videoconferencing		Y		Y	Y	High	Y	Y		Y		Y	High	Y

PROVIDE COMPLETE INSTRUCTIONS

For many learners, Internet collaboration is science fiction. For others, it is the way they while away their spare time. Both groups need clear instructions on how to use Web collaboration mechanisms for learning. Those inexperienced with Internet collaboration tools need simple, explicit instructions and encouragement on getting started. Those who have been chatting and conferencing on the 'net for years need direction on using these mechanisms for learning purposes rather than social exchanges.

Include instructions on tools

Provide a complete online manual for discussion, e-mail, chat, or conferencing system used in the course. Unless you have created your own custom system, you can probably link to the online manuals and tutorials provided by the vendors of your tools. I say "probably" because not all vendors have good instructions written for first-time learners.

Make it easy for learners to print out these instructions. Either combine all topics into one file or assemble them into a special printable file. Better still, consolidate all the manuals for all the systems used in the course into one file with a comprehensive table of contents.

Explain essential actions

Go beyond the basic operations of each tool. Make sure learners know how to prepare and send the kinds of messages necessary in the class. Provide step-by-step instructions for each of these actions:

▶ Send a message to an individual or to a whole group

▶ Reply to messages

▶ Format the message

▶ Quote from an original message

▶ Embed links in messages

▶ Attach files to messages

▶ Post a message on a thread of a discussion group

Supply computer setup instructions

Live events can tax the capabilities of even powerful computers and networks. Instructors and learners need to tune their computers for collaboration. The following example, from an announcement of an upcoming chat session, alerts learners to the event and tells them what they need to do (technically) to get ready for it:

Special tools?	No special tools are needed for the event. The chat application is part of the scenario page. Prior to the event you may want to practice logging in and sending a message. You will know you are successful if you see your message posted in the Message window.
Computer set-up?	Turn off any scheduled maintenance tasks and screen savers. The fewer programs running while you are in the chat session, the quicker will be the response time.

Here are some instructions you may want to include:

▶ Days before the event, verify that all the necessary tools are installed and working.

▶ Close all programs other than your collaboration software and any applications you are going to share. Close background programs, too. If using audio, close any other programs that use audio.

▶ Set screen resolution and color depth to that of the screen being shared.

▶ Disable screen savers and power-conservation features that could dim the screen or slow the processor. Make sure your laptop is plugged in.

▶ Make sure automatically triggered maintenance programs will not run. If you are doing a presentation in the middle of the night to accommodate learners on the other side of the globe, you do not want programs defragmenting your disk, searching for viruses, and archiving your e-mail while you are trying to conduct a demonstration.

PUBLISH A GUIDE FOR MESSAGE WRITERS

Most effective collaboration systems center on the exchange of simple text messages through e-mail or discussion groups. Even when audioconferencing and videoconferencing are available, many learners still prefer the simplicity, convenience, and record keeping of text messages.

However, not all learners know how to craft effective messages and how to manage their message-sending activities well. You may want to monitor how well learners send messages. If problems arise, recommend specific training. Or provide instructions yourself.

The following extended example is a guide to messaging. It is written to learners but applies to instructors as well.

 ## Guide to writing, sending, and managing messages

To learn effectively in this course, you will need to collaborate with fellow learners and with your instructor. Your primary means of collaboration will be through discussion-group postings and e-mail messages. These tools are a means of your learning, not its end. You should spend as much time as possible thinking about the content of messages and as little time as possible dealing with the mechanics of typing, finding, filing, and deleting messages. This guide offers tips and guidelines on how to use messages efficiently.

Follow the policy on collaboration

When you signed up for this course, you agreed to follow the <u>Policy on collaboration</u>. It specifies acceptable and unacceptable practices and behaviors. Please review the policy. It is designed to make the learning experience better for everyone. Follow it completely.

Try discussion groups before e-mail

Make the discussion groups your first stop when checking for information, asking questions, or just hanging out.

Post questions to a forum, rather than e-mailing them to the instructor. The instructor will respond to a forum message just as quickly as to e-mail.

Use your wordprocessor's spelling and grammar checker if spelling and grammar are important.

Reply in the same medium

With so many communications channels (e-mail, chat, forums, videoconferencing, telephone) to choose from, it is sometimes hard to decide which to use.

One general rule will help: **Respond in kind**. That is, reply to a message using the same medium as the message itself. Respond to e-mail with e-mail. Shift media only for specific reasons. Specific reasons for shifting media include these:

A public message needs a private reply. Use a private message (e-mail or private chat) for messages that could embarrass or anger someone if made public. You notice a discussion-group message that misuses terminology. Instead of complaining about it and publicly embarrassing the poster, you point out the problem in a private e-mail. You then let the original poster correct the problem. You make a friend rather than an enemy.

A private message has general applicability. Sometimes the reply to a private message would be useful to more people than the original sender. Say a fellow learner asks you to explain something. Why not post your explanation so others can benefit?

Read more, send less

Read more messages than you send. Write shorter messages than you read. Do not send a message without a good reason.

Say something more than "me, too"

Do not post messages that		
Just say:	**Or:**	**Or just:**
I agree.	I disagree.	Thanks
Yes.	No.	(If you really want to
Ditto.	Are you kidding?	thank someone for taking
Me, too.	Huh?	special pains solving a
Bravo!	No way!	problem for you, send
Hoorah!		them a gift.)

Send only to those who need to know

Send messages only to those who directly need to know. Do not post to a forum an issue that involves only a small number of people. Instead, send an e-mail message to the group of people involved.

Make sure every person in the **To:** or **CC:** fields needs the information. As a conversation goes on, reconsider whether all the recipients are still interested.

When replying to a message, double check who will receive the reply. You do not want to send a private response to a whole group.

Remember the adage, "Praise in public. Disagree in private."

Keep messages short

Keep e-mail messages short. If in doubt, leave it out. If others need more information, they can request more.

Make only one main point per message. Request only one action or decision per message. The recipient is likely to read and respond to the first request and miss the second.

If you have many questions, turn them into a questionnaire and let others fill in a form to answer them all. Keep paragraphs short. Limit them to a maximum of:

    Three sentences

    50 words

    One idea

Do not respond to all messages

Do not feel you have to respond to all messages. You do not reply to all the junk mail you receive. If a message angers you, wait until you calm down. Then decide if it even deserves a response.

Read before you write

Before you hit the keyboard to pound out a witty reply, take time to do a bit more reading.

Check all headers first. Before you reply to a message, scan the headers of all other unread messages in case there is a related message from the same person. Before you take time composing a reply, make sure there is not a later message saying, "Oh, never mind" or "Oops, I was wrong."

Read before posting. Read all the messages before posting a message. Someone may have already answered your question or at least posted it.

Read the FAQ first. Before posting a question to a discussion, make sure the question is not answered in the FAQ.

Lurk before you post. Monitor a discussion before you join in. Make sure you understand the general principles as well as the current topic under discussion before you contribute. Until you are sure which subjects are fair game and which are off limits, keep listening.

Subject subject lines to scrutiny

Aside from the content, the subject line of your message is the most important part. It is the part people see first. It is what most people read to decide whether to read the body of the message. Here are some tips for writing the subject line.

Phrase the subject concisely

Keep the subject line short and to the point. Make the subject a complete phrase but not necessarily a sentence. Remember that people often pick which message to read by scanning a list of subject lines. Put the critical words up front, near the beginning of the line.

Flag the type of message

Use a prefix to help the recipient know how to respond to the message and its urgency. Here are some prefixes that are commonly used:

FYI:	For your information. No reply required.
URGENT:	Important information you must act on immediately.

REQUEST: Please reply with the information requested.

Avoid general words like *information*, *stuff*, and *miscellaneous*.

Revise the subject line as the subject changes

If the subject of a discussion changes over the course of a series of exchanges, remember to change the subject header.

When replying to a message, you need not repeat the original subject header of the message—the one filled in as a default. Change the subject header to one that reflects your contribution to the conversation.

Warn of the size

If posting a long message, warn of the size in the subject heading:

Subject: QMY Report. Note LARGE (50K) file.

Follow conventions

Your instructor may set up specific conventions for subject lines on submissions for class activities. Make sure you understand and follow these.

Conventional parts of a message

What you type in your message is up to you. There are some conventions you should be aware of and should think twice about violating. Let's take a look at the anatomy of a typical message and then consider how we handle each of the parts we find there.

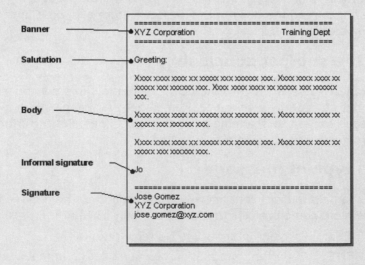

Banner

Like the letterhead of a memo or letter, the banner immediately identifies the source of the message. The banner is optional. Many e-mail programs do not automatically insert a banner but they all let you paste in one.

Use the banner to immediately identify the source and nature of the message. Banners can give a distinctive identity to messages related to the course, messages from you, or messages of a specific nature, such as warnings.

Keep the banner short so it does not push the body of the message into the next scrolling zone.

Salutation

In unsolicited e-mail, begin by explaining who you are and your interest in the recipient. Explain why you are writing to this particular individual. Begin with a neutral greeting:

> **Dear colleague,**
> **Greetings:**
> **Dear fellow learner in PR401,**

Informal signature

Sign your e-mail the way you want others to address you. If you want people to use your nickname, sign that way.

Signatures (footer)

Signatures are text automatically included at the end of messages. In such signatures, include only relevant business information. Do not include information you do not want everyone in the course to have. In a signature include:

> Name
> Title*
> Organization
> Mail address
> Phone
> Fax
> E-mail address**
> Web site*
> Quote*

* Optional. If you include a quote, make sure it is relevant and businesslike.
** In case the message gets separated from its banner.

Attach related materials

In e-mail messages and discussion-group postings you can attach external files to your messages. These files travel along with the text message and can be downloaded by those receiving your messages.

In the message, describe each attachment, including this information:

> File name
>
> Purpose
>
> Format
>
> Size

Make sure the recipient can decompress and open the attachment. Stick to formats approved for the course or at least to widely used file formats. Try sending the message to yourself and opening the attachment.

Do not e-mail or post large files as attachments. As an alternative, you can place the large file on a Web or FTP site and send or post a reference to it.

Do not forget to include the attachments. This error is one of the most common, believe it or not.

Quote wisely

When responding to another message, it often helps if you quote the part you are responding to.

Quote only the part you are responding to

When responding to a message, quote only the part of the message you are responding to, not the whole message.

Make the subject heading of your message reflect the scope of your comment.

> **Subject: Item 17 of your plan. Can we do it this year?**

Flag quoted material

Indicate quoted portions with > characters to the left of the quoted text.

> **> This material is quoted.**

This material is not quoted.

Include only one or two levels of quotations.

>> **This is a quotation of a quotation.**

> **This is a simple quotation.**

This is just some information about the quotations.

After the second level of quotations, just summarize the discussion so far in your own words.

Clarify quotations

Spell out ambiguous pronouns and incomplete names in the quoted portion.

> **Jack [Thompson] promised to send samples to him [Juan Martinez].**

Reply to one point at a time

If the sender asked multiple questions or you are responding to several separate points, quote the first item and respond to it. Then quote the second and respond to it. And so on.

In discussion threads, do not quote

When responding to a message in a threaded forum, do not quote the whole message you are responding to. It is available for anyone to read.

Of course, if you are responding to only one part of a message, then point this out in the subject header and quote the part you are responding to.

Use e-mail conventions wisely

E-mail has evolved its own rules of style, shorthand, slang, clichés, and tone. These conventions apply to discussion group postings and to chat as well. Some conventions compensate for limitations of a text format. Others have no place in learning. Let's take a look at how to use these conventions within this course.

Avoid netcronyms

In e-mail, chats, and discussion groups, many people use abbreviations for common phrases. These are called *netcronyms*, an amalgam of *network* and *acronym*. If you use these, limit yourself to the most common ones and then only if others will recognize them. Some common ones include:

IMHO	In my humble opinion
BTW	By the way

FYI	For your information
FWIW	For what it's worth
TTYL	Talk to you later

Keep in mind that these do not translate well. Best use them only with Americans and English-speaking Canadians.

Do not SHOUT!

Type your messages the way you would if you were speaking or writing a letter. Avoid the practice of CAPITALIZING WORDS FOR EMPHASIS!!!!!!! And multiple exclamation points are not more effective than one. Many people interpret the capital letters and exclamation points as you shouting at them.

Use a few smileys ;-)

Plain text lacks the facial expressions, tone of voice, gestures, and other cues of face-to-face conversations. In e-mail, chats, and forums, many people use smileys (or emoticons) to show the emotion or tone they want attached to their words. To keep the smileys from becoming a private joke, restrict yourself to the most common ones, shown below with their meanings.

:-)	**Smile**	This makes me happy. I am just joking.
;-)	**Wink**	I am making a joke or speaking ironically.
:-(	**Frown**	This makes me sad, too. I do not like this idea any more than you do.
:-o	**Surprise**	Mock surprise.
:-D	**Big smile**	This makes me really happy.

Use emphasizing characters

Plain text lacks a tone of voice. E-mail has evolved conventions to deal with this lack of voice. Here are some conventions in order from least emphatic to most emphatic:

((around words))	For an aside or a very soft whisper.
(around words)	To whisper.
around words	To indicate that the words are underlined or italics.
around words	For emphasis, like boldfacing the words.
ALL CAPS	To shout. Use sparingly. Considered RUDE if overused.
>>!!ALL CAPS!!<	For really strong emphasis with a bit of humor.

Conversationalize

Written language is usually more formal and more constrained than spoken language. Some e-mail conventions restore a bit of the informality of natural conversation. They deliberately bend the rules of grammar, spelling, and syntax for effect. Try the conventions explained here:

Convention	Meaning	Example
... (ellipsis)	A pause or broken off thought. The reader can complete the thought.	And if we do commit to the plan ...
Hmmmmm	I am considering this idea.	We could raise the dividend to attract more investors. Hmmmmmm.
???	Puzzlement or doubt.	ZipECorp says the Zip390 is "sideways compatible"???
?!?	Astonishment.	I click OK and the file is gone?!?
#%&$*	Profanity and other improper language.	How do I feel about the proposal? It is #%&$* %&#$* %#&**.
Bleeping: Use * to replace vowels	Profanity and other improper language **Caution**: Bleeped words may offend some who still recognize the word.	Oh sh*t!
Outlining	To show structure.	Our product line includes: Desktop systems GX21 GX22 Laptop systems GY20 GY21 Hand-held systems GZ11 GZ12

Limit messages to low-ASCII

Unless you know that your e-mail, chat, and discussion group system (and that of each of your recipients) can handle other characters, limit messages to low-ASCII characters. These are the ones not grayed out here:

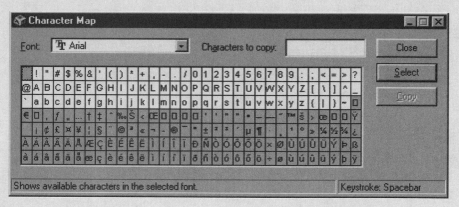

Writing style

The way you write a technical report is not the same as the way you write a love letter. Likewise, the way you write an e-mail or discussion-group message may differ from other forms of writing you do. Here are some stylistic tips.

Conversational tone

Write in a simple conversational tone—not too formal and not too chatty. Write the way you would talk to a respected business associate whom you know professionally but not socially.

Not too informal too quick

Do not immediately use other people's first names or nicknames. Wait until they invite you to do so. Or address others the way they sign their own messages.

Clarify emotion

Clarify your sentiments, especially if they are not clear from words alone. Avoid sarcasm and irony. Subtle feelings are often lost in text messages.

Flag humor and funny language ;-)

If you write something humorous or ironic, make sure that your reader understands that your words are not to be taken literally. One way to do this is to follow the non-literal text with a smiley, such as :-) or ;-).

Use pronouns carefully

Use pronouns only if they refer to nouns in the current message (or the quoted portion of a prior one).

Keep conversations productive

Use discussions to develop, test, and refine ideas. Discuss, debate, question, dispute, and challenge ideas. But keep all discussions positive and disagreements professional.

OK to disagree, but ...

It is OK to disagree and to challenge ideas. It is never OK to abuse, bully, or harass others. Feel free to point out weaknesses in an idea but not criticize the person who offered it.

Vague criticisms without supporting reasons are not helpful. Do not say, "That is the dumbest idea I have ever heard." Just say what you disagree with and why.

Think first

Never send a message when you are angry. Count to ten. Count to one hundred. Sleep on it. Once you launch a message, there's no calling it back and a written record of your action is readily available.

Do not respond in anger to provocative, offensive, insulting, or off-subject messages. Such angry responses just prompt a cascade of more and more irrelevant responses.

Read messages two or three times before you begin to formulate an answer. Read for content and tone and implications.

Consider that the message you are responding to could be a hoax or from an impostor. Maybe the person who posted it was making a bad joke. Or just having a bad day. When you are calm, ask yourself, "Could I possibly have misinterpreted what this person is saying?"

Also consider whether the best response is just to ignore the message. If the message is not relevant to course content, you lose nothing by ignoring it.

Apply the same care to your own messages. Before hitting Enter to send a message, ask yourself how you would feel if someone sent the message to you.

Confront bad behavior

You do not have to tolerate abuse or harassment. As our policies make clear, abusive and harassing behavior is not acceptable. In fact it is your duty to confront and correct such behavior.

If you encounter such inappropriate behavior and you feel it was deliberate, confront the person—politely but definitely. Politely, because the message might have been counterfeit and because you want the person to stop the behavior.

Definitely, so they know you were offended. Do not counterattack; just state the reason for your objection and what you want the person to do: apologize publicly, retract the message, or just stop the inappropriate behavior.

If you do not get a satisfactory response, then contact the instructor or discussion group moderator for help.

Disagree agreeably

When responding to someone's exact words, take care how you respond to their original message.

- If you must disagree, start by stating how you interpreted the other person's words, then list the points on which you agree, and finally explain your points of disagreement.

- If you must criticize, focus on the main issues of disagreement rather than on minor details. No one likes to be nagged.

- Do not nitpick grammar, punctuation, and spelling. Do not mark errors with "[sic]" or make corrections. Just quote.

Beware the pattern of quotation followed by disagreement followed by another quotation and disagreement and so on and on. The person quoted can feel like a punching bag. Mingle in a little praise.

Practice the golden rule of messaging

If you remember nothing else, remember this: **Respond to the messages from others the way you want them to respond to your messages.**

MODERATE DISCUSSION GROUPS

In a *moderated* discussion group the instructor—or someone else—watches over the exchange of messages. This moderator may start and participate in discussions, but the primary duty of the moderator is to ensure that learners have productive discussions with other learners.

Moderators have two main duties. First, they must set up the discussion groups and threads. Second, they must oversee the conversations that take place there.

Pick the right moderator

Normally, the instructor for the course is also the moderator of the course's discussion groups. However, the requirements for a moderator are different from those for an instructor. And the instructor may be too busy to take on both jobs.

Characteristics of a good moderator

A good moderator is knowledgeable, supportive, and articulate.

The moderator should be knowledgeable. The moderator must understand the subject matter, the computer system, and any software used by the discussion group or other parts of the class. Or have ready access to those who do.

The moderator must have a caring nature. The moderator must tactfully endure insults and rude behavior, patiently instruct fumble-fingered technophobes, continually inject enthusiasm into disheartened souls, and calm abused and abusive respondents.

Most of all, the moderator must be a superb communicator. The moderator must be able to listen deeply and accurately gauge the knowledge and emotions of others. Not everyone can do this. The moderator must be someone whom others describe as tactful or diplomatic. And the moderator must be able to express complex ideas and subtle emotions in simple, unadorned prose.

So who are the job candidates?

Moderators can come from several different backgrounds. To pick a moderator, consider the following candidates:

▶ **Instructor**. About 90% of the time the instructor is the moderator. Make this your default choice.

▶ **Teaching assistant**. Often the instructor will delegate moderator duties to an assistant or instructor-in-training. Moderating a discussion group is a great way for a junior staff member to learn about learners.

▶ **Recent graduate.** Learners who have completed the course may be good candidates, especially if they are continuing in the field of the course and want to stay in touch.

▶ **Outside expert.** A practitioner may not have time to teach a course but may be willing to contribute by moderating a discussion group.

If you cannot find an ideal candidate, perhaps you should split up the moderator duties. The computer system manager can handle the technical aspects, while the instructor spot-checks messages and a learner helps out for extra credit.

Set up the discussion group

The moderator sets up the discussion groups. The moderator defines the initial discussion threads and posts messages to welcome learners and start conversations.

Welcome learners

For each major area of the discussion group, welcome learners to the discussion area and explain what and whom it is for. Make the welcome the first message in that area.

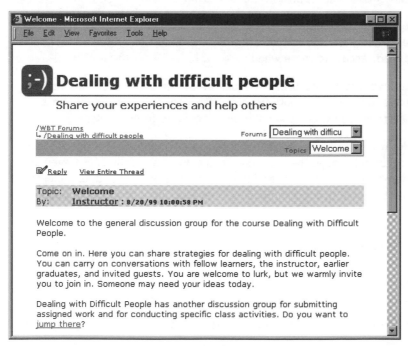

Here is the opening message of a discussion group on strategies for dealing with difficult people.

Make learners feel welcome. Invite them to participate. Help learners decide whether they are in the right discussion group, especially if a class has more than one group. Link to alternative areas such as other discussion groups for a class or public newsgroups on the subject of a class.

Set up needed threads

When learners first arrive at a discussion group they should not find an empty warehouse. Put in some walls and a few rooms. Start a few conventional top-level threads:

▶ **Introduction**. Tell learners what the whole discussion group is about in more detail than on the welcome topic. Put any needed instructions here.

▶ **Summary**. Create a thread to contain a summary or digest of the scattered discussions in the group. Periodically assign learners to write and post summaries to this thread.

▶ **Administrative support**. Provide a place where learners can request help with any aspect of the course other than content.

▶ **General comments**. Plant a general comment thread to collect comments that do not fit any existing thread. The moderator can move these comments to the correct thread or use them to start a new thread.

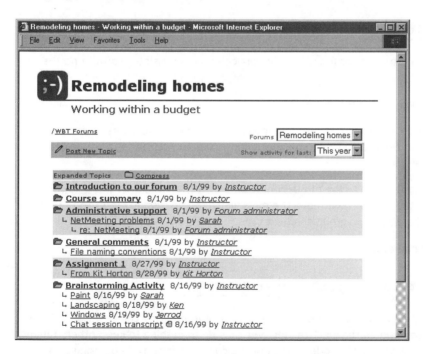

Here you see the messages in a forum on remodeling practices.

Visually style the discussion groups

Clearly distinguish three uses of discussion groups: course content, technical support, and course administration. A different color scheme and prominent graphics remind learners which discussion group they are in.

Establish conventions for routing messages

Set up conventions for labeling submissions. Define rules that ensure that messages are routed to the correct folder. For example, if all learners make the subject header:

> Activity 7.1: Solution

the messages can then be automatically assembled in a specific folder in which the instructor can easily find them.

Keep the conversation lively

The role of the moderator may not be highly visible, but it is never passive. The moderator is like the mechanic for a complex piece of machinery, greasing a squeaky part here, clearing a jam there, flipping a blown circuit breaker when all motion stops. The moderator does whatever it takes to keep the discussion group running at peak efficiency.

Encourage participation

It is the moderator's job to get as many people participating as possible. To this end the moderator should:

▶ Introduce everyone to the system.

▶ Encourage non-participants to join in. The moderator should tell learners up front that they should call or fax if they have not received any communication for a set period of time.

▶ Transfer general messages to the discussion. If an e-mail from a learner has general applicability for the whole class, move the message to the discussion group and ask the learner to use the discussion group the next time.

▶ Help anyone who needs help.

Keep the conversation fresh and vibrant

We have all known people who are always at the center of interesting conversations. Often they are not the ones who do the most talking, yet they do something to keep others talking effectively. The discussion-group moderator can keep conversations lively by using a few proven techniques:

▶ Start new threads by posting interesting, deep questions.

▶ Recruit "guests."

▶ Respond to all inquiries that go unanswered for a few days.

▶ Correct all misconceptions before they propagate.

▶ Remind people of the rules as necessary.

- Create new threads for interesting ideas that spring up deep within existing threads.

- Wrap up tired discussions by summarizing them (or assigning those duties to learners).

Challenge shallow thought

Do not accept mere opinions. Prompt learners to provide the evidence and logical thought behind their opinions. Challenge opinions by responding like this:

> I was intrigued by your answer [Quote it.] Can you explain why you feel so? Did particular experiences, research, or other evidence lead you to this opinion?

If everyone else agrees, take the opposite opinion. Play devil's advocate.

> OK, then answer me this …

> I claim the opposite. Can you prove me wrong?

Throw in a challenging hypothesis.

> But what if …?

> Suppose just the opposite were true. What then?

Perform message maintenance

Messages dashed off in haste can sometimes go astray. A slight miswording can reverse the intended meaning. To maintain message quality, the moderator should:

- Reroute mis-aimed messages to the correct thread.

- Reword unclear or inaccurate subject headers.

- Fix (or have the sender fix) tragic typos or accidental misstatements.

Reject inappropriate postings

The moderator should reject postings that clearly violate course policies. Pacify or expel angry flamers. Remove messages that other learners complain about if you agree they are not appropriate. If you must reject a posting:

- Explain exactly why you rejected the posting.

- Offer the submitter a chance to resubmit after specific changes are made.

- Require an apology if the posting unduly insulted or offended others.

- Point out any violations of a broader policy.

- Explain the consequences of not abiding by the policy.

- Give the submitter a copy of your standards for postings.

Here is an example of a message that rejects a posting to a discussion group.

If messages are posted immediately ...

In some discussion groups, messages are posted immediately without the moderator seeing them. In this case:

► Alert participants to this situation and warn them that some inappropriate messages may slip by.

► Read all new messages frequently, and immediately deal with inappropriate ones.

► If an offensive message slips by, remove it and post an apology to the group.

► Also require that the author of the message post an apology.

Common problems and what to do about them

Here are some common problems encountered in discussion groups and some suggestions on how to handle them.

Problem	Description	Solution
Spamming	Sending self-serving messages, such as advertisements and sales pitches, to the whole group.	Yank the message and remind the sender that it violates course policies.
E-mail bomb	Posting messages designed to disrupt a group by provoking angry responses. Comments on abortion, gun control, political correctness, sexual preferences, or nationalities are all guaranteed to wreck a discussion group for a week.	Remove the message and warn the submitter. Remind other learners how much time they wasted commenting on such messages.
Spoofing	In a conference or forum, pretending to be someone else (other than an assigned role in a role-playing activity).	Remove the message and expel the learner from the class.
Flaming	Making abusive and emotional attacks on someone else.	If the attack is mild, let the group deal with it first. Step in as necessary. Require an apology and warn the sender.
Dominators	Some learners may try to dominate the conversation by intimidating others.	In private e-mail ask the sender to post questions for others to answer. At the same time, encourage others to join in.

Moderate actively but do not dominate

An active moderator should not lead to passive learners. The more actively the forum moderator critiques postings, adds comments, encourages participation, rewords messages, sparks creativity, resolves impasses, soothes tempers, challenges assumptions, and plays devil's advocate—the more active learners become.

Intervene where necessary, but only as much as necessary.

▶ Do not nit-pick. Let pass minor, first-time violations. Many times social pressure will take care of the problem.

▶ Nudge. If minor problems crop up repeatedly, post a gentle general reminder. And give it time to sink in.

▶ Deliver polite requests asking offenders to modify their behavior. Assume they are just careless or too busy to read the rules.

▶ Save high-power interventions for multiple-repeaters and for serious problems. Then pounce.

PREVENT COMMON PROBLEMS

Though collaboration has great potential for education, that potential is often not realized. Often, simple problems get in the way. This section discusses some practical ways to deal with problems that can thwart collaborative activities.

Set realistic expectations for replies

Set realistic expectations for replies from the instructor. After all, some instructors may want to take the weekend off. Some may be 12 time zones away in a country with different political, business, and religious holidays.

If you need help on anything, just contact your instructor. Your instructor will try to respond within 24 hours. If you have not heard back in 48 hours, contact the support desk.

This example lets learners know how soon to expect a response to their e-mail messages.

Instructors who will be unavailable for a longer period should arrange for someone else to handle messages while they are away. Or they should set up their e-mail program to automatically respond to incoming messages with a reply like this:

I will be out of the office until 27 January. I will answer your message then.

Tell learners what parts of the discussion are considered critical announcements and how often they are responsible for checking them. Be reasonable. Giving less than 48 hours' notice is seldom sufficient.

Include make-up activities for missed live events

Record live events so that learners who missed the session can read, hear, and see what they missed [116]. Have make-up work for learners who cannot attend the activity. For example:

Read the transcript of the chat session and write a 500-word summary of the main ideas expressed there.

Set up a speakerphone as a backup (or primary)

Except in vendor demos, voice quality over the Internet is spotty at best. If voice quality cannot be assured, you may want to arrange for the audio portion of an activity to be conveyed by traditional telephone lines connected to speakerphones at each remote site.

Overcome anonymity fog

When meeting for the first time, people tend to categorize one another by gender, physical appearance, personality, social role, and other characteristics [112]. Most of the time, these categorizations do not involve conscious evaluation. They are used to access knowledge and biases, which in turn are used to judge the attitudes, background knowledge, and behavior of the new acquaintances. With most WBT collaboration mechanisms, participants cannot easily categorize others. This lack of knowledge about others can lead to anxiety in addressing them and to some awkward communications.

Help class members get to know one another. Consider having them post their biographies (p 109). Hold icebreaker activities in which learners can gain experience working together. Turn anonymity into an advantage. Remind learners that personal characteristics do not matter. Invite them to create class personas to reflect how they want others to treat them.

Automatically filter messages

Tell users which HTML (or other) formatting codes they can use in messages and which they must avoid. Some HTML codes can wreck the formatting of discussion groups and chat displays. Also limit the use of offensive words. If possible, automatically filter out these format-wrecking HTML tags and common bad words.

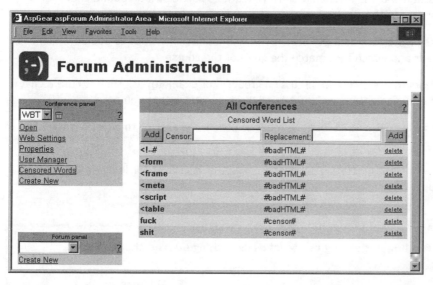

This example shows a censored word list. The code or word in the left column is replaced by the entry in the right column.

This capability is supplied by discussion group software on the server.

Adapt collaboration for small and asynchronous classes

For some courses you may not have enough learners to form frequent classes. In this case you may let learners move through the course at their own pace. Though this has advantages, it can create problems. Collaborative activities can be difficult if learners are not at the same level of knowledge or are not focused on the same issues at the same time.

Modify for nearly-synchronous courses

You can modify collaborative activities to make them work better in classes where not everyone is on the same page. Here's how:

▶ Have learners in later phases of the course assist and tutor those at earlier phases of the course.

▶ Rely more on discussion groups and other asynchronous activities than on real-time ones.

▶ Record all real-time activities for playback by those who cannot attend.

▶ Make real-time activities optional.

▶ Design real-time activities so all levels of learners may participate.

▶ Design courses as a cycle of modules so that learners can take any module first. Learners start when they are ready and quit when they have completed the cycle.

Use public chat and discussion groups

If you do not have enough synchronized learners to ensure a vigorous chat or discussion group, you can still use these mechanisms. Have learners participate in public chat rooms and discussion groups in the general area of your course.

▶ Have learners investigate multiple chat rooms and discussion groups to decide which best suit their needs and which best match the goals of the course.

▶ Require learners to use chat and discussion groups. For example, ask them to use a chat or discussion group to obtain the answers to three questions that you pose.

▶ Have learners use chat and discussion groups to obtain the answer to questions they propose.

▶ Use one of the instant messaging services from AOL or Microsoft for locating ad hoc interest groups.

> Spoon feeding in the long run teaches us nothing but the shape of the spoon.
>
> — E. M. Forster

Substitute asynchronous alternatives for synchronous ones

For courses that may be taught asynchronously, do not require synchronous activities and substitute asynchronous activities for the synchronous ones.

For this synchronous activity:	Substitute this asynchronous one:
Chat	Edited chat archive Discussion group
Instructor-graded activities	Self-graded or computer-scored activities
Scheduled lectures	Recorded lectures
Team assignments	Individual assignments

MOTIVATE PARTICIPATION

Collaboration benefits those who collaborate most actively. But not everybody jumps right in. Why not? And what can we do to get the conversation going?

Understand why people just lurk

Many people forever lurk in the dim shadows of bright discussions. Why do they lurk? Lurkers often say that they:

▶ Lack the technical skills needed to post messages or fear making technical mistakes and appearing stupid.

▶ Fear rejection of their ideas or confrontation with other learners. They worry about making comments that others will find silly, frivolous, or just dull.

▶ Are conditioned by a lifetime of television and lectures to just observe and remain silent. In physical classrooms, instructors tend to do 90% of the talking, but in lively WBT courses instructors post fewer than 10% of the messages [117].

Get learners started

So what can designers and instructors do to turn lurkers into active participants? Here's how to get everyone collaborating:

▶ Encourage purposeful lurking at first. Require it for a few assignments. Have learners report back on what they have observed.

▶ Start with a few very simple assignments to get learners comfortable with the process of posting messages.

> ▶ Continue with a technically simple role-playing activity in which learners can participate anonymously.

> ▶ Form teams and have teams post messages.

Give learners incentives to participate

Make clear the benefits of collaboration. Tell learners what they gain by participating in collaborative activities.

> ▶ Explain what collaboration activities are for and how helpful they can be.

> ▶ Praise good posts. Respond in a positive, encouraging, non-critical way—especially at the start of the course.

> ▶ Base a percentage of the grade on participation in discussions.

> ▶ Give learners a quota of messages to post or respond to in one week.

> ▶ Before class members can view the comments of others, require that they contribute a comment of their own.

Encourage learners individually

Do not let learners get lost in mass education. A little individual attention can motivate a lot of group participation.

> ▶ Early in the course, contact learners individually by e-mail or telephone to encourage them to participate.

> ▶ Contact any learners who exhibit lack of interest or negative attitudes.

> ▶ Contact every learner at least once every few weeks.

> ▶ Require learners to log into the discussion group so you know who they are. After they have lurked for a few times, send them an e-mail inviting them to join in the discussion.

Provoke productive discussion

Ask questions and make comments that people will want to respond to.

> ▶ Post a variety of questions.

> ▶ Hold brainstorming activities.

> ▶ Play devil's advocate.

> ▶ Prime the pump with some good responses. Answer your own question if necessary.

Make everyone feel welcome

Create an environment in which everyone feels his or her ideas will get a fair hearing. Make it a place safe from verbal attacks and abuse.

▶ Establish and enforce rules of appropriate behavior.

▶ Squash flames and personal criticisms.

▶ Use humor lightly and only to encourage, not to harm.

Simplify posting messages

Minimize the effort and knowledge required to collaborate electronically. You do not want the chore of debugging collaboration tools or the task of learning to operate them to steal time from the learning within your course.

Automate posting messages to discussion groups. Provide a form in which the learner can write a message and click a button to route the message to the correct thread.

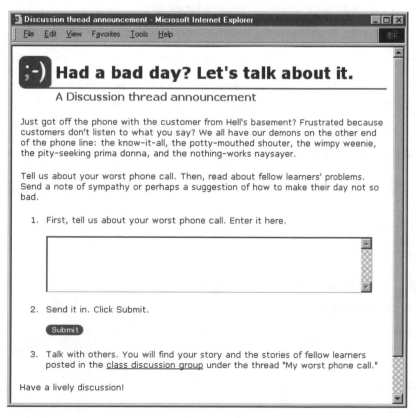

Here is an example of a simple discussion activity. It asks customer-support technicians to share stories about their most difficult phone calls. To post a story, the technicians merely type it into the space provided and click on the **Submit** button.

IN CLOSING ...

Summary

▶ Use Web collaboration mechanisms to enable people to learn directly from other people—much as they do in a classroom. Collaboration makes learners more active and self-reliant.

▶ Make real-time collaboration optional if learners cannot synchronize their schedules. Use e-mail and discussion groups instead.

▶ Start simply, using just e-mail and discussion groups. Adopt the more advanced collaboration mechanisms, like videoconferencing and screen sharing, only after learners have mastered the simpler ones.

▶ Establish and enforce clear policies for acceptable behavior in collaborative activities. Encourage behaviors that foster learning rather than mere social chit chat.

▶ Pick which collaboration mechanisms to use by balancing the media and style of interactions against the technology and skills required for each.

For more ...

See Chapter 9 on virtual classrooms for some advice on how to use collaboration mechanisms in a class. Chapter 6 shows how to integrate collaboration into learning activities.

To find more information on the subjects of this chapter, search the Web for these terms:

computer-supported collaborative work

CSCW

netiquette

virtual conferencing

videoconferencing

Many of the examples shown in this book are on exhibit at:

www.horton.com/DesigningWBT/

9

Teach in the virtual classroom

Designing and conducting instructor-led WBT

Virtual classrooms use Web-based collaboration tools to mimic the structure and activity of a physical classroom course. They feature an instructor who leads a class of learners through an explicit syllabus of material on a predetermined schedule.

WHY CREATE A VIRTUAL CLASSROOM?

Instructor-led Web-based training has several advantages over instructor-less Web-based training [56].

▶ Learners are familiar with the procedures, rhythms, and presentation methods used in the classroom. Classroom courses have been the standard in education for 1000 years or more.

▶ The instructor can answer questions and address concerns immediately and can directly monitor everything going on in the classroom.

▶ The instructor can adjust content and presentation immediately in response to subtle feedback from learners.

▶ The class can combine lecture, question and answer, individual and team activities, reading, and testing.

▶ Learners can work directly with fellow learners and learn from meaningful conversations with them.

▶ The requirement to show up at a specific location on a definite schedule enforces a discipline on learners. Face-to-face contact with the instructor and peer pressure combine to keep learners on schedule.

▶ Being part of a visible group embarked on a common endeavor appeals to a sense of community and tribalism.

ATTEND TO HUMAN FACTORS

Successful virtual classroom courses usually depend more on human interaction than on technological infrastructure. The secret of success seems to be a responsive instructor who attends to the learning needs of all members of the class.

Select a qualified instructor

The quality of instruction in the virtual classroom depends on the preparation and talent of the instructor. No amount of instructional design can compensate for an unprepared or incompetent instructor. The skills required in the virtual classroom are similar to those used in the physical classroom—but with some crucial differences:

▶ **Learners are not physically present**. The instructor must "read" them not through posture and facial expressions but through tone of voice or even their hastily typewritten words.

▶ **The instructor must communicate through the media available**: displayed words, spoken words, slides, sketches, demonstrations, and video. The instructor must be technically proficient in these media and the tools that provide them. A commanding stage presence may be less effective than swift typing skills and an ability to set up and operate multiple computer programs.

▶ **Learners rely less on the instructor**. Lacking direct face-to-face contact with the instructor, learners will communicate among themselves. The instructor must encourage such "talking in class" and make it productive—even if this makes learners less dependent on and attentive to the instructor. The instructor must be willing to move from classroom commander to virtual valet.

Keep the class small

Most instructors recommend keeping virtual classes small. Ilya Zaslavsky, who has taught online geography classes, recommends a class size of fewer than 15 learners [53]. The Fielding Institute in Santa Barbara chooses to maintain an 8-to-1 ratio of learners to faculty in electronic seminars for its Masters program in Organizational Design and Effectiveness [67].

Respond promptly and reliably

Make and keep promises to punctually respond to learners' e-mail messages, discussion group postings, tests, and exercises. Here is such a promise:

> I will check my e-mail in the morning (Dublin time) and evening weekdays only. I will scan forum postings on Mondays and Thursdays. All exercises and tests that are not automatically scored will be returned to you within three business days.

If you will be exploring caves that are not yet wired for the Internet and unable to respond as quickly as promised, have someone fill in for you while you are not available.

HOLD A PRE-CLASS GET-TOGETHER

If practical, schedule a one- or two-day meeting of all participants—learners, instructors, assistants, support technicians, and other staff. Use the meeting to introduce everyone, to overcome initial hurdles, and to motivate learners who may be unfamiliar with virtual classroom courses. Follow a meeting agenda something like the one described in the following example:

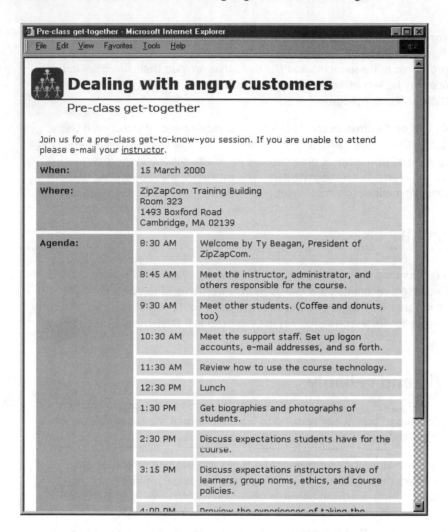

PUBLISH A COMPREHENSIVE SYLLABUS

For virtual classroom courses, the syllabus is the skeleton that articulates the course. It serves as both menu and home page. It lays out the schedule, requirements, and activities of the whole course. The syllabus may be long, but it should be clearly organized and attractively formatted.

Here is a sample that contains most of the elements needed for an effective syllabus. The notes on the right label the content and suggest alternatives.

Agenda

Dealing with angry customers

Instructor: <u>Elicia de Jong</u>

Contents

<u>Objectives</u>
<u>About the course</u>
<u>Modules</u>:

1. <u>Why customers get angry</u>
2. <u>How to calm angry customers</u>
3. <u>Understanding customers' problems</u>
4. <u>Resolving problems</u>
5. <u>When you cannot resolve a problem</u>

<u>Weekly events</u>
<u>Resources</u>
<u>Notes</u>

Objectives

This course will help customer support representatives, sales representatives, and claims adjusters resolve conflicts with angry customers efficiently and without undue stress.

About the course

Make sure you understand the policies and procedures governing this course and that you meet the requirements--before the first class. Also take a few minutes to get to know your instructor and and fellow students.

<u>Policies</u>
<u>Requirements</u>
<u>Grading criteria</u>

Week 1: Why customers get angry (20 Mar 2000)

Events	Readings	Activities
📺 <u>Lecture</u> (20 March 2000 at 20:00 GMT) ✱ ⎯⎯ 🗩 <u>Post-lecture chat</u>	<u>Why customers get angry</u> ✱ ⎯⎯ <u>I'm mad and you're to blame!</u> ⎯⎯ <u>Decline in customer satisfaction in Europe, Asia, and America</u>	🖉 <u>Why do customers get angry?</u> Due: 25 March 2000 ✱ ⎯⎯ 🖥 <u>Discuss why customers get angry</u>. Due: Anytime

---

Title and identifying information

Links to each week's events and to other materials

Because the syllabus may be quite long, include a local table of contents with entries linked to sections of the page.

Objectives

Remind learners what the course is all about.

About the course

Link to materials about the course that the learner may need to refer to before or while taking the course.

Week identifier

Events, readings, and activities

Events are real-time meetings. They can include videoconferences, chat sessions, and other live events.

9

Teach in the virtual classroom

Week 2: How to calm angry customers (27 Mar 2000)

Events	Readings	Activities
📧 Lecture (27 March 2000 at 20:00 GMT) * 🔊 Post-lecture chat 🔊 Role play calming an angry customer*	Calming angry customers * Getting beyond anger	☑ Share a customer complaint you have received Due: 30 March 2000 * 🖼 Brainstorm how to calm angry customers Due: Anytime

[Weeks 3 and 4 are similar]

Week 5: When you cannot resolve a problem (17 Apr 2000)

Events	Readings	Activities
📧 Lecture (17 April 2000 at 20:00 GMT) * 🔊 Brainstorm dealing with unreasonable customers*	When you cannot resolve the problem * Dealing with unreasonable expectations	☑ Simulate dealing with difficult customers Due: 21 April 2000 * ☑Final exam Due: Take between 19 and 22 April 2000 *

Weekly events

These events and activities occur every week, but may not be listed in the week's detailed description:

Lecture: Monday at 20:00 GMT. Required *
Post-lecture chat: Immediately after the lecture
Open forum: Monday at 20:00 GMT
Discussion group: Open all hours

Resources

As you take the class, you may find these general resources useful:

About the instructor   Course discussion group
Roster   Technical support
Biographies of students   Administrative support

Notes

Assignments are due at midnight (00:00 hours UTC) on April 15, then that would make it due by 7:00 PM (19:00 hours) New York time on April 14th (the evening before), or by 1:00 AM (01:00 hours) Berlin time on April 15th.

Lectures are required. We do not take attendance, but we do present information not available through readings or other resources.

Readings are materials learners must read or view. They may include local or Internet materials. Some may be simple Web pages, while others are elaborate multimedia productions.

Activities are things people do. Activities may have deadlines, but learners can generally complete activities on their own schedule. Activities include tests.

In Events or Activities, include milestones or intermediate products for a multi-week project.

Recurring events

List events and activities that occur each week:

Class meetings
Lectures
Chats and other scheduled conferences
Lab sessions

Resources

List resources learners may find useful while taking the course.

Notes

Include any notes, cautions, warnings, or other material that you need to bring to the attention of learners.

Organize the course into bite-sized chunks. If learners are given the complete set of course materials from the start, the very mass of the materials may discourage or overwhelm them. Use the syllabus to divide the mass of course materials into understandable pieces, sort them into logical categories, arrange the pieces into meaningful learning sequences, and set an appropriate schedule for mastering them.

Even if you do not include a formal syllabus, at least suggest a sequence and schedule for consuming the materials—and clearly distinguish high-priority "required" materials from optional ones.

Specify exact dates. When does the week end and begin? Be careful about international differences and time-zone shifts.

> Weeks begin just past midnight Monday morning—GMT!

If possible, fill in actual dates rather than just saying Week 1, Week 2, etc.

Link to everything. Do not require learners to go searching for material mentioned in the syllabus. Link to the materials so that learners can jump to them. For lectures and conferences, link to the page with the embedded conferencing control—likewise for chat sessions. For activities, link to the form learners must fill in and submit to complete the activity.

Flag required items. Use a distinctive icon for required items. Flag any mandatory or date-specific activities in the syllabus and course announcements. Make crystal clear which items affect the final grade and which do not. If an item is optional, but learners who perform the activity can win extra points not available to those who do not participate, is the activity really optional?

PREPARE LEARNERS TO PARTICIPATE

The etiquette for online meetings is far from established or widely known. To help learners know how to behave, publish a guide to participating in live events, something like this extended example:

 # Guide to live learning events

Your class includes several live collaborative events. This guide will help you get the most out of them. It will prepare you to participate effectively in live events. Please review it before the first live event.

Have something to say

In conferences and discussions, make comments that others want or need to hear. If the conversation is lagging, contribute more. If it is full and flowing, make only your best comments.

Chat, not chitchat

Live events are learning tools. Keep conversations on the subject. Keep them professional.

Everybody hears what you say

Remember that everyone sees everything you type and anyone can save a copy. Do not type anything you do not want everyone to remember forever.

Do not greet all participants individually

When entering a conference or chat, do not greet every other participant one by one. A simple "Hi, all!" will do.

Address comments to a specific person

In conferences, distinguish comments intended for a specific person from those for the whole group. Begin the comment with the name of the person you want to respond to it.

Maria, can you explain how you calculated the potential profit?

Indicate the subject of a comment

In chat and conferences, make clear which question you are answering, which point you disagree with, and which problem you are solving. Just begin your comment with a few words identifying its target.

Re the costs, we can economize by …

Wait for people to finish speaking

Wait for people to finish what they are saying. Do not interrupt. Wait for a signal that the other person is through. Be patient with those who have slow typing skills or are a bit awkward speaking in cyberspace.

Over

When you are through speaking, signal so. With the breakups and pauses introduced by network transmission, it may not be clear when a person has stopped speaking and is waiting for a reply. Radio operators typically say "over" at the end of a comment to signal that they are passing control over to the other person. Do likewise by tacking on a closing phrase or comment.

> Let's move on to the second step in the procedure. OK?

> Now you know how I think. How do the rest of you feel about this issue?

Or, you can use trigger phrases: **over**, **period**, and **full stop**.

Roger

Radio operators often use the word "Roger" to signal that they have received the message. Use a similar signal to tell others that you got the message and are preparing a reply.

> Good question!

If you are relying on barely intelligible audio, repeat the question or comment and ask the other person to confirm.

> So, Kerry, you want to know if there are any other costs to the natural regeneration method, right?

If you need more time to think of a reply, say so.

> Let me think about that.

Copy that?

When a message is critical, require a confirmation. When the Capcom wants astronauts aboard the Shuttle to take an action, he or she says something like, "Set your MPU36 switch to the off position, copy?" The word "copy" means "let me know that you understood the message."

Similarly, when the speaker needs confirmation of a message in Chat:

> **Instructor**: Let's go to whiteboard, OK?

> **Learner A**: OK

> **Learner B**: Fine by me

> **Learner C**: Yes

> **Instructor**: Switching to whiteboard. See you there.

Over and out

Say good-bye. When you are ready to leave or end a conversation, give a clear signal. Tell others that you are leaving.

> **Thu:** I think we have covered all the main points. Anyway, I have to rush off to a meeting. Is there anything else that cannot wait?

Peter: Nope, I'm through too.

Maria: No, have a good meeting.

Thu: In that case bye!

Before ending a one-to-one conversation, wait for the other person to acknowledge your good-bye.

MANAGE COLLABORATIVE ACTIVITIES

Virtual teamwork can be frustrating when not managed well [105]. For more successful team efforts, actively manage the effort:

▶ Publish written instructions a week before the activity.

▶ Give the team a definite goal and deadline.

▶ Make sure someone initially assumes leadership of the team. Leadership can shift as the team progresses.

▶ Allocate adequate time. A virtual team will require more time to complete an activity than a physical team. If team members have not worked on virtual teams before, they will require time to learn to collaborate remotely.

▶ Suggest rules or procedures for conducting team activities, reaching consensus, and settling disputes.

▶ Note which learners do not participate in live collaborative activities, and make a point of calling on them by name during the next live event.

TEACH THE CLASS, DON'T JUST LET IT HAPPEN

As the instructor, you must actively lead the class setting the pace, making sure that learners are participating, and overcoming problems.

Contact participants individually. Contact participants individually (phone calls are nice) to let them know you view them as individuals and to listen to any concerns they may have. Visit remote sites and even conduct live activities from there.

Help classmates get to know one another. Have class members post their biographies. Then require each learner to find one common interest or other significant similarity with each other classmate.

Stay on the published schedule. If you publish a schedule, stick to the schedule. Remote learners and those with busy schedules depend on the course schedule to arrange their work and personal calendars to fit the course.

Keep office hours. Most instructors make themselves available about three hours a week at a fixed time [118].

Pace learners. By making assignments week by week, you keep learners from getting ahead of the class and you motivate learners to keep up. However, assign class-long requirements, such as large projects and general readings, at the beginning of the course so that those who want to can start early. You can include the entire syllabus, but have links point to pages that say, "This material will be available starting the week it is mentioned in the syllabus."

Do not spend too much time teaching the course software. Learners become frustrated when too much course time is spent learning how to operate the course software [119]. Refer learners to other sources or teach such skills outside required events.

CONDUCT LIVE EVENTS

Live events are real-time sessions that use some combination of chat, virtual response pads, whiteboards, screen sharing, audioconferencing, and videoconferencing. Live events are complex endeavors that require meticulous preparation, management, and follow-up.

Announce the live event

Announce the live event in plenty of time for learners to prepare for the event and to fit it into their busy schedules.

Calming an angry customer

A role-playing activity

After the lecture on 27 Apr 2000, we will have our usual chat session--but with a difference. We are going to put ourselves in the position of an irate customer, a stressed-out support technician, and the technician's overworked boss.

The scenario, role assignments with descriptions, and a schedule have been posted.

Please read the following information. It answers all the questions you might have about this activity:

| Why? | The purpose of this activity is to let you practice being "on the spot." Chat, although a little slow, will stimulate spontaneity, simulate the "mission-critical" feel of a customer-support desk, and demonstrate how easy it is to be goaded into responding hastily and rudely to a customer. |

Here is an example of an announcement of a live event. It provides complete details about the event and links to related materials.

When?	Monday, 27 Mar 2000 at 21:30 GMT (Log in by 21:25)
Where?	The chat window is embedded in the scenario page. Simply log in and you will be directed to the correct chat session. You will be prompted for your first and last name and a password. Use the password you were assigned when you registered. (E-mail the administrator if you have lost your password.)
Required?	**Yes**. The quality of your participation will count 5% of your final grade.
Preparation?	Carefully read the scenario, the descriptions of the roles, and their assignments.
Special tools?	No special tools are needed for the event. The chat application is part of the scenario page. Prior to the event you may want to practice logging in and sending a message. You will know you are successful if you see your message posted in the Message window.
Computer set-up?	Turn off any scheduled maintenance tasks and screen savers. The fewer programs running while you are in the chat session, the quicker will be the response time.
Alternative?	If you are unable to attend or have technical difficulties, please e-mail the instructor (or call +1.313.555.1234). You will be assigned an alternative activity.
Problems?	If you have any questions about this assignment, e-mail the instructor. If you have difficulties using the chat application, post a message in the technical support forum and the administrator will respond.

Notice how the example above specified the pieces of information required for a live event. Here is a checklist you can use in preparing the announcement of your live event:

▶ **Purpose**. What exactly will learners get out of attending the event?

▶ **Time**. When does the event begin and how long does it last? Remember to specify a time zone or use UTC or GMT times. How early should learners log in? Five or ten minutes before starting time are customary.

▶ **Place**. Where on the Internet or intranet is the event? What is the address of the event host and how do participants enter the event? (Include a hypertext link in the announcement.) Are specific user IDs and passwords necessary?

▶ **Required**? Is attendance mandatory or optional? How much does the event count toward a final grade?

▶ **Tools to be used**. Will the event use chat, audio, video, screen sharing, whiteboard, response pad, or other technologies? Learners should learn to use these technologies before the event, not during it.

▶ **Learning preparation**. What must learners do before the event? What must they read? Are there course modules they should complete?

▶ **Computer setup.** How should users configure their hardware and software for best results? For example, most screen-sharing activities work best if all participants set their screens to the same resolution and number of colors.

▶ **Alternative.** What should learners do if technical difficulties prevent them from entering the event or force last-minute cancellation of the event? What should they do if they are not available at the specified time?

▶ **Contact.** Whom should learners contact for more information?

Prepare for the live event

Good preparation almost guarantees a successful live event. It certainly lowers the anxiety and blood pressure of the presenter. Plan to spend 5 to 10 hours preparing for each hour of the event. How should you spend your time?

Decide roles

Before any live event, spell out the roles of instructor, learners, guests, and others. For each phase of the activity, decide who will lead, who will speak, and who will listen. Also decide who will summarize and evaluate the event. Here is a simple plan for a one-hour guest lecture:

Phase	Person			
	Instructor	**Learner**	**Guest**	**Other**
Introduction (5 min) The instructor introduces the guest speaker.	Presents	Listens		
Presentation (25 min) The guest speaker presents original material.		Listens	Presents	**Director**: Controls the cameras, monitors the schedule, and cues the instructor and the presenter.
Question & answer (20 min) The instructor moderates as learners ask and the guest speaker answers questions.	Moderates	Asks	Answers	
Summary (5 min) The guest speaker recaps the presentation and answers to questions.			Summarizes	
Evaluation (5 min) The instructor reviews the event, notes successes, and suggests improvements.	Evaluates			

Though simple, this plan spells out the main responsibilities and roles of participants during each phase of the event. It forms the basis for more detailed plans.

If the event is complex or involves tight interaction, you may want to prepare and distribute an agenda or script detailing the exact sequence of events.

Specify how to pass control

For chat, audioconferencing, videoconferencing, whiteboard, screen sharing, and other multi-participant activities, all participants must know who has control and how control is passed. Otherwise, frustration dances with chaos.

Modes of floor control

It may help to define modes of control, each with its own rules and expectations. Here are some common modes:

- ▶ **Lecture mode**. The instructor alone can present. Everyone else watches and listens. No one can interrupt the instructor. No one can ask questions.

- ▶ **Q&A mode**. The instructor presents but can be interrupted for questions. All questions are addressed to the instructor (or featured speaker).

- ▶ **Moderated mode**. The moderator leads a discussion. Although all participants have a chance to speak, they can do so only after being recognized by the moderator.

- ▶ **Baton mode**. The instructor introduces the activity and then passes the virtual baton to a participant. The virtual baton is just the symbol of control. While a participant has the baton, he or she controls the presentation. When through, the participant can pass the baton to another participant or back to the instructor.

- ▶ **Free-for-all mode**. Anybody can participate at any time. No one controls or dominates. The instructor is just another participant or just an observer. The only exception is that the instructor can end free-for-all mode.

Spell out the protocol for passing control

Tell learners what phases of activity will take place. Make sure they know how they are to act and when they are to act. Spell out the procedures for obtaining and passing control. For example:

> Remember to ask your question only when the moderator or instructor tells you to. You are allowed one follow-up question. Here is the procedure.
>
> | | |
> |---|---|
> | **Moderator:** | Calls for questions. |
> | **Learner:** | Signals that he or she has a question. |
> | **Moderator:** | Recognizes a learner. |
> | **Learner:** | Asks question. |
> | **Presenter:** | Answers question. |

Moderator:	Asks if the learner has a follow-up question.
Learner:	Either asks another question or says no.
Presenter:	Answers follow-up question.

The procedure repeats until either time runs out or there are no more questions.

Introduce participants before the event

Do not waste time introducing everyone during a live event. Have participants send or post biographies before joining the event or conversation. Include a biography of any guest speaker along with the announcement of the live event. That way the instructor's introduction of the guest speaker can be brief.

Avoid one-way lectures

Do not conduct one-way lectures—or if you do, prerecord them so learners can decide when to view them. Record the lecture ahead of time and let learners play it at their own convenience (p 163). We have all heard horror stories of learners in satellite video courses sending their VCRs to class. Learners would tape the lectures so they could view the presentation at their convenience and could fast forward through the useless parts. There is no reason to require learners to adhere to a schedule merely to receive information.

Send related information ahead

If participants must refer to information during a live conference, send that information ahead of time so that learners can review that material and think of questions. What kinds of materials should you send?

▶ Reports, white papers, position statements, and other reference documents

▶ Detailed examples and case studies

▶ Biographies of the speakers

Pack a conversational first-aid kit

Mark Twain once quipped that it took him more than three weeks to prepare a good impromptu speech. Sometimes the best spontaneous comments are the ones you prepare ahead of time. Prepare comments or questions that will start useful conversations or revive flagging ones. Have them ready in case the conversation stalls. Here are some conversation resuscitators:

▶ Why do you say so?   ▶ Does the plan have any side effects?

▶ Where else might that idea apply?   ▶ What else?

▶ Do you have any doubts?   ▶ And how much would that cost?

Assign pre-event work

Give learners an assignment to complete before the live session. Begin the live event with a discussion of the assignment.

Test the system first

Before holding a real conference (chat, video, audio, whiteboard), hold a 20-minute practice session at the same time of day and day of the week as the real conference. Test for speed and reliability of the system as well as the ability of learners to participate fully.

Rehearse

Rehearse the presentation and collaborative activities. Make sure the tools work reliably and that you are confident using them.

Make a list of things that could go wrong. Write them down on index cards and shuffle the deck. Every five minutes during the rehearsal, draw a card and pretend that the problem on the card just occurred. Practice your response.

Time the rehearsal. The actual class will take 20 to 40% longer than the rehearsal.

Manage the live portion

It's show time! You have prepared. You have rehearsed. You are ready to go.

Hire a director. Have someone other than the instructor, or main presenter, manage the live event. A director can mind the agenda, call time on long-winded speakers, and handle minor emergencies. An active director allows the presenter and instructor to concentrate on the needs of the learners.

Keep learners active. Make presentations dynamic. Use visuals and multimedia to focus attention on key concepts. Never become a talking head. Or worse, an automatic typewriter.

Interact frequently. Never present for more than five minutes without some form of interaction with learners. Spend 40 to 60% of the time interacting with learners.

Call on learners by name. In a physical classroom, the instructor can call on people by just pointing to them or just looking their way. In the online event, the instructor must call on people by name. That means the instructor must have a list of the names of all participants.

Ask more questions than you answer. If you answer a question for a learner, immediately ask the learner a question to test whether they understood. Do not give full answers to questions. Clear up any misunderstandings and point learners to resources they can use to answer their own questions.

Be spontaneous. Script out every session, but leave 30 to 40% of the time free to answer unanticipated questions, go into more detail about issues that deeply interest learners, and interject insights that occur to you at the moment.

Keep a back channel open. In face-to-face meetings, we scan the eye gazes, nodding heads, and smiles of meeting participants. And we listen for vocal utterances like "uh-huh" and "OK." Such signs and signals are called *back-channel responses* [112], and they are an important element in avoiding misunderstanding. In Web collaboration media, instructors must find substitutes to test whether their message is getting through. Keep open an interactive communications channel (chat or voice) so that participants can interrupt if they do not understand something. Consider pausing after each stage of a demonstration or lecture to get feedback.

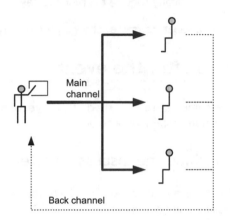

Turn off unused media. Turn off media you are not using at the moment. If you are just talking, turn off the video and leave the audio on. If you are drawing a picture in the whiteboard, temporarily turn off video and audio.

Limit the number of active "speakers." In a live session, no more than 5 to 7 participants can be "talking" at once. Many can listen, but the conversation becomes chaotic if more than a few have the ability to talk at will. Either keep meetings small, or limit which participants can speak without first getting permission.

Maintain control and focus. Without floor-control, no chat, audio, whiteboard, or video conferencing is effective. During synchronous time, learners must all be "on the same page." If questions or discussion drift too far, reestablish the subject under discussion. Terminate activities that continually drift off subject. Give learners a chance to explore the limits and fringes of ideas before jerking them back on course.

Attend to all learners. Give attention to all learners, not just those who stand out. In collaborative activities, those who stand out tend to get more attention and exert more influence than those who blend in [112]. Learners who have their microphones turned up will sound louder than others. Those who sit close to their video cameras will seem larger. Learn to ignore these false cues and give equal attention to all learners.

Make participants visible

Participants in virtual collaboration need a way to know who's there. Since classmates are not visible, learners are not aware of who is listening and watching. They may feel alone or may hesitate for fear of offending unseen watchers. To enhance awareness:

▶ Publish a roster.

▶ Periodically require everyone to say something, even just "I'm still here."

▶ In a separate frame, show a periodically updated list of who is currently logged in.

Follow up after the event

The cameras are all turned off, but learning goes on. After the live portion of an event there is still important work to do.

Continue the discussion after class

To encourage learners to continue conversations started in a class meeting, start a chat session immediately after the class. This gives learners a chance to ask the instructor questions they were too shy to ask in class and enables learners to discuss points that especially interested them during the class.

During the live event, invite participants to contribute to a discussion-group thread on the subject. Start the thread with transcripts of the live event and its follow-up chat session.

Evaluate the event

To improve live events, include a formal evaluation process, something like this:

▶ The instructor critiques the activity, noting what worked well and what could be done better next time.

▶ Learners suggest how they could have done better.

▶ The instructor privately comments on participants' behavior, especially if not appropriate. Common problems include verbally abusing others, dominating the scarce time, and asking questions outside the guest authority's area of expertise.

▶ The instructor or a designated learner writes a summary and lists points of agreement. Everyone reviews the list and concurs.

Thank outside helpers

The instructor (or learners) should write thank-you notes to all those beside staff members who helped them in the live event. A token gift is appropriate for experts who made presentations or consented to interviews.

STAY IN TOUCH AFTER THE CLASS

Learning need not stop at the end of the class—just when learners are beginning to apply what they have learned. Use collaboration mechanisms to let instructors and learners stay in touch and to monitor how successfully knowledge gained in the course is applied on the job.

Maintain collaborative channels

Maintain communication with learners after the class ends. Make it easy and inexpensive for learners to stay in touch.

▶ Provide free e-mail accounts.

▶ Maintain a roster of alumni. Make it available only to alumni.

▶ Invite course graduates to alumni-only chats.

▶ Invite alumni to serve as special tutors, mentors, or teaching assistants.

▶ Keep discussion groups open or set up alumni-only groups.

Monitor the application of learning

Once a month or so, have course graduates discuss how they are applying ideas from the course. Conduct a chat session or open a discussion thread for this purpose. Encourage course graduates to share success stories, ask for help, and offer help to others.

IN CLOSING ...

Summary

▶ Virtual classroom courses use Web technology to mimic the structure and activity of conventional classroom courses.

▶ Use virtual classroom courses when an instructor is necessary to motivate learners, monitor their progress, and answer their questions immediately. Or when the discipline provided by a familiar structure and peer pressure is necessary to motivate learners.

▶ Publish a comprehensive syllabus listing all the events, activities, and readings of the course. Link Web pages, forms, and other required resources. Likewise, include links to the roster, policies, requirements, grading criteria, discussion group, and other resources of the course.

▶ Actively conduct the class. The instructor should contact participants directly, keep them on schedule and focused on the course, and manage collaborative activities.

▶ Plan live events carefully. Ahead of time, assign roles, allocate time, spell out a protocol for passing control, rehearse the event, and send materials needed during the event.

▶ Keep live events lively. Vary the presentation. Require learners to participate.

For more …

For more ideas on using collaboration mechanisms in the virtual classroom, see Chapter 8 on collaboration mechanisms.

If you are not tired of books, you may want to dip into these:

▶ *Building a Web-Based Education System* by Colin McCormack and David Jones [120].

▶ *Web-Based Instruction*, edited by Badrul H. Khan [121].

▶ *Creating the Virtual Classroom* by Lynette Porter [122].

Search the Web for **virtual classroom** or **online classroom** or **virtual university.**

Many of the examples shown in this book are on exhibit at:

www.horton.com/DesigningWBT/

10

Motivate learners

Providing incentive, encouragement, and discipline

It is widely believed that electronic courses have lower satisfaction ratings and higher dropout rates that traditional classroom courses. Dropout rates of up to 85% are claimed [78]. This chapter suggests techniques that designers and instructors can use to keep learners interested, energized, and enthusiastic. You can pick which techniques to use for your course, for your class, and for individual learners.

DOES MOTIVATION MATTER?

WBT is hard for learners. It raises technical hurdles. The rules for social interaction are uncertain. The immediate camaraderie of classroom training is missing. The easiest thing about WBT is clicking on the Quit button.

Successful WBT courses rely on the self-discipline and focus of motivated learners. But can we assume that all our learners are properly motivated?

> One cannot count on the motivation of learners: both learners and professionals have a strong tendency to procrastinate, to fritter away time [123].

WBT demands high levels of motivation, but we cannot depend on learners bringing all the required motivation with them. Our WBT must motivate learners.

Why do learners drop out, slow down, or give up?

The reasons learners give for withdrawing or not fully participating in electronic courses vary. Many of them are the same reasons heard for conventional courses, but some are much more common for electronic courses:

> "The material does not apply to me. It does not help me do my job."

> "The course wastes too much of my time teaching me things I already know."

> "I spent so much time trying to get the technology working that I had little time for learning."

> "It was too lonely trying to learn by myself. I missed having classmates."

> "I am not a herd animal. I learn best alone. I wanted to go faster than the rest of the class."

> "Boring, boring, boring! Just like reading a textbook on the screen. This course is no fun."

> "There was no incentive to try extra hard. No one noticed but the computer."

> "I have a job and a family. The class does not fit my schedule. I cannot just drop everything to attend a chat session that occurs at midnight where I live."

> "There were so many mistakes in the course, and some of the information was out of date. I felt I could not trust it."

> "There was not enough overlap between what the course wanted to teach and what I wanted to learn."

"The course was so full of educational jargon that I felt like a lab rat in an educational psychology experiment."

If you read through this list you will notice inconsistencies and contradictions. Why? People are different. They want different things from a course and they learn in different ways. There is no single technique for motivating everyone, but there are many things that instructors and designers can do to keep most learners motivated.

Pick the right motivators

Learners in WBT courses are motivated by some of the same things that motivate people to work hard at their jobs, to take risks in their lives, and to undertake difficult endeavors. These include both positive motivators that make learners want to take the course and negative motivators that dissuade them. What are some of these magical forces of motivation?

☺ Positive motivators	☹ Negative motivators
▶ Money	▶ Fear of humiliation or embarrassment
▶ Hope of a better job	▶ Boredom
▶ Pride among coworkers, family, and friends	▶ Loneliness
▶ Competition with fellow learners	▶ Technophobia (and real technical problems)
▶ Collecting credentials	▶ Costs
▶ Fun experience	▶ Distrust of the material
▶ Joy of learning	▶ Inconvenience
▶ Independence and flexibility	▶ Lack of time
▶ No need to travel	

Of course, different people are motivated by different forces, events, and rewards. Our task is to design courses that provide the motivators that activate learners while avoiding those that discourage them.

SET CLEAR EXPECTATIONS

The best time to motivate learners is before they begin the course. It is also the best time to avoid frustrations and disappointments. Before the course starts, set clear expectations. Tell learners what they are expected to do, learn, and create. Tell them when and how well they must do these things. Also ask learners what their expectations are of the course. Confirm that the course will meet these expectations.

In one initial offering of the online course "Introduction to Computer-Based Systems" at Purdue University Calumet, learners did not know the format of the course ahead of time. Over half dropped out in the first two weeks [118]. Let learners know what the course requires before they sign up for it.

Tell learners what is expected of them

Tell potential learners what tasks learners must perform to complete the course, when they must do them, and how well they must do them.

What kinds of learning tasks must the learner do to complete the material of the course? Must learners read and view presentations? Do exercises and activities? Take and pass tests? Participate in online discussions, chats, and conferences?

Spell out which activities are required and which are optional. Are passing test scores required before taking advanced sections of the course? Do some optional activities provide "extra credit" toward the final grade?

The place to set expectations is in the course description (p 80). Make sure learners can read the full course description before registering for the course.

> "Will you tell us a story?" said the queen, "one that is instructive and full of deep learning."
>
> "Yes, but with something in it to laugh at," said the king.
>
> — Hans Christian Andersen, *Flying Trunk*

Ask learners what they expect

As part of the registration process (or early in the course), ask learners what they expect to learn. Ask them to state how the objectives of the course relate to their life or career objectives. Such an activity will get learners to commit to the course.

Have the instructor or registrar review their answer. If not realistic, do not accept them in the course.

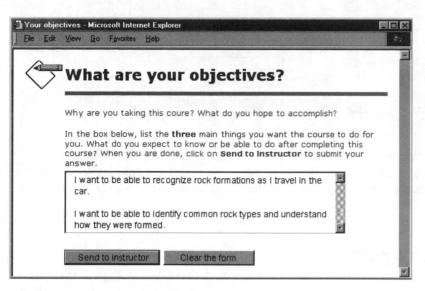

Here is an example of an activity that asks learners to state their objectives for a course.

Have learners rate objectives

Have the learners rate the relevance to them of the objectives stated by the designer. List the objectives of the course and ask learners to state to what degree these objectives agree with their own reasons for taking the course.

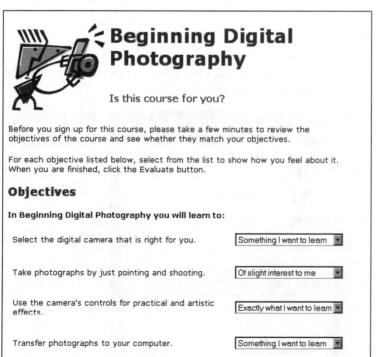

Here we ask learners to state how much the objectives for a course overlap their objectives for study.

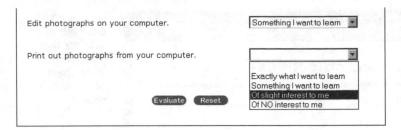

Such a form generates valuable feedback for course designers to tell them what learners really want. It also gets learners to commit to the goals they selected as high priority. The form also warns learners, who might not read the objectives page carefully, that the course does not meet their needs.

REQUIRE COMMITMENT

A lot of the high dropout rate of WBT courses can be explained as a lack of initial commitment. Many dropouts were just "taste testing" the course anyway. Others signed up with the intention of quitting if the course proved at all difficult. Designers and administrators often encourage such shallow commitment by encouraging learners to "just try one of our courses." While we want to let learners sample the goods before purchasing them, we need to demand full commitment when learners enroll in a course in earnest.

Require commitment to finish the course

Before admitting learners to a course, require them to commit to the goals of the course and to pledge to complete the course and stay on schedule.

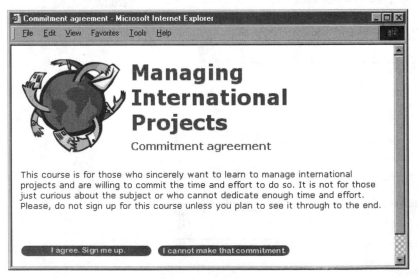

Here is an example of a required page in the registration process.

Do not allow monitoring or auditing. Require at least a minimum level of participation.

Require a positive approach

Learners may be anxious, superstitious, and distrustful of something as new as WBT. Require learners to put aside their distrust, doubt, and suspicion. Explicitly require them to abandon these negative feelings if they are to take the course.

In this example, learners are required, metaphorically at least, to discard fears and negative feelings in order to enter the course. To open the doors to learning, learners must first pass through a negativity detector. To pass through, they must first symbolically discard negative thoughts by dragging them to the trashcan.

Require learners to affirm responsibility

WBT, more than any other form of training, requires learners to actively participate in their learning and bear ultimate responsibility for its success. One emphatic way to communicate this fact to learners is to require them to assent to affirmations of responsibility.

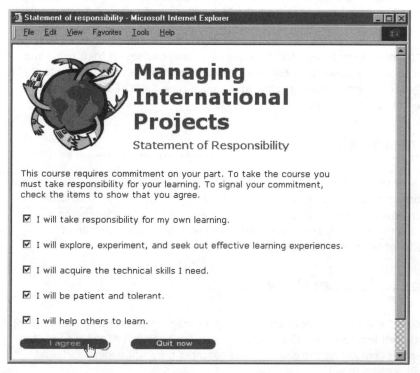

Here is an example that requires just that. To enter the course, learners must check all of the affirmations and then click on the **I agree** button.

Feature the WIIFM

What's a WIIFM? WIIFM is an abbreviation for the question continually asked by prospective WBT learners: "What's In It For Me?" A WIIFM is any credible answer to that question. Think of WIIFMs as the fuel pellets of motivation.

Promote the advantages of online learning

Learners without much experience with WBT or CBT may expect the course to closely resemble classroom instruction. They may feel frustrated because they cannot apply their well-developed skills of classroom learning. They may long for some of the pleasant aspects of the classroom experience, while not noticing or seeking out the better aspects of online learning.

It is up to you to explicitly point out the advantages of electronic learning and of the course in particular. Remind learners that they are acquiring valuable new learning skills that will benefit them for the rest of their lives.

Signal the importance of the course

Let learners know that their organization values training and that it values your course in particular. A clear message from upper management can help. Use of online training at U.S. West Dex increased after e-mail messages from the CEO encouraged employees to take the courses [103].

Set aside time for training. Employees who are required to take courses on their own time may feel that the courses are optional or else that they are an unwanted intrusion into their private lives. Designate times for training. Allocate as much time for WBT training as learners would spend in an equivalent classroom course.

Explain learning materials

Help learners see how the objectives and materials of the course help them accomplish their goals [94]. Tell learners clearly what materials are included, how they help accomplish the goals of the course, how they are related to each other, and how the learner should use them. Without such information, learners are confronted with an incoherent pile of unrelated documents of little interest to them [91].

Specify objectives in learners' terms

Adults quit learning if they do not believe they can apply the information being taught [124]. Clearly and honestly tell learners what they will get out of the course. Tell them what they will be able to do after completing the course, what concepts they will understand, and what skills they will possess (p 90).

Make every objective the kind of answer you would get if you asked learners, "Why are you learning this?" or "What do you want to learn now?" [93]

Create real-world value

Not all learning outcomes are intangible. WBT is rich with opportunities to produce work with monetary and professional value.

Design the course so that by completing it, learners create a valuable intellectual property, which they take away from the course. Create an ongoing project that has as its outcome a valuable work product, such as:

▶ Paper or article ready for submission to a trade or scholarly publication

▶ Action plan for solving a real corporate problem

▶ Computer program

▶ Invention ready for patenting

▶ Proposal for soliciting a new line of business

Have learners complete a realistic class project. At the end of the class, have them post their solutions to the Internet for use by other professionals in their field.

MAKE WBT FUN AND INTERESTING

There are no boring courses, only boring designers. And even the best designers sometimes forget that learning can be a pleasure.

Begin by provoking interest

Begin each segment—especially ones that require extensive reading or are long and difficult—with something to capture the learner's interest and provoke curiosity.

▶ **Tell a story**. Create a scene with people the learner can identify with and care about.

▶ **State a problem that the material will solve**. Make it a problem the learner recognizes.

▶ **Ask a question**. If learners get the answer right, they feel good. If they do not, their curiosity is aroused.

▶ **Show a picture**. Include an intriguing image that draws the learner in. "What is this?"

▶ **Show results** that the learner will be able to accomplish after completing the unit.

Use motivating words

In your description of the course, use words and phrases that make learners want to take the course: *quick, fast, step-by-step, fun, opportunity to ..., leads you through ..., examples, instant feedback, easy, concise, up to date*, and *accurate*. If such words do not apply to your course, do not lie. Just redesign your course.

On the other hand, avoid negative terms. What negative terms? A lot of the terms that are positive and meaningful to instructional designers have a different effect on prospective learners. Take care with educational jargon. Do you really think your learners will take your course because it "eschews prescriptive behaviorism in favor of exploratory constructivism"? Or would they rather take a course that is "quick and filled with examples"?

Ensure high quality

A course with a lot of mistakes, a sloppy layout, and frivolous multimedia loses credibility with learners. Their confidence wanes, as does their participation.

▶ Test your lessons, tests, and activities with actual learners.

▶ Write simply, clearly, actively. Proofread for misspellings, grammatical errors, and lapses of logic.

▶ Make sure that graphics and multimedia justify their download time. Make them as compact as possible and eliminate them if they are just decorative.

▶ Use a consistent, effective layout and visual design scheme.

▶ Check examples for credibility. Make sure the facts and figures you cite in examples and activities are credible. If a learner has experience in the area of the example, he or she will notice the error—and tell all the other learners about it.

Involve learners

Structure the course as a story. Introduce characters the learner will care about or identify with. Empower and imperil them. Make each lesson another chapter in their ongoing adventure, which is resolved only at the end of the last lesson.

To sensitize learners to the issues in a course or lesson, begin by describing situations that involve the issues. Ask the learner what they would do in those situations.

> There is nothing so captivating as new knowledge.
> — Peter Mere Latham

Make WBT more like a game

Why do games appeal so strongly to players? While we may not want to mimic the mayhem of the latest twitch-and-splat videogame, we can still borrow a few of the motivational principles that draw people to computer games.

▶ More activity and interactivity. More doing and less reading.

▶ More examples, case studies, and scenarios—especially from the learner's area of interest.

▶ Simple, clear, appropriate pictures. More show and less tell.

▶ Multimedia, as appropriate and practical.

Vary the content and presentation

For courses, libraries, and museums, you want people visiting the site frequently. One way to draw people to the site is to continually add new material and vary the presentation.

Announce changes

Prominently announce what has changed recently. List changes frequently so that users have a sense that new material is being added and that they should check back often.

Put these announcements on the course home page or in a discussion thread dedicated to course announcements.

Include evolving content

Include content that naturally grows or is updated. Here are some kinds of information you may want to include:

▶ News and press releases

▶ Discussion groups

▶ Digests of discussion groups

▶ FAQs and tips

▶ Lists of related Web sites

You can also create a continually (hourly?) changing page, but do not let this become a distraction.

Incorporate real-time data

Another way to draw interest is to include information that changes continuously. Some examples:

▶ Live data feed from a telescope, video camera, weather satellite, or scientific instrument

▶ Current results from an ongoing experiment or survey

▶ Current orbital positions of the Space Shuttle, the Space Station, or some other satellite

▶ Financial reports or stock prices for various companies

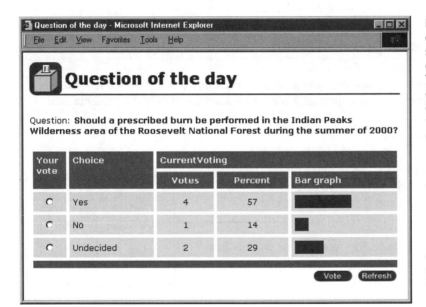

Here is an example that shows the results of a daily poll. The vote totals change continuously throughout the day.

This example uses a virtual response pad (p 361).

OFFER BRIBES (EXPLICIT EXTERNAL REWARDS)

In a conference presentation a couple of years ago, I asked the audience to shout out the methods they used to motivate learners in training. Shouts and laughter followed until one fellow silenced the room with a single word: "Bribes!"

Bribes, in this context at least, are explicit external rewards. External rewards do not themselves increase learning [94]; however, they do get people to pay attention to the material, which is a prerequisite for learning from it. Though they can never replace the inexpressible joy of learning, they can prop it up and urge it on nicely.

What bribes can we offer our learners?

Monetary rewards

Try cash. Dollars, Euros, Yen, Marks, Francs, Kronor, Pounds, and Pence all will do. Take some of the money you are saving by using WBT and spend it on the people who are saving you the money. Consider a simple monetary reward for the first learners to complete a new course or the ones who get the highest scores.

Cash too crass? How about some other rewards of substantial value?

▶ Products your company sells

▶ Stock in your company

▶ A computer

▶ Movie tickets and a dinner

▶ Extra vacation days

▶ Discounts on future courses

Token gifts

Token gifts are rewards with more symbolic than monetary value. They, too, can be powerful incentives to complete a course. Tokens you can use to entice WBT learners include:

▶ Coffee mugs

▶ T-shirts, windbreakers, and sweatshirts

▶ Screen savers and desktop wallpaper

▶ Book bags and satchels

▶ Mouse pads

▶ Posters

Fame and prestige

People stay motivated as long as they are appropriately challenged and their successes are recognized. One way to accomplish this is to provide visible symbols of accomplishment. To bestow fame on successful learners:

▶ Post their name and photo on your site as the "Learner of the Month"

▶ Send out press releases to local media and to their hometown newspaper

▶ Commend them in a letter to their boss

▶ Award them a certificate of accomplishment

Another approach is to establish levels or ranks of achievement. As learners complete part of the course, promote them to the next level.

Tribal membership

Create an exclusive community of successful learners and offer admission as a reward. Members get the status and perquisites of this exclusive community. These may include:

▶ Special discussion groups and chat rooms that celebrities and authorities visit

▶ Access to special advanced areas of the course

▶ Wider choice of future assignments

▶ Special newsletter

Sun Microsystems rewards new sales representatives who take and pass a WBT course by sending them to a weeklong classroom course in California [125].

Contests

Competition motivates. And recognition of competitive victories motivates competitors. WBT learning programs have used contests to motivate the study of difficult material. Perhaps you want to post the names and scores of your top learners.

This example shows a list of the top learners of the month.

Have weekly and monthly contests. Hold contests for various categories. Hold contests for the highest scores on tests and for the largest number of activities performed. Create a Hall of Fame and a Lifetime Achievement award.

Caution: Competition is a powerful motivator and sometimes it motivates the wrong behaviors. If you are teaching teamwork and collaboration, for example, then competition among individuals sends the wrong message.

Some learners, typically those with competitive natures to begin with, place too much importance on the competition and not enough on learning. They try to win at any cost. And that cost is the quality of learning or relationships with fellow learners.

Still other learners find competition silly and childish. One learner described a course competition as "the kind of game designed to appeal to pre-adolescent boys."

My advice: Know your learners. If they are mature enough and appropriately motivated by competition, use it. In any case, make the competition optional and provide other motivations for noncompetitive souls.

PACE AND PROMPT LEARNERS

The timetable of formal classroom training is a strong motivator. The frequent requirements to attend class, submit homework, and take tests help learners stay on schedule. If learners lack the discipline to pace themselves through a WBT course, we may need to create a rhythm of prompting events. Tell learners how important it is to keep on schedule and what to do if they fall behind.

Publish a schedule

Provide a detailed schedule for learners who need a high level of structure. Include a complete outline of the course, including content, activities, and tests. Remember that busy learners may need some time to arrange their work and personal schedules so that they can participate in these events. Make the schedule available before the course begins.

For self-paced courses, suggest a schedule or calculate one for the learner based on the amount of time the learner agrees to devote to study.

Space out activities

Give the course a comforting, consistent, regular rhythm. In an instructor-led class, build in enough evenly spaced instructor-graded exercises and tests so that the instructor can monitor progress of learners, while learners feel they have a partner in learning.

Instead of one long test at the end of a course, include small tests every week or so. Interleave collaboration and activities to break the monotony of extensive reading and to provide frequent chances to practice what is being learned.

Require weekly contributions

To pace a virtual classroom course, reveal the material and assignments in stages. For example, at the start of the week, create a new home page detailing the readings, activities, assignments, tests, and other requirements for the week.

Then, after the week is done, rename the home page to something like "Week7.htm" and create a new home page with the next week's activities. Include links back to previous weekly pages.

Require weekly contributions from every learner. Contributions may include activities and tests completed, postings to a discussion group, or entries in a learning diary.

Remind and encourage learners

Monitor the progress of learners and gently prompt and prod them to stay on schedule. Send e-mail messages to learners to remind them of upcoming special events, milestones, and deadlines. If learners are late with an assignment, send them a reminder message. The assignment may be stuck in the learner's outbox.

Give learners incentives to stay on schedule. Penalize late submissions of activities. Conduct special live events, say an interview with an expert, but require completion of prior course work to attend.

PROVIDE ENCOURAGING FEEDBACK

Respond in a positive, encouraging, non-critical way—especially at the start of the course.

Say it's OK to be a little afraid

Let learners know that it is OK to be a little afraid. They are being asked to use new technology and to learn in new ways without a lot of the familiar, comfortable supports of traditional means. Tell them that they are a part of a great experiment and that things very well may go wrong. Let learners know that in no way will they be penalized for failures of the technology. However, failures of technology will not be accepted as an excuse for not learning.

Encourage learners

Continually give learners encouragement. Make the messages you send them sympathetic and helpful. "You can do this and we will help you."

▶ **Communicate enthusiasm!** If the instructor and the author of the course believe in the course and the learner's ability to master it, the learner will feel the same. Before you write a topic or an e-mail message, ask yourself how you can phrase your message so it communicates enthusiasm.

▶ **Praise accomplishments**. When learners do well, tell them so. Learners do not need lavish praise, just an occasional "Well done." Often learners working alone have no standard against which to measure the quality of their work.

▶ **Praise publicly, criticize privately**. Never, never, never embarrass a learner by criticizing the learner in front of fellow learners, coworkers, or boss. In discussions and chat sessions, you may have to disagree with the learner, but do so gently, without criticizing the learner's thought process or personality.

▶ **Share excellent work with the rest of the class**. One of the best incentives is fame. If a team does an especially effective piece of work, post it as an example for the rest of the class to examine.

Give feedback as soon as possible

Immediate feedback adds motivation [94]. It rewards by acknowledging the learner's progress and provides guidance before the next attempt. Do not make learners wait one nanosecond longer than necessary to learn how they are doing in the course.

▶ Where possible, use automatically scored tests and activities.

▶ Grade all assignments and tests promptly.

▶ Respond promptly to all questions, comments, and suggestions from learners.

BUILD A LEARNING COMMUNITY

In a learning community, learners take responsibility for their own education and training and for that of other members of the community. The concept of a community goes beyond an individual course to empower learners to own the learning process.

Construct a community of learners

Building a community takes efforts at every level of course design and administration. Steps include these tasks:

▶ Let the class decide many aspects of the course, such as the pace and coverage.

▶ Assign class members responsibility to assist in conducting the class—especially in helping learners over technical hurdles.

▶ Use discussion groups, chat sessions, and e-mail to foster learner-to-learner communication. Set up a "learner lounge" where learners can discuss any subject of interest to them.

> ► Set up an alumni association to help learners stay in touch with each other and the instructor after the class. Provide a registry of e-mail addresses and a newsletter with news about alumni.

> ► Stay in touch with learners. Keep former learners informed about follow-up courses and refresher courses.

> ► Create emblems of membership. Provide logos, T-shirts, coffee mugs, and other tokens.

Increase human interaction in the course

Many learners in electronic courses miss interaction with other human beings. They need the encouragement of the teacher and fellow learners. To keep such learners from feeling so lonely:

> ► Post pictures and brief biographies of the instructor (p 94) and learners (p 109).

> ► Meet with learners at the start of the class. If it is not practical for the instructor to travel to the learners, hold an opening videoconference or chat session.

> ► Hold periodic online discussions, conferences, and chat sessions (Chapter 8).

> ► Use collaborative activities (Chapter 8) to encourage learners to motivate each other.

> ► Communicate with each learner every week or so, especially learners who are working alone.

Encourage learners to seek help

Encourage learners to contact instructors, tutors, and other support staff. Make learners feel that they can ask questions, make suggestions, and request help at any point.

> ► Extend a warm invitation. Let learners know you welcome their inquiries.

> ► Post a friendly photograph. Pose the instructor as an approachable peer, not an imperial authority. A smile works, too.

> ► Promise a quick response. And deliver.

Simplify contact. Make contacting you as simple as click-type-click. Here is a response form invoked by clicking on a **Comment** button present on every page. The learner just types in a comment and clicks on **Send**.

INTERVENE WITH UNMOTIVATED LEARNERS

You designed your course to keep learners motivated, and most are doing just fine. But a few are not. Should you take special steps to help them? What can you do?

Identify unmotivated learners early

How can you identify unmotivated learners in time to help them? The instructor must continually be on the lookout for symptoms of failing motivation, such as these:

▶ Lateness in submitting assignments.

▶ Unanswered messages.

▶ Terse, sarcastic, or flippant responses.

▶ Negative comments about the course, instructor, or other learners.

▶ Negative comments by other learners.

▶ Sudden reduction in test scores.

▶ Failure to submit any optional assignments.

In a course without an instructor, a sophisticated computer-managed instruction system can still recognize some of these symptoms, but the system is limited in what it can do to correct the problem. An instructor can do much to remotivate unmotivated learners.

Contact unmotivated learners immediately

Do not wait too long to contact unmotivated learners. An early expression of concern will be more welcome than a later critical inquiry. The longer you wait, the further behind unmotivated learners fall and the more incentive they have to quit the course. If they are far behind, they will be more embarrassed by their failure to keep up.

Remotivate unmotivated learners

Each learner is unique. To remotivate a learner, you must understand why they are not motivated and then work with them and possibly others to craft a solution. There is no formula to follow, but this checklist should help:

▶ **Find out why.** Do not assume that non-participating learners are lazy or in any other way to blame. They may have more important demands on their time. They may have family duties or job responsibilities you are unaware of. If learners are adults, treat them as such. Accept that your course may not be the most important thing in their lives.

> ▶ **Offer a more flexible schedule.** If learners just need a little time to catch up or need to take longer to complete the course, give them that choice.

> ▶ **Help with technical problems.** If technical skills are lacking or technophobia is causing a block, offer resources.

> ▶ **Address the learner as a peer.** Do not be parental. Use neutral language. Express concern, not blame.

> ▶ **Get a response.** If the learner does not respond to e-mail, use other media: postal mail, phone calls, or personal visits.

> ▶ **Keep records.** If failing the course has major consequences, inform authorities. More drastic action may be necessary, and records are essential.

> ▶ **Advise learners of the consequences of not participating.** Tell learners what will happen if they do not complete the course on time, but do not threaten.

> ▶ **Ask for commitment.** Ask the learner to agree to rejoin the course. Get the agreement in writing.

> ▶ **Follow up.** Continue to monitor the learner's performance. Give extra encouragement. Praise all substantive accomplishments.

REDEEM TROUBLEMAKERS

You may have a few learners who are not just unmotivated but are actually negatively motivated. They prevent themselves and others from learning.

These troublemakers are the same type as in the classroom. However, in WBT troublemakers may be more frequent and their behavior more severe than in classroom learning. Research on computer-mediated communication has found that incidents of rude, abusive, and disruptive behavior increase when face-to-face contact is replaced with computer-mediated communication.

Who are the troublemakers?

Although troublemakers come in every size, shape, age, nationality, and background you can imagine, a few behavioral types are especially common and especially noxious. Here is a list of common nightmares:

Bully. The Bully intimidates others through emotional criticism, sarcasm, or personal attack. Of all the troublemakers, the bully poses the greatest threat to other learners.

Pouter. The Pouter refuses to participate in collaborative activities. The pouter communicates tersely if at all.

Whiner. Whiners complain continually about the course, the instructor, and other learners. If everyone complains, then the course may be at fault, but if one person complains, you probably have a whiner.

Know-it-all. The know-it-all has all the answers. Know-it-alls vigorously defend their prejudices and never change opinions. The Know-it-all is often critical of other learners.

Dominator. The Dominator has to win every argument, have the last word in every discussion, and answer every question.

Deal with troublemakers

Dealing with troublemakers is difficult. It requires tact, patience, and an even temper. Those with experience dealing with troublemakers share these suggestions:

▶ **Stay calm**. Do not take it personally. Do not be insulted or let anger direct your response. Wait, if you must.

▶ **Tailor your response to the individual**. Remember that not everyone learns the same way. Perhaps the Pouter is just shy. If that is the problem, offer individual activities as an alternative.

▶ **Do not threaten**. Do not appeal to authority. Never attack the troublemaker's personality or character. Most troublemakers will just react defensively.

▶ **Point out the negative behavior**. Show how the behavior is harming the class, other learners, and the troublemaker.

▶ **Channel the behavior to constructive uses**. Give troublemakers assignments that require them to reverse their negative behavior. Ask the Know-it-all to argue the opposite position. Have the Pouter start and moderate three new discussion threads. Ask the Dominator to serve as a Help desk for other learners. Have the Whiner proofread the course.

▶ **Take decisive action**. A single troublemaker can disrupt an entire class. Expel the troublemaker—but only if his or her behavior is harming others and the troublemaker refuses to change the behavior. Keep thorough records of all your actions.

▶ **Reward good behavior**. Award bonus points of up to 10% of the total grade to learners who practice good netiquette, help their fellow learners, and play fair.

IN CLOSING ...

Summary

► Learners in WBT often give up, drop out, or slow down because they lack the high levels of motivation required to overcome the difficulties posed by WBT.

► Set clear expectations. State your requirements for learners and gather their expectations for the course. Require learners to commit to working hard and finishing the course.

► In every corner of the course—in every activity, on every page—make sure learners know "What's in it for me?" WIIFMs keep learners working hard.

► Make WBT fun and interesting. Make it more like a game than an inquisition. Test and immediately fix annoying glitches. Continually improve the course. Make it dynamic. Incorporate real-world and real-time data into activities. Include evolving content.

► Bribe people to learn. Offer them explicit rewards: money, coffee mugs, membership in a club for successful learners, Learner of the Month awards, certificates of achievement, and whatever else can motivate them.

► Pace and prompt learners. Have learners commit to a schedule. Remind them to stick to that schedule.

► Intervene if you have unmotivated learners or troublemakers. Take corrective steps early to help learners in trouble and to protect others.

For more ...

To help motivate learners, make them aware of the advantages of online learning as spelled out in Chapter 2.

For more ideas on motivating learners, see Chapter 11 [126] and Chapter 21 [127] in *Web-Based Instruction*.

Search the Web for **motivation**.

Many of the examples shown in this book are on exhibit at:

www.horton.com/DesigningWBT/

11

Go global

Designing for the WWW (Whole Wide World)

The first two Ws in WWW remind us that the Web is a global resource, reaching into every continent, every country, and every culture. And putting training on the Web (or the intranet of a multinational company) makes it available around the globe, but availability is not enough. Barriers of language, custom, and expectations limit the use of our training. Local economic and business conditions further restrict who can take our training. Reaching the goal of global training requires solid knowledge of the differences among learners throughout the world—and careful design for these differences.

THE CHALLENGE OF GLOBAL TRAINING

Designing training for the whole world is difficult, expensive, and risky. We must surmount barriers of language, culture, distance, politics, habit, and technology. It is easy to get discouraged before you even start. But the task is not impossible. Let's begin by considering what global training requires and what difficulties we must overcome.

Problematic provincialism

WBT courses and materials designed for one culture or country can fail when used by people from a different background than anticipated.

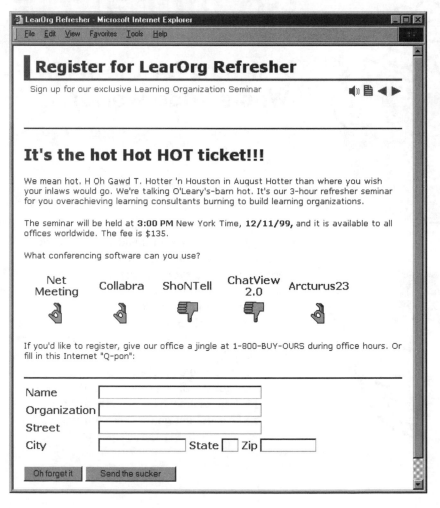

Here is an admittedly concocted example that shows many of the cultural gaffes, goofs, and gaps that plague Web pages developed with only a local focus. How many problems can you spot?

If you only spot a few, return to this example after reading this chapter.

Differences matter

In designing WBT, we must take into account differences among learners around the globe. Differences in language, social values, and accustomed learning styles affect how well training developed for one culture works with a different culture [128]. Let's look at some of the differences among international WBT learners, recognizing that these differences overlap and interact.

Language

Language is usually the biggest cultural barrier in training [128]. For each target group, we must consider how well the group understands the language of the course. How well can the target group:

▶ Read the written language?

▶ Understand the spoken language?

▶ Express ideas in the written language?

▶ Speak the language fluently and clearly?

The answers to these questions determine the need for translation, simplified writing, graphics, and multimedia. The answers can also guide you in choice of collaboration mechanisms and design of team activities.

Culture

Communication is the process of using what we have in common to share what we do not have in common. People of the same culture have more in common than people of different cultures. Hence, communication is easier within a culture.

Language is one aspect of culture, but others are important, too. What other aspects of culture affect the design of training?

▶ **Symbology.** Do learners recognize the same images, icons, and other symbols you use?

▶ **Values.** How does the target group define correct behavior in the classroom, the office, and life in general? What are the expected relationships among people of different ages, genders, and economic classes? Is innovation more important than tradition? Do they value politeness over free expression? What are the relative importance of self, coworkers, family, and authority figures?

▶ **Educational expectations.** How do people expect to learn? Do they prefer theory or practice? Which comes first? Are they accustomed to following a structured agenda or exploring freely on their own? What is the expected role of the instructor: To examine, to lead, or to discuss?

Geographic conditions

Where are your learners located? How does this locale affect how they learn best? What aspects of their work and daily life contribute to their willingness and ability to participate in your course?

▶ In what time zone do they live? How much do business hours at their location overlap business hours at your location?

▶ Where and when can they take lessons? At work during office hours? At work outside of office hours? At home? Are they willing to participate in activities outside of office hours?

▶ What national, religious, and business holidays do they observe?

▶ Who pays for the courses: the employer, the employee, or the government? Are learners paid for the time they spend taking courses?

Technical capabilities

Before prescribing or designing WBT, take into account the technical capabilities of your audience. What systems and skills do they possess? Learners on distant shores may give different answers from those at the home office. Consider:

▶ **Connection speed and quality.** Will learners take the course from a 1-megabit direct connection or a 28K dial-up modem connection? Will they be accessing the course over a local network? What's the average speed? How reliable is the network?

▶ **Computer capabilities.** Do the learners have a network card? Do they have a CD-ROM drive? How fast is their processor? How many colors can they display? How big is their display screen?

▶ **Power and phone service.** Are there frequent power outages? Is phone service reliable and noise-free?

▶ **Internet access.** Is Internet access widely available? Is the cost reasonable? Are learners billed by the connection or by the minute?

WBT can teach globally

The differences among learners around the globe can discourage designers from even trying to deliver training on a global scale. But WBT gives us new capabilities to communicate with those with whom we share fewer common experiences and from whom we are separated by oceans and social customs. With WBT we can:

▶ Reach those who cannot travel to take a classroom course.

▶ Show as well as tell. We can use pictures, animation, or movies to explain concepts that second-language readers find hard to infer from textual descriptions.

▶ Allow learners to repeat segments they did not get the first time—without embarrassment.

▶ Let learners customize training to their local traditions and expectations.

With careful design that attends to the differences among learners, we can take our WBT global.

Not all training is totally global

Not all WBT courses are intended for international use. Some may serve those in similar cultures. Others will be translated and adapted later for particular target markets. Note: Not all the examples in this chapter (or this book itself) follow all the advice of this chapter. Nor should you—unless you are trying to reach the widest audience possible.

GENERAL STRATEGIES FOR GOING GLOBAL

Before we discuss details of how to render graphics or rewrite text, let's look at a few high-level strategies that will make your course more effective for international and local learners alike.

Say what you expect from learners

In the Course description page (p 80) or as part of the registration process, spell out assumptions and expectations, especially concerning language skills, participation, and so forth.

> This course is for business professionals who want to learn to negotiate contracts. There are several ways of learning these skills. Please take a few moments to consider whether this course is the best way for you.
>
> To benefit from this course you should have:
>
> ■ **Strong English-language skills**. You must be able to read and write business English. This course requires reading common business documents and expressing your ideas in writing. None of the tests or other activities are timed, so you can take as much time as necessary to write your thoughts. There are narrated segments, but they are accompanied by text transcripts.
> ■ **Time to study**. This course requires between 5 and 15 hours per week.
> ■ **Commitment**. The course includes several team activities. You must be willing to work as a member of a team.
> ■ **Internet and Web skills**. You should know how to navigate Web pages, fill in on-screen forms, send e-mail, and participate in forums and newsgroups.
>
> If these requirements are too restrictive for you, please consider one of the other courses or books on the resource page for this course.

Here is an example of such a description. It spells out the required language and technical skills, as well as a willingness and ability to participate fully.

Accommodate different levels of technology

If many of your learners lack reliable high-speed communications links or must sometimes access your course over slower channels, design your course so that it still works on these slower channels.

Do not squander bandwidth

Bandwidth is a technical term for the speed of a communications channel, which determines how fast it can download Web pages, pictures, and video clips. If the learner's bandwidth is limited, put your graphics and multimedia on a diet.

Never use a big file to do what a small one does better.

Ask yourself, "Do I really need that 1 megabyte video clip to show how to insert Tab A into Slot B? Or would a 15K animation work as well?"

Provide multiple versions

If you require high-bandwidth media, provide alternative low-bandwidth versions for those who lack high-bandwidth connections.

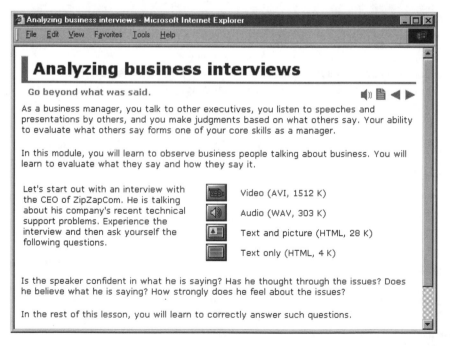

This example offers four versions of an interview, each appropriate for a different speed connection.

This example requires plug-ins to play video and audio.

Video

Clicking on the **Video** button downloads and plays a 1.5-megabyte video clip in which the learner can see and hear the speaker.

Voice

Clicking on the **Audio** button downloads and plays an audio recording of the interview. This version is 20% of the size of the video version.

Text and picture

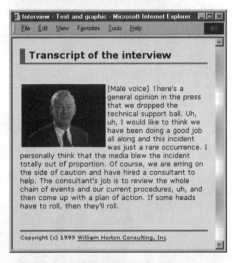

Clicking on the **Text and picture** button loads a Web page containing a picture of the interviewee and the text of the interview. It is 2% of the size of the video version.

Text only

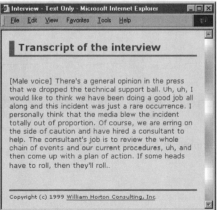

Clicking on the **Text only** loads a Web page containing just a text transcript of the interview. It is 1/250 the size of the original video version.

Accommodate different learning styles

Learners are all influenced by the educational system they have experienced as students. We designers need to think about these different approaches to learning when specifying the organization and access strategy for our courses. For instance, in the United States, Canada, and Australia, adult learners are used to getting immediately to the point. They expect the answers right away and the details only when they are needed. Europeans, on the other hand, may count on a more structured approach with the facts and the details in a predictable, logical order. Asians may be accustomed to learning the theory before getting down to the facts. Younger Americans may prefer a discussion with the instructor and other students. Learners from other countries may be more accustomed to a lecture by the instructor.

How do we accommodate these differing learning styles? One of the best ways is to give learners the navigational choices necessary to take the course in their preferred style. We must provide multiple pathways. Link facts to details, details to theory, theory to facts, and so on. We can suggest a path through the material—perhaps in a table of contents or syllabus—but we should not force everyone to follow that path.

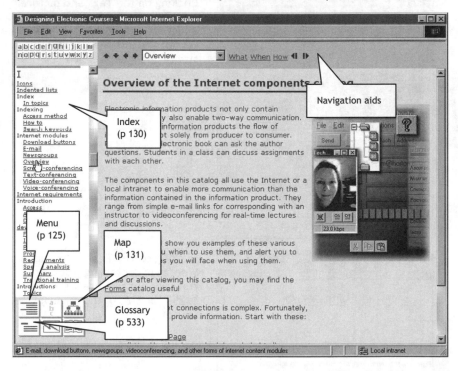

This example shows some of the ways learners can control the path and pace of a course.

This approach to organization has an added benefit. Your WBT course becomes a reference work that learners can consult after completing the course itself.

Be a polite foreigner, not a phony native

There is no generic culture and no totally global viewpoint. Often designers, fearful of offending someone somewhere, purge their course of all cultural identifiers and disguise its viewpoint. Such attempts often end up confusing the very people they avoided offending.

Respect other cultures but do not hide your own. Reveal your nation, your company, and your perspective. Let people know that you are speaking from that perspective and consistently speak from it. Encourage people to interpret symbols in that context. If you must shift perspective, say to show an example, clearly announce the shift.

If your target learners are familiar with your culture and you show respect for their cultures, you can skip much of the rework suggested elsewhere in this chapter.

> Good manners have much to do with the emotions. To make them ring true, one must feel them, not merely exhibit them.
>
> — Amy Vanderbilt

Mix media

Do not rely on text alone to convey your message. Mix text with voice narration, pictures, animation, and other media.

Avoid the Great Wall of Text

One of the biggest barriers in WBT is termed the "Great Wall of Text." It refers to Web pages consisting entirely of great, gray blocks of text. For those who must look up every fifth word in a translation dictionary, scaling the Great Wall of Text taxes endurance and severely tests motivation.

This is the classic Great Wall of Text. Can you imagine anyone reading all of it?

Break up large areas of text

Long passages of unbroken text are boring, intimidating, and look like just too much work. So break up these long passages into smaller, more easily digestible chunks.

▶ **Keep text short.** Edit text to reduce unnecessary paragraphs, sentences, and words. Get to the point.

▶ **Convert paragraphs to lists.** Where possible, use bulleted or numbered lists to highlight the main points of the passage.

▶ **Integrate the text into a graphic.** If your budget and subject matter allow, create a graphic that summarizes the main points you want to convey. Use text for callouts and captions. If you translate, remember to budget for translating the callouts and captions.

Present the same information in multiple formats

As we pointed out earlier, you can use complementary media to overcome the biases or weaknesses of a single medium. For example, you can convert a text-only display to one intertwining text, narration, graphics, and animation:

From this:

Disk shipments on track at 90,000

Disk shipments will hit 90,000 for fiscal year 2000. This number represents a 200% increase over shipments during 1999, which totaled 29,500. Of course, 1999 shipments were below those for 1998, mainly due to fire damage in the Huntsville center. A large part of the growth during FY 2000 can be attributed to working down the backlog of orders which could not be filled from the Huntsville center. Evidence for this comes from the fact that a continuation of the growth experienced during 1995 through 1998 would have resulted in 90,000 units being shipped in 2000.

Shipments for previous years were as follows: 10,200 in 1995, 13,000 in 1996, 21,000 in 1997, and 36,000 in 1998.

To this:

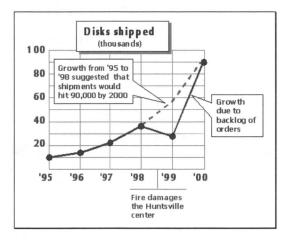

Display the text of narration

Consider displaying the transcript of any voice narration. Such a display has proven to be a great help to those who are not native speakers. You can display just a summary of the voice narration or a full transcript.

If the voice narration is short, you can include the text right in the main display.

This example shows how to replace a network card in a personal computer. The speech balloon contains the actual voice narration. Notice that the displayed text is a more concise version of the spoken narration.

This example uses a Macromedia Shockwave movie.

For a lengthy narration that would take up too much space in the main display area, make full transcript available for display and printing. The following example includes two buttons: one to play the voice narration and another to pop up a separate window containing the text version of the narration, which can be printed out.

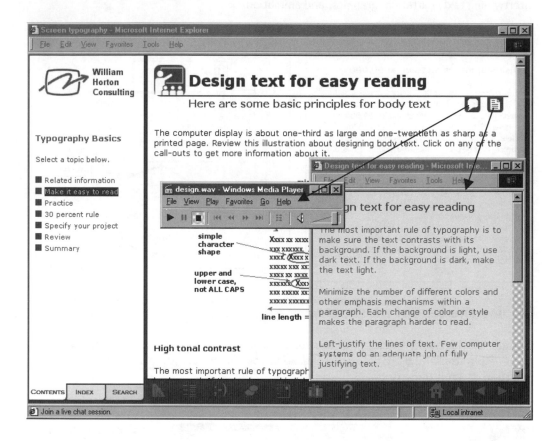

Test, test, and test again

Test your course early and often. Test with members of the target cultures that you will be training. Have your course tested by:

▶ Foreign sales office personnel

▶ Staff in your office who come from the target countries and cultures

▶ Local members of the target cultures

Include a glossary

Include a glossary (p 533) so that learners can look up definitions of words they do not understand. The glossary should define technical and business terms not found in a general-purpose translation dictionary.

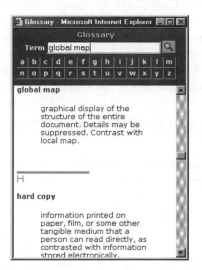

The example to the right displays terms used in a course on designing electronic documents and courses.

You may also want to include links to a general-purpose dictionary that all learners can use to look up non-technical words.

Include a cross-cultural summary

If you cannot design the whole course for a global audience, at least include a cross-cultural summary for the course, for each lesson, and for other critical parts.

Write the summary in simple language (p 469) or provide multiple translated versions. Use graphics to clarify meaning and to break up the text.

Give learners time to absorb information

You are awake at two in the morning so you can participate in a mandatory chat session for your WBT course. As slang-infested messages scroll by, you try to translate them to your language, think of a reply, translate it to the language of the course, and send it off before everyone has forgotten about the message you are responding to. You scan the page for the **Slow down!** Button.

Remember, second-language learners in a different culture may need a little more time than local, native-language speakers. To give them the time they need:

▶ Slow the pace of narration and displayed text.

▶ Do not automatically erase text or other images. Let learners replay any voice, video, music, or sound.

▶ Eliminate timed tests unless reaction speed is a job requirement.

▶ Do not require chat or live conferencing. Allow e-mail and discussion groups as alternatives.

▶ Have a moderator summarize concepts in a simple written recap.

AVOID COVERT NATIONAL CHAUVINISM

National chauvinism can creep into your work in a number of ways. Most of the time it is innocent and unintended. It consists of acting as if your culture and your country is the only one that matters. To avoid national chauvinism, adapt your designs so everybody can understand and participate.

Use generic objects in examples

Are your examples all specific to your locale and culture? If so, broaden them so that learners can see that the concepts apply to them, too.

For example, if you are talking about money, do you automatically show a picture of only the currency of your country?

Copyright © Aris Entertainment, Inc., 1992

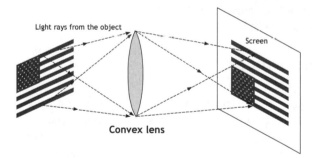

If you need an arbitrary object for an example, is it one associated with a particular nation or culture?

Avoid local expressions

Take care with informal expressions and references to local institutions, sports, TV programs, and so forth. Avoid blunders like these:

▶ "In the testing labs, our product scored a grand-slam home run."

▶ "For an account number, use your Social Security Number."

▶ "... as if Dilbert adopted Garfield and moved into Seinfeld's apartment."

▶ Using "we" and "our" to refer to the citizens of your country.

Substitute internationally known references, and use expressions everyone can understand.

Think from the viewpoint of your learner

Relative directions depend on where things are. Where things **are** depends on where the **reader** is, not where **you** are. For example:

☹ Do not write ...	☺ When you mean ...
What is your destination: domestic or international?	What is your destination: within Canada or outside Canada?
Greetings from the sunny Southland.	Greetings from sunny southern California.
You will meet many other foreigners on the streets of ...	You will meet many other international visitors on the streets of ...

Format addresses flexibly

Many who would like to take your course may find the doors of the registration office locked to them. One of the most common problems in WBT courses is the form of addresses expected. To the right is a common format used by US-based firms. Notice that there is no slot for country. Some countries are divided into provinces, not states; and many of these subdivisions require more than a 2-character abbreviation. What is a Zip? Actually, it is the Zone Improvement Plan devised by the US Postal Service. Very interesting, but what does someone outside the US enter into that slot?

Name	
Organization	
Street	
City	State	Zip

To the right is a revised form that corrects these problems.

If the majority of your learners come from one country, make that the default. Most others will understand why you did so. For an example of this approach, see the Registration page (p 105).

Name	
Organization	
Street	
City	
State or Province	
Country	
Postal code	

MAKE NUMBERS EASY TO UNDERSTAND

Math is a universal language and numbers are numbers, right? Not quite, as this section points out. In international Web pages, we must take special care with how we present numbers, currency, dates, times, and telephone numbers.

SPE££ out ¥our ¢urr€ncy unit$

How much is one dollar worth? Silly question? If you say yes, I will gladly swap you Taiwan dollars for American dollars—one for one. (Each Taiwan dollar is worth about three US cents according to this morning's exchange rate.) Taiwan, the US, Canada, Australia, Singapore, Hong Kong, and New Zealand all have dollars as currency. Similarly, several countries have francs, pounds, and pesos.

Spell out currency units. For example, writing $123 is ambiguous. Instead, write US$123 or $123 USD. If you are referring to Canadian dollars, write $123 Canadian or $123 CAD.

Remember that decimal points are not always dots

One thousand two hundred thirty-four and fifty-six one hundredths is written 1234.56 in the US, but might be written as 1 234,56 in France, and 1.234,56 in Germany.

To avoid such decimal confusion:

▶ Make the country clear—this is especially important anywhere on the Web.

▶ Alert users when jumping from a page produced in one country to one produced in another.

▶ Clarify an ambiguous number. For example change 1,234 to 1,234.0

▶ Use a non-breaking space as a thousands separator. For example, 1 234 567.

> **TechnoTip:** In HTML, you produce a non-breaking space with the code   but this code puts a normal width space between the digits.
>
> Another solution is to use an invisible image. Sounds strange, but here's how it works. You create a GIF image whose single pixel is transparent or at least the same color as the background of your page. Where you want the space to occur, include the image. Within its IMG tag include a WIDTH attribute set to the number of pixels of space you want to include. Here's how it looks for a 3-pixel wide space:
>
> ```
> <IMG SRC="onepixel.gif" WIDTH=3 HEIGHT=1>
> ```
>
> This solution works, but it makes your HTML messy and can interfere with the screen readers used by the blind.

State dates clearly

Format dates unambiguously. The date 01/02/03 could be 1 Feb 2003, 2 Jan 2003, 2 Mar 2001, or 1 Feb 1903. Make the date clear to everyone. Any of these forms work:

▶ 1 February 2003

▶ 1-Feb-2003

▶ 2003-02-01

▶ February 1, 2003

Note: For dates stored in databases, follow ISO Standard 8601, which formats the date as 2003-02-01.

Make your time zone known

What time is 9 AM? Even in the United States this is ambiguous. Is this Eastern, Pacific, Mountain, or Central time?

> The teleconference begins at 9:00 AM, New York time.

Be sure to include an international time zone. You might say "3:00 PM New York time (20.00 UTC)." UTC stands for Universal Time Coordinated and is what was called Greenwich Mean Time or GMT in more Anglo centric times. Also, many countries use 24-hour time. 3 PM could be 15.00 in Sweden or 15h00 in France.

State the day too. When it is Tuesday morning in India, it is Monday evening in California.

Include both international and American units

State measurements in both metric and American units. Say:

> ... 3.17 meters (10.39 feet)   - or -   ... 10.39 feet (3.17 meters)

Put the unit familiar to the largest number of your learners first.

When you convert the number, state both values at the same degree of precision. Do not equate an approximate value with one of great precision.

☹ **Do not say ...**	☺ **When you could say ...**
... about a thousand acres (404.7 hectares)	... about a thousand acres (400 hectares)

Include international telephone numbers

In telephone numbers, remember to include the international calling code for the country.

> Call our Tokyo office at **+81**-3-5421-7698 or our
> Denver office at **+1**-303-555-6782.

The plus sign before the number is just a convention. It is not dialed as part of the number. It says, "After you dial the digits to start an international call, continue with these digits." To find a list of country codes, search the Web for the phrase **international calling codes**.

Be sure to include a separate telephone number for people outside your toll-free zone. Most US toll-free numbers work only inside the US or in the US and Canada.

If you do not answer telephone calls 24 hours a day, clearly state your hours.

> Please call during business hours—9 AM to 5 PM New York time
> (14:00 to 22:00 UTC).

BE CAREFUL WHEN SHOWING PEOPLE

Nothing embodies a specific culture more than an image of a person. Avoid using images of people or parts of the human body as symbols. If you must use an image of a person:

Dress people modestly. Use common conservative business attire as your model. Avoid loud patterns, bright colors, high fashion, or overly casual wear. A hemline that is chic in Paris may be "blatant sexist exploitation" in San Francisco and "pornographic" in Dhahran.

Minimize indicators of social and economic class. Again, use simple business attire and avoid accessories that imply wealth or position, such as jewelry, furs, exotic cars, etc. Avoid emblems of religious value.

Keep relationships between people simple. Show people interacting in a polite and not too casual way. Make clear that the power to make decisions stems from job assignment or recognized expertise, not merely gender, social laws, or age.

Keep hands generic. When showing an operation involving the use of a hand, make the hand as generic as possible. Minimize racial and gender differences. Even better, use a cartoon hand. Instead of a hand of a particular gender or race, prefer a cartoon hand.

☹ No    ☺ Yes

The goal of the graphic is to focus attention to the task the hand is performing rather than on speculation about what kind of person it is attached to. Oh, by the way, if only one hand is to be shown, make it the right hand, because in many Arab countries the left hand is reserved for toilet tasks.

Use cartoon characters when appropriate. With cartoons you can avoid problems associated with race and gender. One word of caution: Because of their frequent use for humor, cartoons may not be appropriate for highly formal situations.

MAKE MEDIA GLOBAL, TOO

Graphics and multimedia can help bridge chasms of language, but not without careful attention to differences in the ways people experience these media. Here are some media-specific tips to help make the media you use work for a global audience.

Pictures

Pictures are independent of language but only if they are properly designed. Create images that have the same meaning in all cultures. Avoid symbols with offensive or emotional associations.

Suppress unimportant details

Details that could inform one audience can confuse or distract another. To make symbols international, design objects that are abstract enough to avoid cultural associations. There is a fine line between making an image recognizable and making it culturally specific. Choose graphics that your international readers can identify, but take care to include only those details that enhance recognition. Some suggestions are:

- ► **Disguise or diminish national differences** like national clothing styles or the shape of power plugs.

- ► **Hide audience-specific details** by deleting them, blurring them, or picking a viewpoint that does not show such details.

- ► **Use an icon or simplified drawing** instead of a realistic drawing or photograph.

- ► **Obscure or omit textual labels**. For instance, show keyboards with blank keys. Indicate particular function keys by position, not by name or label.

- ► **Show all possible instances if you cannot disguise variable features.**

Pick universal visual symbols

The symbols we use to encode meaning or to decorate a graphic can have vastly different associations in different cultures. We must ensure that these associations do not contradict our intended meaning.

Common problems

Many symbols have rude, offensive, or strongly emotional meanings to certain groups of people. Here are some categories to avoid:

Gestures

This gesture may mean OK in North America, but it can mean zero or worthless in France, and in South America it refers to a part of the anatomy not normally exposed in public.

Every hand gesture is obscene or rude somewhere in the world. Avoid projecting fingers (any finger, any number of fingers) and clenched fists.

Mythological beings

The grim reaper was supposed to represent the act of halting a process in a manufacturing operation. The reference meant nothing in much of Asia.

Avoid gods, angels, demons, and other mythological creatures. We do not all share the same religious and mythological heritage.

Puns

The balance scale was used to represent the scale of a map. Such a use only works for English speakers because in English these two meanings share a common word. Puns seldom work with second-language learners, and they defy translation.

Body parts

The eye used as a symbol for conducting an inspection was interpreted by some as giving an enemy the evil eye, that is, placing a curse on them.

Hands easily become obscene gestures. An ear can symbolize gossip; the lips, a sexual suggestion; and the bare feet, an accusation of poor hygiene.

Religious symbols

This icon was supposed to represent assistance in diagnosing and solving problems, sort of first aid in troubleshooting. The Red Cross is a standard symbol for medical care in Christian countries, but in Islamic countries the same aid is provided by an organization called the Red Crescent.

Question any symbol that has religious associations. Such symbols can slip in quite innocently: A charting program may use six-pointed stars and crosses when plotting data points; a crescent might seem a good symbol for nighttime.

Totems

This owl was used as the logo for online training until its creators discovered that in southeast Asia, the owl symbolizes stupidity and brutality and in Central America it represents witchcraft and black magic.

Do not use images of animals for symbols. We do not all agree on which of its characteristics the animal represents.

People

This button was used to run a computer program, but many sought meaning in the individual person shown.

When we show an image of a person, we reveal someone of a particular race, gender, age, and economic class that may not fit the viewer's expectations of the role symbolized.

Respect national symbols

Do not casually diminish the flag, currency, coat of arms, or other emblems of a country. This can often happen quite innocently. Imagine a symbol of European economic unity that shows a businessman wearing a suit made of the flags of the European countries. Somebody is the lapels and somebody else the seat of the pants.

Pick appropriate grading marks

When marking right and wrong answers, take care with your choice of symbols. The check and X-marks used to grade school papers are not used consistently throughout the world.

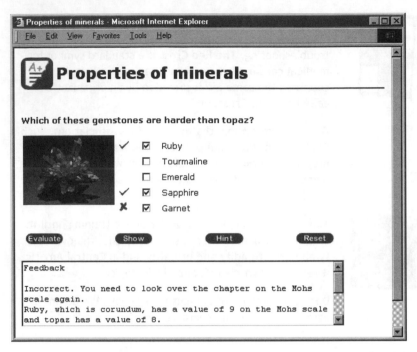

The marks used in this test use the meanings common in North America. However, in Scandinavia, their meanings of right and wrong are the opposite of what they are in North America.

As alternatives to check marks and X-marks, you can use:

○   and   🚫

😊   and   ☹

+   and   —

Avoid even inadvertent political statements

Check and double-check your work for unintended messages. The eagle used in the emblem on the left worked fine as a symbol of accomplishment, until someone noticed that it resembled the eagle on the right.

Draw on common imagery

Science, TV news, movies, and international sports provide us with a palette of shared images we can use for symbols and examples.

Space exploration

Who has not seen a Space Shuttle launch? Or marveled at photographs of earthrise over the moon or an astronaut or cosmonaut floating free in space?

Medicine

Around the world, medical doctors wear stethoscopes around their necks, administer injections with hypodermic syringes, and prescribe pills.

Transportation

Just about everybody who takes WBT is familiar with trains, plains, busses, and automobiles.

Sports

Most nations compete in the Olympics. Formula 1 auto racing spans five continents. The World Cup may draw an audience of a billion or so. Avoid local forms such as American football.

Business

People's homes differ much more than their offices. The fax machine used to send a message in Tokyo looks a lot like the one that receives it in Cairo.

These sources work well because they are emotionally neutral or positive and, with the possible exception of the World Cup, none of them has strong religious or political associations.

Narration

Voice narration can help international learners understand your course. Voice narration relieves the tedium of lengthy reading—especially if the narration is easy to understand. Voice narration can also make understanding displayed text easier.

Select a narrator carefully

Picking a narrator that everyone can understand requires care. Here are some characteristics to look for:

► An expressive range—not a monotone.

► A moderate pitch—neither too high to seem shrewish, nor so low that inexpensive computer speakers rumble.

► An understandable accent—for English narration, use a narrator with a middle-class London accent or someone trained to speak like a US news reporter.

► An appropriate level of authority—the narrator must be believable in his or her role.

E-nun'-ci-ate'

If your budget doesn't allow for hiring professional voice talent, here are some tips to help you record the best narration possible:

► Stand up while recording.

► Speak at a moderate pace, about 150 words per minute.

► Maintain a constant volume level.

► Enunciate clearly and precisely.

► Repeat numbers, technical terms, and abbreviations.

► Pause often.

Help learners understand the narration. Eliminate background sounds and music while the narration plays.

Voice-over rather than lip-sync

There are two ways to use voice narration: *voice-over* and *lip-sync*. In voice-over narration, the voice comments on events happening in the animation or video but is not associated with any particular person or cartoon character. Voice-over narration is the omnipresent voice behind the curtain or off to the side. With lip-sync narration, the voice is synchronized with the lip movements of a person or cartoon character in the scene.

Unless all learners have high-speed connections, I suggest sticking to voice-over narration. Voice-over narration can usually be stored separately and need not be precisely synchronized with movements. Relaxing the requirement for tight synchronization makes for smoother sound and movement, avoiding the stammering audio and stuttering video common with lip-sync narration over slow communications channels.

Even if your learners do have a high-speed connection, there are still reasons to prefer voice-over narration. Lip-sync narration is difficult to redub after translation. Remember those badly dubbed science-fiction movies made in the late 1950s?

Music

When was the last time you saw a movie or television program without background music? Music is an omnipresent accompaniment to visual entertainment, and even news programs have theme music. However, music can be closely linked to a particular culture. Here are some guidelines to help you select music for international multimedia:

Stick with "safe" forms. With just a few exceptions, you can safely use instrumental versions of European classical music, Western pop music, and mainstream jazz.

Watch out for melodies that may have different meaning in different contexts or countries. For example:

▶ The recurring theme in Smetana's "Die Moldau" is used as the basis for the (informal) Israeli national anthem.

▶ "God Save the Queen" in the British Commonwealth becomes "My Country, 'Tis Of Thee" in the United States.

▶ The melody of the German national anthem, "Einigkeit und Recht und Freiheit," is also familiar as Hayden's "Glorious Things of Thee Are Spoken" (String Quartet in C Major, op. 76, no. 3) and as a Lutheran hymn. Many, however, remember it as the Nazi anthem, "Deutschland über Alles."

Avoid music with strong regional or national associations. For example: Reggae, Bluegrass, Dixieland, and Polkas. Such music will distract from your message. (Unless, of course, those genres or regions are relevant to your message.)

Animation

With animation you can distill the subject to just the essentials, eliminating unnecessary details that might distract your viewer. As a result, simple hand-drawn animations can be more effective than complex rendered animations or full-motion video segments. Plus, simple animations usually require fewer system and network resources to run.

I once used a simple stick figure as the main character in an animation about career paths. The dejected fellow to the right has a flat-line career path. Using familiar cartoon conventions, I was able to make the character sympathetic and expressive with a minimum of detail.

Cartoons appear around the world, and their conventions are well understood. You can use that fact to your advantage when designing animation sequences for international audiences. Just remember, all of the tips for designing graphics apply here, too: hiding irrelevant details, avoiding the use of religious or mythological symbols, and showing people only when necessary.

Video

Video is the medium of last resort. Use it only where it is important to convey emotion, depict fact or history, or show the natural movement of the subject. For most uses, however, its realism gets in the way of the message. Video shows too much detail about people, their dress, race, gender, age, mannerisms, and speech. It can distract the viewer from your real message. On the technical side, video requires substantial bandwidth and processing power. It is expensive to produce. And, it is even more expensive to localize.

If video is what's needed to adequately express your message, mimic the style of video used by CNN International or SKY News. And always make it easy for learners to replay video segments.

Discussion groups

Discussion groups are becoming a staple in WBT courses. For classes composed of people of different cultures, you must make sure that cultural differences do not interfere with the potential benefits of the exchange of ideas.

The most important requirement for multicultural discussion groups is an active moderator who is familiar with how cultural factors can affect people's participation in a computer-mediated discussion. The moderator must screen messages before they are posted and may delete some messages or require the submitter to rewrite the message before it can be posted. Here are some rules for the moderator:

▶ **Require civility.** Squash flames, personal attacks, and overly emotional criticism. Remember, many participants find overt criticism distasteful or intimidating.

▶ **Edit messages.** Help those with limited fluency to express their thoughts. Simplify complex messages so that all participants can understand the messages. With the sender's permission, correct misspellings and grammatical errors.

▶ **Prompt nonparticipants** with specific questions. Some class members may not be used to offering their ideas in class.

▶ **Allow criticism of ideas but not of other people.** Encourage people to find ways to improve ideas submitted by others.

Conferencing and chat sessions

In conferences and chat sessions, participants exchange messages without a delay. For such a session, a moderator cannot screen messages before they are posted. How can we make sessions more productive to an international and multicultural audience?

▶ **Publish a "code of conduct"** that requires participants to respond professionally, write simply, and assist their fellow students who need help.

▶ **Make participation optional.** Differences in time zones, national and religious holidays, and work schedules may make it impossible to find a date and time when everyone can participate.

▶ **Prefer low-bandwidth media.** A chat session or discussion group requires much less bandwidth than an audio conference or videoconference. In a discussion group, those with limited language skills can read text at their own pace. The quality of voice in audioconferencing and videoconferencing is often hard for second-language learners to understand.

▶ **Post an edited transcript** of the session for those who could not participate live or who had trouble following at the rapid pace of the exchange.

▶ **Moderate after the fact.** Point out behavior and ask participants to be more considerate. Creatively nudge the discussion away from personalities and other irrelevant issues and back toward the subject of the discussion.

ENCOURAGE LEARNERS TO FORM "NATIONS"

Medieval universities drew students from many countries. The students from each country would often band together into groups, called *nations,* for self-protection in a foreign land, to combat homesickness, and to study more effectively. Within their nations, students could discuss in their native language the lectures delivered in Latin or in the language of the host country.

Our courses can take a similar approach. Let learners set up discussion groups and chat sessions where they can help one another in their native language. Consider letting learners with the same language and culture work together on projects and in activities.

DISPLAY AND PRINT AS INTENDED

Web pages used internationally require attention to a few technical details to guarantee that they display and print the same for all learners.

Use escape sequences for high-ASCII characters

Even though your word processor or HTML editor will let you type in accented letters and other high-ASCII characters, use escape sequences instead. High-ASCII characters are characters other than these:

```
a b c d e f g h I j k l m n o p q r s t u v w x y z
A B C D E F G H I J K L M N O P Q R S T U V W X Y Z
0 1 2 3 4 5 6 7 8 9
~ ! @ # $ % ^ & * ( ) _ + { } | : " < > ? ` - = [ ] \ ; ' , . /
```

Escape sequences are sequences of characters used to display special characters.

If you want to display:

> Encyclopædia X © 1999 Jørgen Lervåg
> ($85 US, £50 UK)

Enter:

```
Encyclop&aelig;dia X &copy;
1999 J&oslash;rgen Lerv&aring;g
($85 US, &pound;50 UK)
```

Although you can specify all characters by their numeric code, these characters will display correctly only on systems using the standard ISO Latin 1 character set. To find a list of the named and numeric codes, search the Web for **iso8859**.

Some word processors substitute escape sequences when they save documents as HTML and some do not. Test a sample before you assume all is well.

Define character sets with meta-tags

You want learners to read your text as you wrote it, not as a garbled mess that looks like encrypted e-mail from Mars. You must make sure the browser displays the page using the right symbols for letters and numbers. In the head section of the HTML file, use meta-tags to define the character set used for the text.

```
<html>
<head>
<meta http-equiv="Content-Type"
    content="text/html; charset=iso-8959-2">
```

Here are some of the character sets you may need to use, especially when translating to specific groups of languages:

charset =	Name	Covers these languages
iso-8859-1	Latin1	Western European languages: English, French, Spanish, German, Portuguese, Italian, Dutch, Danish, Norwegian, Swedish, Finnish, Icelandic, Irish, Scottish, Catalan, Basque, and Albanian. Latin1 also includes Afrikaans and Swahili.
iso-8859-2	Latin2	Central and Eastern European languages: Czech, Hungarian, Polish, Romanian, Croatian, Slovak, Slovenian, and Sorbian.

charset =	Name	Covers these languages
iso-8859-3	Latin3	Maltese and Esperanto.
iso-8859-4	Latin4	Estonian, Latvian, Lithuanian, Greenlandic, and Lappish.
iso-8859-5	Cyrillic	Russian, Serbian, Bulgarian, Byelorussian, Macedonian, and Ukrainian.
iso-8859-6	Arabic	Arabic
iso-8859-7	Greek	Modern Greek
iso-8859-8	Hebrew	Hebrew
iso-8859-9	Latin5	Turkish
iso-8859-10	Latin6	North Polar languages: Inuit, Lappish, Icelandic.

As browsers, operating systems, and other tools perfect their support of Unicode, which combines most common character sets into one, this step will be unnecessary. But for the time being, we must take care to display the characters we intend.

Print on all sizes of paper

Some of your learners will need to print out parts of your course. Make sure they can do so on the paper already loaded in their printers. There are two standard paper sizes you must accommodate. The US Letter size (8½ by 11 inches) is used mostly in the United States and Canada. The A4 size (210 by 297 mm) is used throughout much of the rest of the world. A4 is taller and narrower than US Letter size. If our Web pages and other materials must print out successfully, we must design them to fit on the overlap between these two sizes.

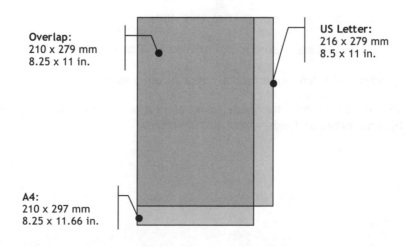

Overlap:
210 x 279 mm
8.25 x 11 in.

US Letter:
216 x 279 mm
8.5 x 11 in.

A4:
210 x 297 mm
8.25 x 11.66 in.

As the graphic shows, we must design materials to print out on a page as narrow as A4 (8.25 in., 210 mm) and as short as US Letter (11 in., 279 mm).

For documents in Adobe Acrobat (PDF) format, we can set the page size precisely. For HTML pages printed from the browser, we have less control. Browsers vary in how they lay out pages and how much margin they include. Without heroic actions, we are limited to controlling only the width of the page.

TechnoTip: We can control the width of the page with Cascading Style Sheet features supported by Version 4 browsers. Or we can simply put the entire page within a table of a fixed width and limit graphics to a width that fits within this table. For example, suppose we determine that the appropriate width is 640 pixels:

```
<body>
<table width="640">

        [The content of the page goes here.]

</table>
</body>
```

Leave room for translation

When translated to another language, text tends to expand. This is especially true when translating from a very compact language, such as English. It is also true when dealing with technical terms that may have no exact matching term and hence will require a phrase to replace a single word. Consider how this menu bar expands as it is translated from English to other European languages:

English	**File Edit View Print Help**
Spanish	**Archivo Editar Ver Imprimir Ayuda**
German	**Datei Editieren Anzeige Drucken Hilfe**
Italian	**File Modificare Visualizzare Stampare Aiuto**
French	**Fichier Édition Visualisation Impression Aide**

Leave room for text to expand if translated. Leave extra space in and around page layouts, callouts in figures, text-entry fields, names, and addresses.

WRITE IN INTERNATIONAL ENGLISH

If you write in English, write in a simple, direct style that minimizes reading problems for those who read English as a second language. This style is sometimes referred to as *international English*.

If you are writing in another language, the general requirements for simplicity and directness apply, as well, though the exact rules may vary a bit.

Advantages of international English

Writing in international English benefits several different groups of people (and automated systems). Use international English if you are concerned about how well any of the following can understand your text:

- ▶ Second-language readers abroad or in your own country

- ▶ Translators and localization experts

- ▶ People with reading difficulties, dyslexia, and limited literacy

- ▶ Impatient readers who skim, scan, and skip a lot

- ▶ People who are reading from the computer screen

- ▶ Automatic translation systems

Use words that everyone will understand

Pick words that all your learners will understand—or can find in their pocket translation dictionaries. Use and spell these words in their accustomed ways.

Can the cool slang, dude

It is easy to get caught up in the slang and informality of language used on the Web, especially on sites for sales and marketing. You may want to substitute more standard expressions for ones like these:

> For a totally tubular Internet learning experience surf on over to our gnarly site.

> ... the most bandwidth-boggling videoholic in Webdom.

> Lay a click on us. We're good to go!

Just say what you have to say in an interesting but understandable way.

Avoid faddish and I-just-made-it-up words

Much about the Web and WBT is new, and we want to convey the excitement of such innovation in our language. There is a tendency to use popular expressions without thinking whether more established ones would be easier to understand.

☹ Do not write ...	☺ When you mean ...
Impactful	Effective
Address a problem	Solve a problem
Innovising	Suggesting ideas
Interface with the team	Meet the team
Deinstall	Remove

Gender-neutralize with care

If you want to avoid using *he* as a generic pronoun, take care how you do so because some alternatives are more understandable than others. For example, if we wanted to revise this passage:

> The prospective investor should read the prospectus carefully. Then he can decide wisely.

We have several alternatives, but not all are equally effective.

☹ Do not say ...	☺ When you could say ...
... Then **he/she** can decide wisely.	... Then **the prospective investor** can decide wisely.
... Then **s/he** can decide wisely.	**You** should read the prospectus carefully. Then **you** can decide wisely.
... Then **(s)he** can decide wisely.	
... Then **they** can decide wisely.	**Prospective investors** should read the prospectus carefully. Then **they** can decide wisely.

Keep in mind that some gender-neutral forms do not fare well with automated translation systems, such as the one in the following example:

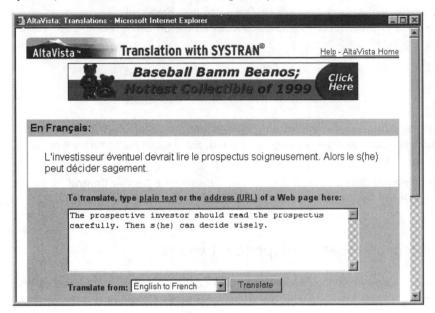

The input is at the bottom and the resulting translation is right above it. Notice how one of the alternatives from the previous list gets translated to French.

Cut down on multi-word verbs

One of the hardest tasks in learning English is learning multi-word verbs. These verbs usually combine a common verb with one or two prepositions. Native speakers use them to express many different meanings. Consider the different meanings of *get up*, *get at*, *get on to*, *get on with*, *get over*, *get in*, and *get by*. The meanings of most of these combinations must be memorized.

If a single-word alternative says the same thing, use the single word.

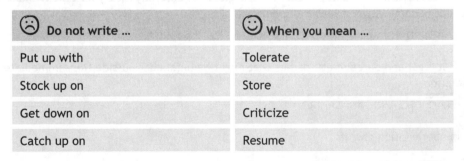

☹ Do not write …	☺ When you mean …
Put up with	Tolerate
Stock up on	Store
Get down on	Criticize
Catch up on	Resume

Mind how you use sets of words with multiple meanings

In English, many words do double or triple duty. One word may have multiple meanings or serve as multiple parts of speech. For example, consider all the different meanings of each of these words:

Set	Take	Mind
Make	Fix	State

The word *set* is so versatile that the *Oxford English Dictionary* requires 250,000 words to fully define it. Such versatile words are not easy to avoid. But we can make sure we never write something like this:

> To improve display of data on the display monitor, display the Display Control Panel and adjust the Display Frequency control until the display monitor displays correctly.

Take care with pronunciation-dependent words

Be careful with words whose meaning depends on pronunciation. They are among the easiest words to misinterpret. Pronounce each of these words in its various meanings:

Conduct	Record	Invalid
Progress	Extract	

If you use words like these, make sure the context (or pronunciation in narration) makes the meaning clear.

SOMA (Spell Out Most Abbreviations)

Use few abbreviations and define them in the glossary. Carefully read your text to make sure it has not become clogged with abbreviations.

> DXP's PII PCs come with DVD, 2X AGP, and 2 Mbps IRDA.

Spell out legal and bureaucratic names that might be unfamiliar outside their immediate jurisdiction:

> FDIC, FTC, VAT, ASPCA, IRS

Use an abbreviation only if:

▶ The term is used repeatedly.

▶ The term is over three words long.

▶ The abbreviation is better known than the full term.

Gimme hi-quality spelling

Spell words in their standard way. Use the primary spelling found in an established dictionary.

☹ Do not write ...	☺ When you mean ...
Gimme	Give me
Lite	Light
Hi or lo	High or low

Write sentences everyone can understand

Even if the words are familiar, the sentences and paragraphs may still baffle readers. For clarity, we must combine understandable words in straightforward ways.

Avoid long, intensive modifier strings

In business and technical documents, there is a tendency to stack up a long train of words all modifying the final word or other words in the train.

☹ Do not write ...	☺ When you mean ...
Primary Internet access and service provider	Primary provider of Internet access and service
Select the Start, Warm, and Stir buttons.	Select the Start button, the Warm button, and the Stir button.

As a rule, allow just one modifier before the word it modifies.

The passive should be avoided

The passive form, which uses the recipient of the action as the subject, has its place—but not when it obscures or inappropriately disguises the agent of the action.

☹ Do not write ...	☺ When you mean ...
The Enter key should be pressed.	Press the Enter key.
The room was locked by Police Officer Diaz.	Police Officer Diaz locked the room.

Use fewer of them (pronouns that is)

Pronouns are those words like *she*, *it*, and *they* that substitute for nearby nouns. They save space and add variety, but they can confuse readers if the original noun (the *antecedent* of the pronoun) is not clear.

Repeat the noun if the noun is short.

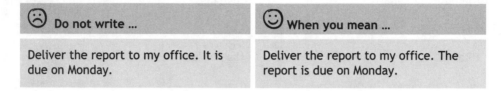

☹ Do not write ...	☺ When you mean ...
Deliver the report to my office. It is due on Monday.	Deliver the report to my office. The report is due on Monday.

Do not use pronouns to refer to distant nouns.

Keep in mind that the noun to which a pronoun refers may have scrolled off the top of the window. As a rule, use a pronoun to refer to a noun in the current or preceding sentence—within the same paragraph. Do not use a pronoun to refer to a noun in a different paragraph.

Do not use the same pronoun in one sentence with two antecedents.

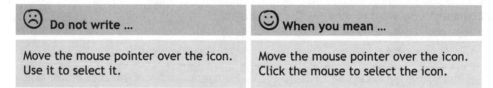

☹ Do not write ...	☺ When you mean ...
Move the mouse pointer over the icon. Use it to select it.	Move the mouse pointer over the icon. Click the mouse to select the icon.

Note: Use alerting words

Alerting words prepare us to read the words that follow. They reveal the sequence of ideas, warn us of shifts of viewpoint, and flag important announcements. They are especially helpful for second-language readers struggling to understand the structure of a passage of text. Alerting words include:

- ▶ First, second, third, …
- ▶ First, next, then, finally, last
- ▶ And, but, yet, nevertheless, however
- ▶ Note, remember, caution

Craft simple, by which I mean not complex, sentences

Do not overload readers. Give them a full stop to digest your latest thought. Let learners read one simple sentence. Then another. Then another.

☹ Do not write ...	☺ When you mean ...
After having the proposal signed by your supervisor, submit it to the steering committee where it will be considered by the individual members for two weeks before being voted on by the committee as a whole.	First, have your supervisor sign the proposal. Then, submit it to the steering committee. The members of the committee will each consider it. After two weeks, the committee will meet. At this meeting, the committee will vote on your proposal.

Avoid or cut down on the use of too many words

Do not use three words when one or two will do. Avoid wordy phrases that can be replaced with a single common word.

☹ Do not write ...	☺ When you mean ...
Provides support for	Enables
Past history	History
In some manner or other	Somehow
Visible to the naked eye	Visible

God save the Queen's English

Not everyone who speaks English speaks your variety of it. The English spoken and written in Britain differs considerably from that used in the United States. Canada, Australia, and India each add their own variety. Many of the differences are subtle but pervasive. Note the kinds of differences between American and British English.

	American English	British English
Spelling	Color	Colour
Grammar	The company is ...	The company are ...
Punctuation	We say, "Yes."	We say, "Yes".
Meaning	To table = consider later	To table = consider now

Instructors and authors must keep these differences in mind to avoid misunderstandings. Instructors must allow for such differences when grading submissions from around the world and when leading and moderating discussions. "Shall we table this question?"

Should you translate?

Should you translate your WBT and all its materials to the native languages of all your learners? Yes, of course. Learners perform best when text and narration are in their own language. But can you afford to translate into multiple languages? Or would the money and effort be more effectively spent on simplified writing and better graphics?

First, consider the need and scope for translation.

▶ What percentage of your target audience does not read your language? In other countries? In your own country?

▶ Into how many languages would you translate?

▶ How much content would you translate?

▶ How often does your content change?

Against the advantages of translation you must weigh the costs. The basic costs of translating text vary depending on the complexity of the writing and subject matter and on the target language. I have seen prices ranging from $25 to $75 USD per page per language. And I would not even guarantee that range.

To these visible costs you must add the hidden costs. Some hidden costs stem from changes made necessary by translation, for example, adjusting the layout to fit the translated text. They also include revising the text in all graphics as well as re-recording narration and redubbing all lip-sync video. Sometimes these hidden costs exceed the visible ones.

If you do translate, employ native speakers of the language who have not spent too many years away from the target country. A lot of embarrassment can result from a sloppy translation performed by a non-native speaker who does not know the idioms of the language as currently spoken in the target country.

PRACTICE INTERNATIONAL NETIQUETTE

The ways people greet and interact with one another vary from culture to culture. Learners often take their local expectations with them into cyberspace as they write e-mail messages, post to discussion groups, and participate in chat sessions and videoconferences. For collaboration involving multiple cultures, we must carefully consider the proper formality, deference, and forms of address.

> Nothing more rapidly inclines a person to go into a monastery than reading a book on etiquette. There are so many trivial ways in which it is possible to commit some social sin.
>
> — Quentin Crisp, *Manners from Heaven*

Show proper respect

The breezy informality and immediate camaraderie common among Web-savvy Americans may seem rude and childish to senior business executives from a more formal, structured society. The world is not a classless society. Instructors and learners must show the proper degree of politeness and deference, especially upon first contact with strangers.

Here's a brief etiquette lesson for first contacts with new acquaintances.

When addressing ...	Take this approach initially
Stranger	Formal politeness and slight deference until the person's status is clear
Higher level manager	Courtesy and deference
Older person	Courtesy and deference
Peer of the opposite gender	Formal politeness but not intimacy
Peer of the same gender	Informal politeness if well known with some intimacy permitted

Use the other person's name with care

Do not automatically use other people's informal names when addressing them in e-mail, chats, and discussion groups.

If you must address a person by name, refer to the person by an honorific and family name. Mr. Chen, Suzuki San, Dr. Gonzalez. Keep in mind that the family name is not always the last name.

Use people's first or informal names only when you are sure they want you to. In general, Americans, Canadians, Australians, and Swedes do not object to being called by their first names—after being introduced. For other groups, wait until you are invited to use the first name. This is especially true for countries in which the language distinguishes between formal and informal pronouns. If someone signs an e-mail message "Regards, Connie" you can probably shift from "Constance" to "Connie" in how you address her.

Never substitute a nickname until you are told to do so. One does not refer to the Prince of Wales as "Chuckie Windsor." In general, use people's informal names only if:

▶ They invite you to.

▶ They use your informal name.

▶ They sign that way.

▶ Everyone else in the discussion group, class, or working group does.

BON VOYAGE

Thanks to the Web, communications satellites, and international commerce, the world is becoming a smaller place. We hear the same music, we see the same movies, and many of us get the same news reports. Communicating across boundaries of culture is difficult but getting easier.

Maybe what we have been talking about in this chapter is nothing more than good manners, that is, "speaking" in a way that is easy for others to understand and making our audience feel welcome and appreciated.

IN CLOSING ...

Summary

- ▶ The goal of global training requires designing WBT for people with different cultures, languages, economic conditions, and expectations for learning.

- ▶ Set clear expectations for learners. State requirements for language skills, commitment, participation, and technical capabilities. Make your cultural perspective and viewpoint clear.

- ▶ Accommodate different levels of technology. Provide simple text and graphics as alternatives for larger multimedia presentations. Substitute lower-bandwidth chat for videoconferencing.

- ▶ Let learners take the course in a way consistent with their preferred learning style. Provide menus, an index, and a map to guide them.

- ▶ Use expressions, examples, and formats that work for learners of all cultures and countries. Clarify dates, times, telephone numbers, currency amounts, measurement units, and numeric quantities.

- ▶ Avoid culture-specific symbols such as those based on animals, hand gestures, religious symbols, or images of people. Draw on common imagery provided by international business, sports, transportation, medicine, and space travel.

- ▶ If you are not translating your text, write in a simple, direct style of English, free of slang, complex expressions, ambiguous words, unfamiliar abbreviations, and convoluted sentences.

- ▶ In collaborative activities, show proper respect and reserve, especially when addressing people of other cultures.

For more ...

For a concise view of cross-cultural issues in WBT see Chapter 10 of *Web-Based Instruction* [129].

For a fascinating case study of the kinds of cultural differences that you must overcome to take your WBT global, see Chapter 12 of *Distance Training* [130].

You may want to consult one of these general guides:

▶ *Developing International User Information* by Scott Jones and others [131]

▶ *Do's and Taboos Around the World* by Roger Axtel [132]

▶ *International Technical Communication* by Nancy Hoft [133]

▶ *International Dimensions of Technical Communication*, edited by Deborah Andrews [134]

For even more ideas, search the Web for **globalization**, **localization**, and **translation**.

Many of the examples shown in this book are on exhibit at:

www.horton.com/DesigningWBT/

11

Go global

12

Overcome technical hurdles

Making WBT available to more learners and more organizations

WBT has established a robust beachhead, successfully teaching technology skills within American computer and telecommunications companies. This is only logical. These companies have great training needs, the skills are ones for which WBT is well suited, and these companies have the computers and networks in place to host WBT courses.

These factors help, but one of the most important reasons why WBT sprouts and thrives in such environments is that these organizations have the ability to overcome common technical problems. The workforce in such companies is already highly skilled at using and maintaining computers. Such companies, who cannot afford to have expensive workstations and even more expensive employees idle, provide omnipresent in-house technical support. No wonder WBT caught on in such companies first.

However, if WBT is to break out of this enclave—and it is already doing so—non-technical learners without benefit of local technicians must get up and running on their own. And they must spend their time learning productively instead of tinkering with frustrating software.

TECHNICAL COMPLEXITY BARS EFFECTIVE TRAINING

Technical complexity threatens WBT from two sides. First, technical complexity frustrates, distracts, and discourages learners, who either waste valuable time in the course or else give up outright. Second, dealing with technical problems can overload instructors and other staff to such a degree that they have little time and energy to devote to the learning activities of the course. They lose enthusiasm for their jobs, and learners sense this.

Technical difficulties are common. When a Web-based course on coaching, developed for the American Management Association, was pilot tested by over 1000 learners at six Fortune 1000 companies, 40% of learners had performance problems [57]. In the same project, four of the six Information Technology departments had trouble distributing and installing the Shockwave plug-in. And the Shockwave plug-in is among the easiest to install. In a project by Mortgage Bankers Association of America, learners had problems downloading and installing plug-ins for Adobe Acrobat documents and PowerPoint slides [58].

Software rots. Your computer worked fine yesterday. You have not changed anything since then. Why is it not working now? The facetious, though painful, answer is that software rots. Programs write where they shouldn't on the disk. A speck of the disk surface flakes off. A cosmic ray from a distant pulsar reverses the magnetic polarity of a tiny patch of your disk or zaps a few bits in memory just before they are written to disk. An update for a totally unrelated program installs a new and improved version of software also used by the browser. Who knows? It happens and will afflict instructors and learners in the course. Even if we get learners over initial hurdles, the road is full of speed bumps and potholes.

Technical support is necessary. At the beginning of the 21st century, it is not realistic to assume that the majority of our learners can take courses without any special technical help. As designers make things simpler, users attempt more ambitious tasks. And designers respond by offering more complex tools to help in those tasks. It is called progress.

PLAN FOR TECHNICAL SUPPORT

The time to plan for technical support is while you are designing the course, not after the network crashes during the final exam. A plan for technical support need not be complex, but it should cover the main issues likely to arise as you introduce and conduct your course.

Consider all issues

What should your support plan include? The rest of this chapter can serve as a general checklist. But first, here are a few general issues for the list:

▶ How will learners obtain the tools and technologies they need for your course?

▶ Who will answer questions about them?

▶ Who will help learners when they have problems?

▶ How will instructors and administrators receive training on the tool or technology?

Do not proceed until you have answers to these questions.

Plan for disasters

Put on your most pessimistic, cynical, jaded attitude and list all the disasters that could befall your course. The server breaks down, the network fails, and the database crashes. The Tourette5 virus changes every fifth word in your course to an obscenity. The company decides to replace high-performance workstations with television sets running WebTV™. For each plausible disaster (and some of the implausible ones) create a plan of action:

▶ How will learners recognize the problem and know how to act?

▶ How long should they wait for the problem to be corrected by someone else?

▶ What action should learners then take on their own?

▶ How do learners continue to learn while the problem persists?

At a minimum, specify how instructors and learners should contact one another in case a server or network failure disables Web and e-mail channels. Have learners print out a copy of these instructions early in the course. Provide learners with:

▶ Instructor's phone number, postal address, and office number

▶ Contact information for checking on network and server availability

▶ Alternative non-network resources (listed in the syllabus)

Consolidate support for multiple courses

If you offer several courses built on the same technologies, have the courses share common technical-support resources, such as these:

- ▶ FAQ file

- ▶ Tutorials

- ▶ Test pages

- ▶ Setup activities

- ▶ Help desk

Assemble the specific pieces needed for a particular course from this pool of common resources.

> I know so little about the typewriter that I once bought a new one because I couldn't change the ribbon on the one I had.
>
> — Dorothy Parker

> I have yet to see any problem, however complicated, which, when you looked at it in the right way, did not become still more complicated.
>
> — Poul Anderson

LOWER THE HURDLES

Far too many potential learners never get started with WBT. They never even try. They take a look at the long list of technical requirements for taking the course and walk away, muttering, "Who do they design these courses for?"

Identify technical barriers

No course is effective unless learners can and will take it. The surest way to prevent learners from taking a course is to require more computer resources and skills than learners possess. Take a look at the following list of requirements and see what barriers you spot.

If you want to ensure that few take your course, require a rigid and impossibly high set of requirements:

▶ A more powerful computer than most learners will have.

▶ Faster network connection than many will have. Remember, some may need to take courses from home or hotel room over a modem.

▶ Many obscure, unsupported, or beta-version plug-ins that learners must download and install.

▶ Extensive changes to basic browser settings.

And do not bother providing help meeting the requirements or testing compliance.

On the other hand, if you want as many learners as possible to take your course, reduce requirements and help learners meet them.

Reduce technical requirements

Even the most humane WBT designers are subject to bouts of *gizmania*, also known as *bell-and-whistle syndrome*. This disease manifests it with symptoms of excessive (some say obsessive) use of large numbers of trendy technologies for reasons apparent only to the designer. Gizmania leads to courses that only play on advanced workstations after hours of downloading and days of installing software and then only between frequent reboots of the workstation.

The only known cure for gizmania is voluntary restraint and renewed focus on the needs and abilities of learners.

Do not require unnecessary technology

If you do not need a feature, do not use it. If you do not need certain media, omit them. If you can substitute media that play without a plug-in for ones that require a plug-in, make the substitution. Creativity and cleverness can usually find a better way to say something with less technology.

Do not use a plug-in (or any other added technology) to do something the browser does just as well without a plug-in. With JavaScript, style-sheets, and Dynamic HTML, you can create sophisticated animations, fancy typography, and rich interactions with just a Version 4 browser.

Require an up-to-date browser if this eliminates the need for a couple of plug-ins. On one project, upgrading to 4.0 level browsers eliminated the need for two plug-ins and a considerable number of slow-to-download graphics.

Do not require users to download more than they need. If certain features are used on only a few modules, say so and let users decide whether they need those features.

Select supported technologies

Buy and implement technologies that are fully supported by their vendors. Use only browsers, plug-ins, delivery systems, and other tools that:

▶ Have 24-hour-a-day, 7-day-a-week telephone support. They should also have Web-based troubleshooting.

▶ Offer complete documentation and a tutorial.

▶ Reliably auto-install themselves.

▶ Have an uninstall program or button.

Do not require lowering settings

Do not require learners to **lower** their settings to take your course. For example, if they have their display set to 1024 by 768 pixels, do not require them to back it down to 800 by

600 just to take your course. Establish minimum requirements, but make your course run on systems that exceed these requirements. Have your 800 by 600 course run in a window of that size or adjust to any size screen.

Limit the number of new technologies

Design your course so that it does not require learners to master three new ways of communicating and a half-new computer program. Consider what technologies and communications media your learners are already familiar with. Which do they use regularly for their own purposes? If necessary, conduct surveys to find out what technologies your learners can use.

Technologies impose complexity on two levels. On the surface, they require learners to operate the tools. And on a deeper level, they require someone to install and set up the underlying server software.

Here is a migration path through WBT technologies. Each phase represents another level of sophistication. I'd recommend asking learners to advance no more than one or two levels per course.

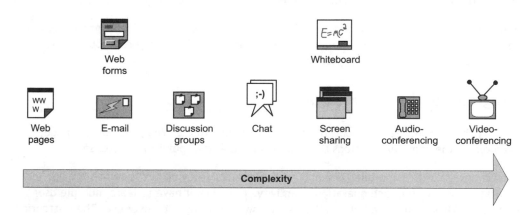

If learners are comfortable with discussion groups, you can introduce chat or even whiteboard or screen sharing. However, if your users are still trying to get e-mail working, I would not recommend asking them to install, set up, and operate an audioconferencing system.

Simplify and integrate technology

Once you have chosen the technologies to use in your course, determine how to provide these technologies so they do not overwhelm learners with unnecessary complexity. Simplify technologies. Adopt tools that package multiple capabilities behind a single, simpler user interface. Integrate tools right into Web pages. Also consider creating a custom installation program to simplify the process of acquiring and setting up the necessary tools.

Pick multipurpose tools

Reduce the number of separate tools the user must deal with. If one tool handles multiple functions, prefer it. Two kinds of multi-purpose tools are common:

▶ **Media players.** Apple's QuickTime player and Microsoft's Windows Media Player, for example, can each play several video and sound formats that otherwise might require separate players.

▶ **Collaboration tools.** Some combination tools, like Microsoft's NetMeeting, provide chat, whiteboard, screen sharing, audioconferencing, and videoconferencing in one package.

Although combination tools seldom provide the most powerful individual components, they do reduce the number of:

▶ Potentially incompatible programs running at once

▶ Separate files the learner must download and install

▶ User interfaces the learner must master

▶ Vendors who can blame each other for incompatibilities and related problems

Before you decide on a consolidated tool, honestly decide how many of its separate features you will really need. Resist gizmania. If you only need a couple of features, you may do better with a simpler, single-purpose tool or two.

Integrate tools into the page

Simplify the user interface of tools by integrating them into the Web page. On the page, expose only the knobs and buttons that learners need at that point in the course.

The advantage of this approach is simplicity for learners. They do not have to start up separate programs for each operation or activity. They do not have to learn multiple user interfaces. They do not see buttons, knobs, and switches they will never use. Their attention does not stray from the point being discussed on the Web page.

Integrating tools into pages puts needed services right on the page where they logically occur in the instructional sequence. Such integrated tools match the look and feel of the rest of the course. Because all learners use the same software, you can prepare a single set of instructions, FAQ, help, and tutorial.

And this approach puts everyone on the same level, sort of like school uniforms. Technical expertise is less of a status factor or unfair advantage.

Here are some approaches I have used on various projects to integrate tools into Web pages:

Create a form interface to discussion groups. Create a form that posts the learner's response in the correct thread of the correct discussion group. Likewise, allow learners to read discussion group messages through a form interface.

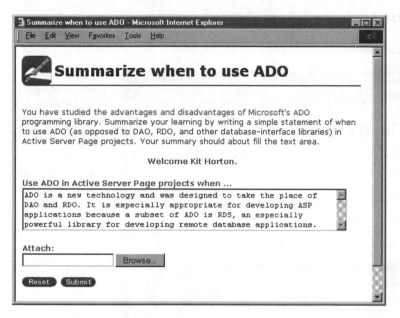

This example shows a form interface to a discussion group. To post a message to the designated thread of the discussion group, the learner fills in the form and clicks on the **Submit** button.

This example uses an Active Server Pages file-upload server component.

Embed a minimal chat control or applet on the Web page where needed. Just show the conversation, the comment the learner is composing, and buttons to send the message. You can also add controls for sending a private message to another chatter.

This example both announces an activity and lets learners carry it out without having to switch to a separate tool or window.

At the bottom of the window are areas where the learner reads posted messages and types new messages.

This example uses a Macromedia Director Shockwave object to communicate with the Macromedia MultiuserServer.

Embed a control or applet for video- and audioconferencing so that the video window appears right on the Web page. Again, reduce the number of buttons to just those necessary for the activity being performed.

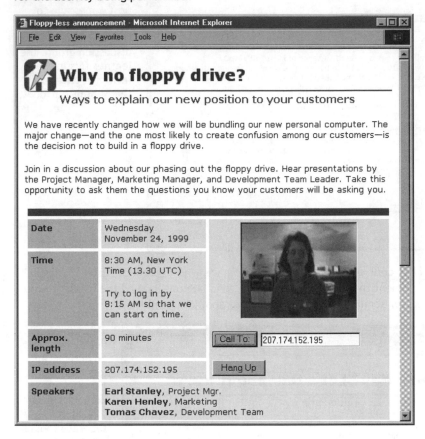

This example puts the window for an online conference onto the page that announces it. To join the conference, the learner need only click on the **Call To:** button.

This example uses the Microsoft NetMeeting ActiveX control.

Simplify the login procedure. Have the Web page identify the conference or forum the person is logging on to and the account of the learner. That way the learner just has to enter a password.

Of course, someone, the designer usually, has to build the tools into the interface. The first requirement is tools that come as configurable and embeddable components, which increasingly they do. The second requirement is a wee bit of programming. To set up the three examples above required a couple of days. To set up additional pages like these would take only a few minutes each.

Create an integrated installation program

If your course requires a late-model browser, a few specific fonts, and several plug-ins, the separate downloads and installations may prove too much for any but the most dedicated learners. In cases like this, consider creating an integrated installation program that in one operation installs everything learners need to play your course and configures the components the way your course requires. Offer the combined installation program both from a Website and on CD-ROM.

Though creating such an integrated installation program is a lot of work for you, it eliminates a lot more work, error, and frustration for potential learners. For help with creating an installation program, you may want to consult one of the vendors of installation software, such as InstallShield (www.installshield.com) or Wise Solutions (www.easyforyou.com).

Do not tempt fate

Do you climb the tallest tree around so you have a better view of the thunderstorm overhead? Do you roller-skate backwards down the middle of the freeway? Did you buy a home over a toxic waste dump because you liked the bubbling sound emanating from the backyard? If so, here are a few more thrills for you:

▶ Create Web pages that require loading files larger than your computer's memory. Actually anything over about 10% of the memory should do it.

▶ Display media that require multiple plug-ins to be running at the same time. For a real thrill, require plug-ins from rival companies.

▶ Specify beta-version plug-ins. Or even Version 1.0.

▶ Figure Java is Java. If it worked on a Sun workstation, it will probably run on Windows 95's Java Virtual Machine, right?

▶ Encourage course authors and instructors to use whatever media they individually like.

Obtain safe conduct through firewalls

Firewalls are combinations of hardware and software that protect an intranet from some of the evils of the big, bad Internet. They filter what flows into the intranet from the Internet. Firewalls can block parts of your course. A firewall may be configured to block Java applets, video clips, logins to secure servers, or proprietary file formats such as Shockwave or QuickTime.

If firewalls pose a potential problem for your courses, work with computer security staff to see if the restrictions can be relaxed, if only for specific courses.

If media cannot scale the firewall, invite them in through the front door. With approval from your security and network administrators, bring the entire course or just the banished media inside the firewall. One option is to install the course onto a server on the same side of the firewall as the learners. Another is to use a hybrid CD-ROM course that stores media on a CD-ROM and accesses them from there.

> Computer in the future may weight no more than 1.5 tons.
> — *Popular Mechanics*, 1949

Require some computer skills

WBT requires some computer skills. It is dangerously naïve to think otherwise. State the expertise requirements of your course ahead of time—and enforce them.

Make clear that the lack of computer skills is no excuse for failing to complete course work. Unless your course is about using learning technologies, you cannot afford to spend class time teaching these basic skills.

Reduce the technical requirements to a minimal level and then require that level of expertise of learners.

SOLVE PROBLEMS BEFORE THE COURSE STARTS

Use the weeks before the course officially starts to iron out technical wrinkles. Help learners meet technical requirements. Provide access to a gauntlet of automated tests and directed activities to identify problems. Make all technical support materials available. Provide access to technical support discussion groups and staff.

Let learners know that they are expected to have everything working by the first day of the class.

Help learners meet requirements

Do not leave learners on their own to meet the technical requirements of your course. Clearly enunciate the requirements and provide resources to test compliance and to meet the requirements.

This diagram shows one scheme for getting learners started. It consists of three kinds of interlocking components. A technical Requirements page, a collection of tests, and comprehensive setup instructions.

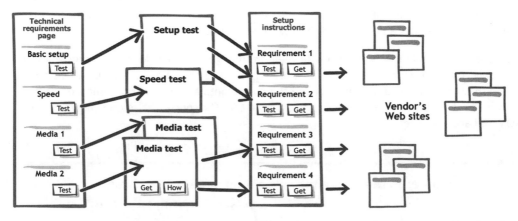

Learners start with the Technical Requirements page (p 494), which lists all the technical requirements for the course. Each requirement or group of related requirements is linked to a Test page (p 497) to let learners confirm whether their system meets the requirement. Each Test page is linked to the part of the Setup Instructions page (p 504) that tells how to obtain and install the resources necessary to meet the requirement. Both the Test page and the Setup Instructions page contain links to vendors' Web sites where learners can obtain needed resources and support.

Throughout the diagram are buttons that link the pages. These buttons let the learner get assistance in meeting a requirement:

▶ **Test**. Confirm whether the learner's system meets the requirement.

▶ **How**. Get instructions on how to download needed software, set up the browser, or make other adjustments.

▶ **Get**. Download needed software.

Why are Technical Requirements and Setup Instructions each a single page, while Tests are on separate pages? The reasons are pragmatic. To meet the requirements, learners must often install new software. Installing new software may require closing the Web browser or even restarting the computer. Learners find the process easier when working from a printout that does not disappear every few minutes. Single pages are easier for learners to print out.

Tests, on the other hand, require separate pages because mixing too many different tests on a page can make the tests unreliable and unduly complex.

Specify requirements fully

On a single Technical Requirements page, list all the hardware and software required for taking the course. Specify what problems learners will encounter if they cannot meet a specific requirement.

Give learners choices and let them know the compromises required. Identify alternative browsers and other software. Tell learners what they will miss by not meeting a particular requirement. Let them decide.

Include links to pages for testing whether the learner's system meets the requirement and links to sources of needed software.

Hardware

Tell learners what kind of computer they can use to take the course. Provide sufficient details so that learners can verify whether their current computer is adequate—or so they can buy a new computer that is.

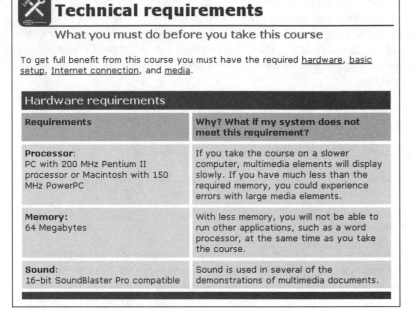

Here is an example of the section of Technical Requirements page specifying the computer hardware.

Help learners verify compliance

Although it is possible to have learners download and run a program to test compliance with these requirements, this is not done in this example. Separate programs would be required for each separate hardware system and perhaps operating system.

If learners will not know the specifics of their computers, you can link these requirements to a page that tells them how to verify such things.

List special requirements, too

In your list of hardware requirements, remember to include any special hardware that may be needed for collaboration, lab activities, or special versions of a course:

- ▶ Speakers for listening to sounds, music, and video

- ▶ Printer for printing out forms and other materials

- ▶ Microphone for recording voice or audioconferencing

- ▶ Video camera for recording video clips or videoconferencing

- ▶ Scanner for capturing paper documents and drawings

- ▶ MPEG video decoder circuitry for full-screen video

- ▶ CD-ROM or DVD drive for hybrid courses that use disk storage

Basic setup

The basic setup includes the fundamental pieces of software and their basic settings required to display the course.

Basic setup	Test basic setup
Requirements	**Why? What if my systems does not meet this requirement?**
Operating system: Windows 95, 98, or NT 4.0 or Macintosh OS/7 or later	This course will run on some UNIX systems, though some multimedia elements will not be available.
Screen size: At least 600 by 800 pixels How	With a smaller screen size you cannot see all of the course window without scrolling.
Screen colors: At least 16-bit color (thousands of colors) How	If you have 8-bit color (256 colors), you can still take the course, though some graphics will have streaks or bands of solid color. No colors will be entirely accurate.
Browser: Internet Explorer 4.0 or Netscape Navigator 4.0 How Get for PC Get for Mac	This course uses the style-sheet and Dynamic HTML features of Version 4.0 browsers.
JavaScript Version 1.1 installed and enabled How Get for PC Get for Mac	Interactive portions of this course require Version 1.1. Without it, JavaScript errors will be frequent.
Java enabled How	Although this course does not use Java applets, Java is required by some of the examples it shows.
Cookies enabled How	This course uses temporary storage elements called cookies to keep track of who you are from page to page. You **must** enable cookies.

Operating system

In theory Web technologies are independent of operating systems. In practice, we test and we pray and we specify limitations. Not all versions of all browsers run on all operating systems. Fonts and multimedia seldom display the same on all platforms. Rather than disappoint learners and balloon your tech support costs, you may want to specify exactly which operating systems your course runs on.

Display settings

The browser displays on a screen. That screen must be large enough and must display enough colors for your course to appear as you designed.

Browser version

The most important part of software for WBT is the browser. Specify the brand, level, and version of each acceptable browser. You may also need to specify which version of JavaScript the browser must support, since the JavaScript version can be updated independently of the browser.

Browser settings

You may also need to specify how learners must set up their browsers to correctly display your course. Keep this list short, as learners may hesitate or lack the technical skills to reconfigure their browsers. Here are some common requirements:

- ▶ Display graphics

- ▶ Accept cookies

- ▶ Enable Java

- ▶ Enable JavaScript

- ▶ Enable ActiveX controls

- ▶ Get a new version of the page with every access

Internet connection

To take a Web-based course, the learner must have access to the Web or at least to the portion containing the course. For corporate learners this is seldom an issue; however, for individuals, you may need to spell out the requirements, for example:

Internet connection	
Requirements	**Why? What if my system does not meet this requirement?**
Internet connection: Access to the Internet, either through your organization's intranet or through an Internet Service Provider with whom you have an account. Test	If you cannot access the Internet, you cannot take this course. If your company's firewall blocks certain media, you may not be able to view these media.
Connection speed: Connection speed of at least 56 kbps. Test	If you are patient, you can take this course with a slower connection. You will have to wait longer for large graphics and multimedia elements to download.
E-mail address: An e-mail address accessible from the Internet Test	Your password and other information are sent to your e-mail address.

Media players and resources

In order to display more than simple text and graphics, the learner may need media players, plug-ins, and other resources to extend the capabilities of the browser. You can specify the particular component the learner will need or you can specify the media the learner must play and let the learner pick the best plug-in. If your course must run on different operating systems and in different brands of browsers, you will probably need to take this last approach, since the same medium may require one plug-in for Internet Explorer on Windows 2000 and another plug-in for Netscape on a Macintosh.

12

Overcome technical hurdles

Media players and resources	
Requirements	**Why? What if my system does not meet this requirement?**
Adobe Acrobat Reader 4.0 Test Get for PC Get for Mac	Several case studies are in Acrobat (PDF) format. The case studies are required activities.
Macromedia Shockwave Director 6.0 player Test Get for PC Get for Mac	This course uses 20 Shockwave Director animations to illustrate important concepts.
Player for QuickTime 4.0 movies Test Get for PC Get for Mac	This course contains 12 QuickTime movies, about 30 seconds each. They are not essential.
Fonts: Verdana and Webdings Test Get for PC Get for Mac	Without Verdana, text will not look as pretty and some lines may break awkwardly. Without webdings, some special symbols will be missing.

Here is an example specifying the media requirements for a course.

Test compliance with requirements

Do not assume that all learners know what software is installed on their computers, how the software is set up, or what speed Internet connection they have. Someone else may have set up the computer or the learner may be taking the course on a borrowed computer. Or the learner may have forgotten reinstalling QuizWhiz 3.0 after version 4.0 crashed.

Many users may not even know what browser they are using. Large companies often customize the basic browsers provided by Microsoft and Netscape, renaming them and putting in their own logos. Some Internet service providers, such as AOL or WebTV, provide their own customized version of a Netscape or Microsoft browser.

Create a series of pages that test—or tell learners how to test—their connection, software, and skills to see if they are ready to take the course.

Automatically test fundamental requirements

Automatically detect and warn about technical requirements that learners may not meet. Set up a "sniffer" page to detect or infer their computer resources, browser setup, and communications speed.

Basic setup

Test to verify that the learner has the basic software and display settings needed to properly view the course.

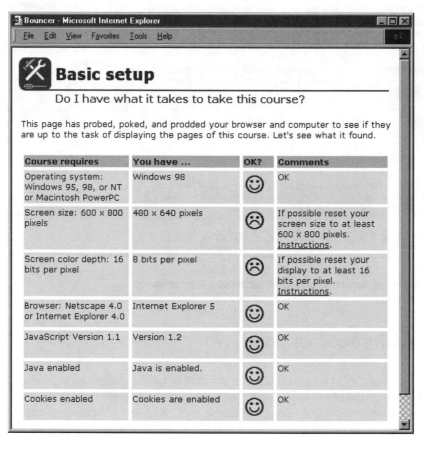

Here is an example of a sniffer page and what it found about my setup.

Guess I need to make some adjustments.

For requirements not met, the sniffer page can recommend corrective action. Where the problem requires obtaining new software, it can link to instructions on how to obtain the software.

TechnoTip: How does the example page know so much about my computer? It uses JavaScript to examine the properties of the browser's **navigator** and **screen** objects. It tests the ability to store cookies by trying to write one and then read it back.

Connection speed

If connection speed is critical, you may need to provide learners a way to test it by measuring the time from the beginning to end of the download of a large Web page.

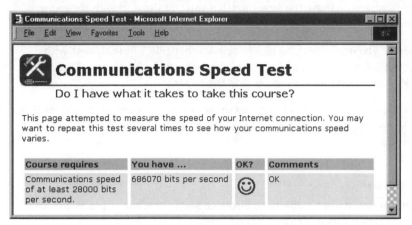

As this example shows, my local network is zipping along nicely today.

The test page is made large by including a large amount of text hidden within HTML comment tags.

Test the display of individual media

Also set up a "media petting zoo" consisting of pages that visually verify the learner's ability to display the various media of the course.

What to test

Test all the media your course uses. Do not leave any out. Include samples of the latest versions of the media that you will use in your course. Learners who can display Shockwave Flash 3.0 may not be able to display 4.0. Learners may think they have Version 4 of the player installed when they really have only 3.

Set up test pages for:

▶ **Graphics** of the file format, number of colors, and color palette used by graphics in the course.

▶ **Video**, using all the specific codecs used to create the video. The word *codec* is short for code-decode and it describes the precise method used to compress the frames of video. Even though you have the right player, it cannot play video without the right codec.

▶ **Specific fonts** required, e.g., for special text, formulas, symbols.

▶ **Character sets** (symbols for letters and numbers) for multilingual courses.

▶ **Authoring tool plug-ins.** Test a module of the maximum size and complexity that will occur in your course. Create it with the version of the authoring tool you will use for course modules. For example, if you use Authorware 5, create a module that exercises all the features you will use. Then convert it to Shockwave format exactly as you will in real life.

► **Office documents.** If you are using documents for common office suite or desktop applications, create a sample using the exact version you will use and with the same fonts and other display characteristics that the actual content will have.

► **Document images.** If you use something like Adobe Acrobat (PDF) format, test with a document formatted using the fonts and features you will use in the course. Test ability to display the document image inside and outside the browser.

► **Other media.** Do not forget any. Do you use any sound, music, animation, or video? How about that one picture in PNG format? It is easy to forget about background images and music. Test them all.

Media test pages

Media test pages confirm the learner's ability to display a single medium. Here is an example that tests the learner's ability to play sound files.

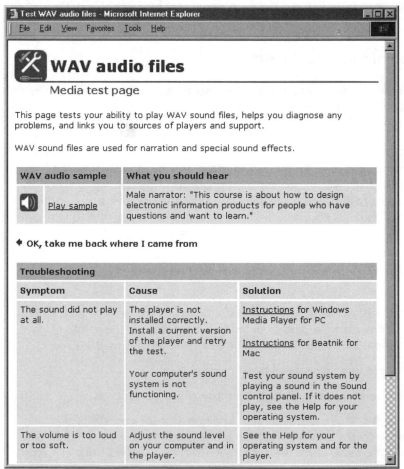

Note that the page contains both test and troubleshooting information, along with links to instructions for installing the needed player and to sources for downloading it.

Although it is tempting to put related media onto a single page rather than creating single pages, do not do so. Trying to test multiple media on one page can make the testing process slow and unreliable. The various media take longer to load and they may interact in unpredictable ways. It may appear that Sample A is working fine but Sample B is in trouble. However, the problem may just be that Sample B's plug-in is allergic to Sample A's plug-in. The allergy may be caused by a programming error in A's plug-in, not B's.

> **A browser is a piece of software that misdisplays Web pages on all computers. Java is a programming language that crashes equally well on all operating systems. A plug-in is a software suppository.**
>
> — Thorndon Killabit

Schedule early collaboration activities

Set up self-guided activities to confirm a learner's ability to use the basic collaboration mechanisms of the course. Automate these tests where possible. At least minimize the effort required by the instructor. Simplify the instructor's role to saying, "Yeah, I got your message."

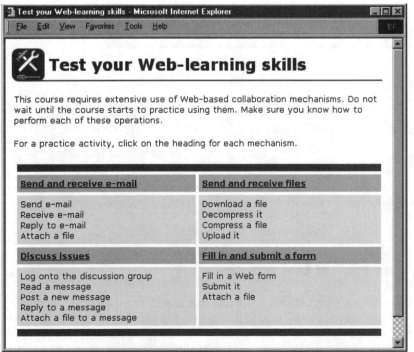

This example lists the required skills in four areas. The headings for each area are links to tests. For example, selecting **Discuss issues** takes the learner to ...

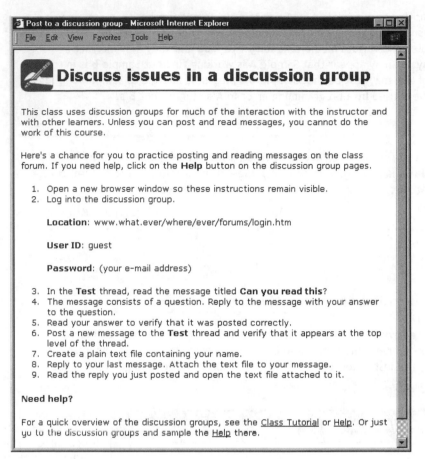

... this test activity, which requires them to read and write messages in a discussion group

> There is no reason anyone would want a computer in their home.
>
> — Ken Olson, President and founder, Digital Equipment Corporation

Create a "petting zoo" of test questions

If you are using more than the simplest text-entry and multiple-choice questions, there is a danger that some learners may not know how to manipulate the test items to properly enter their answers. To prevent this problem, create a sample test using all the different types of questions you will use. Make the questions so simple that the answers are obvious.

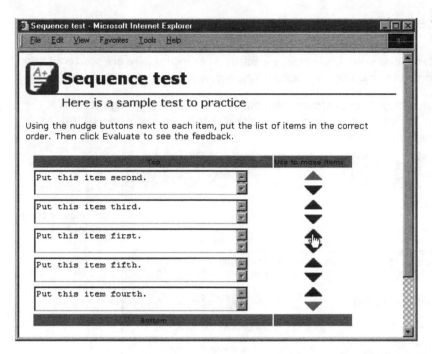

This example lets learners practice putting items in sequence by clicking on nudge buttons.

In the "petting zoo" learners concentrate on mastering the techniques of answering questions without having to think about the answers. You may want to make the test the first activity of the course and require a passing score before allowing learners to continue with the course. Do not, however, set a time limit on this pretend test.

Practice live events

Schedule test sessions for all the live-event mechanisms to be used. These include:

Chat. Have everyone log in and greet others. Have each learner practice sending a private message to the instructor and to another learner.

Whiteboard and screen sharing. Announce ahead of time exactly what the instructor will demo. Have learners acknowledge, via chat or e-mail, that they saw the demonstration. If sessions will be interactive, have each learner in turn take over control and take a specific action that the instructor can observe.

Audioconferencing. In the test, ask a simple question. Have learners confirm by answering the question by chat or e-mail—or if audioconferencing is two-way, by speaking their answers.

Videoconferencing. Show a simple object and require learners to respond with its name, using whatever feedback mechanism you will use in videoconferencing sessions.

Schedule these sessions frequently, up to once a week, and keep them simple and short— just enough activity to test ability to use the mechanism.

Provide complete setup instructions

Getting a computer set up is no simple task, especially when instructions are scattered over five Web sites, seven read-me files, and some FAQs, and nobody can remember which one.

Consolidate all setup instructions onto one Web page formatted for printing out. This is especially helpful if a procedure requires closing the Web browser, and essential if it requires restarting the computer.

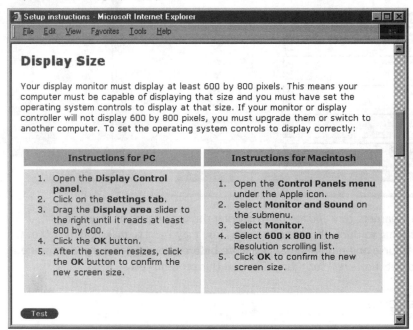

This example tells learners how to adjust the color settings of their computers.

Link to sources of software. If setting up the computer requires installing software, link to a location site from which the learner can obtain the software and instructions for installing it. If the software is freely available from the Web, tell learners how to obtain and install all the components. For each component, link learners to instructions on how to download, decompress, install, configure, test, and uninstall the component.

Tell how to obtain support. For each component, direct learners to the support provided by the vendor. Link to:

▶ Download site for getting the latest version

▶ Troubleshooting and problem-solving pages

▶ Web-based support

▶ Internet newsgroups on the product

▶ Vendor's database or knowledge base of bug fixes, workarounds, and technical tips

Also provide telephone numbers for free and pay-per-incident numbers.

If the course requires specific plug-ins, rather than general capabilities, put the contact information directly on the page that tests the plug-in (p 500), rather than in the setup instructions. That way, learners can test, troubleshoot, and get help on the plug-in from one page.

Help pick the right plug-in. If several plug-ins provide the needed capabilities, help learners pick which one to use. Include a decision table or questionnaire form that guides them in making a choice. Also provide a second choice if the first does not work.

Help learners prepare exercises and activities. For hands-on computer activities, explain how to obtain the sample data and how to set up the computer software used in the activity, for example:

> The exercises and activities of this course are based on the "typical" installation of Microsoft Office 2000. They assume that the Office 2000 settings have not been changed since installation. If you have customized Office 2000, some of the screen displays may not appear exactly as shown in this course and some of the procedures may differ slightly. If you are an experienced Office 2000 user, you should be able to adjust to these differences. If you find the differences troublesome, you can reinstall Office 2000 taking the "typical" option.

SUPPORT LEARNERS DURING THE COURSE

Once the course is underway, problems can still occur and learners still need help. Much of this help can come from the vendors whose tools you are using. But first you must help learners diagnose their problems, solve the simple ones, and contact vendors or others for support.

Designate a starting point

Give learners one place to start their search for support. This starting point can be a simple page that lists all available resources, or it can be the primary source of support itself. Here is one such design.

This drawing illustrates how learners are encouraged to start their search in the Help facility. Help not only contains useful information itself, but also has direct links to the course FAQ, tutorial, discussion group and other forms of support.

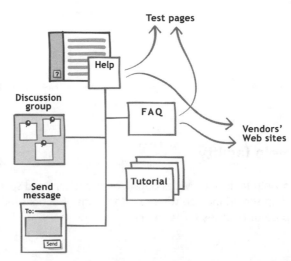

Create necessary support resources

Create and link together the resources learners need to diagnose and solve their own problems. Here are some resources learners may need:

- ▶ Help file covering all the main procedures and tools of the course (p 506)
- ▶ FAQs—Frequently Asked Questions file (p 508)
- ▶ Tutorial or instructions on the course (p 509)
- ▶ Discussion groups for technical problems
- ▶ Interactive troubleshooting guide
- ▶ Downloadable manuals for the course-delivery software, collaboration tools, and media players
- ▶ Phone number and hours for Help desk
- ▶ Web form for requesting assistance or reporting problems (p 121)

List items in the order in which you want learners to try them.

> It is characteristic of all deep human problems that they are not to be approached without some humor and some bewilderment.
>
> — Freeman Dyson

Help facility

A Help facility provides detailed instructions and specific assistance with the task at hand. Help should include topics on the kinds of actions learners must perform frequently or that pose difficulties for learners.

? Help desk

Welcome to the Help desk. Click on an item to learn more.

Getting started

- Using the correct course URL
- Logging in to the course
- Marking your place

Finding your way

- Using the buttons in the Navigation Bar
- Going sequentially through a course
- Finding a particular lesson in the course
- Contacting your classmates
- Obtaining reference resources

Searching for information

- Using the index
- Using the glossary
- Using the search facility
- Searching the Internet

Using videoconferencing software

- Obtaining the software
- Installing the software
- Testing the software
- Making a call
- Sharing an application
- Taking control of an application
- Adjusting the video
- Adjusting the audio
- Using the chat window
- Using the whiteboard
- Videoconferencing protocol

Administrative details

- Selecting a course
- Completing the Registration Form
- Paying for a course
- Attending a pre-course meeting
- Obtaining a student ID and password
- Reviewing your records and grades
- Changing address, phone, or e-mail
- Withdrawing from a course

Getting technical support

- Reading instructions
- Checking the FAQs
- Posting a question to the support forum
- Contacting technical support
- Program-specific support

All about tests

- Scoring
- Timing
- Computer or network malfunctions
- True-false tests
- Multiple choice tests
- Fill-in-the-blank tests
- Matching tests
- Click-in-picture tests
- Crossword puzzles

Using the class forum

- Obtaining a password
- Logging in to the forum
- Finding a particular thread
- Posting a message
- Attaching a file

Using an embedded chat window

- Logging in
- Chat protocol
- Broadcasting a message
- Logging off

Getting course-work support

- Contacting your instructor
- Posting a question to the class forum

This is the table of contents for a comprehensive Help facility called the **Help desk,** in this case. Use this list of topics as a model for your own Help facility.

Make help context-sensitive. Context-sensitive help displays information for the current situation of the learner. It tries to detect or infer what the learner is trying to do and respond accordingly. The Help is context-sensitive in that it describes the current page, its buttons, and entry options.

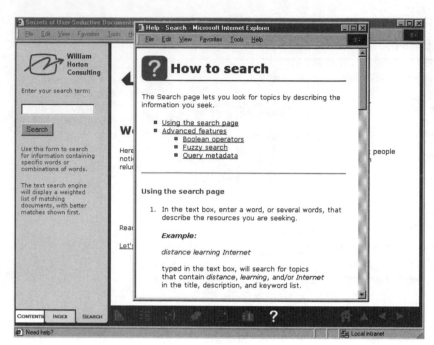

In this example, the learner pressed the Help button immediately after clicking on the Search tab. As a result, the learner receives help on conducting searches.

Frequently Asked Questions—FAQs

Frequently Asked Questions are just what their name implies: answers to questions that many learners ask. FAQs are not a comprehensive list of questions but just the high-priority ones.

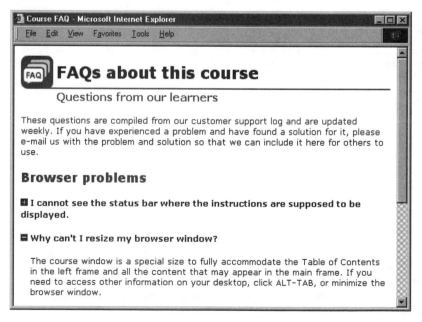

This example shows a list of questions and answers. They are arranged in a few main categories and updated weekly. Clicking on a question or the button beside it reveals the answer to the question.

Use FAQs to handle information created after the course is produced but before it is revised. Include an FAQ topic for each common question not adequately answered by the guided tour or Help, or not easily noticed. If a question is asked more than about three times, add it to the FAQ topic.

If the FAQ comprises only a few scrolling zones of information, just put it into one page. If it is longer than a few scrolling zones, make it easy for learners to scan a short list of questions and then reveal their answer:

▶ List the questions at the top of the Web page. Make each question a link to its answer later in the page. At the end of each answer, include a "Back to top" link to zip the learner back to the questions.

▶ Put a list of questions in a separate frame where they serve as a menu. Clicking on a question makes its answer appear in an adjacent frame.

▶ Make questions expand to reveal the answer when clicked on. You can do this with Dynamic HTML.

▶ Make the FAQ a thread in the course discussion group. Put the question in the Subject line and the answer in the body.

Course instructions/tutorial

It is not heresy to suggest including a short tutorial on how to take your course. Instructions are almost always required. Even the simplest course may need some instructions.

Start with simple instructions

I prefer a simple set of instructions rather than a complete course for getting learners started in a course. I find learners seldom have the patience for more than a few scrolling zones of information. Let's look at a sample set of instructions for a course.

 Course instructions

Key points
Navigating this course is quite simple. Click on underlined text or buttons to jump to another part of the course.

To see where a link takes you, point to the link with the mouse. An explanation will appear in the status bar at the bottom of the browser window.

Always begin this course by opening `start.htm` to ensure that the proper scripts are loaded and the course appears in the correct window.

For more help, select the **Help** icon.

- Screen layout
- Main navigation buttons
- Access mechanisms
- Narration buttons
- Organization
- Taking lessons
- Taking tests
- Quitting the course
- Getting help
- Technical requirements
- Limitations

The instructions begin with the most important ideas stated in a concise form so they fit in the first scrolling zone. Also at the top is a table of contents linked to the rest of the content that appears later in the file.

Screen layout

The screen is divided into three main areas:

Presentation area, where the main content of the course appears.

Main navigation buttons, which are buttons for the main components of the course.

Access area, containing the table of contents, index, and search facility.

If the course is displayed in frames, start with an overview. Point out the function of each.

Main navigation buttons

The table of contents and index share the frame at the left of the window. They also share a common set of buttons.

Jumps to a map of the course

Jumps to the glossary

Sends an e-mail message to the instructor or the Foundation of Knowledge and Competence Development

Jumps to a list of additional resources for creating electronic courses

Jumps to a schedule of upcoming chat sessions

Jumps to the log In page for the class forum

Opens a help window

Jumps to the top level of the course

Jumps up one level

Moves forward in the topic sequence

Moves back in a topic sequence

Explain the primary buttons for:

▶ Navigating through the course

▶ Bringing up auxiliary windows

▶ Jumping to navigation aids, such as a map of the course or a glossary.

Access mechanisms

You can find pages in four main ways:

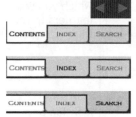

Click on the **Next** and **Previous** buttons to go through the course in sequence.

Select the **Contents** tab to reveal a hierarchical table of contents. To jump to an individual page, click on its item in the table of contents.

Select the **Index** tab to reveal an alphabetical list of subjects. Clicking on a subject displays the page about that subject.

Select the **Search** tab to enter a word or phrase and find pages that contain that word or phrase.

Highlight the main ways of finding pages, especially ways of finding them out of sequence or looking them up again later.

Narration buttons

Some topics have optional voice narration. Such topics display these buttons for controlling narration at the top of the page:

 Plays the voice narration.

 Displays the text of the narration.

Tell learners how to play media elements such as sounds, animation, and video.

Organization

The course is organized in a hierarchy of three levels as shown in the course Contents. If the table of contents is displayed, you can tell where you are by looking for the highlighted item in the table of contents. If no item is highlighted, you are at the top level of the current lesson.

Preview the organization of the course and help learners imagine the structure they must navigate.

Taking lessons

We suggest taking the lessons in the order they are presented in the table of contents. You may select each page in sequence from the table of contents, or you can repeatedly click the Next button in the navigation bar.

To look up information on a specific subject, select the index and find the subject alphabetically.

Suggest a way of proceeding through the content of the course, even if only as a default.

Taking tests

Tests contain their own instructions and are relatively simple. Just answer the test questions and select the **Evaluate** button. Some tests include a **Hint** button to reveal clues to the correct answer.

Relieve any anxiety learners may have about taking tests by explaining how tests work.

Quitting the course

To leave the course, make a note of where you left off and then close the window. There is no automatic bookmarking facility with this course.

Tell learners of any actions they have to perform, such as logging out, to leave the course.

Getting help

Specific help on a topic is available by clicking on the Help button in the navigation bar. This help explains how to manipulate and navigate that particular kind of topic. For instance, it explains how to log on to the forum or take a particuar type of test. The help does not cover the content of the topic.

You can also click Support in the main table of contents. From there you can access the Help desk as well as the FAQ.

Also, there is a support thread in the class forum. Check there frequently to see if others have had the same problem.

Tell learners how to get more help. Mention sources of help in the order in which you want learners to try them.

Limitations

The limitations of Web browsers limit how you can navigate the course.

- **The Back command works on frames.** Sometimes you will need to click Back twice to get back where you came from.
- **Bookmarks do not work reliably** with a multi-frame document like this.

Mention any unexpected constraints the course imposes.

Suggest a strategy for taking the course

Point out different ways learners can take the course and recommend one as a default. At least suggest a strategy for taking the course. For example:

> If you have been with ERLCo for more than three years, you can skip or skim the first three lessons and dive into Lesson 4. If you are new to ERLCo, go through the first three lessons to make sure you understand the markets we serve.

> The lessons on grammar and pronunciation are important—but pretty boring. We suggest you take the first few topics of each to get the basics under control. Then, as you proceed through the other lessons, periodically return to the lessons on grammar and pronunciation as you feel a need to know more.

Link to a course on taking courses

If the course is complex or if many learners are new to your kind of course, link to a short, simple course on taking courses. Some tools vendors include courses on how to take courses created with their tools.

Publish a student handbook

Consider consolidating all necessary details about the course into one document. ZDU, a purveyor of Web-based courses about information technology, collects all the separate pages of instructions, policies, and procedures into a single document that learners can view online or print out. ZDU call this the *ZDU Handbook* [135]. This 50-page document contains an overview of ZDU, policies on membership and billing, technical requirements for taking courses, instructions for taking courses, lists of course materials, information on obtaining certificates of completion, and the legal terms and conditions of enrollment.

Learn from problems

As problems occur, solve them and make sure that they do not occur again. Here's one strategy. It shows a plan for moving support knowledge from where it was painfully discovered to where it can be productively applied.

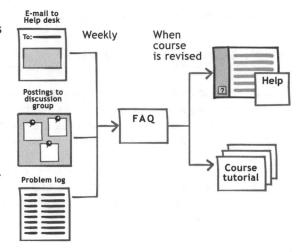

Once a week, the keeper of the FAQ file scans reports of problems and solutions. If problems seem common or critical, a question and answer is added to the FAQ file.

When the course is revised, the knowledge that has accumulated in the FAQ is added to the Help facility and course tutorial.

TEST YOUR COURSE

Test your course as learners may experience it. Install it on a computer that barely meets the minimal requirements and test the most common operations. Better still, have learners test for you.

Test on a minimal system

Test your course on a system that just meets the minimum requirements stated for your course. Be sure to test with:

▶ Earliest version of the operating system, installed with the default or minimum set of features

▶ Minimal required amount of memory (RAM)

▶ Earliest specified version of the browser

▶ Slowest speed connection allowed

Set aside an old computer that barely meets your minimum requirements. Reformat its disk and install the operating system and browser from scratch. This ensures that you do not have any extra fonts, plug-ins, or updates that would not be on the minimum required system.

Then test your complete system, installing each required additional component exactly as stated in your instructions. Better still, have a prospective learner do the test.

TechnoTip: For speed tests, always turn off caching and empty the disk and memory cache.

Test on all supported browsers

Test your course on all the versions of all the browsers you plan to support, not just the earliest versions you support. Sometimes something works in Version 3.1 of a browser and then in 4.0 it does not work. That neat feature you depended on in an early version may be declared a bug or security risk and programmed away in the very next version.

If you do not have time to test every version of browser, at least test "at the corners." Let's say your course is designed to run on versions 3 through 4 of Netscape and Microsoft browsers. You would then test on Netscape and Internet Explorer Version 3.0 and again on Version 4.0 of those browsers.

Test the most common operations

Test the features that matter most to the success of your course. Test everything that could cause your course to fail.

Technical problems	Content problems	Human factors problems
► Missing link destinations	► Inaccuracy of factual statements	► Legibility on older monitors
► Misaimed link triggers	► Incorrect names of people, places, and organizations	► Color-blindness, especially red-green distinctions
► Missing images		
► Misdisplayed images	► Out-of-date information	► Link destinations that surprised learners
► Orphaned pages (no links to them)	► Differences between the terminology of users and that of the document	► Places where learners got lost
► Missing or incorrect <title> tags		► Expressions of anger, frustration, or confusion
► Long download times	► Spelling errors	► Flailing—just trying one link after another
► Pages that print out incorrectly		

TechnoTip: Examine the server's error log after testing. There you can spot which files the server could not find along with other surprising problems you may not otherwise notice.

Focus your testing

Few of us have time and budget enough to test every aspect of a course thoroughly. We can take heart in the thought that not everything must be perfect. Focus your testing and redesign on the parts of your course that are:

▶ Critical for success of the course

▶ Taken by more people

▶ Taken by unmotivated users

IDENTIFY SOURCES OF SUPPORT

For each component in your entire learning system, identify a source of support. Who can answer questions about it? Who can help solve problems caused by the component? In most projects, support comes from a mixture of four sources: training staff, Information Technology department, tool vendors, and learners themselves.

Training staff

Training professionals are caring, sympathetic, and technically knowledgeable. They would seem to be the ideal candidates to provide technical support. Learners know how to contact their instructors and administrators. And training organizations want to offer complete training solutions.

Unfortunately, many training organizations underestimate how much support learners will require and are then swamped with requests. It is not unusual for instructors to spend the majority of their time handling technical problems rather than doing anything that advances learning.

The training staff may want to serve as the initial contact for learners with technical problems but quickly refer them to other resources that can more effectively solve the problem. You may want to set up a Help desk which learners can access by chat, discussion group, or telephone. Have the Help desk identify problems and direct learners to other resources that provide solutions.

Information Technology department

Most large companies and universities have a department in charge of ordering, installing, setting up, and maintaining computers and networks. Such departments are often called *Information Technology* (IT), *Information Systems* (IS), or *Management Information Systems* (MIS).

IT may provide general support. The IT department may be limited in how much direct support it can provide your learners and instructors. The IT department may contain experts in operating systems and desktop applications used by everyone in the company, but probably lacks expertise in various training tools. IT experts cannot explain why a Java applet created from a Macromedia Director movie plays OK on Macs but not on PCs. They can, however, provide support on the basic operating systems, networking software, and standard applications on which your course may rely.

Work with your IT department. Recognize that your mission and that of the IT department may clash. Their mission is to keep computers and networks working efficiently. Yours is to train. When **your** training courses clog **their** servers with gigabytes of multimedia and your videoconferencing systems slow **their** network so people start buying postage stamps again, you will not have to wait long for the IT manager to come knocking on your door.

Work with your IT department **before** you develop your training. Understand the limitations of computer and network resources and how to avoid points of vulnerability. Agree on what software and media you will use and the amounts of file storage you will require.

Tool vendors

Referring problems to the vendors of tools has some dangers, but it helps both the learner and the vendor in the long run.

Tool vendors are experts in their own tools, and many provide free Web-based support. A few even provide free telephone support. However, not all tool vendors are prepared to interact with individual users. Many prefer to deal with system administrators who analyze and summarize problems.

Reporting problems to tool vendors is something of a civic duty. Unless users of tools report problems, vendors may not even know of the problems. Unless lots of people report a problem, vendors may have slight incentive to fix it.

Since vendors are continually refining their support tools, remodeling their Web sites, and upgrading their products, only they can provide detailed instructions on locating, downloading, installing, and setting up their products. Although sending a learner to the vendor's site might feel like asking a child to cross a busy street alone, it really is the only practical solution unless you have a large staff to monitor vendors for changes and immediately rewrite your instructions.

Learners themselves

Ultimately, learners must help themselves if they are to become effective at taking WBT. Having learners solve their own problems fosters patterns of self-reliance that are valuable throughout the course and future courses.

However, some learners may resent the amount of time given over to solving problems. Set clear expectations. It is not unusual for learners to spend 10% of their time dealing with technical issues during their first few WBT courses.

Set expectations early. From the beginning, let learners know that they will encounter technical problems, that others will help them overcome these problems, but that they are primarily responsible for helping themselves.

Distribute the computer wizards. Spread the more computer-competent learners among teams. That way, each team has a resident expert, and the experts do not fight for the mouse [35].

Encourage peer counseling. Help learners to help each other. Informal peer counseling programs have proved effective in teaching basic computer skills [136]. Computer users learn basic skills more effectively working together than alone [137]. This is especially true for learners anxious about their computer skills. So establish a peer-support discussion group and award bonus points for contributions made to it.

IN CLOSING ...

Summary

The technical complexity of getting and keeping WBT systems running prevents many learners from taking WBT. To help learners over technical hurdles:

▶ **Limit the amount and sophistication of technology required** for your course. Design your course to run on the computers learners already have. Minimize the number of plug-ins, add-ons, and other special software that learners must download and install. Suggest alternatives. Flag optional items.

▶ **Provide clear instructions**. Tell learners how to download, install, and configure the browser, add-ons, and any other software.

▶ **Require learners to use the system early**. Require them to submit assignments, enter into a discussion, participate in chat, and use other features of the system during the first week. Design these first activities so learners can concentrate on the mechanics of the process.

▶ **Plan for technical support**, especially the kinds of disasters that can disrupt your course.

▶ **Set up a "testing gauntlet" and "media petting zoo"** where learners can verify their ability to take the course—before they start the course. Likewise, schedule practice sessions with chat, videoconferencing, and other real-time collaboration tools.

▶ **Provide complete computer set-up instructions** with links to vendors' Web sites so learners can obtain needed software and technical support.

▶ **Support learners** with such tools as an FAQ file, Help facility, course tutorial, problem-reporting mechanism, and support discussion group.

▶ **Allocate support duties** among the training staff, IT department, tool vendors, and learners themselves.

For more ...

The Help Desk Institute (www.helpdeskinst.com) sponsors conferences and conducts seminars on the subject of providing technical support to computer users.

If you can stand a shameless self-promotional plug, I'd suggest that you can learn a bit about creating a Help facility by reading *Designing and Writing Online Documentation [2]*.

For even more ideas, search the Web for **Help desk**, **Help facility, setup,** or **installation**. Most of the results will not be useful, but if you scan them, you will find a few relevant examples.

Many of the examples shown in this book are on exhibit at:

www.horton.com/DesigningWBT/

13

Venture beyond courses

WBT for the other million ways we learn

We learn not from courses alone—and certainly not from conventional courses alone. In this chapter, we consider some alternatives and adjuncts to conventional courses. Some of these can be used in place of conventional courses. Others can replace a lesson or two. Still others can be added to conventional courses to augment or extend them. A few aim not to teach knowledge but to eliminate the need for it. They all belong in the WBT designer's toolkit.

Here's a quick preview of the various alternatives and adjuncts to courses:

Construct	Descriptions	Page
Libraries	Organized collections of electronic documents and other reference resources.	520
Museums	Organized collections of interesting objects, each extensively annotated.	525
Glossaries	Dictionaries of the terms and abbreviations used by a specialized group.	533
Job aids	Tools to provide reminders, calculate numbers, guide decisions, and generally make work easier.	536
Mentors	More experienced professionals who provide guidance through e-mail and other Web collaborative media. Telementoring.	542
Conferences	Professionals getting together in cyberspace to view presentations, discuss issues, view new products, and make friends.	548
Guided tours	Self-guided demonstrations of interactive computer systems and Web sites.	554
Field trips	Tours through real or imaginary sites with relevant commentary on each site.	559
Simulations	Interactive environments that mimic real systems or devices.	567

Note: In this chapter I refer to these constructs by their simple names. I have omitted the overused preceding word *virtual* or *online,* as well as the prefixes *tele-* and *e-,* when talking about them. Feel free to pencil in these missing lead-ins. Use ink, if you own the book.

LIBRARIES

The basic idea of libraries has not changed much since ancient Alexandria. It has not needed to. Libraries make knowledge accessible by collecting the best and most needed works, labeling them, organizing them, cataloging them, and enabling people to find them on their own. Web-based libraries extend that idea by making many more types of knowledge resources—not just books—available to learners. And Web-based libraries keep longer hours.

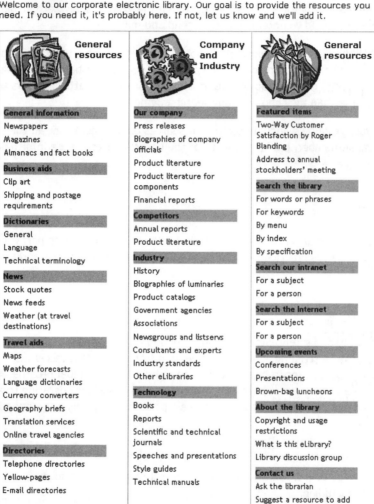

This example shows the home page for a corporate library. Notice the wide variety of resources and access methods provided.

To find more examples of libraries, search the Web for **virtual library** or **online library**.

When to create a library

In a sense, the whole Web is like a library ... after an earthquake. The Web contains the equivalent of trillions of pages of information, but finding the one you want requires a lot of rooting around in disorganized piles.

Before you start creating a library for a subject area, search the Web to see whether one already exists. Perhaps you could volunteer to help extend and maintain it.

If you determine that a library does not exist, think about what your library will offer that fifty public search engines do not already offer. The one thing you can probably offer is an application of your knowledge of a field so that users of your library get better answers to their questions in less time than they can with any search engine.

Verify the quality of your resources. Include the best resources on a subject, not all the resources on a subject. Remember, one of the goals of the librarian is to reduce information overload.

Tips for better libraries

Design your library not as a monumental shrine to dusty books, but as an inviting portal to self-education. Make the library practical, helpful, and fun. Tailor it to the needs and tastes of its users.

Grow the library gradually

Grow your library smoothly and surely. Start with an extended Course Resource page (p 113). As it grows to several scrolling zones, put a menu in front of it. As it increases beyond a few hundred resources, incorporate a database to hold the individual records. As you begin offering more and more kinds of resources and services, consider migrating to a true knowledge-management system. Start simple and adopt technology only as you need it.

Include a wide range of media

Do not limit yourself to Web pages. Make your library a portal to whatever resources learners need. Consider including:

- ▶ **Electronic books and other documents**. These may be in HTML, plain text, or Adobe Acrobat PDF formats.

- ▶ **Word-processor files**. If your organization has a standardized file format, use that one. If you use multiple wordprocessors, consider an exchange format such as RTF.

- ▶ **Photographs**. Let people see as well as read about a subject. Make available photographs that people will want to view or use in their own works.

- ▶ **Multimedia**. Make available video clips of presentations, audio recordings of speeches, and virtual reality models of proposed buildings and other environments.

- ▶ **Job aids.** Include calculators, converters, and other useful utility programs. Also consider posting quick-reference summaries and checklists. See Job aids (p 536) for some ideas.

- ▶ **Electronic communities.** Link to newsgroups (p 349) on the Internet and your intranet.

- ▶ **Pre-Web Internet resources.** Some very useful resources were put on the Internet before the evolution of the Web. Government agencies and universities still maintain WAIS and Gopher archives, FTP download sites, and Telnet ports. Include a Web interface to any of these that are needed by your audience.

Link to other repositories

Your library cannot contain everything everybody needs. Cover the specific needs of your field and your users. Then refer library patrons to other sources. Link to other Internet libraries, especially those specializing in areas of interest to your library patrons. Also, link to your various corporate libraries.

If you are setting up an extensive library and will be exchanging information and resources with other libraries, get to know the emerging standards for electronic descriptions of educational and bibliographic resources. The two main ones are:

- ▶ ANSI/NISO Z39.50 and ISO-23950 for interchange of bibliographic information (lcweb.loc.gov/z3950/agency/)

- ▶ IMS metadata standards for learning resources (www.imsproject.org/metadata/)

Publish a usage policy

Make clear what users of your library can do with resources they find there. Specify what rights users have to read, share, copy, reuse, and modify the materials available through the library. Some items may be ones you own, while others are ones you have rights to display only. Still others may be resources you do not possess but provide links to.

One practical solution is to include a blanket rule that is quite restrictive and to flag items, such as clip art, for which learners have additional rights.

Provide several modes of access

Make it possible for everybody to find just what they need, regardless of their knowledge of sophisticated search engines and access techniques. Provide simple mechanisms to let users find information by these methods:

- ▶ **Full text.** Search for words and phrases within the title or body of the item sought.

- ▶ **Keyword.** Search by words that describe the content sought but that may not actually occur within the item sought.

- ▶ **Index.** Pick from an alphabetical list of subjects linked to works on that subject.

▶ **Menu**. Select through a hierarchical list of categories, sub-categories, and sub-sub-categories.

▶ **Specification**. Find items with certain combinations of characteristics, such as cost, medium, and file format.

Scoop rather than type

The effort required to create and maintain a catalog of Web-based resources is daunting to the budgetarily limited. One way to hold down costs is to automate the process of entering and updating descriptions of Web-based resources. On one project, we developed a process called *scooping* to periodically visit a site known to hold descriptions of learning resources, retrieve these descriptions, parse them to extract relevant information, and enter the information into our database. It took a couple of months of programming work but eliminated the need for a staff of several librarians to do the same work.

Unite your library and museum

Build and manage a library and a museum (p 525) as one operation. They are separate institutions in the physical world only because they warehouse different kinds of objects: paintings and sculpture in art museums, books in libraries. On the Web, all objects are just bits.

The missions of libraries and museums are complementary. Museums contain unique original two- and three-dimensional objects and provide tiny plaques of commentary on them. Libraries provide extensive commentary on everything imaginable but only low-fidelity reproductions of objects of interest.

You may still want to maintain separate user interfaces for the library and museum—at least until patrons seem ready to accept a merger. Behind the interface, the two institutions can share a common Web server, database, and access mechanisms.

Using libraries in WBT courses

Libraries have been an important part of education since the Great Library at Alexandria. Educational institutions run some of the world's largest and best libraries. Sending students off to the library for a bit of research is a tradition in education—one that WBT designers can well capitalize on to integrate libraries into WBT courses. Here are some ways you can get started using libraries in your courses:

▶ Create a guided tour (p 554) of the library to show learners around. Focus on items related to your course.

▶ Conduct scavenger hunts (p 204) to familiarize learners with the organization and search mechanisms of the library.

▶ Assign guided research activities (p 207) that get learners in the habit of using library resources.

▶ Use library-based materials throughout the course.

MUSEUMS

A museum is an organized collection of exhibits gathered in one place. Exhibits consist of informative objects, such as paintings by van Gogh and sculpture by Rodin, annotated with relevant facts. A Web-based museum is much the same, except that the place where objects are gathered is not a building made of granite and marble but a linked set of Web pages.

Virtual museums have been used to showcase objects as diverse as human organs, paintings by a second-grade class, and airsickness bags. In this section, we will explore the kinds of virtual museums that a corporation or training group might set up.

Web-based museums are also called *virtual museums*, *e-museums*, *virtual galleries*, *online museums*, and *online galleries*.

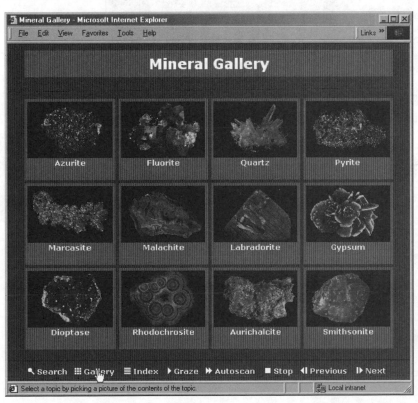

This example shows a small museum of minerals. It contains pictures of minerals and information about them.

Here in the virtual gallery, visitors see small images of the minerals and their names. A visitor can pick a mineral by appearance or by name to jump to the exhibit of that mineral.

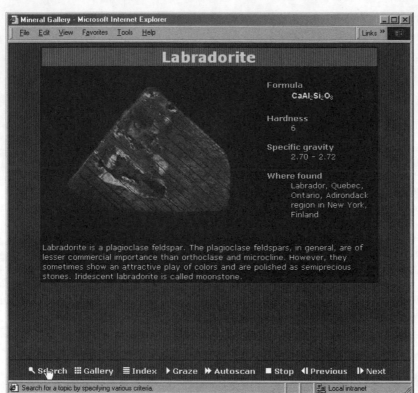

The individual exhibit shows a single mineral. It also provides technical details about the mineral along with a brief description of it.

The **Next** and **Previous** buttons take the visitor forward and backward through all the minerals in the museum. The **Graze** button starts advancing through the exhibits at a rate of about six seconds per exhibit. **Autoscan** does the same at a rate of one per second. The **Stop** button stops the browser on the current exhibit. Graze and Autoscan are useful if the visitor can recognize a mineral, but does not know what it is called.

> In large calm halls, a stately museum shall teach you the infinite lessons of minerals,
> In another, woods, plants, vegetation shall be illustrated - in another animals, animal life and development.
>
> — Walt Whitman, *Leaves of Grass*

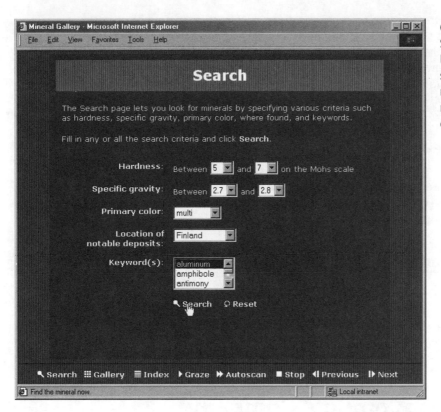

Clicking on the **Search** button lets the visitor search for minerals that meet specified characteristics.

To find more examples of Web-based museums, search the Web for **virtual museum** or **online museum**.

When to create a museum

Museums organize large numbers of separate objects into meaningful collections. Museums are useful to:

▶ Make available the artifacts of a field of endeavor—or of an organization engaged in that endeavor.

▶ Provide access to concrete instances of objects from a field being studied.

▶ Enable learners to discover patterns and trends among separate objects and instances.

Every day, busy companies with crowded offices and cramped disk drives archive their history with the trashcan and the Delete key. Years later, their leaders wonder why employees have no sense of the tradition or heritage of the great company they work for.

A museum is a great way to preserve and organize the artifacts of an organization's formative years and epic struggles. I am not suggesting you exhibit a virtual reality walkaround of the polyester leisure suit worn in 1978 by the current president of the company or digitally enhanced photographs of the scandalous behavior at last year's Christmas party. No, the best use of the virtual history museum will be to display how the organization got where it is today and why certain traditions exist.

Exhibit your treasures

With virtual museums, space limitations do not exist. The only limit to size is how well you can organize the collection. Organize well and you can include a wide variety of materials to educate and delight visitors to your museum.

Include a variety of exhibits

What do you have that people need or want to see? Probably more than you realize. Here is an example of the Home page of a company history museum. Notice the wide variety of resources and access methods provided. Notice also how it resembles the home page for the corporate Library (p 521).

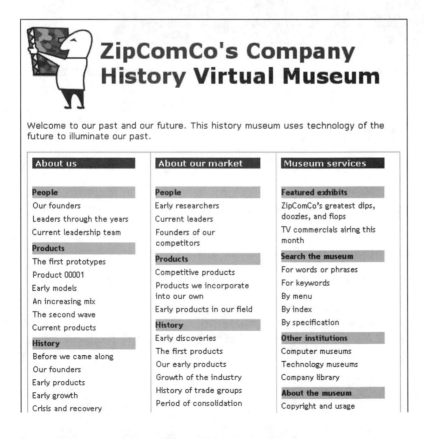

ZipComCo's Company History Virtual Museum

Welcome to our past and our future. This history museum uses technology of the future to illuminate our past.

About us	About our market	Museum services
People	**People**	**Featured exhibits**
Our founders	Early researchers	ZipComCo's greatest dips, doozies, and flops
Leaders through the years	Current leaders	TV commercials airing this month
Current leadership team	Founders of our competitors	
Products		**Search the museum**
The first prototypes	**Products**	For words or phrases
Product 00001	Competitive products	For keywords
Early models	Products we incorporate into our own	By menu
An increasing mix	Early products in our field	By index
The second wave		By specification
Current products	**History**	**Other institutions**
History	Early discoveries	Computer museums
Before we came along	The first products	Technology museums
Our founders	Our early products	Company library
Early products	Growth of the industry	**About the museum**
Early growth	History of trade groups	Copyright and usage
Crisis and recovery	Period of consolidation	

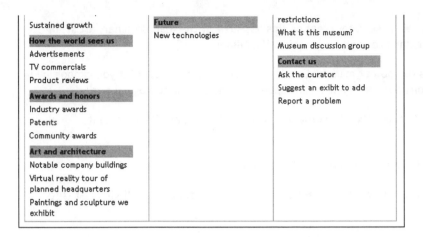

Invite submissions. You never know what individuals have squirreled away and would be willing to donate to your museum—especially since they can donate and keep the object, too.

Include a variety of media

Most museums consist simply of photographs and text. But consider enriching your museum with other media as well. Here are some candidates:

▶ **Scanned documents**: Print advertisements, covers of annual reports, articles of incorporation, the first stock certificate, and critical patents.

▶ **Video clips** of important events: Speeches, technical presentations, product demonstrations, experiments, product tests, award presentations, TV commercials.

▶ **Audio recordings**: Speeches, presentations, jingles from commercials.

▶ **Virtual reality**: Models of prominent or proposed buildings, walkarounds of important objects, conceptual models of a field of research.

Annotate exhibits thoroughly

Label items you exhibit. Provide concise but thorough details for each item on exhibit. Here is a checklist of the kinds of details people may want to know. No individual item will need all these details, but this checklist will make sure you consider all possibilities.

▶ **Name.** Include both official and unofficial names. Include the formal, legal, scientific name of an object along with its informal common name.

▶ **Description.** What is the object? What does it exemplify? Why is the object on exhibit here? What is important about it?

▶ **ID Number.** What is the product number, model number, or serial number of the item?

▶ **Dimensions.** What are the object's height, width, depth, weight, area, and volume?

▶ **Creator**. Who is responsible for creating this object? List the lead designer, artist, or project manager. Link to their biographies, if available.

▶ **Date**. When was the object manufactured, completed, or discovered? If you cannot give a specific date, consider specifying a time span, historic era, or geological period.

▶ **Medium**. Of what materials is the object constructed? What are its important components?

▶ **Owner**. Who owns the actual object? Who holds copyright on its design?

▶ **History**. How and when was the object conceived, created, and modified? What is its provenance?

▶ **Classification**. Does the object fit into a defined taxonomic scheme? Does it fit a standard industry category? Does it illustrate an artistic or design movement?

▶ **Rating**. How does this object compare to comparable objects as rated by the curator of the museum, by an industrial rating agency, or by museum patrons?

▶ **Sales**. If the object is a product, how many were sold and for how much money?

▶ **Price**. If the object is for sale, what is its price?

▶ **Keywords**. How is the object indexed? Link each keyword to other objects indexed with the same keyword.

▶ **Links to details**. Link the annotation of the object to more complete materials about it.

Put visitors in control

Let museum visitors choose the exhibits they want to see. Guide them through the collection, but let them decide which exhibits to view and which objects to study in detail.

Give private tours

A virtual museum has no fixed floor plan, no permanent arrangement of exhibits, no limitations on available space. The use of search engines and databases makes it possible for visitors to the museum to have an experience custom-tailored to their individual needs. Here are some ways to custom tailor the display:

▶ Display just the subset of interest to the individual visitor.

▶ Arrange the exhibits to reveal trends and patterns of interest to the visitor.

▶ Generate custom maps and menus that reveal what the visitor is interested in learning.

Let visitors make their own tours

Let learners search the museum for exactly what they want to see right now. Do not force them to plod through the whole Louvre if all they want to see is the Mona Lisa. Here are some ways to make it easier for visitors to find the exhibits they want to see:

Index the whole museum. Provide a conventional alphabetical index listing each object in the museum by its name and by what it illustrates.

Menus. Provide several menus that let learners search by whatever characteristics are important to them. For example, a corporate history museum might contain menus organized by time period, by current product line, by underlying technology or market, and by person in charge.

Visual gallery. Let visitors pick objects by scanning thumbnail images of all objects on exhibit. Also let them graze the display by having it automatically advance from item to item at a rate of about one per second until the visitor says, "Stop, that's the one I want."

Linked keywords. Assign keywords to each exhibited item to describe it. Let visitors search for items indexed with a particular keyword. Also display the keywords on each exhibit. Make them links so that clicking on one displays a list of other items indexed with that same keyword.

Search by characteristics. Include a search engine that lets learners search by specifying detailed characteristics of the object sought.

If many paths through the museum are possible, suggest a simple one. Or provide a tour (p 554) conducted by a docent.

Let visitors choose what to download

Museums can contain a lot of large graphics and multimedia. This is appropriate to their mission. What is not appropriate is to fail to warn visitors before starting a lengthy download. Here are some common-sense courtesies to practice:

▶ **Preview the object**. Describe the object in words or display a small thumbnail image. Then let the learner decide to download it.

▶ **Specify the size** of the download.

▶ **Consider providing both high- and low-bandwidth versions**. For example, for a photograph, you might provide a large JPEG image optimized for quality along with a smaller version optimized for maximum compression.

Let learners inspect an exhibit in detail

Let learners enlarge photographs to inspect items of interest. Make the image of an exhibit into an image-map with each object in it linked to an enlargement of it. Or overlay the illustration with a grid of rectangular areas, each triggering display of an enlargement of that area.

Tips for better museums

Museums are lofty institutions but their success often depends on a few mundane details. Here are a few suggestions of the mundane ilk to guide you along:

Position your effort wisely

Before you create a new museum for a subject, search to see whether there is already one available on the Internet or your company intranet. One consolidated effort will certainly outperform three under-funded, part-time efforts.

Merge the virtual museum with the virtual library (p 524). Both perform analogous functions and can use the same underlying database and search engine.

Communicate the theme of the museum

Make clear the specialty and scope of the museum. What organization, field, or subject does it cover? In words and graphics make clear what it includes and what it does not. Set the expectations of visitors before they are disappointed.

Invest in technology

Tracking dozens of characteristics of each of hundreds of exhibits is an invitation for error, frustration, and wasted effort. Consider using a database as the core of your museum if it contains more than a couple of hundred exhibits and you store more than a few characteristics of each exhibit.

Forego the 3D metaphor

Good news. It is no longer mandatory for museums to contain rendered 3D images of dimly lit marble corridors where museum visitors must click again and again to advance past trapezoidal views of photographs of paintings or photographs on the simulated walls. We can now replace this slow and tired cliché with newer faster clichés. Or just well-organized menus and perhaps an index or search engine.

Using museums in WBT courses

Think about your last visit to an art museum. Close your eyes and imagine yourself walking through one of the galleries. What do you see? Fine art, for sure, but what about the people you see? Do you see a shushing teacher herding a gaggle of giggling third-graders? Do art students from the local university languidly sketch the exhibits between trips to the espresso bar? Do parents with children in tow sidestep around the perimeter of the room, dutifully reading the plaques of every painting? Museums are places where many different kinds of people can learn many different things in many different ways.

Wandering a virtual museum on your own may be a pleasant way to while away an afternoon, but it is not automatically a learning experience. Here are some tips to increase the learning that takes place in the galleries of your museum and to make the museum a part of your WBT course:

▶ Create a learner's tour (p 554) of the museum, pointing out the galleries and exhibits of interest to learners in your course.

▶ Assign scavenger-hunt activities (p 204) that require learners to comb the museum for relevant exhibits. Call them "Treasure Hunts," though.

▶ Craft guided-research activities (p 207) that use the museum's assets as resources.

▶ Organize specialized tours through exhibits to reveal patterns and trends you are teaching.

▶ Assign learners the task of finding relevant objects of personal interest.

GLOSSARIES

A glossary defines terms and guides readers in their use. Most Web-based glossaries are really what most people call *dictionaries*, but their usefulness goes beyond what we call them.

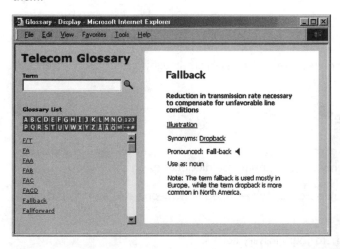

Here is an example of a sophisticated Web-based glossary. It contains terms from the telecommunications industry. Users can look up terms by two methods. Users who know the spelling of the term can type in the term in the text box at the upper left and click the search button beside it. If the term is found, it is displayed in the area to the right.

Or users can click on a letter button to see a list of terms beginning with that letter. Once they find the term in the displayed list, they can click on it to display its definition and other details. In addition to the definition, this example includes:

▶ A link to an illustration. The illustration, of course, could have been displayed here instead.

▶ Synonyms and other related words, each linked to its definition.

▶ Pronunciation, both spelled out in text and linked to a voice pronunciation.

- ▶ Part of speech of this word.

- ▶ Usage notes to help the reader use the term appropriately.

To find more examples of glossaries, search the Web for **glossary** or **dictionary**.

When to create a glossary

A glossary makes strange words familiar and guides us in their use. It can teach concepts, as well. Consider creating a glossary for areas in which:

- ▶ Practitioners use many specialized terms and abbreviations. Every complex endeavor is subject to the Tower-of-Babel effect.

- ▶ Correct use of terminology is crucial to success. There are legal penalties or just severe embarrassment for misusing terms.

- ▶ People of different specialties (and hence different vocabularies) must collaborate. An architect may use a technical term for something that a general contractor refers to by its common name and the construction worker calls by yet another term.

- ▶ Specialists and non-specialists must work together. Often reports written by a specialist must be typed and edited by those not versed in the esoteric terminology of the specialist's field.

Tips for better glossaries

Glossaries are relatively easy to create. Effective glossaries, though, require close attention to linguistic and technical issues.

Focus on a particular field

Focus on a specific area of knowledge. A glossary is not a replacement for a general-purpose dictionary. There are already plenty of general-purpose dictionaries on the Web.

Before you start your glossary project, check to see whether someone else already publishes a glossary for your field.

Don't forget to clearly label the field your glossary covers.

Evolve your glossary

Start simple and make your glossary more sophisticated as you increase its size and functions.

1. Start with a simple list of words and definitions in a single Web page.

2. If the list gets longer than 5 or 6 scrolling zones, add some letter buttons at the top to jump directly to the first term beginning with a letter.

3. As the list grows beyond a size that will load quickly, break it into separate files, one for each letter or group of letters.

4. If your glossary grows beyond a couple of hundred terms, or if it needs frequent revision, consider storing the terms, definitions, and other data in a database and generating each definition in response to a request from the user.

5. Add advanced search features. For example, let users search for words whose definitions contain specific words. Or let users look up words by how they are pronounced.

Write clear definitions

Writing good definitions is an advanced skill. I cannot tell you how to write good definitions, but I can warn you off the most common mistakes. First, word the definition as a phrase completing this statement: "A *whatever* is ..." If something in the definition refers to something besides the term, make it a complete sentence.

> **Linked list** – a data structure in which each member stores an item of data and a pointer to the next member in the list. In double-linked lists each member contains pointers to both the previous and next member in the list.

Do not use a term in its own definition.

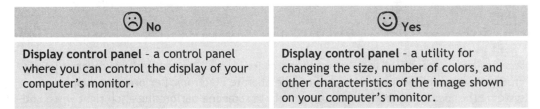

☹ No	☺ Yes
Display control panel – a control panel where you can control the display of your computer's monitor.	**Display control panel** – a utility for changing the size, number of colors, and other characteristics of the image shown on your computer's monitor.

Provide general definitions before specific ones. For each specific definition, begin with the area in which this definition applies.

> **scope** – the range or breadth over which something applies. In computer programming, the routine or library within which a variable has meaning.

Separate term and definition

Format the term and definition so they are clearly separate. This is crucial for multi-word terms.

☹ No	☺ Yes
peep-hole effect misinterpretations caused by receiving information without being aware of the context in which it applies.	**peep-hole effect** misinterpretations caused by receiving information without being aware of the context in which it applies.

Link related definitions

If the definition of one term includes words defined elsewhere in the glossary, consider linking each of these terms to its definition. This is especially important in a field where novices would have trouble understanding definitions otherwise.

Using glossaries in WBT courses

Glossaries are almost mandatory in courses that contain terminology not familiar to learners and courses that aim to teach correct use of terminology. So your course needs a glossary. How do you provide it?

▶ Link to someone else's glossary on the Web. Glossaries exist for most technical and business subjects, and most are free.

▶ Create a special glossary just for your course.

▶ Create a glossary covering the subject of your course and put the glossary on the Web for everyone to use.

This last solution is a bit more work, but think of it as community service.

JOB AIDS

Job aids are a category of tool, rather than a specific tool. The term *job aid* covers a lot of ground from a recipe on an index card to an elaborate electronic performance support system. The idea of a job aid is to provide help to someone performing a job right when and where they need it.

Job aids are not considered as training, but they can reduce and shape the need for training and in some cases can substitute for training.

To find more examples of job aids, search the Web for **job aid** or **online job aid**. Or search for the type of job aid you want, such as **calculator**.

Types of job aids

Let's look at some common types of job aids implemented using Web technologies. They range from simple instruction sheets and checklists to sophisticated calculators and virtual consultants.

Task-specific instructions

Most products come with paper or online documentation. However, the documentation provided by the vendor is generic. It tells how to do general tasks and how to use standard components of the program. Often that falls short of what employees need to do their jobs. While one section of the manual might tell how to format text and another might tell how to send a fax, and an office guide might tell how to write a business letter, that information would be of little use to the poor clerk charged with faxing a customer a letter on the company letterhead.

A job aid would tell the clerk exactly what to do to accomplish this very specific task.

Faxing a letter to a customer

To fax a letter to a customer:

1. Open the letter template

Select **File** then **Open**.

When the dialog box appears, in the File Name field enter:

`c:\Program Files\Microsoft Office\Templates\ZZCo\Z1.dot`

Click **Open**.

2. Fill in the address

When the letter opens:

Click on <**Enter customer name**>

Type in the name of the customer to receive the letter.

Do the same for <**Enter customer address**>

3. Fill in your name and position

At the bottom of the letter:

Click on <**Enter your name**>

Type in your name

Do the same for <**Enter your position**>

4. Fill in the body of the letter

Click on <**Enter your message here**>

Type in your message.

5. Save the file

Select **File** and then **Save**.

Specify where you want the copy saved.

Click on **Save**

6. Send the fax

Select **File** and then **Print ....**

In the Printer Name drop-down list, select **ZZFax**

Click on the **OK** button.

In the Phone Number field, enter the number of the person to receive the fax.

Click on **Send**.

Note: If you send faxes frequently, you may want to print out this job aid.

Checklists

Many problems defy analytical procedures, yet succumb to a systematic application of common sense. Checklists are a valuable job aid in such situations. They remind the practitioner to consider all of the items on the list. They prevent lapses in memory and discourage jumping to conclusions. Checklists take several forms:

▶ Reminders of questions to ask, solutions to try, or ideas to consider.

▶ List of things to do, though not in any particular order.

▶ Self-audits to count the symptoms, and hence calculate the severity of a problem.

Is my password secure?

Could someone learn your password and use it to obtain classified information from our systems? Take this simple self-audit to see how secure your password really is.

☐ Is your password just letters or just numbers?

☐ Is it shorter than 8 characters?

☐ Is it made of a single common word?

☐ Is it based on your birthday or that of a spouse or child?

☐ Is it based on your Social Security Number or driver's license number?

☐ Is it based on the name of a child, spouse, or close relative?

☐ Have you had the same password for more than two months?

☐ Is your password written down somewhere not under lock and key?

If you answered yes to any of these questions, you are a security risk. Change your password **now**.

Here is an example of a self-audit. It guides employees in assessing the security of their passwords.

Reference summaries

Reference summaries condense essential information to a single Web page or piece of paper. They are sometimes called *crib sheets*, *cheat sheets*, or *pocket reference cards*.

Reference summaries are an especially popular form of computer documentation (if any form of computer documentation can be called popular), where they present information that otherwise would have to be memorized. These include keyboard shortcuts for menu commands, arbitrary codes for fields in databases and configuration files, commands in programming languages, and object models for programming libraries. Reference summaries can contain other forms of condensed knowledge for other fields: organization charts for corporations, critical procedures for a piece of equipment, commonly used tables of values, emergency procedures, and Miranda warnings for police officers.

Menu Editor – Keyboard shortcuts		
Move the cursor		
By lines	Up one line	↑
	Down one line	↓
	Up to top line	Shift ↑
	Down to bottom line	Shift ↓
By relationship	To parent item	←
	To first child item	→
	To next sibling item	Alt N
	To previous sibling item	Alt P
Move the item		
By lines	Up one line	Ctrl ↑
	Down one line	Ctrl ↓
	Indent one level	Ctrl →
	Outdent one level	Ctrl ←
By relationship	Before previous sibling	Ctrl P
	After next sibling	Ctrl N

This simple example contains the keyboard shortcuts for a program used to edit hierarchical menus.

Show and hide items		
Collapse the current item		Ctrl ·
Expand the current item		Ctrl +
Collapse all items		Shift Ctrl ·
Expand all items		Shift Ctrl ·

If you want to print out this summary, use the <u>printable version</u>. It fits everything snugly onto a single piece of paper.

Reference summaries are **not** training. They are for refreshing the memories of those already trained. They may, however, reduce the amount of rote memorization that takes place in training.

Calculators

On-screen calculators reduce the reliance on pencil and paper for common calculations. They also eliminate the need to memorize complex formulas.

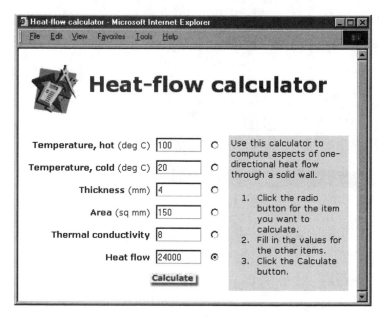

Here is an example to help engineers calculate heat flow through a wall or surface. The user just clicks on the item to be calculated, fills in all the others, and then clicks the **Calculate** button.

Such calculators are easy to create in Web pages. They require a little expertise with Web forms and JavaScript, but nothing that would require a professional programmer.

You can incorporate such calculators into your course to relieve learners of the tedium of manual calculations. Such calculators also make useful reminders of the course, especially if emblazoned with the course logo.

Consultants

Consultants give advice. A Web-based consultant is a form that the user fills in to describe a problem—a virtual interview. When the user clicks the **OK** or **Submit** button, the form analyzes the user's answers and presents its recommendations.

The following eConsultant helps managers decide how to deal with security violations by employees. Choices include a written warning, quarantine away from secure information, dismissal, or prosecution. This Web page replaces a complex, three-staged if-then diagram in the employee handbook.

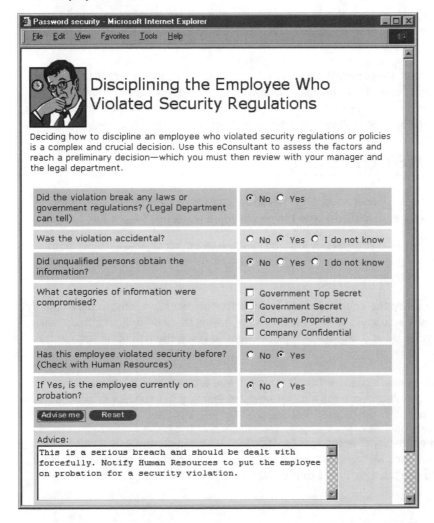

You can think of consultants as calculators for more than numbers. Use them when a situation has a lot of conditions mixed with irregularities and exceptions.

Most consultants can be implemented using just Web form elements and a bit of JavaScript. The difficult part is figuring out the rules that lead from inputs to recommendation.

Tips for better job aids

Designing job aids is not difficult so long as you keep in mind that they are first and foremost tools for use in the work environment.

Design for how the job aid will be used. If a job aid will be used to guide users in performing a procedure on the computer screen, keep it compact so it does not cover up too much of the user's work area. If the job aid guides a procedure done away from the computer, design it for printing out.

Keep job aids compact and concise. As a rule, design the job aid so it fits in a single scrolling zone of the browser at its default size, or on a single piece of paper, if it will be printed out.

If printing out, format for paper. If a job aid will be printed out, make sure it prints on a single sheet of paper. Consider formatting the printable version in Adobe Acrobat (PDF) format so that you can control the layout more precisely than with HTML. And remember to allow for differences between A4 and US paper sizes (p 467).

Using job aids in WBT courses

Job aids complement WBT courses nicely. They make courses more efficient, provide reminders afterwards, and help advertise the course. Here are a few suggestions.

Do not make job aids into tutorials. A job aid is not a training tool. Making it into one destroys the unique value it has as a job aid. Use job aids to supplement and complement training but not as training.

Use job aids to simplify the course. Just as job aids simplify work, so too can they simplify taking a course. Use calculators to relieve learners of having to make tedious calculations. Use reference summaries and task-specific instructions to guide them in using tools in the course.

Do not let job aids remove the need for learning. If you are teaching a concept or procedure, do not give learners a job aid that obviates learning the concept or procedure. At least teach the concept or procedure first, and then let learners have the job aid.

Use job aids as mementos. Give learners job aids that they can continue using after the course. These mementos will remind them of what they learned and where they learned it. Put your logo onto the job aid. Link it to your Web site.

MENTORING

The term *mentor*, meaning a wiser and more experienced person who guides development of a less experienced person, comes from the character Mentor in Homer's *Odyssey*. When Odysseus sailed away to sack Troy, he left his son, Telemachus, in the care of Mentor, who was charged with the proper upbringing of the lad. And when Athena wished to advise the lad, she did so in the voice and form of Mentor.

Today, the concept of mentoring remains an important force in the development of knowledge, skills, and judgment. The terms *telementoring* and *online coaching* refer to the traditional acts of mentoring performed using e-mail, videoconferencing, and other Web technologies.

Though most implementations of telementoring have paired pre-university students with industry practitioners, its use is by no means limited to young protégés. In this section we will consider how it can be used to guide the career development of adults.

To find more examples of Web-based mentoring, search the Web for **telementoring, online coaching,** or **mentoring.**

How does mentoring work?

In its most common form, mentoring pairs mentors with protégés in an ongoing one-to-one relationship. The mentor provides guidance, advice, and knowledge as requested by the protégé. Exchanges can take place by e-mail, videoconferencing, or plain old telephone calls.

Beyond that, there are no precise rules for how the partners interact. The nature of the mentoring relationship is personal and dynamic. It can evolve into what best accomplishes the goals of the partners.

Why use mentoring?

Mentoring provides learners with a more knowledgeable and mature partner from whom they can learn much more than facts.

What mentors provide

Mentors provide real-world experience, perspective, and maturity. In recruiting mentors, consider what they can offer.

- ▶ **Detailed subject matter knowledge**. Mentors know their field. They may have specialized or esoteric knowledge.

- ▶ **Emotional maturity**. A good mentor is patient, self-confident, and resilient. Mentors take problems in stride.

- ▶ **Perspective**. Good mentors have broad experience in their companies, their industries, and the world.

- ▶ **Knowledge of the way things really work**. Mentors know what matters and what does not. They know which aspects of theory make a difference in practical application.

▶ **Business savvy.** Good mentors understand how their organizations do business and how the goals of a department or field contribute to those of the organization as a whole.

▶ **Analytical skills.** Good mentors are good problem solvers. They know how to dissect complex situations and how to manage their parts.

What mentoring does for learners

Mentoring lets learners take advantage of the knowledge and experience of others. Mentoring is an effective way to:

▶ Motivate learners by showing that what they are learning applies in the real world

▶ Help learners decide where to focus their learning efforts

▶ Infuse learning with the authority possessed by real-world practitioners

▶ Teach subtle subjects that require more individual attention than the instructor alone can provide

Learners can form important relationships

Mentoring can extend far beyond offering advice on the narrow subject of a course. Some mentoring relationships develop into friendship. Eighth grade student Erin had this to say about her mentor:

> Good friends come along once in a lifetime. I met mine on the computer screen in the Global Schoolhouse where I met Steve who was a professor at Cornell University. I struck up a conversation with him and this spawned a long distance relationship. Steve and I send e-mail to each other often, and we discuss everything from musical instruments to school [138].

There is no reason that a mentoring relationship struck up during a course needs to end at the end of that course. Web-based mentoring is too new to sport many long-term success stories, but good Web-based mentoring relationships should weather job changes, overseas assignments, and busy schedules better than face-to-face counterparts.

Tips for better mentoring

Successful mentoring programs require careful planning, hard work, and adequate time. You must recruit, train, and motivate mentors. You must match mentors with protégés who must negotiate their relationship and learn to work together. If you do all this, you can integrate mentoring into your organization and your training efforts.

Recruit good mentors

Where do you get mentors? Once you have an idea what characteristics you are looking for in mentors, start the search. Here are some likely candidates:

- ▶ **Managers** of the teams where learners may eventually work

- ▶ **Senior professionals** in the area of study

- ▶ **Consultants** with specialized knowledge or broad experience in a field

- ▶ **Recently retired** managers and professionals

- ▶ **Company "old-timers"** (which may mean those with three years of experience at Here2Day.com, Inc.)

- ▶ **Recent graduates** who are knowledgeable in a new technology or techniques that others in the company must learn

Remind potential mentors what they stand to gain from the experience of mentoring someone else. What's in it for them? Mentors not only get to share wisdom, they gain knowledge, too. They can refresh their skills and catch up on new developments in their field. They also get a chance to spot talent among students and to enjoy fellowship with other mentors.

Prepare mentors

Help mentors become familiar with the kinds of tasks they may be asked to perform and the questions they will be called on to answer:

- ▶ Let them examine e-mail, chats, discussions, and other transcripts of mentoring sessions

- ▶ Show them feedback from prior learners and mentors

- ▶ Let them talk to prior mentors

Match mentor and learner carefully

Match mentor and learner based on what the learner wants and needs and on what the mentor has and is willing to share. Make sure their goals are compatible. Involve the learner, the mentor, and the instructor in the decision. Learners know what they want, instructors know what learners need, and mentors know what they can offer.

You may want to use a discussion group to match learners and mentors. Have mentors fill in forms describing themselves and what they want to get out of the experience. Post the forms' contents to a Protégé-wanted thread. Do likewise with the learners so their answers are posted to a Mentor-wanted thread. Let learners, mentors, and the instructor examine all the requests before making matches.

Negotiate individual contracts

Mentoring is an individual relationship between the mentor and the protégé. Each pair must negotiate contributions to the relationship. Agenda for discussion should include:

▶ How much time will the mentor contribute?

▶ What tasks will the mentor perform? Brainstorm? Make suggestions? Conduct research? Answer questions? Critique drafts and prototypes?

▶ How often will the mentor and protégé communicate? How quickly will each respond to messages from the other? Who will act and who will react?

▶ How soon should they follow up on unanswered requests?

Allow time

Establishing a successful telementoring program can take months of active development and vigilant monitoring. It takes time to recruit and train mentors, match them with learners, get them working together, and wait for them to learn to work together effectively. Do not expect overnight success, and do not give up too soon.

Variations of mentoring

In addition to the ongoing one-to-one mentoring relationship, some alternative forms are also in practice. Though strictly speaking some might not qualify for the term mentoring, they are interesting applications of the general idea of coaching.

Ask somebody who knows

In some programs, experts serve as information resources for learners. In such "ask somebody who knows" or "ask the expert" programs, the experts make themselves available to answer questions on a subject.

Such an approach can be very effective in answering subtle questions for which learners cannot just look up an answer. It can be inefficient, though, if learners tend to ask the same questions over and over again or if they refuse to try to find answers on their own. In the Passport to Knowledge Project, over half the questions sent to mentors were duplicates of ones in the questions archive—even though learners were instructed to check the archive first [139].

Though such one-shot interactions minimize the load on experts, they offer little in the way of an ongoing relationship.

Mentor advises an entire class

Some classes may employ a single advisor for the entire class. The advisor gets to know the goals and needs of the class, and the class has a permanent resource. Sometimes the advisor is a paid consultant.

Having just one advisor per class limits the amount of individual attention each learner gets. However, it does have the advantage of reducing the costs and effort of having individual mentors for each learner.

Team mentoring

Advice can come from teams of experts organized on the model of a telephone support help desk that is available 24 yours a day, 7 days a week. Advice can be provided through an ongoing chat session. Or learners may select an advisor from a database of available experts.

In such a plan, mentors serve in shifts so that a few are always available. The duties can be distributed across multiple time zones girdling the globe. That way, experts can serve during office hours or on whatever schedule they prefer.

Using mentoring in WBT courses

You can make mentoring a standard part of your courses by integrating it into the routine activities of the course.

Make mentors needed but not essential

Design activities with important roles for mentors. Says Kevin O'Neil of the CoVIS project:

> To make a telementoring program succeed, the hardest part is in crafting the learner's work so learners can see telementoring as necessary to the success of the work, but not so indispensable that it is a crisis if the person goes away for two or three days [140].

In the course syllabus, note the role of mentors and ensure that mentors contribute to the outcome but do not determine it.

Make mentors more than pen pals

Although friendship may be a wonderful outcome of a mentoring relationship, it should not be the primary goal. To focus mentoring relationships on learning goals, give learners a specific project to complete with the help of their mentors. Specify goals, milestones, and deadlines.

Monitor mentoring

To get mentoring off to an effective start, the instructor should monitor interactions between mentors and protégés. Simply require that both include the instructor in the "cc:" list for all e-mail messages. Be sensitive to the desire for privacy and discontinue the monitoring when it seems that the partners are working together effectively.

CONFERENCES

Practicing professionals attend conferences to update their knowledge, view the latest products, meet their peers, and have fun. Now they can attend conferences without leaving their computers.

An online conference has speakers, attendees, papers, presentations, panels, vendor exhibits, and even sightseeing tours just like a physical conference [141]. Only nobody has to travel, because the conference is on the Web.

Here is the home page for an online conference. After paying your fee at the registration booth, you can proceed through any of the doors to partake of the activities of the conference.

To find more examples of conferences, search the Web for **online conference** or **virtual conference**.

Why hold a conference?

The online conference offers several advantages over physical conferences:

▶ **Costs are less.** Participants save the costs of travel, lodging, restaurant meals, and bar tabs.

▶ **More people can participate.** Since participants do not all have to be in the same place at the same time, more can take part. Participants can attend while still working part time. Or even full time.

▶ **Participants can attend every session.** Because most events are asynchronous, taking place over a period of days, participants do not have to choose between simultaneous presentations.

▶ **Nobody has to take notes.** Complete handouts are available before the conference. Participants have access to the actual presentation materials used at the conference.

▶ **Presentations can evolve.** Presenters do not have to "freeze" their presentations months beforehand in order to meet the deadline for the conference proceedings. Presenters can submit "preview" copies and keep revising. Presenters can incorporate audience feedback, revising their presentations to deal with issues raised and interest shown by conference participants.

▶ **Presentations are more complete and thoughtful.** Presenters are not limited to a short time slot. Participants can ask as many questions as they want. Presenters can think before answering questions. They can answer questions fully.

What does a conference contain?

Give the online conference the metaphorical structure of an earth-bound conference. Capitalize on participants' knowledge of conventional conferences to make yours seem familiar. Here's what an online conference might include.

Location	Component	How implemented
Main auditorium	Keynote	The conference kicks off with a 30-minute presentation that is broadcast by videoconferencing, audioconferencing, and simultaneous transcription into chat.
	Featured presentations	Featured presentations use audioconferencing broadcast and simultaneous transcription into chat. They are typically 15 to 30 minutes long.
	Panel discussions	Panels consist of a chat session in which the panelists can type in messages. Everyone else can just read the messages, until the question-and-answer period.

Location	Component	How implemented
Meeting rooms	Regular presentations	Regular presentations consist of Web pages or PowerPoint slides (to download) that cover a topic. Each regular presentation may have a scheduled question and answer session. All have an ongoing discussion.
	Q&A session	Participants can join an optional chat session with the presenter of a regular session. These are scheduled at the convenience of the presenter, but do not overlap other live events.
	Ongoing discussion	Each presentation has a thread in the conference discussion group.
Registration desk	Registration form	Participants register by filling in and submitting a Web form.
	About the organization	The organization running the conference is described in a Web page.
Exhibition hall	Floor layout	The "expo" is an image-map of the floor showing the location of the booths of vendors. The more expensive booths are most prominent, but all are legible. Clicking on a booth displays the Web page for the booth.
	Booth	Each booth consists of a Web page for the vendor. All the Web pages for booths look alike since they are produced from templates. Each booth contains the company name, logo, and information about the vendor's products and services. The booth also contains a chat or videoconferencing window, along with a schedule of demonstrations, presentations, and question-answering sessions.

Each booth also contains links to the company Web site and an e-mail link to the company. Some conferences supply vendors with special conference e-mail addresses, such as:

vendor-name@conference-name.com |
| Sponsors | Banners | Throughout the conference, screens contain small and large banners naming the sponsors of the conference. |
| Registration packet | Name badge | Attendees are listed in the conference directory. They also receive a password to admit them to events and an at-conference e-mail address (persons-name@conference-name.com). |

Location	Component	How implemented
	List of attendees	The conference provides a roster of participants (who agree to release their names to other participants).
	Schedule	The schedule is a calendar with links to each of the scheduled events.
	Feedback form	Feedback is gathered by a Web form.
Speakers' lounge	Practice area	The practice area provides a place where presenters can post their materials and try out chat and conferencing systems ahead of time.
	Helper	In the speakers' lounge are the E-mail address or chat-window for a person to help speakers resolve problems.
Private reception	VIP party	The conference may include a special chat or conference session just for speakers and other contributors to the conference.
Bookstore	Exhibits	The bookstore contains pictures of the covers of books by presenters and other books on the subject of the conference. Each is linked to a Web-based bookstore.
Hotel bar	Sit at the bar	The bar provides a chat room for social issues and anything else.
	Sit at a table	Tables in the bar center on discussion group for various topics only peripherally related to the subject of the conference.
Information desk	Helper	The Information desk has scheduled chat sessions and an ongoing discussion group about the conference and its speakers.
	Finder	To help participants find their way, the conference includes an index, a menu, and a search facility.
Sightseeing	Postcards	In the gift shop, participants find images of postcards that they can print out and send to friends and relatives.
	Wild stories	Participants can pick from a selection of "you won't believe what happened to me at the conference" stories to tell co-workers and friends.

Announcing the conference

On the conference announcement, tell prospective participants everything they need to know to decide whether to attend. Set positive, yet realistic expectations.

The Wired Builders' Alliance presents the ...

First Annual Builders' Online Conference

The only conference dedicated to helping building contractors use the Internet to get more business.

Live events: 14 – 19 August 2000

Ongoing discussions: 14 August – 30 September 2000.

Keynote: George Pardue, CEO, Bilt2Last

Topics:

- You can't download a house: How buyers shop for a builder.
- When builders build a Web site.
- Building bridges to customers: E-mail, chat, discussion groups, and beyond.
- Virtual reality for previewing construction.
- I know hammers, not HTML: Overcoming technical concerns.

Fee: $75

To register

Technical requirements

Version 4.0 browser

Microsoft NetMeeting

Co-sponsored by Building Technologists and Schoniker Tools

Here we see the announcement of an online conference. It contains much the same information as for an earth-based conference— with a few additions.

Tips for better conferences

Online conferences are a new medium, and their success is not certain. A focus on the needs of participants can, however, put the odds in your favor.

Price the conference reasonably

Even though participants save a lot of money by not having to travel to the conference, few will be willing to pay more than 10 to 25% of the registration fee for a physical conference. Charge a moderate fee for access during the live period of the conference, a small fee for access afterwards, and no fee for access to the conference digest.

Minimize technical difficulties

Minimize the technical requirements. Design materials to play on as many browsers as possible. Spell out technical requirements and provide help meeting them (p 481).

Hold several practice sessions before the conference so that participants can learn to use chat, discussion groups, and other media you will use in the conference.

Control attendance

Require participants to register beforehand, even if the conference is free. Otherwise, you do not know who will be there and what their interests are.

Restrict attendance to those who can learn from the conference and who can participate effectively in it. You may, however, want to grant a few "press credentials" for outsiders to observe the proceedings.

Schedule for the convenience of participants

The main reason to attend an online conference rather than a real one is simple convenience. So make your conference as convenient for participants as you can:

▶ Let the conference run over a long enough time period, say two weeks. That way, more people can participate, and the discussions can run their course.

▶ Publish the schedule of live events well before the conference so that people can arrange their calendars.

▶ Make preliminary papers and other materials available a couple of weeks before the start of the conference. That way, participants arrive ready to discuss the papers.

▶ Schedule live events during weekends and evenings. Or do a survey to find out when most participants prefer to have the events.

▶ Make all presentation materials, papers, examples, and archived live events available for months afterwards. Publish a digest of the conference and keep it available forever.

Layer presentations

Keep live presentations very short, chat sessions moderately short, and let discussion groups run on for weeks.

Follow each presentation with a chat session and then a discussion thread. Clearly label which thread discusses which presentation.

Integrate with conventional conferences and publications

Online conferences blend well with conventional conferences and scholarly publications. Here are a few common relationships:

▶ The presentations of the online conference are published in an industry or scholarly journal after the end of the conference.

▶ The presentations are published in a proceedings volume or as a book.

▶ The online conference houses the papers and continues the discussion from a physical conference that occurred earlier.

▶ The online and physical conferences occur at the same time. Presentations at the physical conference are Webcast (p 195) to online participants.

Using conferences in WBT courses

An online conference is quite different from a course in structure and in purpose. However, conferences are valuable resources for learners. Here are some ideas for using them to enhance a WBT course.

▶ **Have learners attend.** If a conference of interest overlaps the term of the course, negotiate a group-registration fee and send the class. Give learners specific assignments of sessions to attend, people to meet, and products to view.

▶ **Have learners assist.** Running a conference is a lot of work. Have learners volunteer to help out. It is a great way to meet luminaries in the field and strike up friendships.

▶ **Make a presentation.** Volunteer the class to provide a part of the program that overlaps the content of your course. Have the instructor lead learners in preparing and delivering the presentation.

▶ **Conduct your own conference.** As a class project, create and administer a conference on the subject of your course. Doing so will take a commitment of 6 to 12 months, so the project may have to span several classes, but it does let learners meet prominent practitioners in the field and make a résumé-worthy contribution to it.

GUIDED TOURS

The guided tour demonstrates an interactive computer system, such as a computer application, a Web site, or a WBT course itself. It does not teach how to operate the software, but does give an overview of its structure and a preview of its capabilities.

Here is an example of a guided tour. It shows the tour incorporated into the intranet-based knowledge management system called KNACK. The KNACK user can embark on the tour from any KNACK page by clicking on the **Tour** button.

This displays the start of the tour and opens a separate tour window that guides the user through the tour.

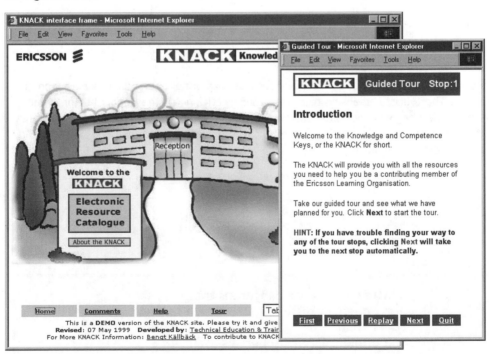

The introduction (called Stop 1), welcomes the tourist, briefly describes the subject of the tour, and tells how to continue the tour. The tourist clicks on Next to advance to the next stop.

The tour continues through the major sections of the system. Here we are at the fourth stop.

Notice that the tour describes the stop and suggests exploring it—like going ashore from a cruise ship. The tourist can always rejoin the tour by clicking on the **Replay** button, which resets the underlying window to the current stop in the tour. Other buttons also give the tourist choices. **Previous** lets the tourist return to the previous stop, and **First** restarts the whole tour from the beginning.

A little learning is a dangerous thing;
Drink deep, or taste not the Pierian spring:
There shallow draughts intoxicate the brain,
And drinking largely sobers us again.

— Alexander Pope, *An Essay on Criticism*

At the end of the tour, tourists are returned to the point where the tour started and are given a brief summary of what they saw.

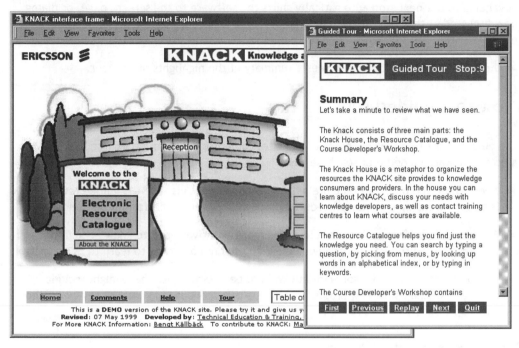

The **Quit** button dismisses the tour and lets the tourist return to work.

To find more examples of guided tours, search the Web for **guided tour** or **virtual tour**.

How guided tours work

Typically, the user starts the tour by clicking on a Tour button or command in the main software or Web site. This action pops up the tour window where the software guided tour runs.

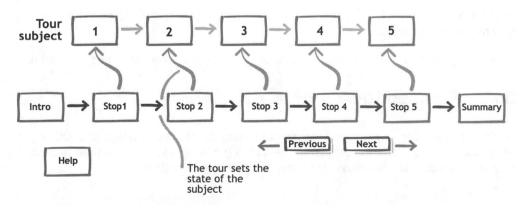

The guided tourist begins the tour in earnest after a brief introduction, which states the purpose and subject of the tour.

At each stop on the tour, pertinent features of the software are pointed out. In some tours advancing to the next stop automatically shifts the software to the screen, page, or dialog box discussed at that stop of the tour. In others, the user receives instructions on how to navigate within the software to find the next stop.

At the end of the tour, the tourist sees a summary of the highlights of the tour.

When to use a guided tour

Use guided tours to orient people in a Web site, computer program, or WBT course. Provide a quick software guided tour for those who:

▶ Need to see the big picture before getting lost in the details. Use the guided tour to walk learners through a complex procedure before asking them to perform it on their own.

▶ Just want an overview. For example, sales representatives need to know enough to demonstrate a product and its advantages, but do not have time to learn to operate it.

▶ Will be involved with the software but will not be operating it. These might include managers of the operators, prospective buyers of a product, and product reviewers too lazy to actually use the product.

Tips for better guided tours

A good tour leaves tourists excited, satisfied, and confident that they can now travel on their own.

Keep the tour focused. A tour is not a tutorial, a Help facility, or an instruction manual. A tour provides a broad overview of how the pieces fit together.

Encourage tourists to explore the sights at each stop. Suggest things to click on. Map out a side excursion or two. Give tourists a **Rescue Me** button to get back to the tour at any point.

Start with a preview telling what is on the tour. Promise only an overview and tell learners how to proceed on the tour.

Clearly flag activities, that is, places where the tourist can do more than just look and read.

Variations of guided tours

Guided tours are one way to orient learners to a piece of software or a Web site. Other techniques you may want to consider are field trips (p 559) and virtual museums (p 525), both of which can take learners step by step through subject matter.

Using guided tours in WBT courses

Though software guided tours do, in a sense, teach, their primary purpose and best use is to preview a piece of software or a Web site and to orient prospective users. That still leaves several ways to use guided tours in WBT courses.

▶ **Tour the course**. Introduce your course with a tour of its major areas of content, pointing out the types of presentations and activities it includes.

▶ **Tour the user interface**. Show learners the main knobs and levers they will use to navigate your course. (Some course vendors provide guided tours of the user interface of their tools.)

▶ **Preview software used in the course**. If your course requires using a software package, create a tour to point out the features that will be used in the class.

▶ **Preview software you are teaching**. If you teach the use of a software package, use tours to preview difficult procedures before instructing learners in how to perform them.

▶ **Tour resources**. Lead learners on tours of virtual libraries, virtual museums, simulations, and other Web-based adjuncts to your course. On these "learners' tours," point out features important to participants in your class.

FIELD TRIPS

The field trip lets learners explore a real or conceptual space. It consists of definite stops where the learner can observe and learn. Field trips are also known as *virtual tours* or *online tours*.

The following example is a virtual field trip showing the variety of pure and mixed architectural styles in one neighborhood in Boulder, Colorado. (And yes, it is the neighborhood in which your humble author lives, though not in a house so grand, alas.)

The tourist traverses the field trip by repeatedly clicking the **Next** button, or backs up by clicking the **Previous** button.

> Experience is not a matter of having actually swum the Hellespont, or danced with the dervishes, or slept in a doss-house. It is a matter of sensibility and intuition, of seeing and hearing the significant things, of paying attention at the right moments, of understanding and coordinating. Experience is not what happens to a man; it is what a man does with what happens to him.
>
> — Aldous Huxley, *Texts and Pretexts*

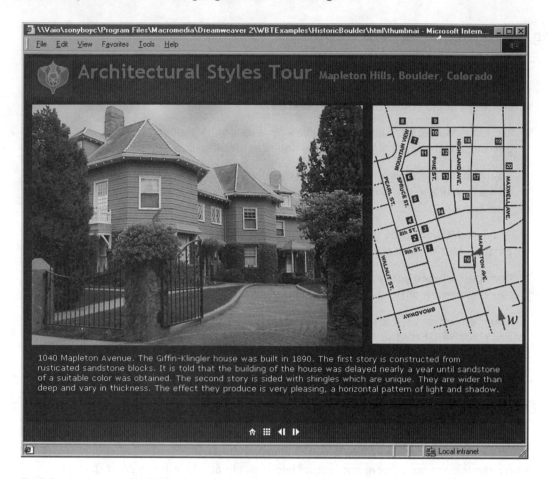

Each basic stop on the field trip contains a picture of a house and commentary on it. It also contains a you-are-here map showing the location of the house and the direction of the view shown in the photograph. Some stops have alternative views that the tourist can select in the you-are-here map.

Clicking the **Gallery** button brings up a page that shows thumbnail images of all the houses on the field trip. Here the tourist can chose to visit a particular house by clicking on its image.

Art is not to be taught in Academies. It is what one looks at, not what one listens to, that makes the artist. The real schools should be the streets.

— Oscar Wilde

To find more examples of field trips, search the Web for **virtual tour** or **online tour**.

How field trips work

The field trip begins with an introduction and then proceeds through a series of stops. Each stop describes one object in the area of the tour.

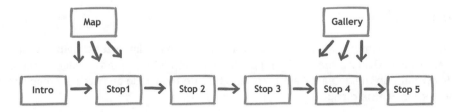

Some tours include a map showing an overview of the path of the tour and a gallery providing thumbnail images of all the stops. The map and gallery serve as menus. Users can jump from the map or the gallery to any tour stop.

When to use a field trip

Use field trips to help people explore a place they cannot visit in person. The place visited can be a real locale or an imaginary one. Use field trips when the locale to tour is:

▶ **Too far away**. To travel to the real locale would be expensive and time consuming.

▶ **Too spread out**. A field trip can include stops in Stockholm, Smolensk, Sydney, Santiago, San Diego, and Smallville. The only airfare is a mouse click.

▶ **Too dangerous**. Toxic vapors, bullets, and the vacuum of outer space cannot penetrate the computer screen.

▶ **Imaginary**. How about taking learners to a place where everything is done by the book and all theories are made real?

Tips for better field trips

The secret to an effective virtual field trip is a balance between simplicity and freedom. Learners must not get lost, yet must feel free to explore on their own.

Keep the field trip simple

Keep the user interface for the field trip simple so that users focus on the material on the tour rather than the navigation mechanisms.

Keep the layout stable

When designing field trips, keep the layout stable. If the layout varies, put the **Next** button at the top so it is always at the same location in the window.

TechnoTip: In HTML, specify the size of all images. That is, include WIDTH and HEIGHT attributes in all IMG tags. That way, the browser can lay out the page before all the graphics finish downloading. Including WIDTH and HEIGHT attributes prevents the squirmy page-dance that sometimes occurs as incoming graphics shove text blocks around the page.

Show spatial relationships

If the spatial relationships among objects on the field trip are important, help people see the relationships. Overlap the stops so that the next stop is visible in the edge of the current stop. Show both on the you-are-here map. And be sure to include an overview map showing all the stops in the field trip.

Let people inspect objects of interest

On the field trip, let people inspect objects of interest. Let them click on an object to enlarge it and read commentary about it. Let people select among various viewpoints at a stop.

Let people go off on their own

Let people pick their own tour or design their own. Provide an overview map and gallery from which people can pick destinations in any order they choose. If there is any danger that people will wander too far afield, include a **Rejoin field trip** button to rescue them. Or start digressions away from the field trip in a separate window so the field trip remains on the screen.

Narrate stops well

Tell field trippers what they should notice on the tour. Otherwise they may flail or become distracted by all the pretty pictures. For each stop, explain what the scene shows. What are the names of the objects shown? From what direction is the scene viewed? What in particular is significant about the objects shown in this stop?

If technical conditions permit, consider providing the narration by an authoritative voice as well as in text.

Anchor each stop with a visual

For each stop, display a compelling visual image. It should be attractive, but it is more important that it clearly communicate the main idea of the stop.

Variations of field trips

The basic design of field trips welcomes variations and alternatives to suit the constraints of the subject matter and the needs of trip takers.

Personal travel diaries

A simpler form of virtual field trip resembles a personal travel diary illustrated with snapshots. Such tours can present an individual person's experience of a subject in a direct and interesting way.

Geology along the Peak-to-Peak highway

As it parallels the continental divide, Colorado's Peak-to-Peak highway provides some of the most breathtaking scenery in North America. For the geologist, the beauty is not just in vistas of distant summits but closer to the road—right beside the road in fact. To the geologist, the Peak-to-Peak provides some of the most interesting road cuts in the inner Solar System. Come with us as we travel north from Nederland to Estes Park and Rocky Mountain National Park with a side trip to Brainard Lake and the Indian Peaks Wilderness.

Here we are about 1.1 miles outside of Nederland, looking north at Mt. Audubon (13,233 ft). It is a beautiful late summer morning. There's not a cloud in the sky.

We have Ogden Tweto's Geologic Map of Colorado with us. According to it we are traveling through a region of Precambrian biotitic gneiss, schist, and migmatite. These metamorphic rocks range in age from 1.7 to 1.8 million years old and are derived mostly from sedimentary deposits.

About 3.6 miles from Nederland we stop alongside this roadcut. The rock appears shiny and a little green. We think this must be

some of the schist we read about. The regular platy fractures are really spectacular and seem to be caused by the flat-faced sheets of mica. There is quite a bit of what appears to be iron staining on these rocks, too. What we thought was especially interesting is a seam of a black, shiny rock running through the cut. We took a hand sample with us and, if our Audubon Field Guide can be believed, the specimen is amphibolite. I would have thought that the amphibolite would be harder than the surrounding schist.

At about mile 6.1 we pull off the road for a truly "Kodak" moment. The left edge of the road just drops away and we find ourselves looking out upon an enchanted landscape of granite pinnacles. It's hard to explain, but I feel as though I'm looking through a stereopticon. The sense of depth seems artificial. I'm sure it has something to do with the feathery appearance of the fir trees.

Consulting our geologic map, this granite appears to be Precambrian in age (1.6 to 1.7 million years). You can see how the edges of this formation have spalled away, giving the rocks a rounded appearance.

Reluctantly, we get into our van and take off. We want to get to Brainard Lake in time to cook some lunch.

This example leads the learner on a tour of the geology of the Rocky Mountain region. This example structures the tour as a personal journal recounting an automobile trip northward along the Peak-to-Peak highway in Colorado. It consists of a series of annotated photographs of the vistas and road cuts along the way.

The photographs and commentary continue for another page. Here is the last stop—Brainard Lake.

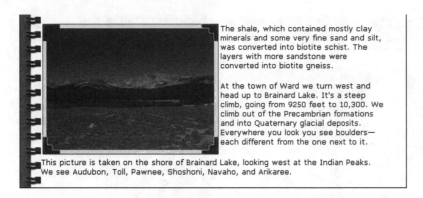

The shale, which contained mostly clay minerals and some very fine sand and silt, was converted into biotite schist. The layers with more sandstone were converted into biotite gneiss.

At the town of Ward we turn west and head up to Brainard Lake. It's a steep climb, going from 9250 feet to 10,300. We climb out of the Precambrian formations and into Quaternary glacial deposits. Everywhere you look you see boulders— each different from the one next to it.

This picture is taken on the shore of Brainard Lake, looking west at the Indian Peaks. We see Audubon, Toll, Pawnee, Shoshoni, Navaho, and Arikaree.

13

Venture beyond courses

Self-guided tours

Self-guided tours enable people to explore a space on their own. Use virtual reality or just a linked series of image maps to let people navigate through space by clicking in a picture to indicate where they want to go next. Use self-guided tours for demonstrating the interior and exterior of buildings, vehicles, public places, natural settings, and so forth.

Tours of imaginary worlds

Let people explore virtual locales. Provide tours of imaginary worlds and of physical objects they could not tour in reality. Here are some examples of imaginary tours.

▶ The human brain. That movie screen over there is the visual cortex and those things that look like trans-Atlantic telephone cables are the *corpus callosum*.

▶ An imaginary town with exactly one example of every architectural style.

▶ A cave through all the major kinds of rocks found on earth.

▶ The atom. Scuba dive thorough electron clouds and dodge shark-like neutrons.

For a menu, create a schematic map or scene containing all the features you need to display.

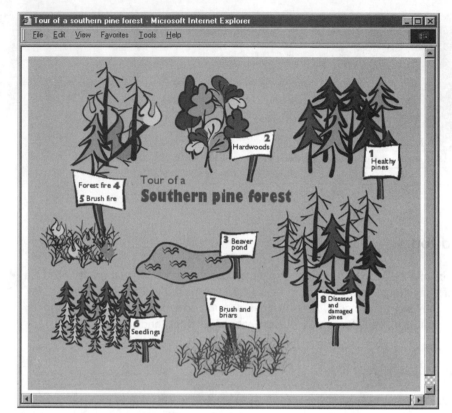

Here is the overview map for a tour of a pine forest in the southeastern United States.

Alternative forms

The field trip has characteristics in common with guided tours and museums. Like a guided tour (p 554), the field trip has definite stops where the user observes and learns. However, the guided tour describes a separate piece of software or window, while the virtual field trip provides the content it describes.

The virtual field trip is also like a virtual museum (p 525). In a museum the items of interest have been brought indoors. That is, they have been collected into a precisely organized collection that the museum visitor can view in several different sequences. In the field trip, the items of interest are seen in context. Usually, only one sequence through the stops is provided.

Using field trips in WBT courses

Get learners out of the virtual classroom. Send them on a virtual field trip. Field trips easily fit as activities within a WBT course. Use them to let learners see how concepts taught in the course are applied (or misapplied) in the real world. Use them whenever you would recommend a real field trip, but schedule and budget say no.

Require specific learning outcomes. Make the field trip more than a vacation away from the responsibilities of learning. Give learners specific assignments they must accomplish on the field trip—objects they must find, patterns they must notice, or principles they must infer.

SIMULATIONS

Used for tests (Chapter 7) and activities (Chapter 6), simulations also form the basis for an entirely new kind of course—though many would not call it a *learning environment* rather than a course. The kinds of simulations we talk about here are ones that are used for learning and that are complete enough to teach everything needed through simulation.

Here is an example of a simple Web-based simulation used for learning. It is called SomeWoods and is modeled on the popular computer game SimCity. It is designed to help private landowners in the southeastern United States learn to manage their forests more effectively regardless of their particular goals.

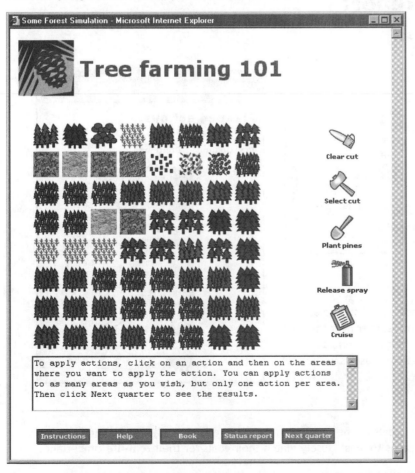

This simulation runs quarter by quarter for up to 50 years. Each quarter, the learner reviews the results from the last quarter and decides what actions to take. Actions include things like selectively cutting an area, clear-cutting it, replanting it, conducting a controlled burn, or having the area appraised. Actions can be applied to each of the 100 stands on the map individually.

The results for a quarter depend on actions taken by the learner, and also on variables such as rainfall, fluctuations in prices for saw timber and pulp wood, emergency needs for cash (daughter gets accepted at Harvard), forest fires, and disasters, such as tornados and lightning.

Just as in the real situation, learners must look beyond the superficial appearances. To do so, they can call up a detailed status report.

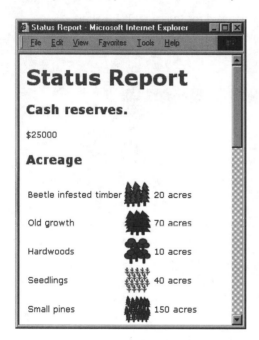

The status report shows the land use and conditions of trees.

The status report also lists the actions ordered by the learner over the next quarter. This list gives learners a chance to reconsider actions, just as in the real world.

Learners can set the goals of the game. Goals can mix economic, aesthetic, and environmental concerns to most closely match their goals for their real-life timberland.

To find more examples of simulations, search the Web for **learning simulation**.

How simulations work

In a typical learning simulation, users start by reading the instructions or at least the goals and main rules of the simulation—just enough to get started. The simulation itself consists of rapid cycles of interaction: The learner acts and the simulation provides immediate feedback. These action-feedback cycles continue as the learner pursues the goals of the simulation. If the learner has any questions about how to interact with the simulation, he or she can access Help or the instructions.

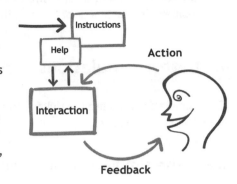

When to use simulations for learning

Developing effective simulations is difficult, time-consuming, and expensive. Getting them to work well over the Web makes development even harder. When are simulations worth this effort?

Costs of failure are high. If the potential consequences of inadequate training are severe, the costs per individual can be justified. Failures that endanger life, public safety, and financial success are good candidates. Brain surgeons, nuclear power plant operators, and stock market investors must perform at a high level of skill.

Learners need individual training. Simulations are self-customizing. Each participant experiences a unique series of events in response to his or her own knowledge, skills, and instincts.

Many people must be trained. Since the major costs for a simulation are in developing and perfecting it, training additional learners adds little to the total costs. Spreading the costs over a few hundred or few thousand learners recovers those costs.

Tasks are complex and time is short. Simulations can provide high-performance training, telescoping weeks of training into days. Inside Edge, a simulation that taught sales and negotiation skills to inside sales representatives for GE Supply, replaced 40 hours of classroom training with 20 hours of 15-minute modules [142]. Royal Coaching Journey, a four-hour simulation for the Royal Bank Financial Group of Canada, replaced 10 hours of classroom training. According to an article in *Chemical Engineering*, a simulator-based training program qualified Conoco refinery operators in six months rather than the twelve to eighteen months required for conventional training.

Skills to be taught are subtle or the knowledge complex. Simulations work well for subjects in which the greatest challenge is not acquiring factual knowledge but applying knowledge, skills, and beliefs in complex, unique situations. Training experts interviewed for an August 1998 article in *Training & Development* all strongly agreed that simulations could teach soft skills [142].

You have time and budget to see the project through. Simulations may be effective, but they are seldom easy or inexpensive to develop. Simulations can require over 500 hours of development for each hour of learning [81].

Tips for better simulations

Good simulations require careful design and extensive refinement. Here are a few tips to speed you on your way.

Make the simulation meaningfully realistic

Many novice designers equate realism with photo-realistically rendered 3D graphics or virtual reality worlds. For learning purposes, though, realism has a somewhat different meaning. The simulation need not mimic closely the task for which it provides training so long as it exercises the skills and knowledge needed in the real task [143]. A simulation is realistic (hence effective) if it:

▶ Implements the causal relationships and principles of the real-world system that learners must master

▶ Contains details necessary for the learner to map components of the simulation to their real-world counterparts

▶ Lets learners control the aspects of the simulation they would control in the real world

▶ Makes learners feel they directly control the subject of the simulator without awkward intermediate steps

In other words, it is more important that the simulator works like the real-world system than that it looks like the real-world system.

Design the required elements well

Commercial computer and videogames can cost millions of dollars and take years to develop. Few training organizations have budgets that large. On the other hand, I have seen effective learning simulations created by one person in a week. A good learning simulation requires good design more than it requires massive amounts of programming and intricate graphics.

If you are creating a learning simulation, focus your early design efforts on defining the core elements of the simulation—and only later worry about how you will portray them to learners. Here is a checklist of the essential ingredients of an effective simulation.

Key goal expressed as a specific task.

In the simulation, exactly what are learners to accomplish? Give learners a single, understandable goal against which their results can be measured.

☹ No	☺ Yes
Invest in stocks, bonds, and real estate to see how markets work.	Invest so you double your money within three years.
Run the nuclear reactor so that no humans or equipment are damaged.	Scramble the reactor, keeping radiation exposure below prescribed levels for all reactor staff and citizens while keeping maintenance and replacement costs for equipment within budget.
Make money-raising trees.	Over 50 years, make an average of $50 per acre per year without reducing the acreage or basal area in trees.

Scenario—a pretend world

Create an imaginary world for learners to interact with. This may include:

▶ **Definite roles for the learner**. Define a character or characters for the learner to play. Give the character specific motivations and abilities.

▶ **Objects for the learner to interact with**. Provide tools the learner must use to accomplish difficult tasks. Tools include control panels of devices, sources of information, vehicles, and in some cases, play money.

▶ **Adversaries and allies**. A simulation may include other characters to help or hinder the learner. These characters may be other live participants in the simulation or may be simulated characters.

▶ **An environment**. The environment organizes and structures the simulation. It sets the scene and provides a context for the interaction. The environment includes everything the learner **does not** interact with directly—things like imaginary streets, buildings, rooms, and furniture.

Well defined characters

When simulating interpersonal relationships, provide learners with well-fleshed-out descriptions of the characters they will encounter in the simulation or test. If possible, include photographs or drawings of these characters. Encourage learners to print or display these descriptions in a separate window.

Model of the subject

The most important part of the simulation, for learning purposes, is the underlying model it represents. The model is the core knowledge you are trying to teach. The model consists of the principles that govern how the real-world system or organization works. The model determines how the simulation reacts to each input from the learner, how it is affected by events outside the control of the learner (weather, luck, enemy action), and how it evolves over time.

The model must be simple enough that you can economically implement it and the learner can infer its principles within a simulated lifetime. The model must be rich enough that the simulation seems as varied and capricious as the real-world system it mimics.

Challenges

What challenges will learners face in accomplishing the goal of the simulation? These challenges should mimic the ones learners will face in real life and be crafted so that they provide opportunities for learning, not just frustration. Include obstacles that learners know about and can anticipate and plan for. Also include some unexpected events that require spontaneous action.

Initial call for action

I have seen learners stare at the first screen of a simulation for 10 or 20 minutes before making a motion. To get learners past this blank-page phenomenon, require action within a short amount of time: "We need your decision in 5 minutes" or "An alarm just sounded on the master control panel. Better check it out." Smoothly and naturally propel learners into their roles within the simulation.

Program variety into the simulation

Design simulations so that the answer or response is different each time. That way, learners can repeatedly run the simulation. They cannot cheat by knowing the answers ahead of time. Either design the simulator to generate a new problem each time, or inject vagaries from the world being simulated: weather, equipment failures, outbreaks of the flu, or market fads.

Let learners play multiple roles

In simulations, let learners play multiple roles. Have them play once "by the book," again "on gut instinct," and finally "as bad as you can be." Simulations let learners experience the consequences of alternative behaviors. To teach the consequences of negative behavior, assign learners the persona of an evil or careless person, and let them experience life from that perspective. Instead of telling learners why they should follow rules, let learners break the rules and experience the consequences.

Provide instructions and context

Make sure that the challenge of the simulation comes from the subject simulated, not from learning to operate the simulator. Learning the rules of the simulated world is hard enough without having to learn the rules of the simulator as well. Provide explicit instructions on operating the simulator. Cover these points:

▶ **What is the goal?** What is the learner to accomplish in the simulation? How is success defined? Can learners set goals for themselves?

▶ **What roles do learners play?** Are learners expected to play the role of a particular character? What are the motivations, values, and goals of that character?

▶ **How do I get started?** Learners often hesitate to take the first step. To get the simulation under way, suggest a starting strategy ("Why don't you begin with safe investments?") or a hint ("Psssst! Look in your in-basket").

▶ **What are the rules?** If the simulation mimics a situation, spell out the rules that people in that situation would know. If the simulation behaves in unrealistic ways, make these exceptions clear. You do not need to tell learners how to beat the simulation, just how to play it well enough so that they are learning the things they would learn in the real world.

▶ **How do I operate the simulation?** Tell learners how to operate the user interface of the simulation. How do they translate real-world actions, such as making a phone call or selling a stock, into clicking, typing, dragging, and dropping? In some designs, this information is in a separate Help facility.

Go beyond trial-and-error learning

Supplement trial-and-error learning with other methods, too. Learning by trial and error is suspect anyway. Those who learn by trail and error alone, without guidance or time for reflection, do not always acquire the most effective problem-solving strategies [143]. Learning by trial and error can be frustrating, and there is the danger that learners remember their first attempts, not the correct ones.

Variations of simulations

Simulations are as varied as the subjects they simulate and the imaginations of designers. Here are a few common varieties of simulations.

One-shot simulations

For a simulation of a complex system, let learners make changes to many separate parameters and immediately see the results. Learners can tweak and tune their answers as much as they want to.

In the following example, learners practice ordering restaurant meals to meet specific dietary requirements. This task is more complex than it appears. Meals consist of several different foods, each with different nutritional ingredients. Dietary goals are seldom simple, often involving seemingly contradictory objectives.

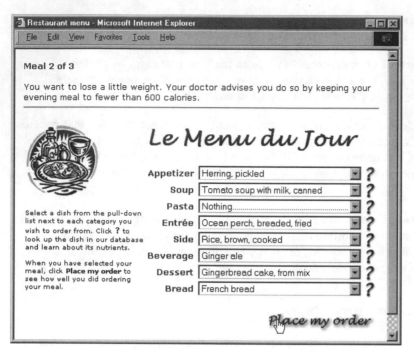

In this simulation, learners pick foods for several courses. After placing their order, they see how well they did. Learners can go back and make adjustments to try different combinations of foods.

Learn-by-example simulations

In learn-by-example simulations, learners intervene in incidents to determine the course of events and then observe the consequences of their actions. Here is the typical sequence in a learn-by-example simulation:

1. Learners view, listen to, or read about an incident, typically one involving conflicts among a group of people.

2. At key points in the incident, learners make choices about how to proceed.

3. Learners observe the consequences of their decisions.

4. This cycle repeats as the story unfolds.

At the end, learners are asked to summarize what they have learned.

Such simulations are easy to implement and require no programming, just a clever linking of HTML pages.

Microworlds

Seymour Papert at MIT developed the concept of microworlds. A microworld is a special form of simulation that provides an abstract environment or a simplified representation of a physical environment. Within the microworld, objects react to each other and to the learner according to defined principles that allow complex behaviors to result [144].

Microworlds are an effective way to teach highly complex activities that cannot be reduced to a few simple principles—or even to a few dozen simple principles. Microworlds, however, are complex to design and construct. They require intricate knowledge of the "world" being simulated and meticulous attention to the relationships among its many components.

Using simulations as WBT courses

A typical learning simulation starts with a brief introduction that frames the simulation by telling what is simulated and what will be learned in the simulation. At this point, I like to give the learner a choice of learning by the simulation or by a conventional tutorial. Most pick the simulation. Surprised?

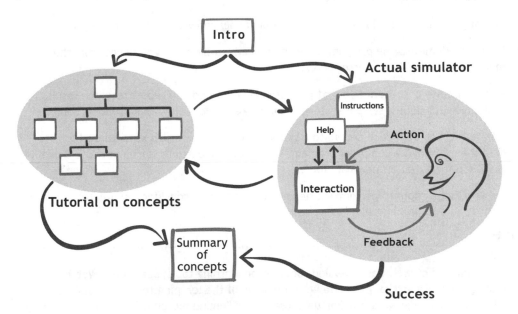

At some point, the learner realizes that to achieve the goal of the simulation, it would help to know more about the subject of the simulation. Then the learner jumps to the conventional tutorial for a little study. After learning a bit more about the subject, the learner returns to the simulation. Learners may switch back and forth several times during the course.

Once the learner achieves the goals in the simulation, there follows a quick review of the concepts. There is no test, because the simulation is the test. If learners can perform the task in the simulation, they can do it in the real world.

Of course, there are many variations possible in this flow. Some learners prefer to start with the tutorial and learn about the subject before trying their hand at the simulator. Others forgo the simulation altogether, and others never taste the tutorial.

IN CLOSING ...

Summary

- ▶ People learn as much outside the classroom as inside it. People learn by visiting museums and libraries, by looking things up in glossaries, by taking guided tours and field trips, by attending professional conferences, and by getting advice from wiser colleagues. We can use Web technologies to create online analogues of all the ways people learn.

- ▶ Create **virtual libraries** and **museums** so learners can find the documents, examples, case studies, and other resources they need.

- ▶ Prepare **glossaries** and **job aids** to help people apply knowledge right on the job.

- ▶ Set up a **telementoring** program so inexperienced learners can get advice from their more knowledgeable and wiser peers.

- ▶ Hold an **online conference** so that professionals in a field can report research results, exchange techniques, swap war stories, and make friends—all without leaving home.

- ▶ Create tours to introduce people to a system or locale. Use a **software guided tour** to lead them through a computer program, Web site, or electronic document. Use a **virtual field trip** for a real or imaginary locale.

- ▶ For teaching people to perform subtle and complex tasks, consider a **simulator**.

For more ...

To find examples of Web-based versions of common learning tools, search the Web by combining the word **virtual** or **online** with the name of the learning tool. For example, for Web-based museums, search for "virtual museum" or "online museum."

Many of the examples shown in this book are on exhibit at:

www.horton.com/DesigningWBT/

14

Contemplate the future

Fearless predictions about how we may learn

We end this book by daring a few predictions of how WBT and the functions it serves will continue to develop.

WBT WILL BREAK OUT OF TECHNICAL TRAINING

Most successful applications of WBT seem to teach technical subjects within technical organizations. The technologies of WBT are well suited to structured technical knowledge. And technical organizations and their employees have the technical skills required by WBT. As tools and technologies of WBT are made easier to use, more people will use them in more environments for more subjects.

Among training experts, the overwhelming consensus seems to be that WBT cannot teach soft skills. Whenever so many experts agree so strongly that something cannot be done, I expect the breakthrough any moment.

STANDARDS WILL MUDDLE ALONG

There is great need for interoperability between systems so that designers can intermix training content and systems from different vendors.

I believe the AICC standard for interoperability (www.aicc.org) will continue to gain acceptance, though as of October 1999 only three course-management systems were certified as compliant. IMS (www.imsproject.org) has promised more sophisticated standards, and vendors have promised to follow such standards. The promises, at least, are promising.

If vendors would curb their lusts for a temporary competitive advantage, meaningful standards could advance rapidly. If not, standards will advance only as purchasers of courses and tools attach standards to their requests for bids.

One technical standard does seem ready. I expect to see WBT make a slow but sure transition from HTML to XML, which seems well suited to the highly structured nature of training materials and the need to customize materials to special groups and even individuals. With XML, every element of a "page" can be generated and modified from scripts and its appearance controlled by style sheets (CSS and XSL).

WBT WILL DEVELOP A MARKETPLACE

A marketplace of training will develop on the Web. Competition will emerge in common subject areas, and courses will compete like books. Costs will drop and quality will improve.

For popular subjects, mass markets will develop over time. Already, some classes at the Open University in the United Kingdom have an enrollment of 10,000 [80]. The Web should enable even larger markets for courses.

Such mass markets will produce economies of scale—and enormous profits. They will also create secondary markets for more handcrafted WBT for smaller audiences on narrower subjects.

EDUCATION AND TRAINING WILL MERGE

In the past, the terms *education* and *training* had clearly distinct meanings. Education was what went on inside schoolhouses and on university campuses. Training took place within industry or in trade schools. Today, corporate "training departments" teach conceptual engineering courses, basic ethics, and social etiquette, while universities offer degree credit for courses in operating Photoshop 5.5. With WBT, the distinctions vanish altogether.

> The folks who think there's a difference between training and education have profoundly misunderstood education—Roger Schank [145].

And training, I might add. In the future, universities will become course vendors to industry, not just to other universities. At the same time, much of the standard university curriculum will be taught in courses developed by private firms.

Continuing education will move to the big tent and out of the sideshow. Gradually, universities and private industry will acknowledge that education, though more intense in early years, continues uninterruptedly throughout life.

TRAINING AND PUBLICATIONS WILL MERGE

Back when training was conducted in classrooms and publications required printing presses and warehouses, it made sense for corporations to have separate departments for training and publications. It made sense for schools to be separate from libraries. After all, most organizations are structured not by their objectives, but by the types of assets used to accomplish those objectives. Once both functions are performed primarily over the Web, we will need to ask whether the division makes sense.

The logical outcomes of a merger of publications and training are knowledge management systems on the large scale and knowledge objects on the small scale. Knowledge management systems ensure that workers in an enterprise can get the knowledge they need in the form they need it, when they need it, right where they are. Kind of like just-in-time training for the whole enterprise.

Knowledge objects are self-contained modules that deliver that knowledge in whatever forms it is needed. To the person who needs a course, the knowledge object is a course. To the person who needs a detailed reference manual, it is that manual. To the person who needs a simple job-aid, it is a quick-reference card.

THE CLASSROOM WILL BLOSSOM

WBT will not kill the classroom but renew it. WBT will free the classroom from the burden of trying to do what WBT or other media do better. In the future, the classroom will be used to put small numbers of learners together where, free of distractions, they can see, hear, smell, and touch one another. Together, they and an instructor or facilitator will collaborate in intense, highly efficient learning experiences.

GIZMANIA WILL RUN OUT OF BATTERIES

Gizmania is a code word for designers' fascination with technology for its own sake and the need to use every technology available. Remember the ransom-note typography when writers first got Macintosh systems? Writers used 27 fonts on every page. Or how about the refrigerator art that infested corporate memos when color printers became common? These outbreaks of gizmania were temporary problems. People soon tired of gewgaws and began to notice the powerful effects of good, restrained design. The same will happen with WBT. Soon, we hope.

WBT (AND THIS BOOK) WILL DISAPPEAR

WBT will continue to grow and advance. Soon every product sold will have WBT available from the manufacturer or an enterprising freelance trainer. WBT may even become the predominant way of delivering training.

Along the way, WBT will transform from emerging technology to submerging technology. In a decade—or two, at most—WBT will become such a normal, customary way of delivering training that we hardly notice it. Nothing worthy of a name. Or a book.

By then, anyone anywhere will be able to learn anything at any time.

# References

1   Brandon Hall. *The Web-Based Training Cookbook*. New York: John Wiley & Sons, 1997.

2   William Horton. *Designing and Writing Online Documentation*. New York: John Wiley & Sons, 1994.

3   William Horton. *The Icon Book: Visual Symbols for Computer Systems and Documentation*. New York: John Wiley & Sons, 1994.

4   William Horton. *Illustrating Computer Documentation*. New York: John Wiley & Sons, 1991.

5   William Horton, Lee Taylor, Arthur Ignacio, *et al. The Web Page Design Cookbook*. New York: John Wiley & Sons, 1996.

6   M. G. Moore and Greg Kearsley. *Distance Education: A Systems View*. Boston: Wadsworth Publishing, 1996.

7   Herbert Simon. "Designing Organizations for an Information-Rich World." In *Computers, Communications, and the Public Interest*. Baltimore, MD: Johns Hopkins University Press, 1971.

8   Marianne Kolbasuk McGee and Jennifer Mateyaschuk. "Educating the Masses." *InformationWeek Magazine*, 15 February 1999.

9   T. C. Doyle. "Why Johnny Can't Configure: The IT Education Crisis." *Solutions Integrator Magazine*, 1 February 1998.

10 Norm Ainslie. "Facilitated or Instructor-Led Online Learning - the Role of the Instructor." *Journal of Instruction Delivery Systems*, Spring 1998.

11 Dick Schaaf. "What Workers Really Think About Training." *Training Magazine*, September 1998, 59-66.

12 National Center for Educational Statistics. *Profile of Older Undergraduates: 1989-90*. Washington, DC: U.S. Department of Education, Office of Educational Research and Improvement, 1995.

13 Unattributed. "Industry Report 1998: An Overview of Employee Training in America." *Training Magazine*, October 1998.

14 Christa Degnan. "Taking the E-train." *PCWeek Online*, 31 May 1999.

15   Unattributed. "The 1999 CBT Report: Executive Summary." Web page. http://www.ittrain.com/exec-sum.html. *Inside Technology Training* Magazine. July 1999.

16   Platte Clark and Brian Johnson. "Moving from ILT to WBT: A Novell Education Case Study." *WBT Producer Conference Proceedings*. San Diego, California: Influent Technology Group, 1999.

17   Ann E. Barron and Catherine Rickelman. "Creating an Online Corporate University: Lessons Learned." *ASTD International Conference & Exposition*. Atlanta, GA: The American Society for Training & Development, 1999.

18   Patrick Porter. "Boeing's Big Experiment." Web page. http://www.ittrain.com/archive/MarchLO_99_8.html. *Inside Technology Training* Magazine. July 1999.

19   Tom Barron. "Harnessing Online Learning." *Training & Development*, September 1999, 28-33.

20   Teri Kestenbaum. "Educational Benefits of Online Learning." Microsoft Work document. http://support.blackboard.net/components/Benefits_of_Online_Learning.doc. Blackboard, Inc. 5 July 1999.

21   Marie Kascus. "Converging Vision of Library Service for Off-Campus/Distance Education." *Journal of Library Services for Distance Education*, 1997, 1 (1).

22   Deborah Schreiber. "Organizational Technology and Its Impact on Distance Training." In *Distance Training*. San Francisco: Jossey-Bass, 1998, 3-18.

23   Lisa Shaw. *Telecommute*. New York, NY: John Wiley & Sons, 1996.

24   W. E. Souder. "The Effectiveness of Traditional vs. Satellite Delivery of the Management of Technology Master's Degree Programs." *The American Journal of Distance Education*, 1993, 7 (1), 37-53.

25   Brandon Hall. "Mastering Online Enterprise Training: a Survival Guide." Web page. http://www.pathlore.com/archives/bhall_cover_story.html. Pathlore Software. 5 July 1999.

26   David Becker. "Training On Demand." *TechWeek*, 11 January 1999.

27   Luisa Kroll. "Good Morning, HAL." *Forbes Magazine*, 8 March 1999.

28   Kathleen Maher. "Inventing the Virtual Classroom." *Interactivity Magazine*, August 1998.

29   Bill Gillette. "Taking Training Online." *Corporate Meetings & Incentives*, October 1998.

30   D. Picard. "The Future in Distance Training." *Training*, November 1996, s5-s10.

31   ASK International. "A New Training Concept, JUST IN TIME." http://www.askintl.com/concept.html. ASK International. 22 June 1999.

32   Marianne Kolbasuk McGee. "Save On Training." *InformationWeek Magazine*, 22 June 1998.

33   Bronwyn Fryer. "MCI Goes Live." *Inside Technology Training*, October 1998, 18-22.

34   Lisa Terry. "Slash Your Costs! Here Comes Web-Based Training." Web Site. www.solutionsintegrator.com. Solutions Integrator. 22 September 1999.

35   Beth McGrath. "Partners in Learning: Twelve Ways Technology Changes the Teacher-Student Relationship." *T.H.E. Journal*, 1998, 25 (9).

36   Lawrence Lesser. "Technology-Rich Standards-Based Statistics: Improving Introductory Statistics at the College Level." *T.H.E. Journal*, February 1998.

37   L. C. Baron and E. S. Goldman. "Integrating Technology with Teacher Preparation." In *Technology and Education Reform*. San Francisco: Jossey-Bass Publishers, 1994.

38   Bryan Alexander, James Crowley, Deanne Lundin, *et al.* "E-COMP: A Few Words About Teaching Writing with Computers." *T.H.E. Journal Online*, September 1997.

39   Silva Karayan and Judith Crowe. "Student Perceptions of Electronic Discussion Groups." *T.H.E. Journal Online*, April 1997, 69-71.

40   CCA Consulting. "Annual Distance Learning Spending in Higher Education Expected to reach $1.5 billion during the 1997-1998 Academic year." Web page. www.cca-consults.com/press.html. CCA Consulting, Inc. 9 July 1999.

41   Walter Baer. "Will the Internet Transform Higher Education?" In *The Emerging Internet: Annual Review*. Queenstown, MD: The Aspen Institute, 1998.

42   B. Ives and S. Jarvenpaa. "Will the Internet Revolutionize Business Education and Research." *Sloan Management Review*, 1996, 37 (3).

43   Suzanne Swope. "The Approaching Value-Added Education." *Educational Record*, 1994, Summer, 17-18.

44   Thomas Russell. "The No Significant Difference Phenomenon." Web site. teleeducation.nb.ca/nosignificantdifference/. Thomas Russell. 12 July 1999.

45   M. W. Goldberg. "CALOS: First Results From an Experiment in Computer-Aided Learning." *ACM's 28th SIGCSE Technical Symposium on Computer Science Education*. New York, NY: Association for Computing Machinery, 1997.

46   V. F. McAlpin. "On-line and F2F Students: Is There Really Any Difference?" *2nd UNC Workshop on Technology for Distance Education North Carolina State University*. Raleigh, NC: North Carolina State University, 1998, 6-7.

47   J. Ward. "Community College Student Perceptions of Online Instruction Experiences." *Education at a Distance*, 1998, 12 (3), 6.

48   G. D. Garson. *The Political Economy of Online Education*. Raleigh, NC: North Carolina State University, 1996.

49   D. L. Wilson. "Self-Paced Studies." *Chronicle of Higher Education*, 1996, 62 (21 (Feb. 2)), A19-A20.

50   M. Moore and Greg Kearsly. "Research on Effectiveness." In *Distance Education: A Systems View*. New York: Wadsworth Publishing, 1996.

51   Bill Orr. "A Significant Difference." Web Site. tenb.mta.ca/anygood/asigdiff.shtml. 12 July 1999.

52   Robert B. Pankey. "Piloting Exercise Physiology in the Web-Based Environment." *T.H.E. Journal*, December 1998.

53   Microsoft Corporation. "San Diego State University Case Study." http://www.microsoft.com/education/hed/studies/caseh55.htm. Microsoft Corporation. 5 July 1999.

54   Jane Whitney Gibson and Jorge M. Herrera. "How to Go from Classroom Based to Online Delivery in Eighteen Months or Less: A Case Study in Online Program Development." *T.H.E. Journal*, January 1999.

55   Jerald G. Schutte. *Virtual Teaching in Higher Education: The New Intellectual Superhighway or Just Another Traffic Jam?* Northridge, CA: California State University, 1997.

56   Barry Ellis. "Virtual Classroom Technologies for Distance Education: The Case for On-line Synchronous Delivery." Web page. www.detac.com/solutoin/naweb97.htm. DETAC Corporation. 2 July 1999.

57   Kevin Kruse. "Real World WBT: Lessons Learned at the Fortune 500." *ASTD International Conference & Exposition*. Atlanta, GA: The American Society for Training & Development, 1999.

58   Therese Monahan. "Disseminating Time- and Regulation-Sensitive Information: Online Training Seminars at Mortgage Bankers Association of America." In *Distance Training*. San Francisco: Jossey-Bass, 1998, 137-154.

59   Microsoft Corporation. "Toys "R" Us Case Study." Web page. http://www.microsoft.com/Windows/NetMeeting/InAction/toysrus.asp. Microsoft Corporation. 4 June 1999.

60   Tom Kubala. "Addressing Student Needs: Teaching on the Internet." *T.H.E. Journal*, 1998, 25 (8), 71-74.

61   Linda Cooper. "Anatomy of an Online Course." *T.H.E. Journal*, February 1999.

62   John Niemi, A. K. Owens, and Barbara J. Ehrhard. "Video-Teleconference Distance Education HRD Graduate Classroom." *National Meeting of American Association of Adult Continuing Education*. Cincinnati, OH: American Association of Adult Continuing Education, 1997.

63   Stanley L. Kroder, Jayne Suess, and David Sachs. "Lessons in Launching Web-based Graduate Courses." *T.H.E. Journal*, May 1998.

64   Jim O'Keefe. "Online Learning Fills Immediate Need for Employee Technology-Skills Training." Web page. http://www.amcity.com/albany/stories/1997/10/06/focus4.html. Capital District Business Review. 18 June 1999.

65   Docent. "Lucent's Wireless University." Web page. www.docent.com/solutions/success/lucent.htm. Docent. 9 July 1999.

66   Barney Dalgarno. "Constructivist Computer Assisted Learning: Theory and Techniques." *Proceedings of ASCILITE '96*. Adelaide, South Australia: University of South Australia, 1996.

67   Barbara Mahone Brown. "Digital Classrooms: Some Myths About Developing New Educational Programs Using the Internet." *T.H.E. Journal*, December 1998.

68   David Iadevaia. "An Internet-Based Introductory College Astronomy Course with Real-Time Telescopic Observing." *T.H.E. Journal*, January 1999.

69   Linda Harasim. "A Framework for Online Learning: The Virtual U." *Computer*, September 1999, 44-49.

70   Jane Whitney Gibson and Jorge M. Herrera. "A Pilot Study to Set Up an Asynchronous Web-Based Distance Learning Program in Undergraduate Business." *7th Annual Lifelong Learning Conference*. National University, CA: National University Research Institute, 1998, 1-5.

71   Geoffrey Moore. *Crossing the Chasm: Marketing and Selling Technology Products to Mainstream Customers*. San Francisco, CA: Harper Business, 1995.

72   Jonathan Grudin. "Groupware and Social Dynamics: Eight Challenges for Developers." *Communications of the ACM*, 1994, 37 (1), 92-105.

73   Marjo Favorin. "Towards Computer Support for Collaborative Learning at Work: Six Requirements." http://www-cscl95.indiana.edu/cscl95/favorin.html. 20 October 1995.

74   Philip Rutherford. "Annotations: The Key to Collaborative Teaching and Learning on the Internet." http://elmo.scu.edu.au/sponsored/ausweb/ausweb96/educn/rutherford/paper.html. 5 November 1996.

75   Stephen Bostock. "Designing Web-Based Instruction for Active Learning." In *Web Based Instruction*. Englewood Cliffs, New Jersey: Educational Technology Publications, 1997, 225-230.

76   Aniruddh H. Patel. "Syntactic Processing in Language and Music: Different Cognitive Operations, Similar Neural Resources?" *Music Perception,* 1998, 16 (1), 27-42.

77   Marlene Scardamalia and Carl Bereiter. "An Architecture for Collaborative Knowledge Building." In *Computer-based Learning Environments and Problem Solving.* Berlin, Germany: Springer-Verlag, 1992, 41-46.

78   Andy Sadler. "How to Make WBT Drive Profits - Not Drain Productivity." *Technical Training,* September/October 1999, 20-24.

79   Margaret Driscoll. *Web-Based Training: Using Technology to Design Adult Learning Experiences.* San Francisco: Jossey-Bass/Pfeiffer, 1998.

80   Alfred Bork. "The Future of Computers and Learning." *T.H.E. Journal Online,* June 1997.

81   Douglas M. Towne and Allen Munro. "Simulation-Based Instruction of Technical Skills." *Human Factors,* 1991, 33 (3), 325-341.

82   Steve Alexander. "Transform That Product Manual into Top-Notch Training Material." *Inside Technology Training,* September 1999, 50-51.

83   Ron Oliver, Jan Herrington, and Arshad Omari. "Creating Effective Instructional Materials for the World Wide Web." http://www.scu.edu.au/sponsored/ausweb/ausweb96/educn/oliver/. 5 November 1996.

84   Thomas E. Cyrs and Eugenia D. Conway. *Teaching at a Distance with the Merging Technologies: An Instructional Systems Approach.* Las Cruces, NM: Center for Educational Development, New Mexico State University, 1997.

85   Elissa Smilowitz. "Do Metaphors Make Web Browsers Easier to Use?" *Designing for the Web: Empirical Studies.* Sandia National Laboratory, Albuquerque, NM, 1996.

86   Timothy Slater, Michelle Larson, and David McKenzie. "Bringing Physics of the Sun to the Public." *T.H.E. Journal,* October 1998.

87   David E. Hailey, Jr. and Christine Hailey. "Hypermedia, Multimedia, and Reader Cognition: An Empirical Study." *Technical Communication,* 16 April 1998, 330-342.

88   Virginia Junk and Linda Fox. "Making the Most of Home Pages, E-mail, The Internet and Presentation Graphics." *T.H.E. Journal,* August 1998.

89   Sharon McDonald and Rosemary J. Stevenson. "Effects of Text Structure and Prior Knowledge of the Learner on Navigation in Hypertext." *Human Factors,* 1998, 40 (1), 18-27.

90   Jutta Degener. "Editing and Publishing." Web page. http://kbs.cs.tu-berlin.de/~jutta/ht/writing/editing.html. Jutta Degener. 24 September 1999.

91   Katy Campbell. "The Web: Design for Active Learning." Web page. http://www.atl.ualberta.ca/articles/idesign/activel.cfm. Academic Technologies for Learning, University of Alberta, 7 July 1999.

92   H. Kim and S. C. Hirtle. "Spatial Metaphors and Disorientation in Hypertext Browsing." *Behaviour and Information Technology,* 1995, 14 (1), 239-250.

93   Michael A. Hughes. "Active Learning for Software Products." *Technical Communication,* 1998, 45 (3), 343-352.

94   Lawrence J. Najjar. "Principles of Educational Multimedia User Interface Design." *Human Factors,* 1998, 40 (2), 311-323.

95   Valerie J. Shute, A. Gawlick, and Kevin A. Gluck. "Effects of Practice and Learner Control on Short- and Long-Term Gain and Efficiency." *Human Factors,* 1998, 40 (2), 296-310.

96 S. S. Lee and Y. H. K. Lee. "Effects of Learner-Control Versus Program-Control Strategies on Computer-Aided Learning of Chemistry Problems." *Educational Psychology*, 1991, 83 (4), 491-498.

97 Kurt Kraiger and Janis A. Cannon-Bowers. "Measuring Knowledge Organization as a Method for Assessing Learning During Training." *Human Factors*, 1995, 37 (4), 804-816.

98 Jasmine Solomonescu. "Virtual Labs for Real-Life Scientific Training." Web page. http://www.telelearn.ca/g_access/news/virtual_labs.html. TeleLearning Network of Centres of Excellence. 18 June 1999.

99 Ruth Colvin Clark. *Designing Technical Training*. Phoenix, AZ: Buzzards Bay Press, 1994.

100 Curtis Jay Bonk and Thomas H. Reynolds. "Learner-Centered Web Instruction for Higher-Order Thinking, Teamwork, and Apprenticeship." In *Web-Based Instruction*. Englewood Cliffs, New Jersey: Educational Technolgy Publications, 1997, 167-178.

101 Eleanor Bicanich, Thomas Slivinski, Susan Hardwicke, *et al.* "Internet-Based Testing: A Vision or Reality?" *T.H.E. Journal Online*, September 1997.

102 Bob Filipczak. "Training Gets Doomed." *Training*, August 1997, 25-31.

103 Lauren Gibbons Paul. "Cyber Coaching for Soft Skills." *Inside Technology Training*, November 1997, 20-26.

104 Richard Mayer. "Multimedia Learning: Are We Asking the Right Questions?" *Educational Psychologist*, 1997, 32 (1), 1-19.

105 Don Scott, Catherine Cramton, Stéphane Gauvin, *et al.* "Internet Based Collaborative Learning: An Empirical Evaluation." http://ausweb.scu.edu.au/proceedings/donscott/index.html. 9 July 1997.

106 Murray Turoff. "Designing a Virtual Classroom." *1995 International Conference on Computer Assisted Instruction*, 1995.

107 Sheizaf Rafaeli and Fay Sudweeks. "Interactivity in the Nets." In *Network & Net Play: Virtual Groups on the Internet*. Menlo Park, CA: AAAI Press/The MIT Press, 1998.

108 A. Lauzon. "Integrating Computer-Based Instruction with Computer Conferencing: An Evaluation of a Model for Designing Online Education." *American Journal of Distance Education*, 1992, 6 (2), 32-46.

109 Christian Pantel. "A Framework for Comparing Web-Based Learning Environments." Master of Science. http://www.telelearn.ca/g_access/showcase.html. Simon Fraser University. 28 October 1997.

110 Phyllis Blumenfeld, Ronald Marx, Elliot Soloway, *et al.* "Learning With Peers: From Small Group Cooperation to Collaborative Communities." *Educational Researcher*, November 1996, 37-40.

111 Winfred Arthur, Brian Young, Jeffrey Jordan, *et al.* "Effectiveness of Individual and Dyadic Training Protocols: The Influence of Trainee Interaction Anxiety." *Human Factors*, 1996, 38 (1), 79-86.

112 Susan Fussell and I. Benimoff. "Social and Cognitive Processes in Interpersonal Communication: Implications for Advanced Telecommunications Technologies." *Human Factors*, 1995, 37 (2), 228-250.

113 Felicie Barnes and Bennie Lowery. "Sustaining Two-Way Interaction and Communication in Distance Learning." *T.H.E. Journal*, March 1998.

114 Deborah Schreiber. *Interactive Video Handbook*. Washington, DC: American Association of Retired Persons, 1995.

115 Karen Jarrett Thoms. "Teaching via ITV: Taking Instructional Design to the Next Level." *T.H.E. Journal*, April 1999.

116 Jack M. Wilson. "Distance Learning for Continuous Education." *Educom Review*, March/April 1997.

117 David Raths. "Is Anyone Out There?" *Inside Technology Training*, June 1999, 32-34.

118 Judy Ann Serwatka. "Internet Distance Learning: How Do I Put My Course on the Web?" *T.H.E. Journal*, May 1999.

119 Philip Davis. " How Undergraduates Learn Computer Skills: Results of a Survey and Focus Group." *T.H.E. Journal*, April 1999.

120 Colin McCormack and David Jones. *Building a Web-Based Education System*. New York: John Wiley & Sons, 1998.

121 Badrul H. Khan, ed. *Web-Based Instruction*. Englewood Cliffs, New Jersey: Educational Technology Publications, 1997.

122 Lynette Porter. *Creating the Virtual Classroom: Distance Learning With the Internet*. New York: John Wiley & Sons, 1997.

123 Elliot Soloway, Mark Guzdial, and Kenneth Hay. "Learner-Centered Design: the Challenge for HCI in the 21st Century." *Interactions*, April 1994, 36-48.

124 Jerold W. Apps. *Mastering the Teaching of Adults*. Melbourne, FL: Krieger Publishing, 1991.

125 Lynn Densford. "Sun Microsystems: Finding new ways to put training in context." *Corporate University Review*, November/December 1998.

126 Richard Cornell and Barbara L. Martin. "The Role of Motivation in Web-Based Training." In *Web-Based Instruction*. Englewood Cliffs, New Jersey: Educational Technolgy Publications, 1997, 93-100.

127 Philip Duchastel. "A Motivational Framework for Web-Based Instruction." In *Web-Based Instruction*. Englewood Cliffs, New Jersey: Educational Technolgy Publications, 1997, 179-184.

128 Doo H. Lim. "Organizational and Cultural Factors Affecting International Transfer of Training." *Performance Improvement*, March 1999, 30-36.

129 Betty Collis and Elka Remmers. "The World Wide Web in Education: Issues Related to Cross-Cultural Communication and Interaction." In *Web-Based Instruction*. Englewood Cliffs, New Jersey: Educational Technolgy Publications, 1997, 85-92.

130 Manon Ress and Patrice Sonberg, ed. *Skills-Based Distance Training for a Global Environment: Malaysia's Virtual University*. San Francisco: Jossey-Bass, 1998.

131 Scott Jones, Cynthia Kennelly, Claudia Mueller, *et al. Developing International User Information*. Bedford, MA: Digital Press, 1992.

132 Roger E. Axtel. *Do's and Taboos Around the World*. New York: John Wiley & Sons, 1990.

133 Nancy Hoft. *International Technical Communication*. New York: John Wiley & Sons, 1995.

134 Deborah Andrews, ed. *International Dimensions of Technical Communication*. Arlington, VA: Society for Technical Communication, 1999.

135 ZDU. "ZDU Handbook." Web site. http://www.zdu.com/handbook/wholehandbook.asp. ZD Inc. 18 June 1999.

136 Peter Dolton. "The Economic Evaluation of Peer Counseling in Facilitating Computer Use in Higher Education." *Education Economics*, 1994, 2 (3), 313-326.

137 Carolyn M. Keeler and Robert Anson. "An Assessment of Cooperative Learning Used for Basic Computer Skills Instruction in the College Classroom." *Journal of Educational Computing Research*, 1995, 12 (4), 379-393.

138 Yvonne Marie Andres. "Scientist on Tap: Video-Conferencing Over the Internet." Web page. http://www.gsn.org/teach/articles/sot.html. Global SchoolNet Foundation. 18 June 1999.

139 Margaret Riel. "Tele-Mentoring Over the Net." Web page. www.iearn.org/circles/mentors.html. Margaret Riel. 3 September 1999.

140 Dorothy Bennett and David Neils. "Establishing the Telementoring Project." Web page. http://nsn.bbn.com/telementor_wrkshp/confnote/panel2.html. National School Network. 22 June 99.

141 Yu-mei Wang. "Online Conference: A Participant's Perspective." *T.H.E. Journal*, March 1999.

142 Jennifer J. Salopek. "Workstation Meets Playstation." *Training & Development Magazine*, August 1998, 26-35.

143 Daniel Gopher, Maya Weil, and Tal Bareket. "Transfer of Skill from a Computer Game Trainer to Flight." *Human Factors*, 1994, 36 (3), 387-405.

144 Seymour Papert. *Mindstorms*. New York: Basic Books, 1980.

145 Roger Schank. "End Run to the Goal Line." *Educom Review*, January 1995.

Index

Index

M

Index